BATTLE Angel ALITA™

1

STORY & ART BY YUKITO KISHIRO

BATTLE ANGEL ALITA
RUSTY ANGEL
Vol. 1
Action Edition

Story and Art by Yukito Kishiro

Translation/Fred Burke, Sterling Bell &
Matt Thorn
Translation Assist/Lillian Olsen
Touch-up & Lettering/Mary Kelleher
Cover & Graphics Design/Sean Lee
Editor 1st Edition/Trish Ledoux
Editor Action Edition/Elizabeth Kawasaki

Managing Editor/Annette Roman
Editor-in-Chief/William Flanagan
Production Manager/Noboru Watanabe
Sr. Director Licensing & Acquisitions/
Rika Inouye
V.P. of Sales & Marketing/Liza Coppola
Sr. V.P. of Editorial/Hyoe Narita
Publisher/Seiji Horibuchi

Printed in Canada

Published by VIZ, LLC
P.O. Box 77010
San Francisco, CA 94107

Action Edition
10 9 8 7 6 5 4 3 2 1
First printing, December 2003
First English edition, 1995

www.viz.com

CONTENTS

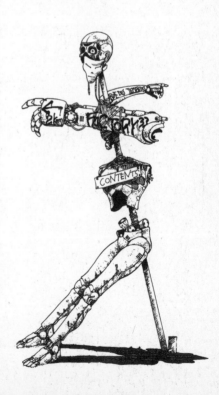

RUMB RUMB

THRRRMMMM

THE SCRAPYARD. HOME TO RUBBISH AND REFUSE -- BOTH HUMAN AND NON -- OF TIPHARES, A UTOPIA ABOVE THE CLOUDS.

RUMMM MMMM

KREK KAKREK

TWINK
TWINK
TWUNK

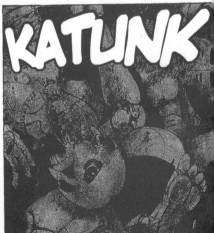

KATUNK

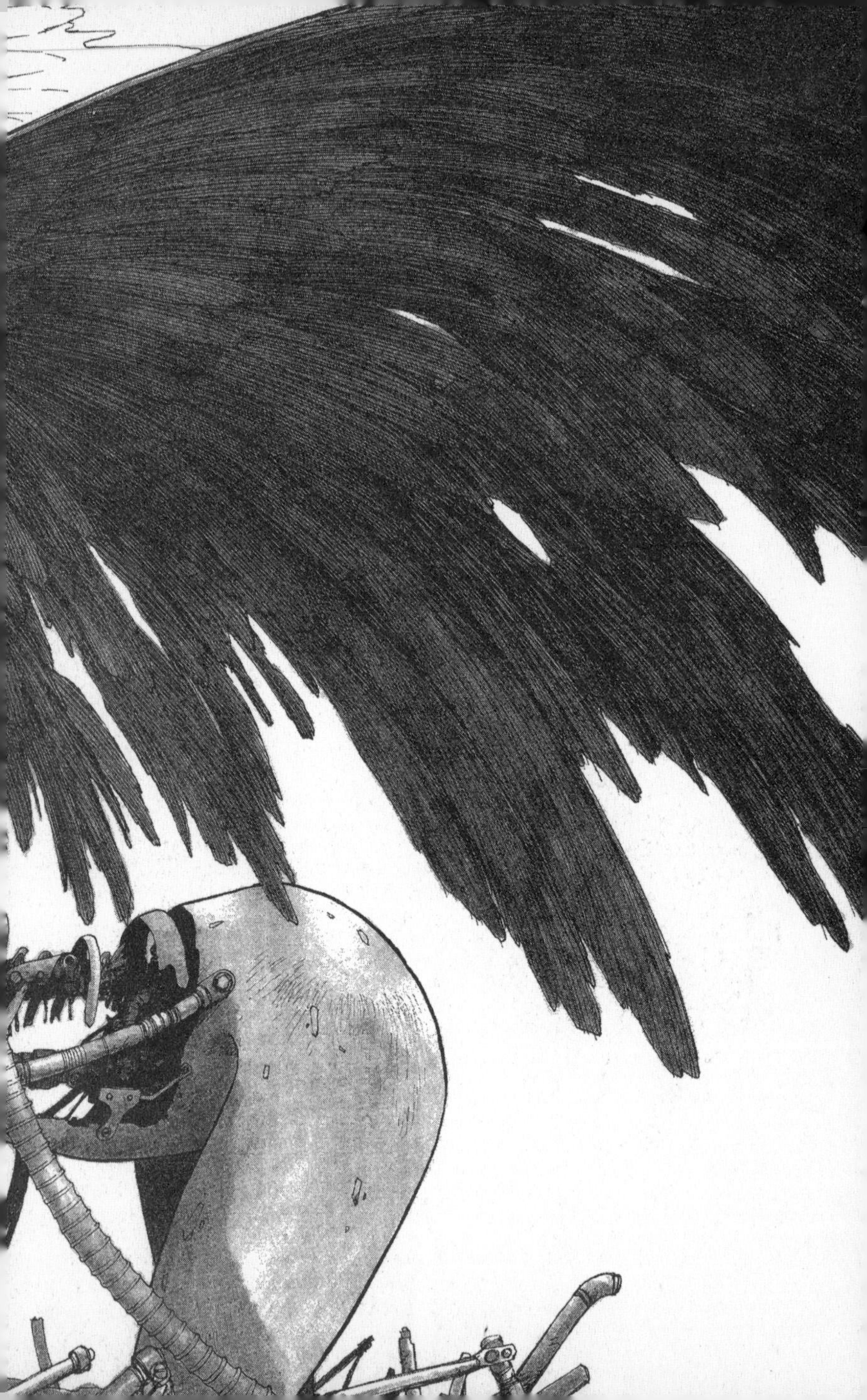

RUSTY ANGEL
BATTLE 1: RECLAMATION

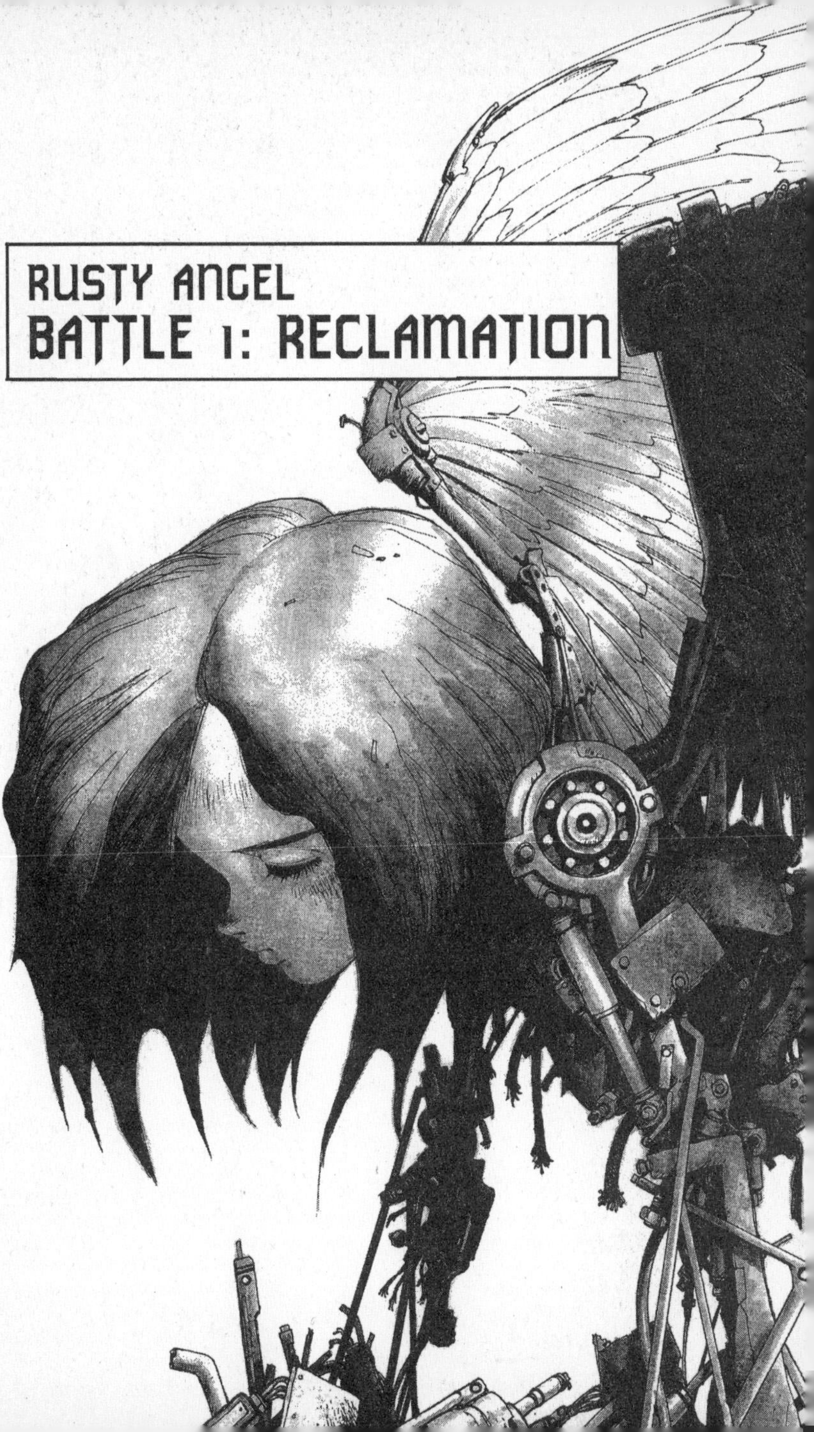

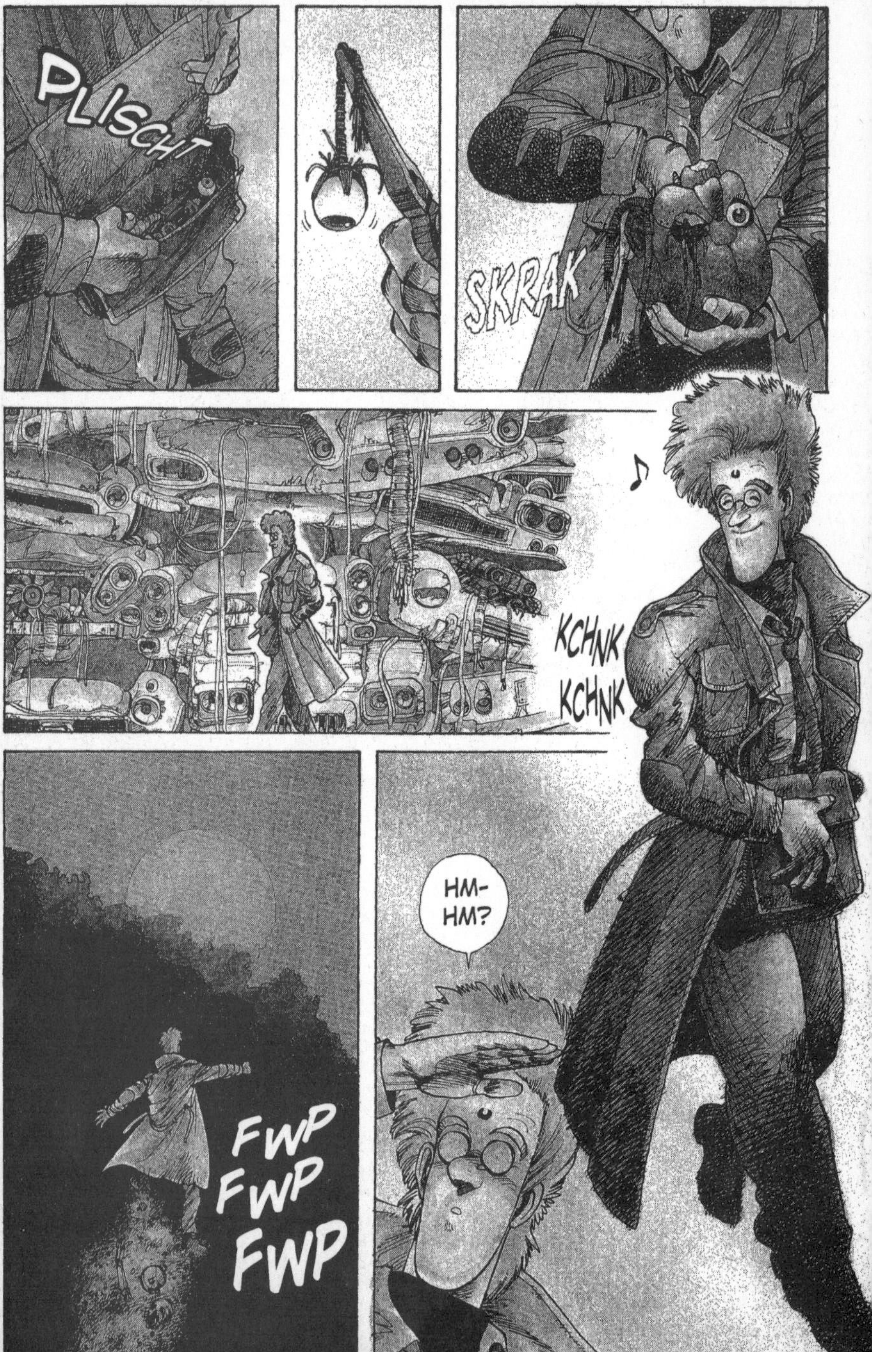
SKRAK
PLISCHT
♪
KCHNK
KCHNK
HM-
HM?
FWP
FWP
FWP

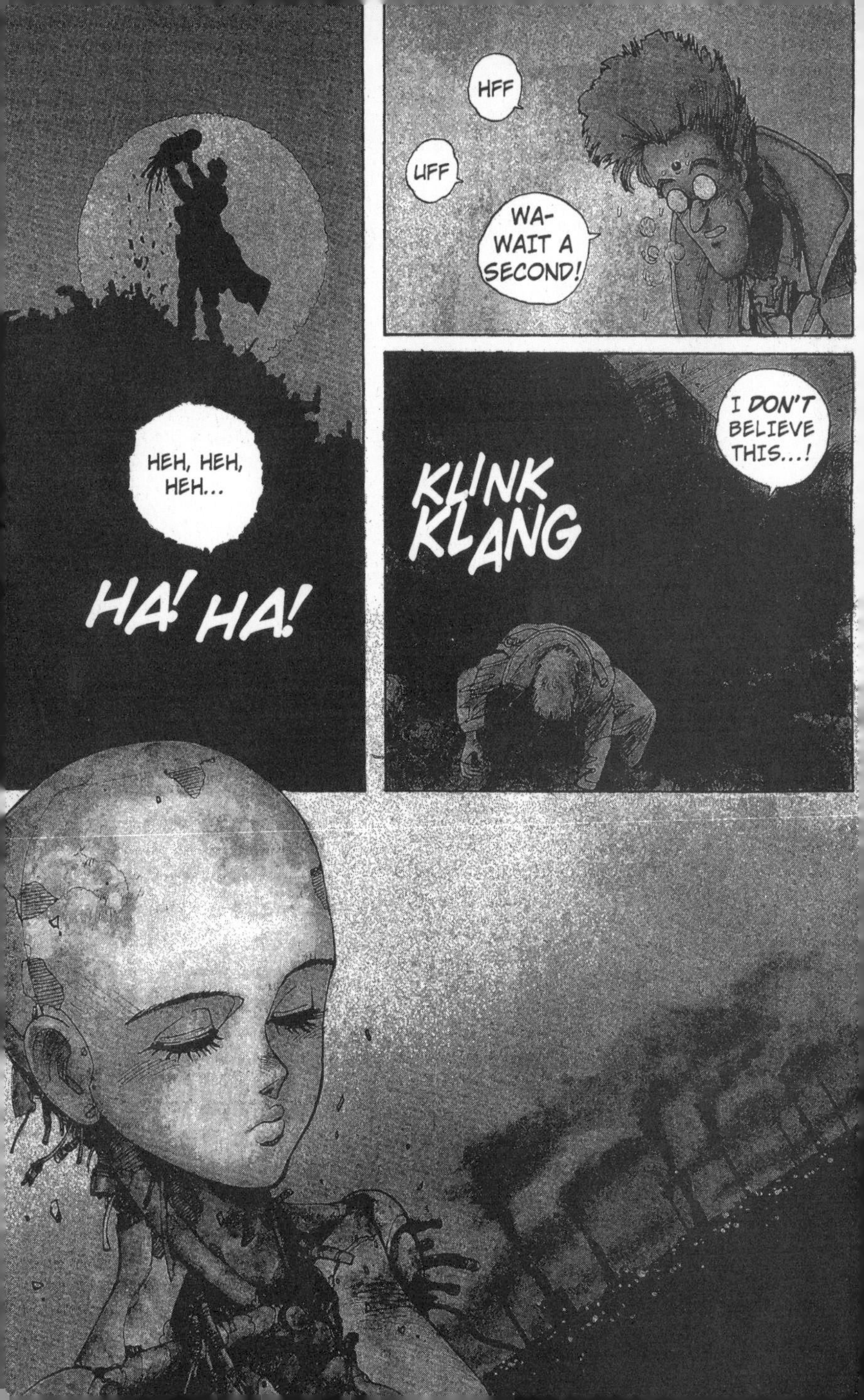
HFF
UFF
WA- WAIT A SECOND!
I DON'T BELIEVE THIS...!
KLINK KLANG
HEH, HEH, HEH...
HA! HA!

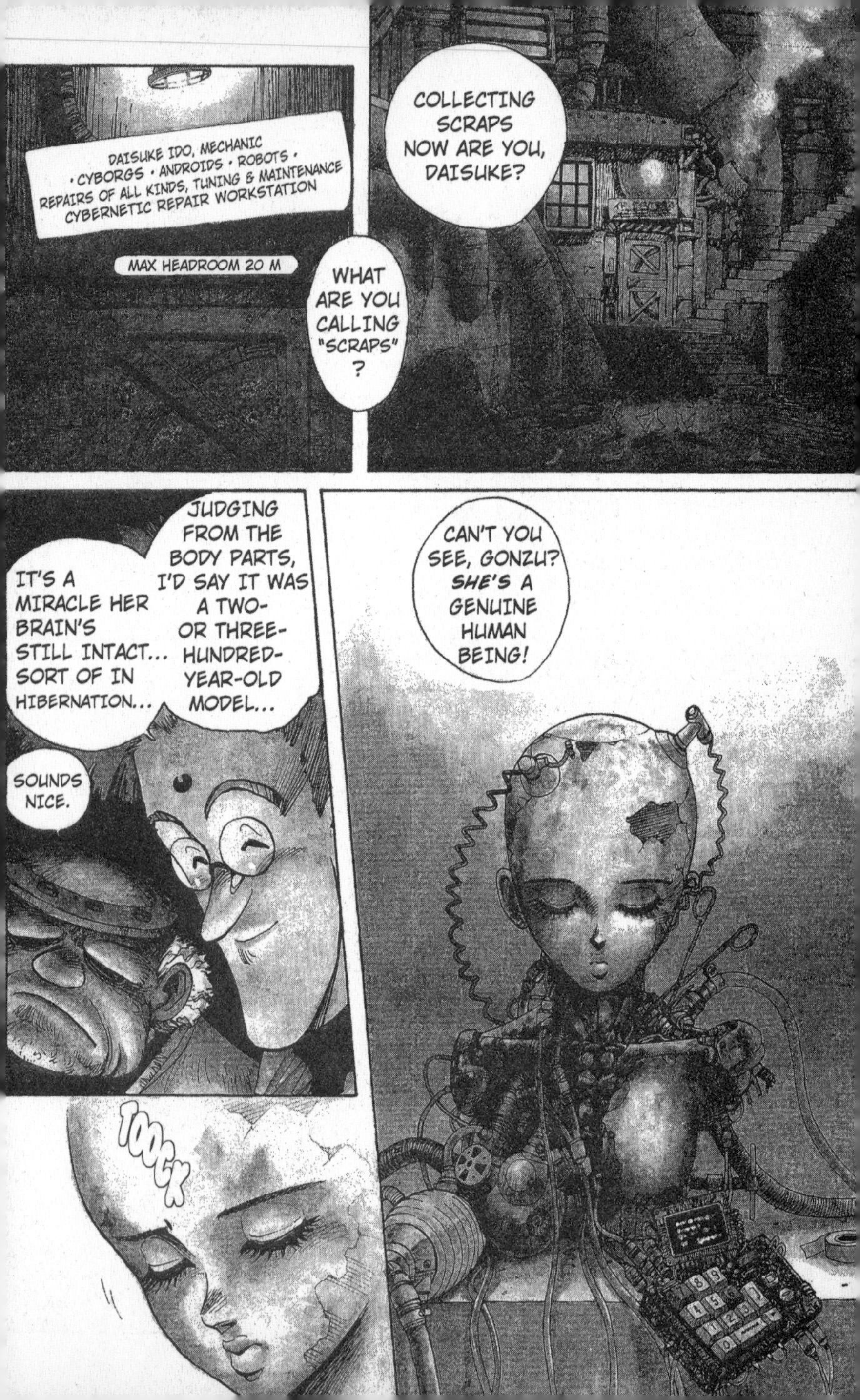
COLLECTING SCRAPS NOW ARE YOU, DAISUKE?
WHAT ARE YOU CALLING "SCRAPS"?
DAISUKE IDO, MECHANIC
• CYBORGS • ANDROIDS • ROBOTS •
REPAIRS OF ALL KINDS, TUNING & MAINTENANCE
CYBERNETIC REPAIR WORKSTATION
MAX HEADROOM 20 M
CAN'T YOU SEE, GONZU? SHE'S A GENUINE HUMAN BEING!
JUDGING FROM THE BODY PARTS, I'D SAY IT WAS A TWO- OR THREE-HUNDRED-YEAR-OLD MODEL...
IT'S A MIRACLE HER BRAIN'S STILL INTACT... SORT OF IN HIBERNATION...
SOUNDS NICE.
TOOCK

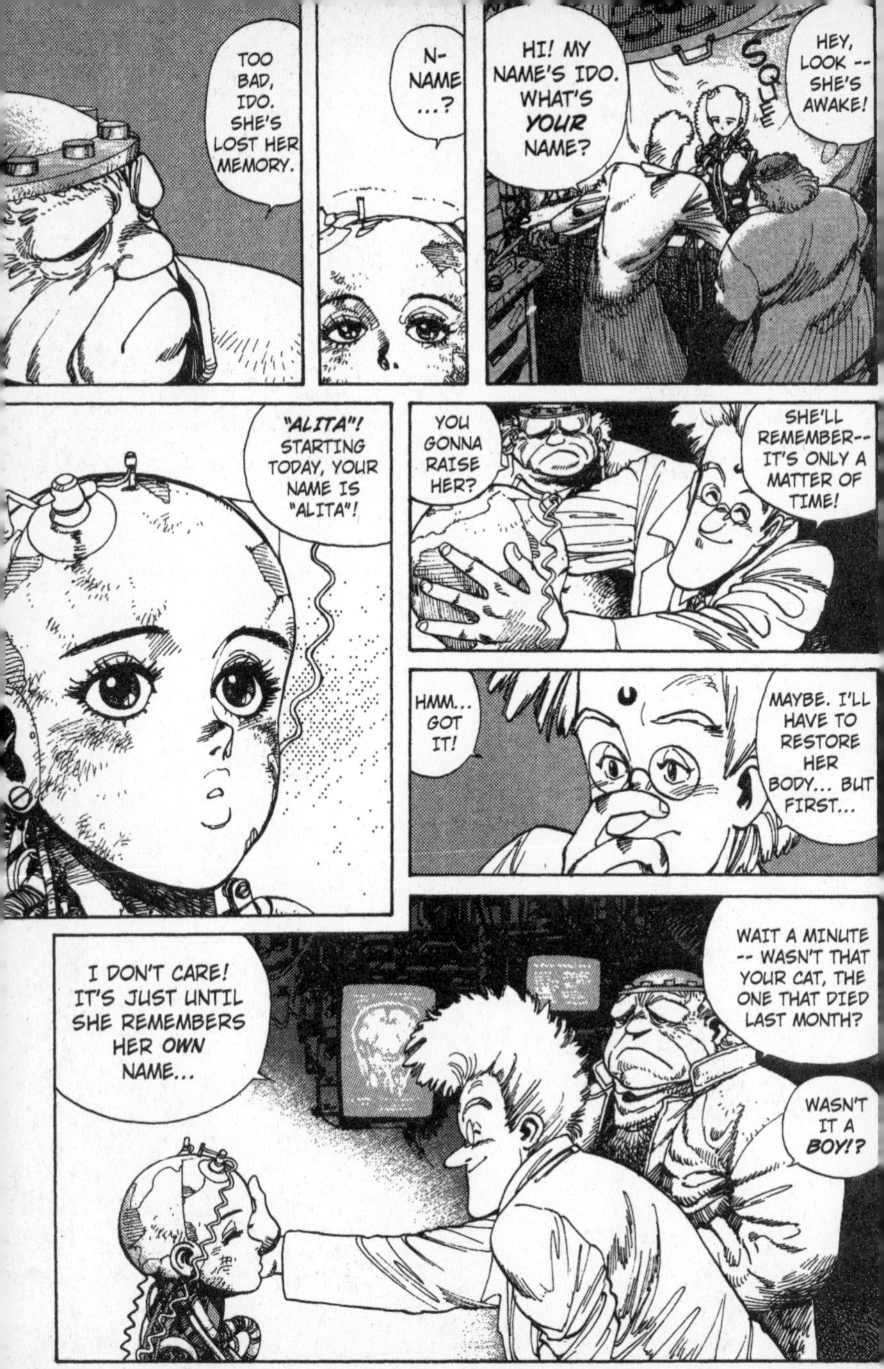
HEY, LOOK -- SHE'S AWAKE!
HI! MY NAME'S IDO. WHAT'S *YOUR* NAME?
N- NAME ...?
TOO BAD, IDO. SHE'S LOST HER MEMORY.
SHE'LL REMEMBER-- IT'S ONLY A MATTER OF TIME!
YOU GONNA RAISE HER?
MAYBE. I'LL HAVE TO RESTORE HER BODY... BUT FIRST...
HMM... GOT IT!
"ALITA"! STARTING TODAY, YOUR NAME IS "ALITA"!
WAIT A MINUTE -- WASN'T THAT YOUR CAT, THE ONE THAT DIED LAST MONTH?
I DON'T CARE! IT'S JUST UNTIL SHE REMEMBERS HER *OWN* NAME...
WASN'T IT A *BOY!?*

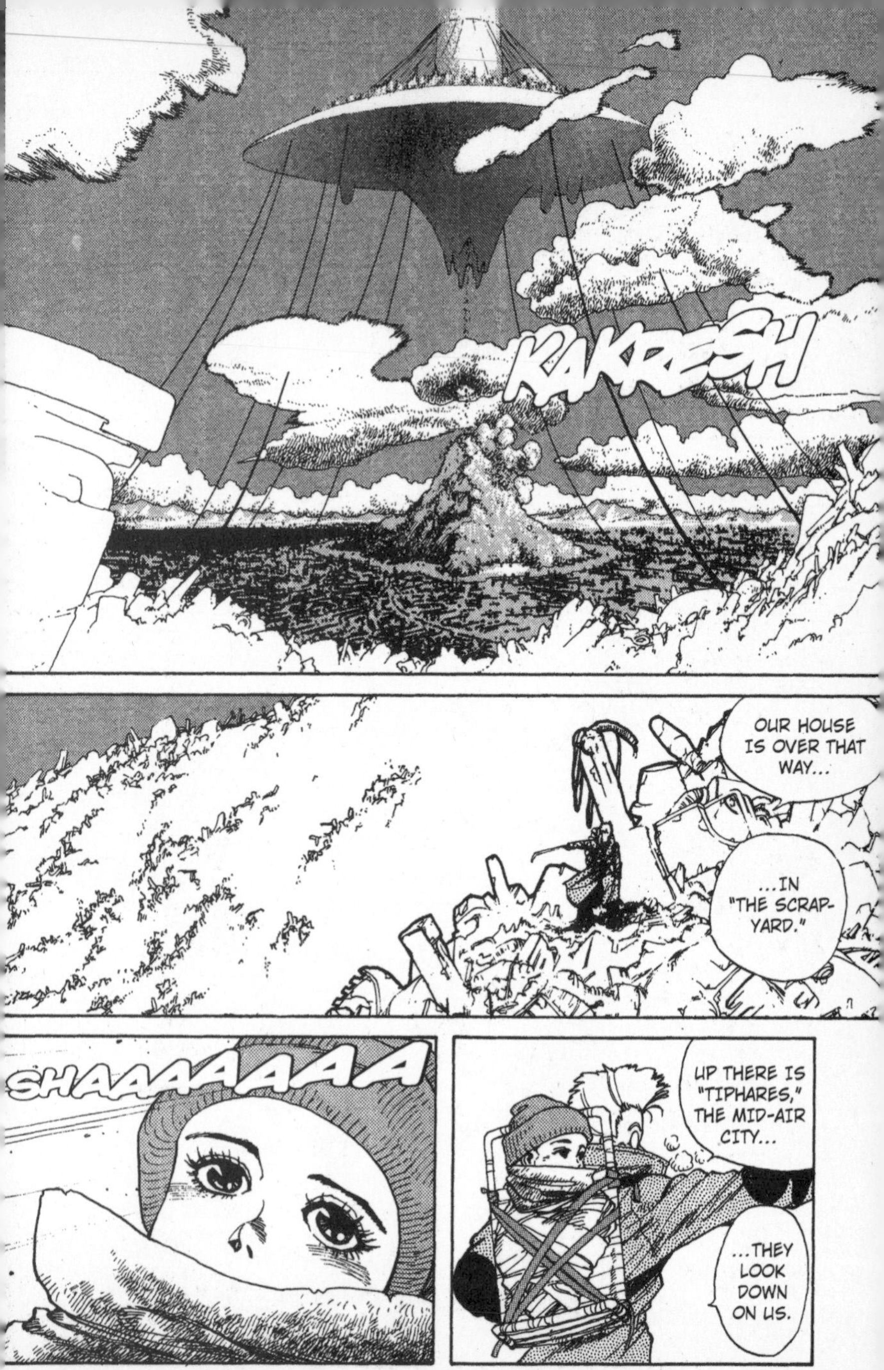
KAKRESH
OUR HOUSE IS OVER THAT WAY...
...IN "THE SCRAP-YARD."
UP THERE IS "TIPHARES," THE MID-AIR CITY...
...THEY LOOK DOWN ON US.
SHAAAAAAA

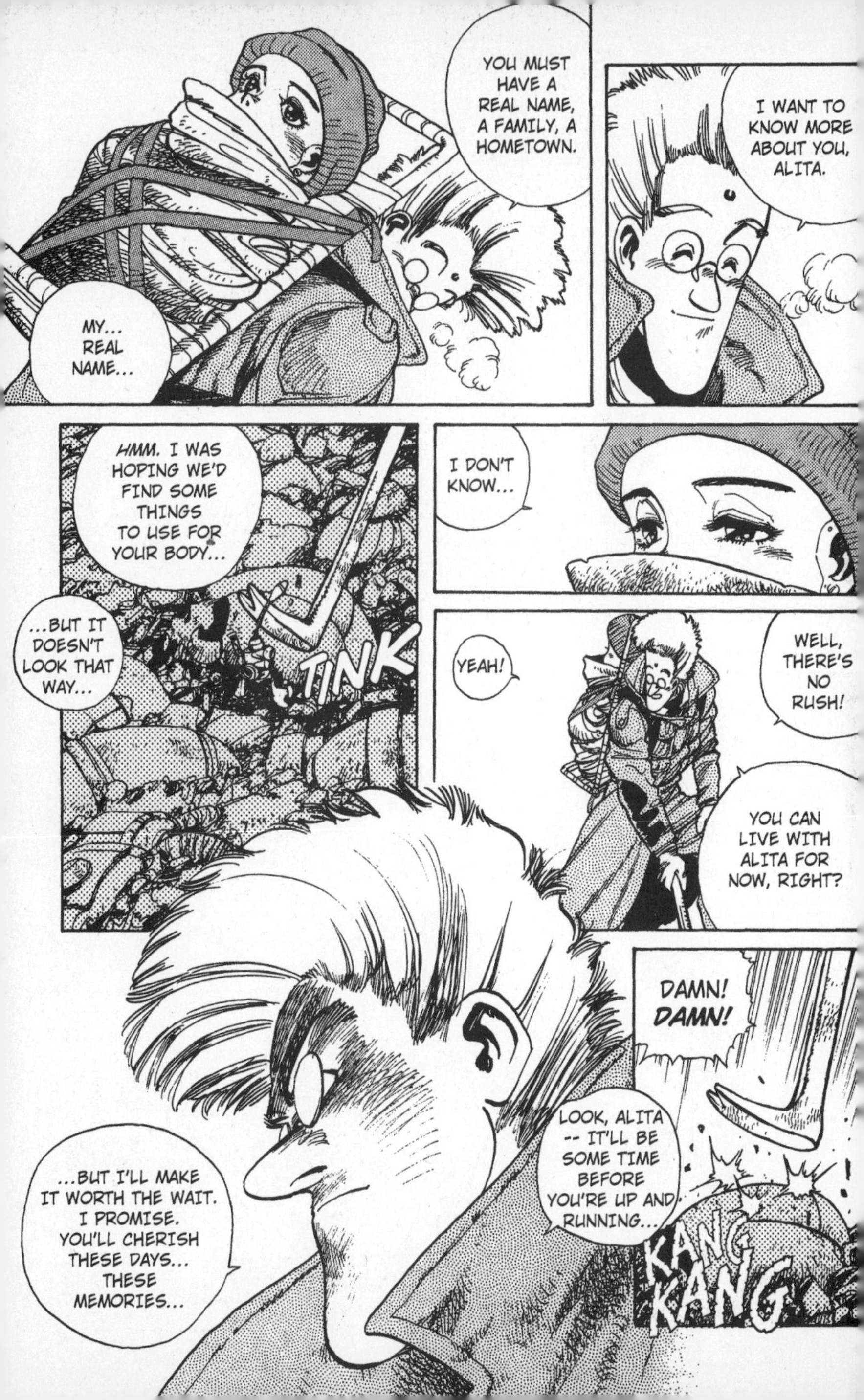
I WANT TO KNOW MORE ABOUT YOU, ALITA.
YOU MUST HAVE A REAL NAME, A FAMILY, A HOMETOWN.
MY... REAL NAME...
I DON'T KNOW...
WELL, THERE'S NO RUSH!
YEAH!
YOU CAN LIVE WITH ALITA FOR NOW, RIGHT?
HMM. I WAS HOPING WE'D FIND SOME THINGS TO USE FOR YOUR BODY...
...BUT IT DOESN'T LOOK THAT WAY...
TINK
DAMN! *DAMN!*
KANG KANG
LOOK, ALITA -- IT'LL BE SOME TIME BEFORE YOU'RE UP AND RUNNING...
...BUT I'LL MAKE IT WORTH THE WAIT. I PROMISE. YOU'LL CHERISH THESE DAYS... THESE MEMORIES...

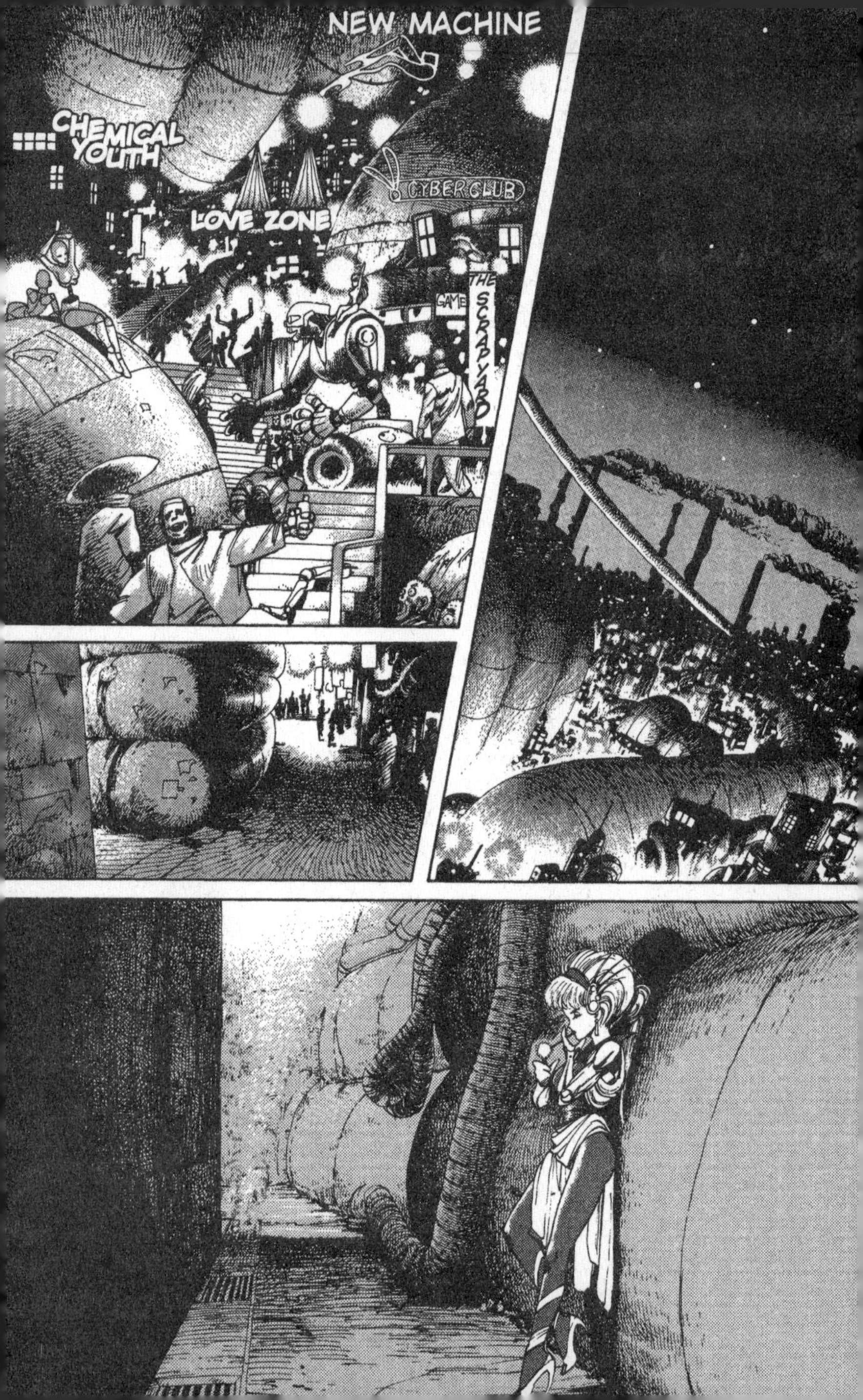
NEW MACHINE
CYBERCLUB
CHEMICAL YOUTH
LOVE ZONE
THE SCRAPYARD
GAME

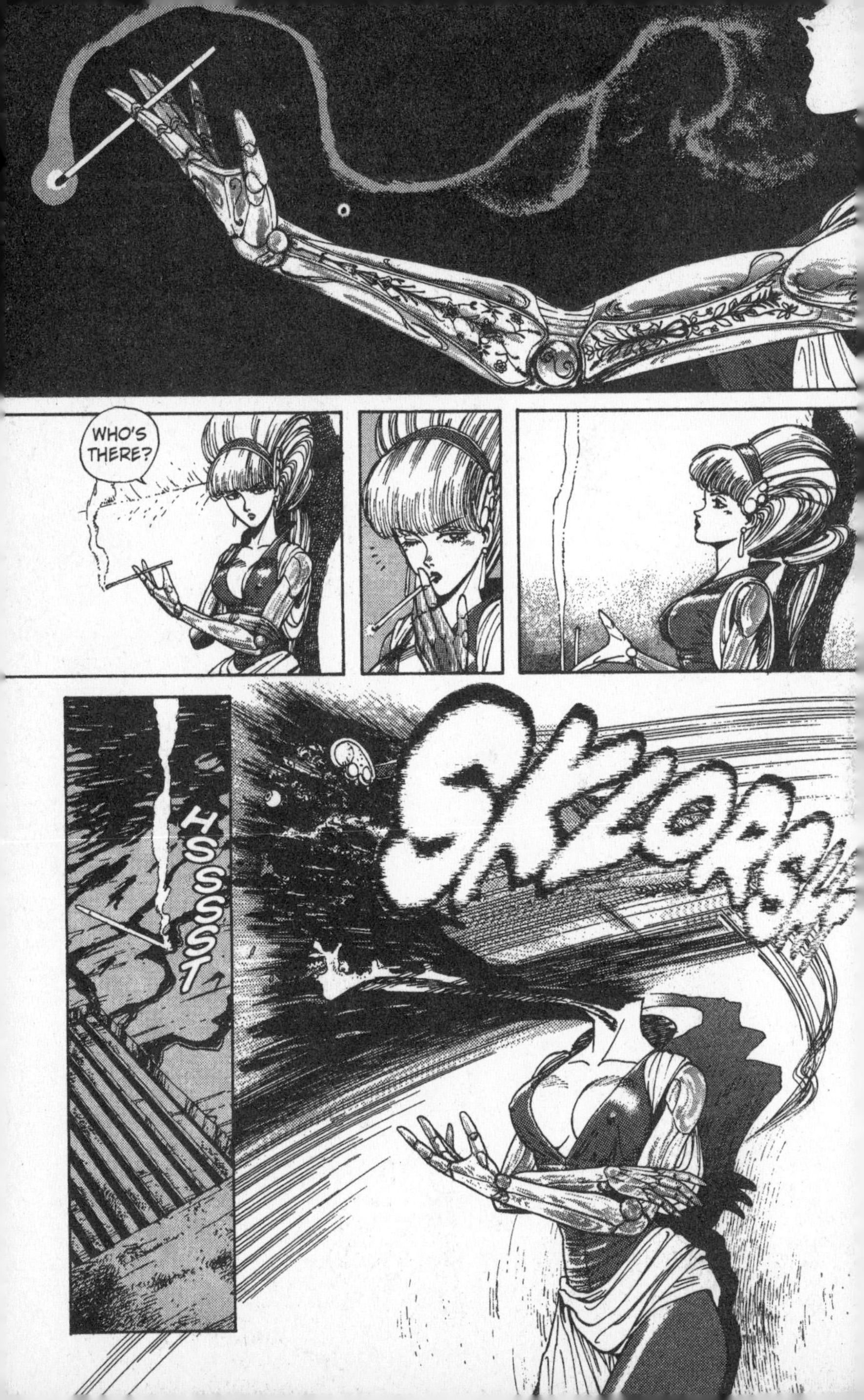
WHO'S THERE?
HSSSST

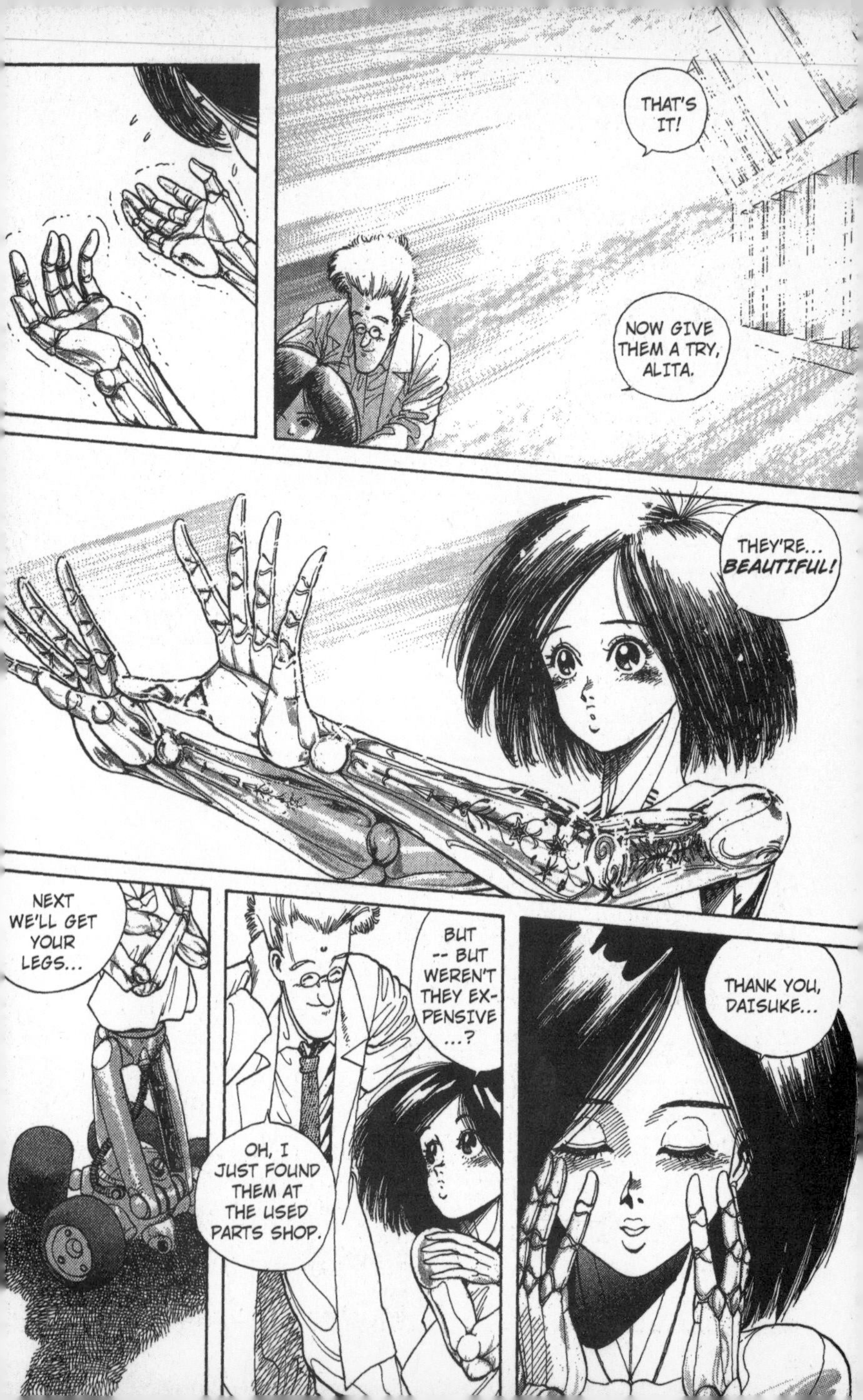
THAT'S IT!
NOW GIVE THEM A TRY, ALITA.
THEY'RE... **BEAUTIFUL!**
THANK YOU, DAISUKE...
BUT -- BUT WEREN'T THEY EX-PENSIVE ...?
OH, I JUST FOUND THEM AT THE USED PARTS SHOP.
NEXT WE'LL GET YOUR LEGS...

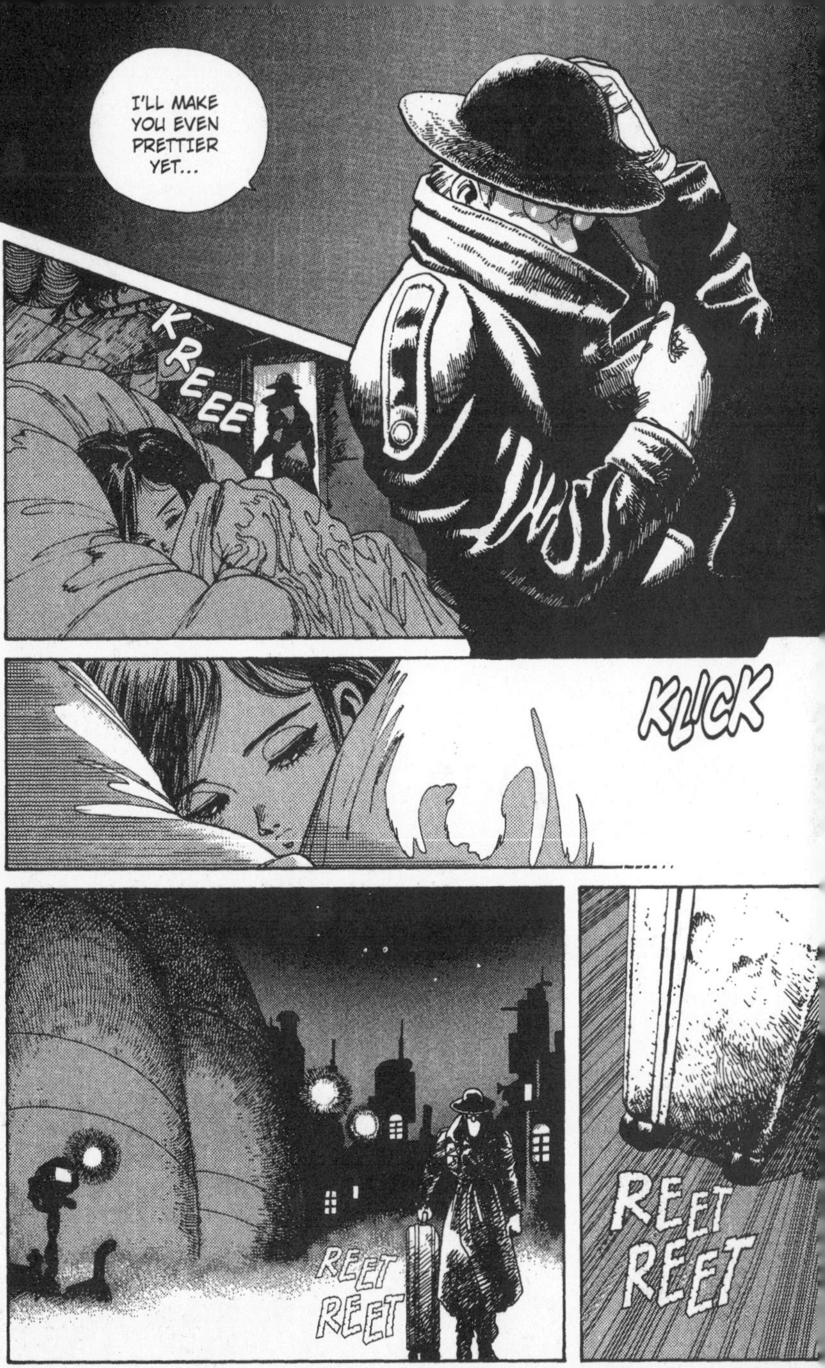
I'LL MAKE YOU EVEN PRETTIER YET...
KREEEE
KLICK
REET REET
REET REET

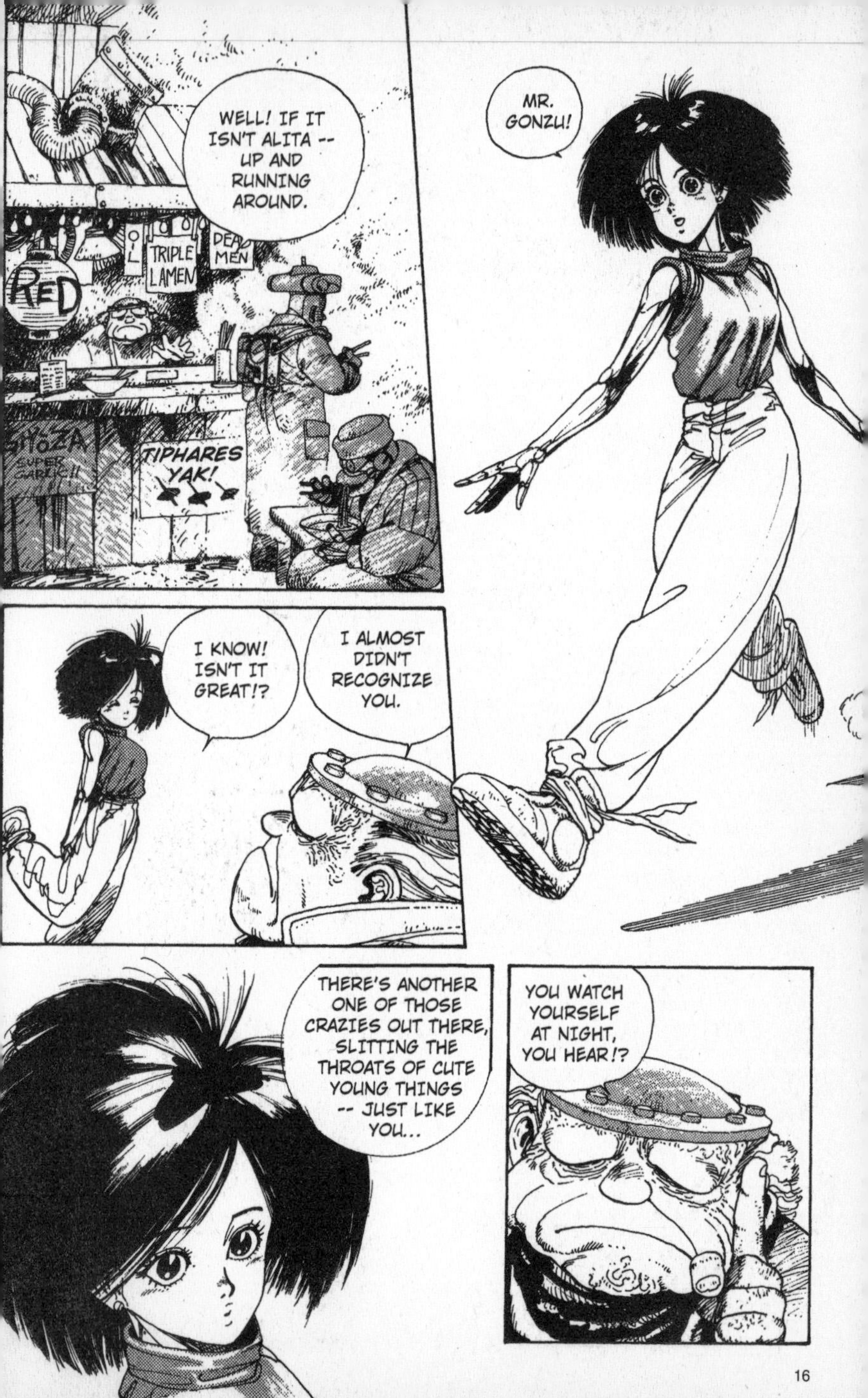
MR. GONZU!
WELL! IF IT ISN'T ALITA -- UP AND RUNNING AROUND.
OIL
DEAD MEN
TRIPLE LAMEN
RED
TIPHARES YAK!
I ALMOST DIDN'T RECOGNIZE YOU.
I KNOW! ISN'T IT GREAT!?
YOU WATCH YOURSELF AT NIGHT, YOU HEAR!?
THERE'S ANOTHER ONE OF THOSE CRAZIES OUT THERE, SLITTING THE THROATS OF CUTE YOUNG THINGS -- JUST LIKE YOU...

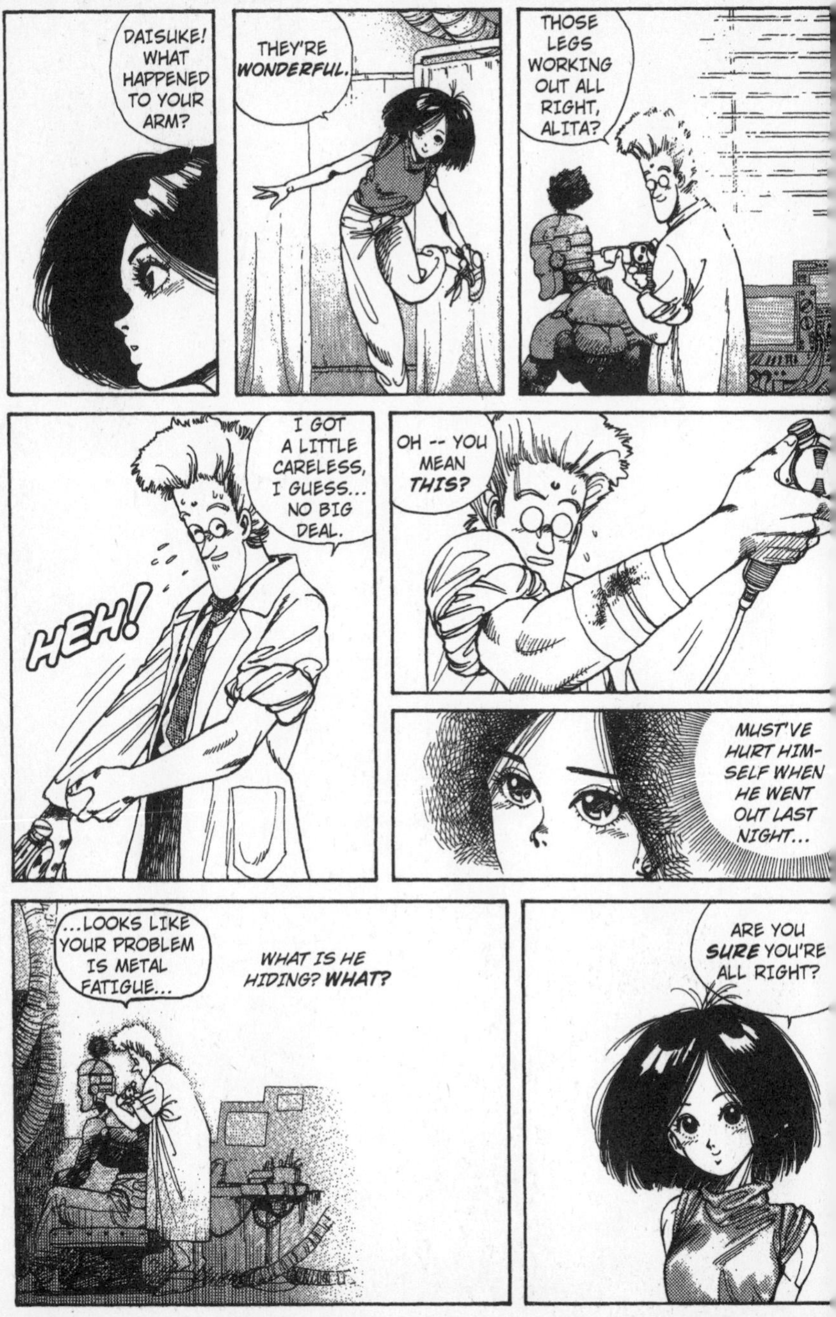
THOSE LEGS WORKING OUT ALL RIGHT, ALITA?
THEY'RE *WONDERFUL.*
DAISUKE! WHAT HAPPENED TO YOUR ARM?
OH -- YOU MEAN *THIS?*
MUST'VE HURT HIM-SELF WHEN HE WENT OUT LAST NIGHT...
I GOT A LITTLE CARELESS, I GUESS... NO BIG DEAL.
HEH!
ARE YOU **SURE** YOU'RE ALL RIGHT?
...LOOKS LIKE YOUR PROBLEM IS METAL FATIGUE...
WHAT IS HE HIDING? WHAT?

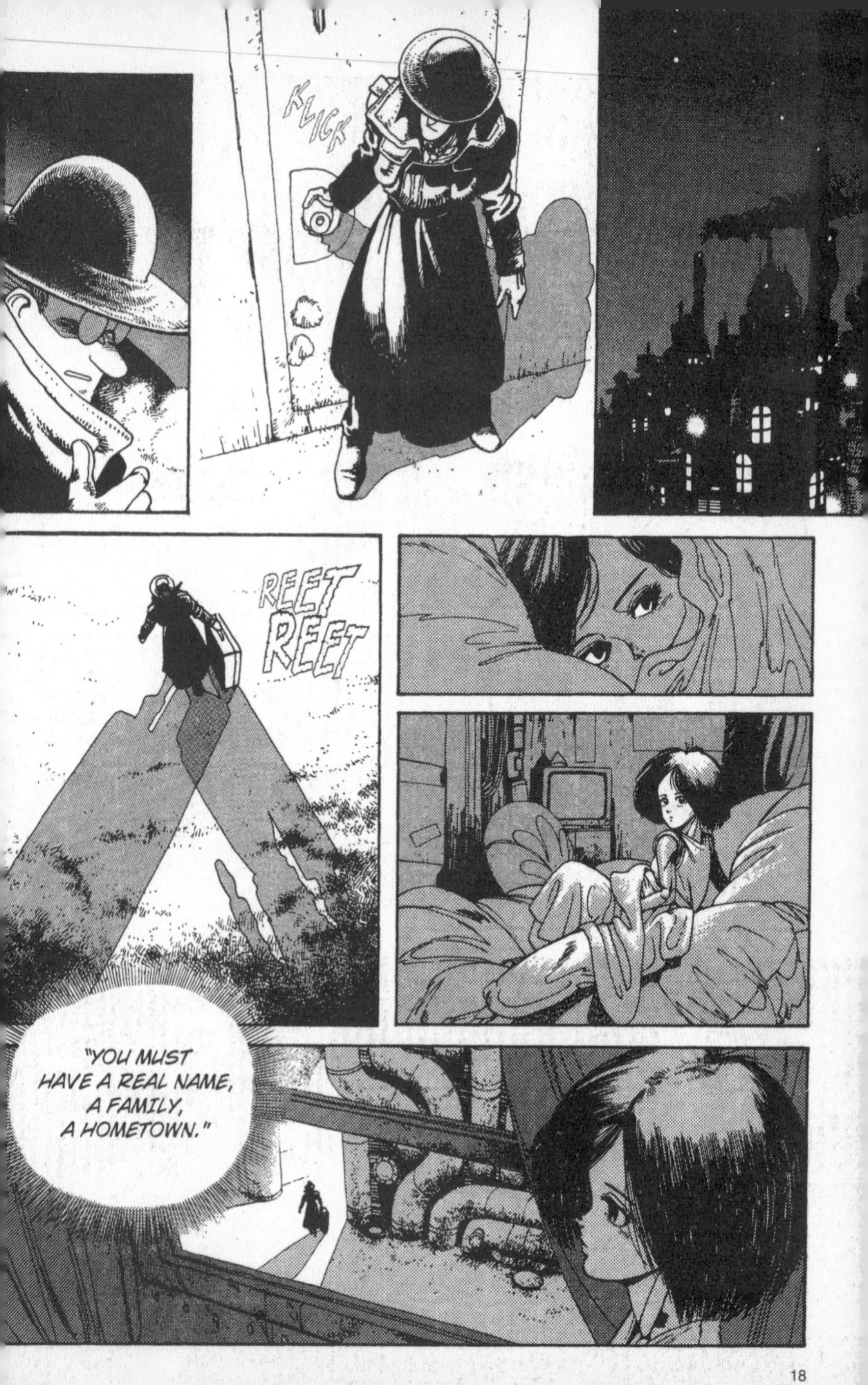
KLICK
REET REET
"YOU MUST HAVE A REAL NAME, A FAMILY, A HOMETOWN."

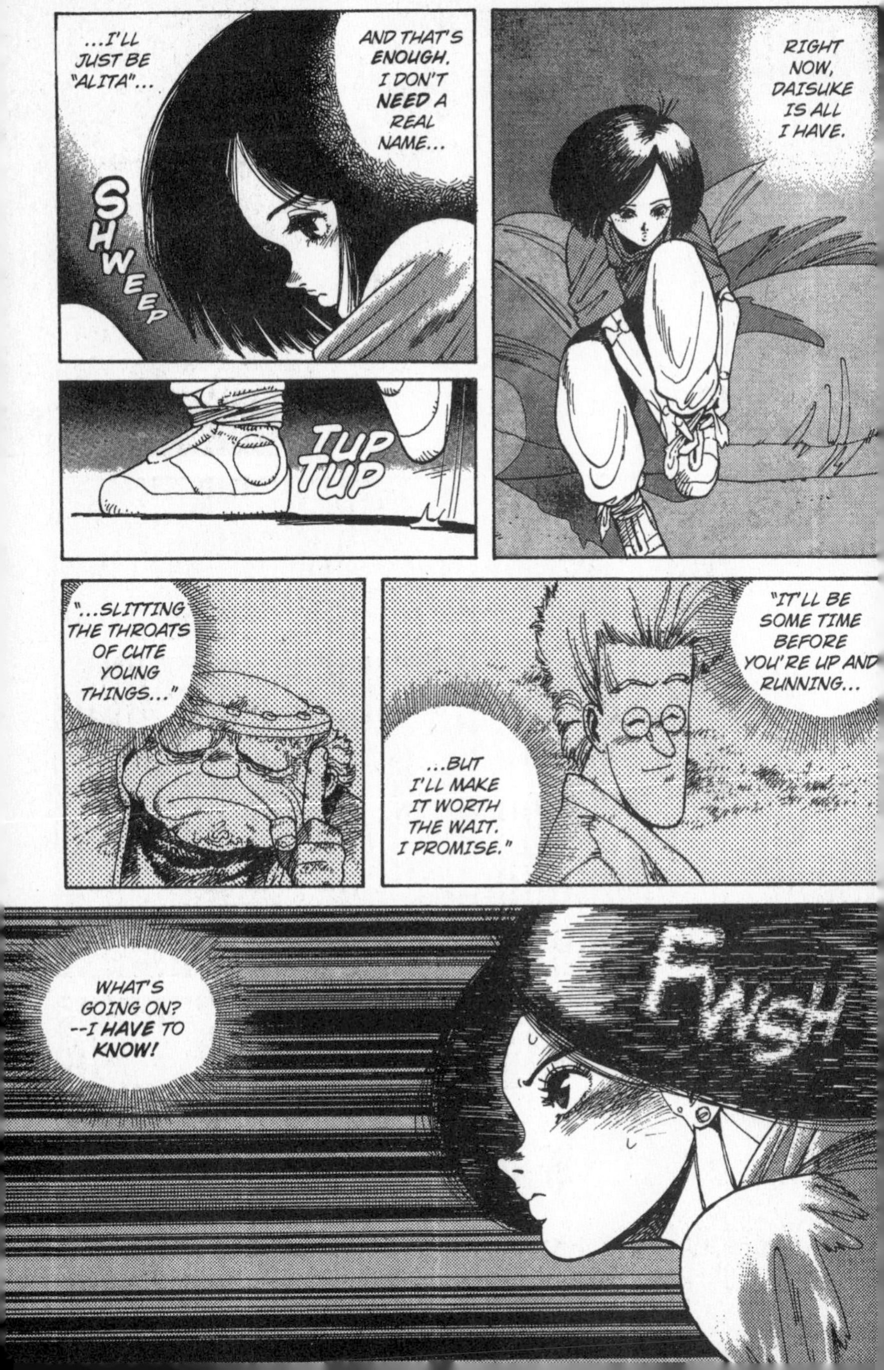
RIGHT NOW, DAISUKE IS ALL I HAVE.
AND THAT'S ENOUGH. I DON'T NEED A REAL NAME...
...I'LL JUST BE "ALITA"...
SHWEEP
TUP TUP
"IT'LL BE SOME TIME BEFORE YOU'RE UP AND RUNNING...
...BUT I'LL MAKE IT WORTH THE WAIT. I PROMISE."
"...SLITTING THE THROATS OF CUTE YOUNG THINGS..."
FWSH
WHAT'S GOING ON? --I HAVE TO KNOW!

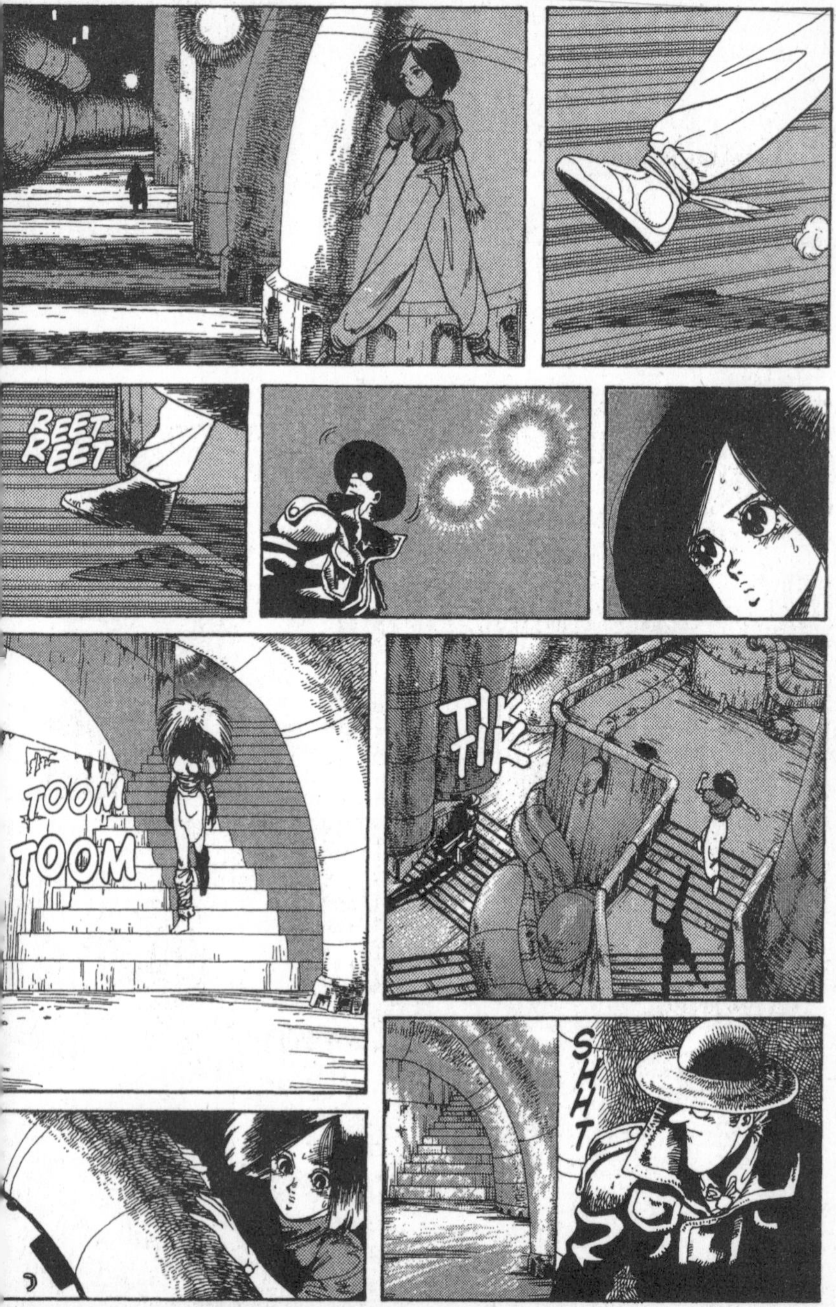
REET REET
TIK TIK
TOOM TOOM
SHHT

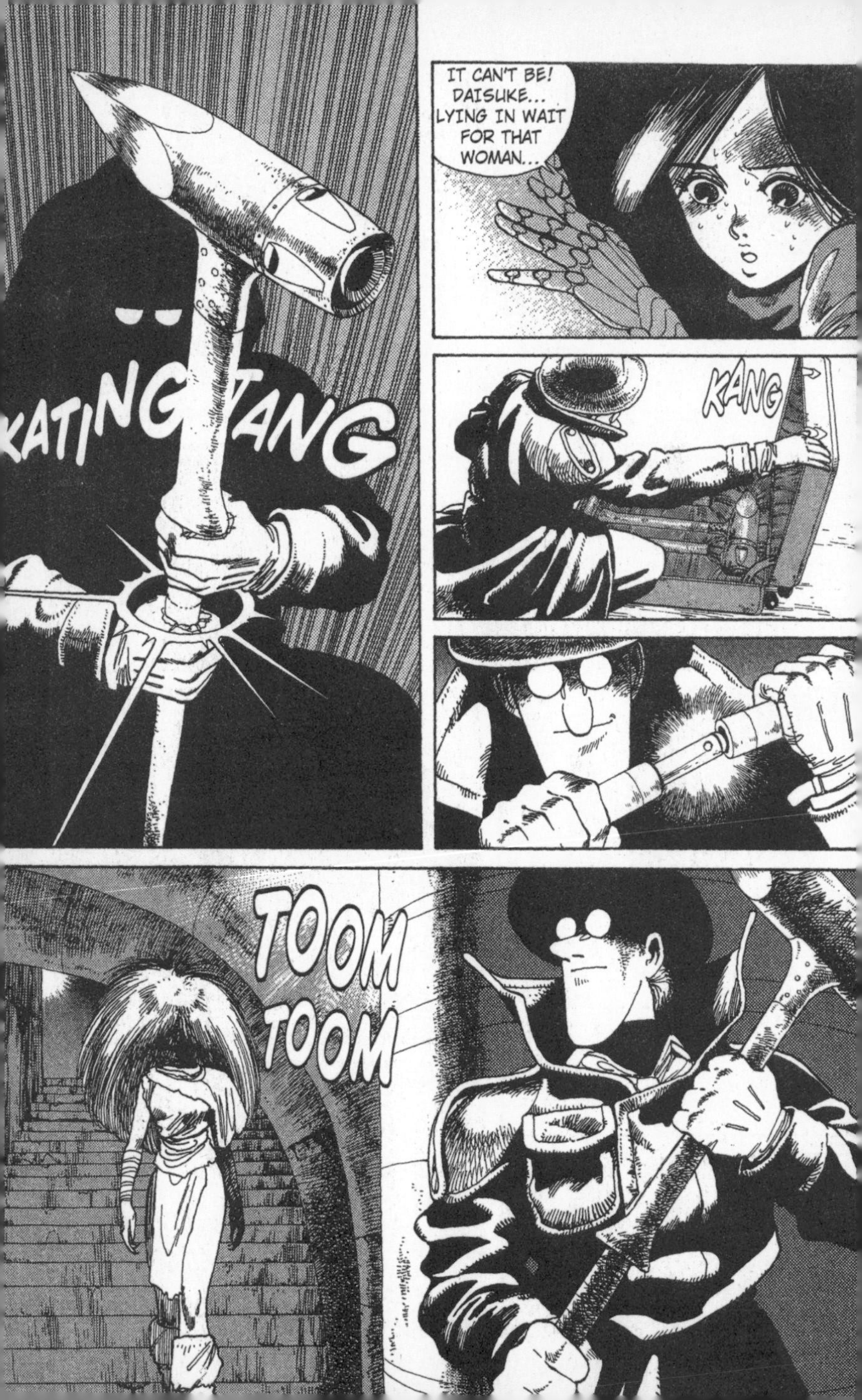
IT CAN'T BE! DAISUKE... LYING IN WAIT FOR THAT WOMAN...
KANG
KATING TANG
TOOM TOOM

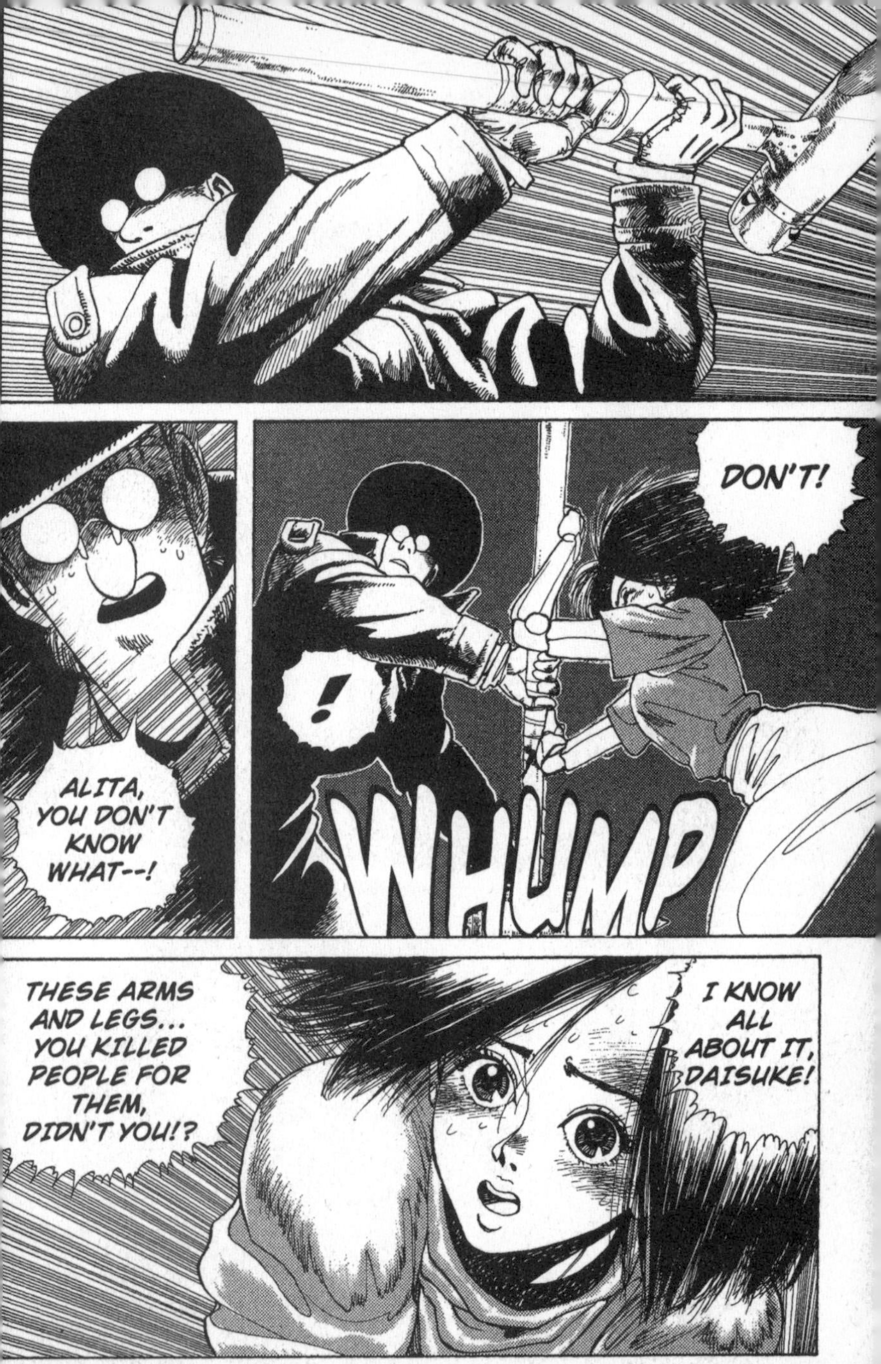
DON'T!
!
WHUMP
ALITA, YOU DON'T KNOW WHAT--!
I KNOW ALL ABOUT IT, DAISUKE!
THESE ARMS AND LEGS... YOU KILLED PEOPLE FOR THEM, DIDN'T YOU!?

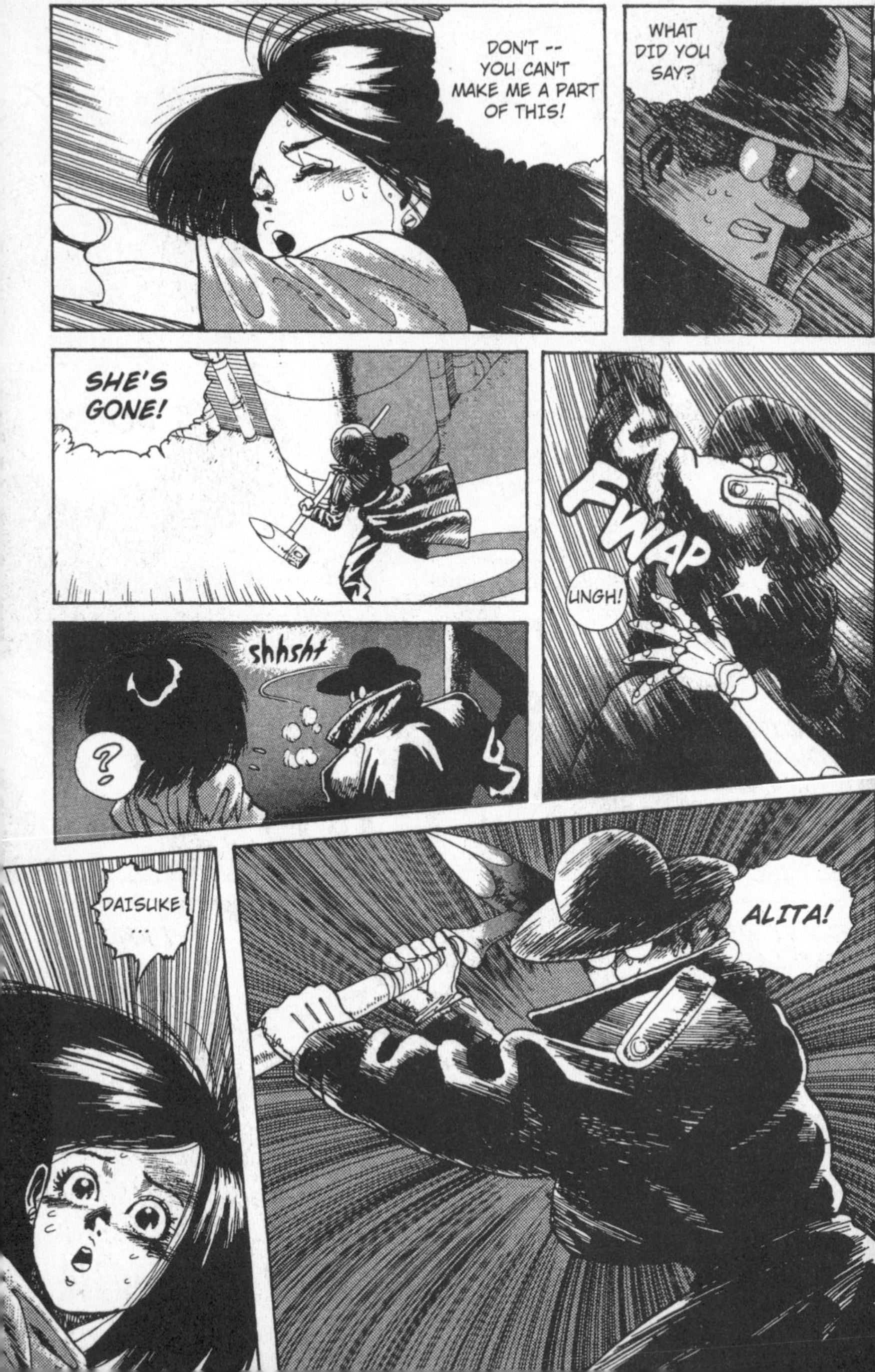

WHAT DID YOU SAY?
DON'T -- YOU CAN'T MAKE ME A PART OF THIS!
FWAP
UNGH!
SHE'S GONE!
shhsht
?
ALITA!
DAISUKE ...

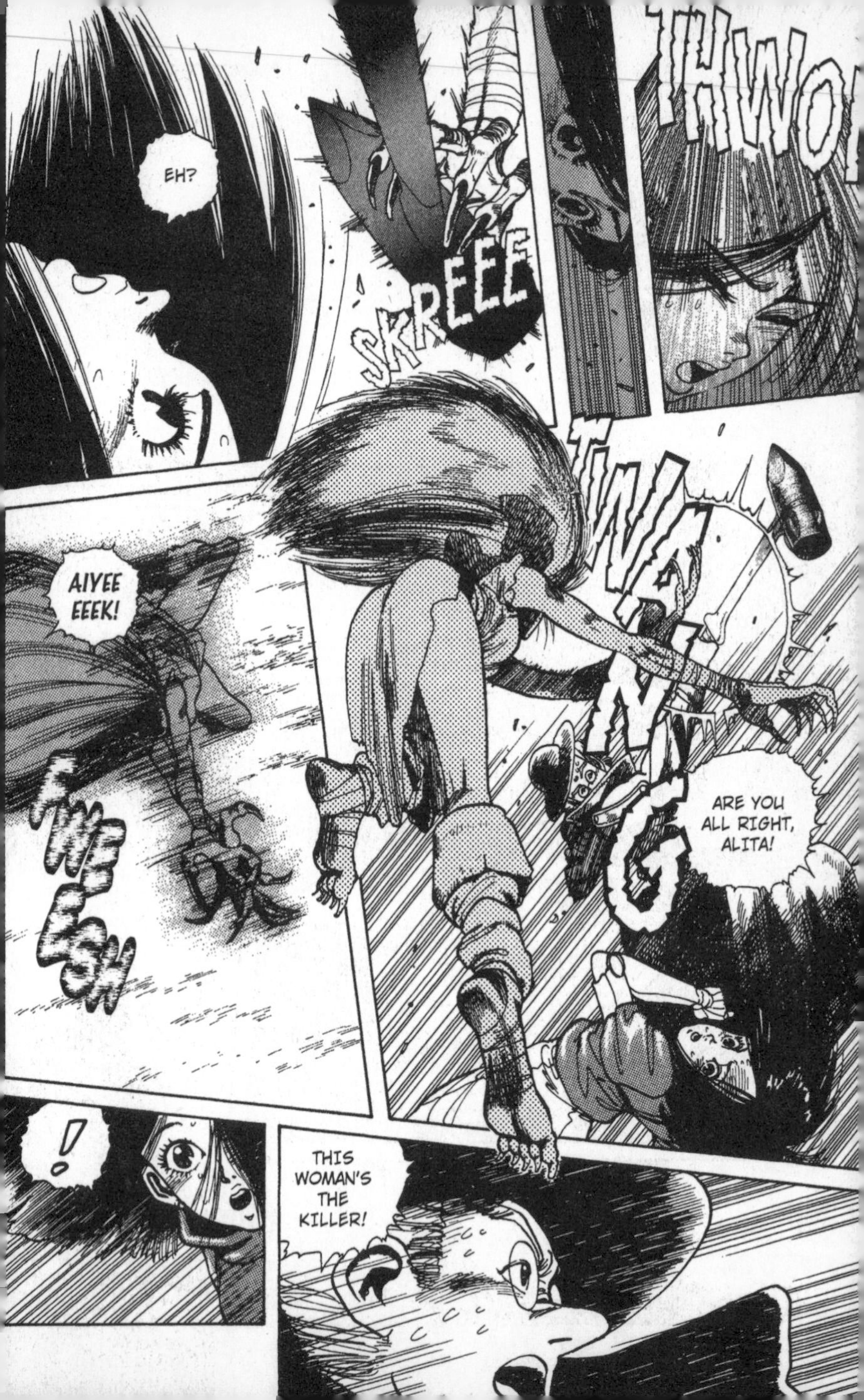
THWO
SKREEE
EH?
TWANNG
ARE YOU ALL RIGHT, ALITA!
AIYEE EEEK!
FWEESH
THIS WOMAN'S THE KILLER!
!

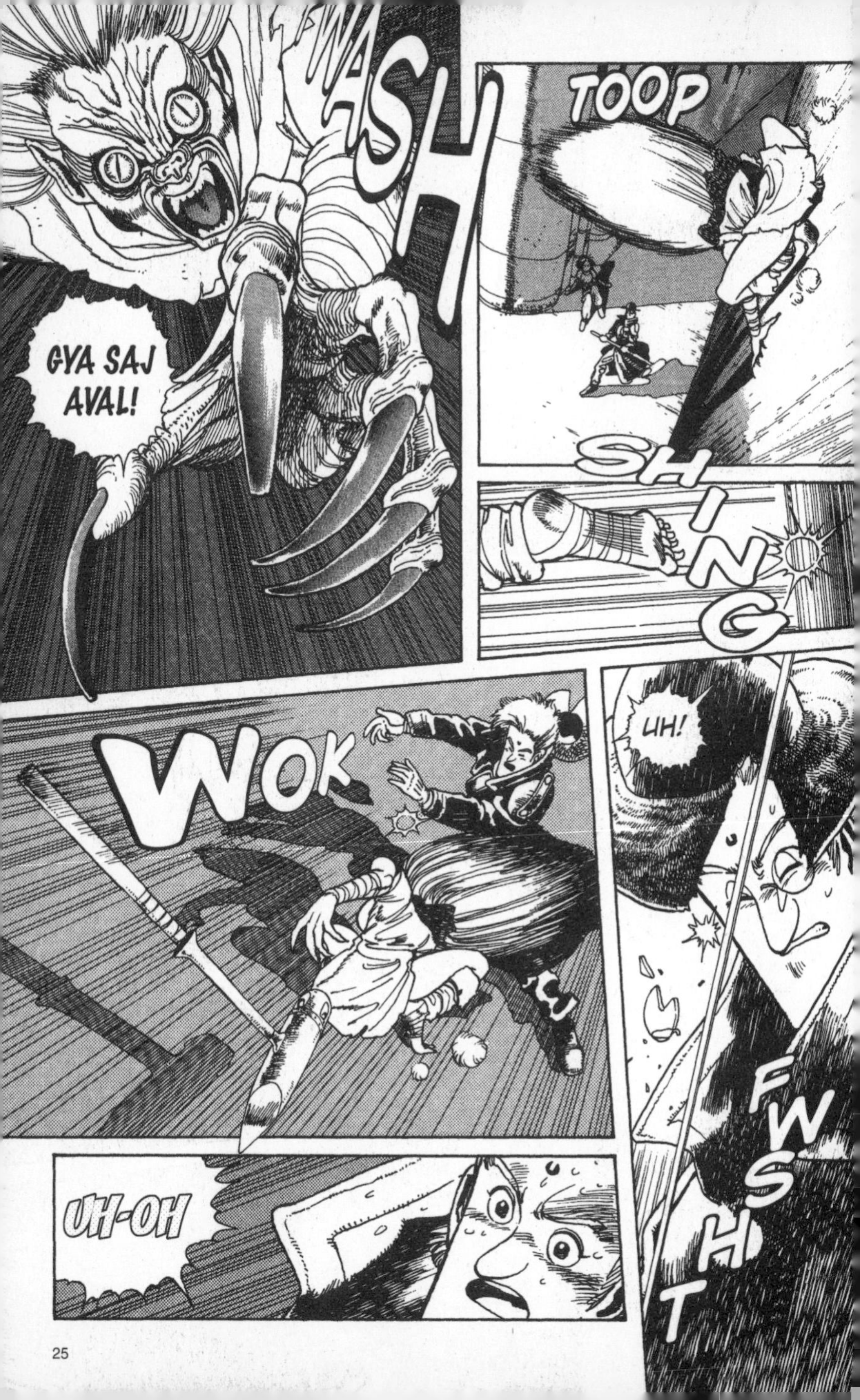
TOOP
SHING
FWASH
GYA SAJ AVAL!
UH!
FWSHT
WOK
UH-OH

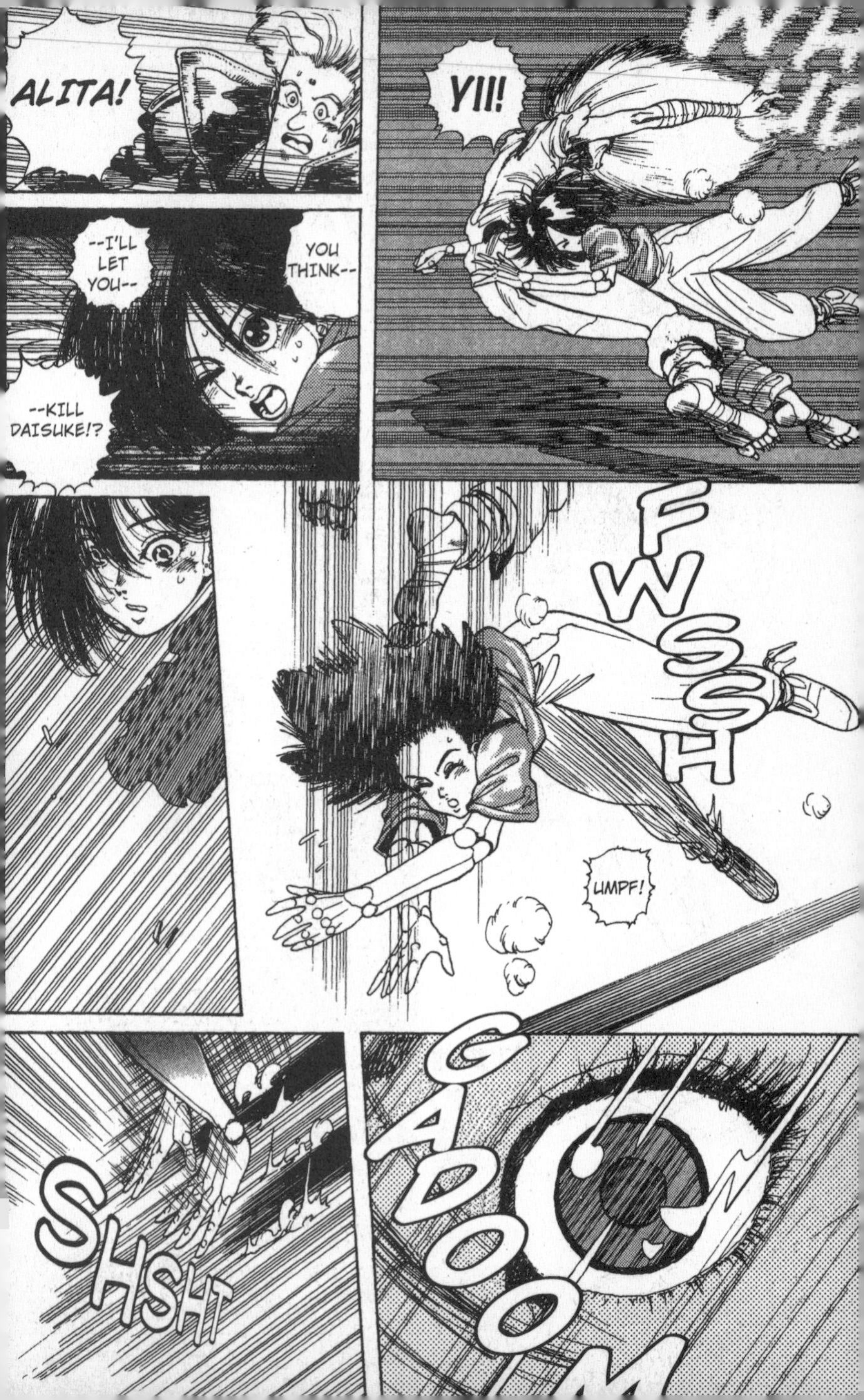
YII!
ALITA!
YOU THINK--
--I'LL LET YOU--
--KILL DAISUKE!?
FWSSH
UMPF!
GADOOOM
SHSHT

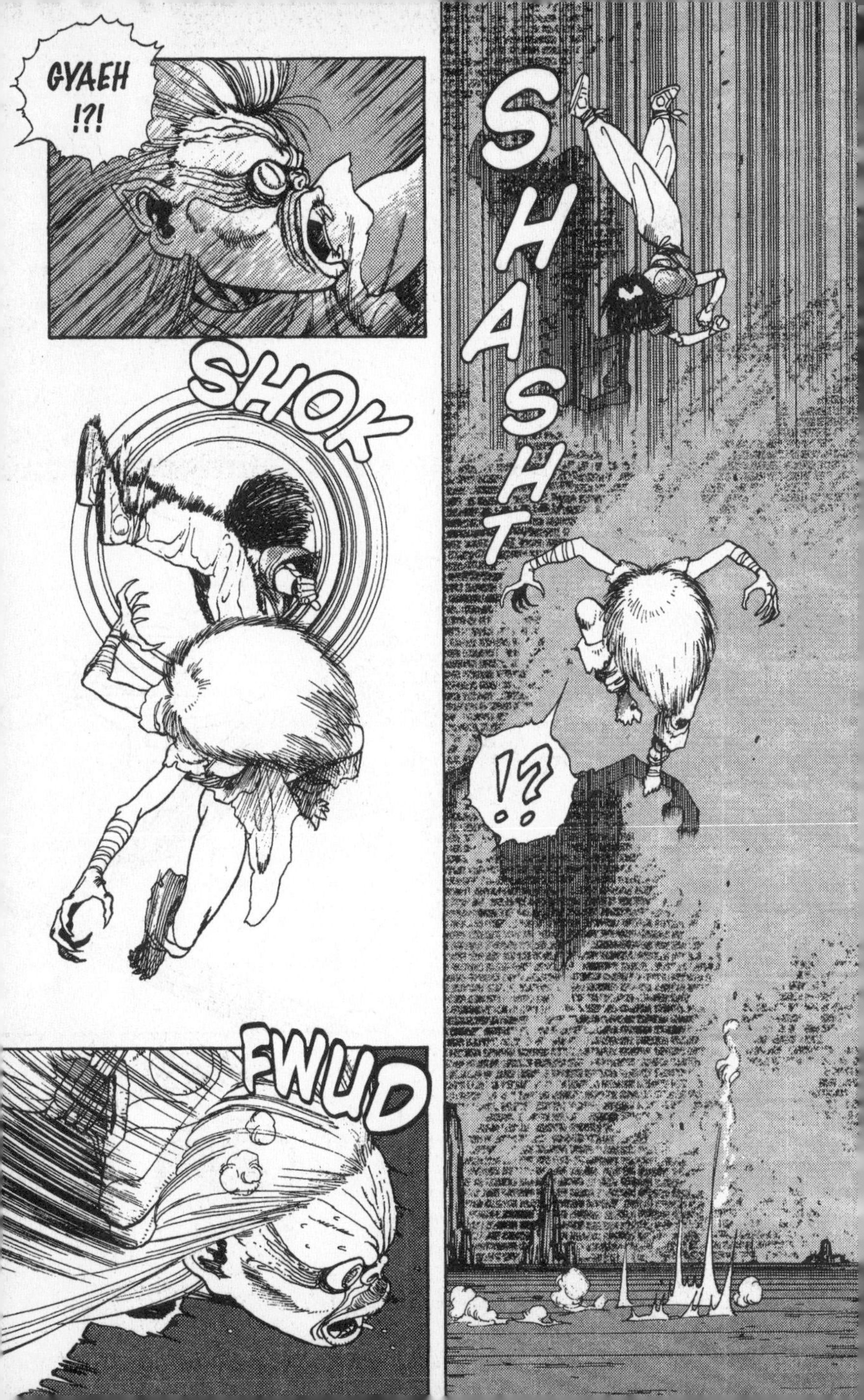
SHASHT
!?
GYAEH !?!
SHOK
FWUD

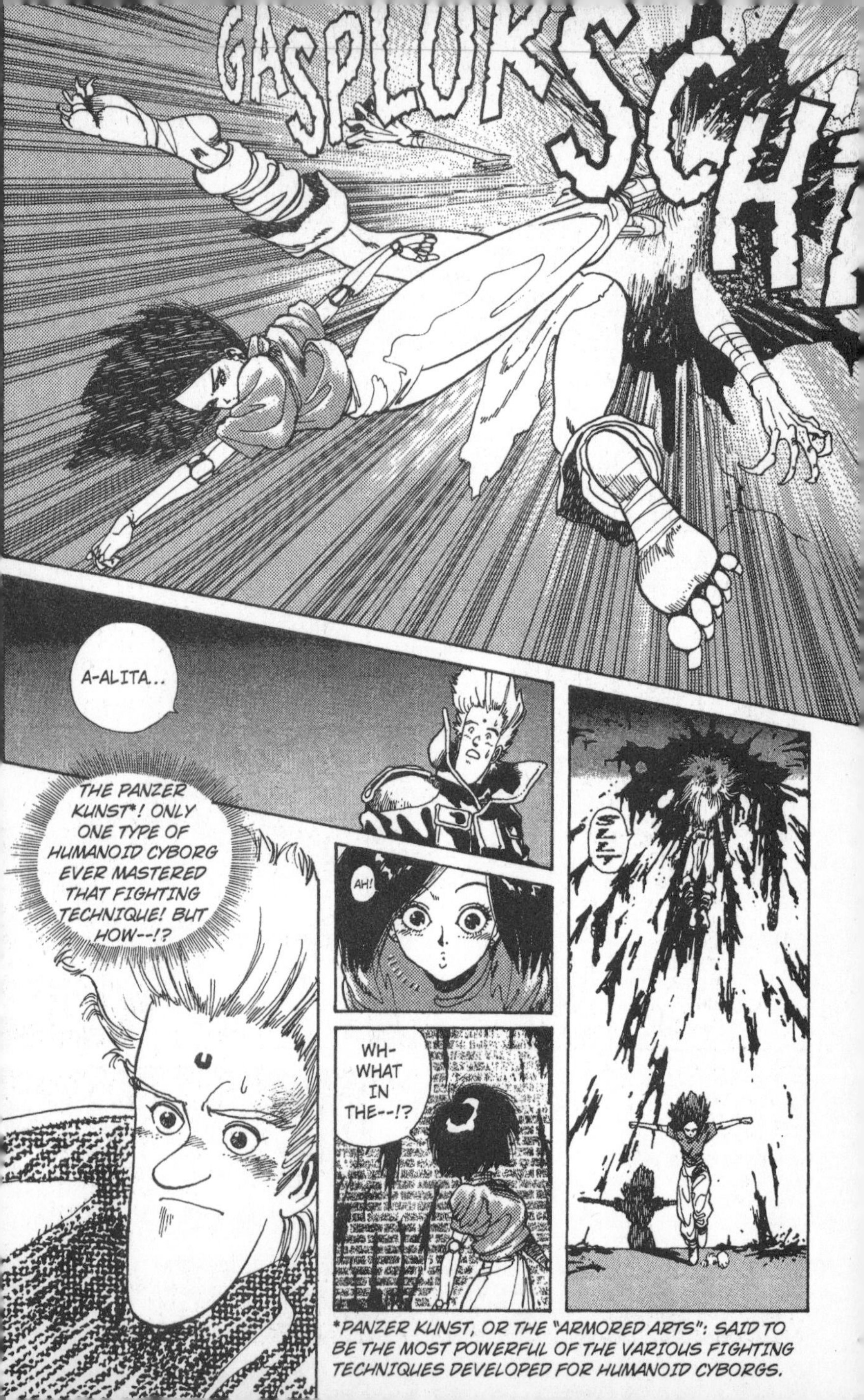
GASPLUK
SCH
A-ALITA...
AH!
WH-WHAT IN THE--!?
THE PANZER KUNST*! ONLY ONE TYPE OF HUMANOID CYBORG EVER MASTERED THAT FIGHTING TECHNIQUE! BUT HOW--!?

*PANZER KUNST, OR THE "ARMORED ARTS": SAID TO BE THE MOST POWERFUL OF THE VARIOUS FIGHTING TECHNIQUES DEVELOPED FOR HUMANOID CYBORGS.

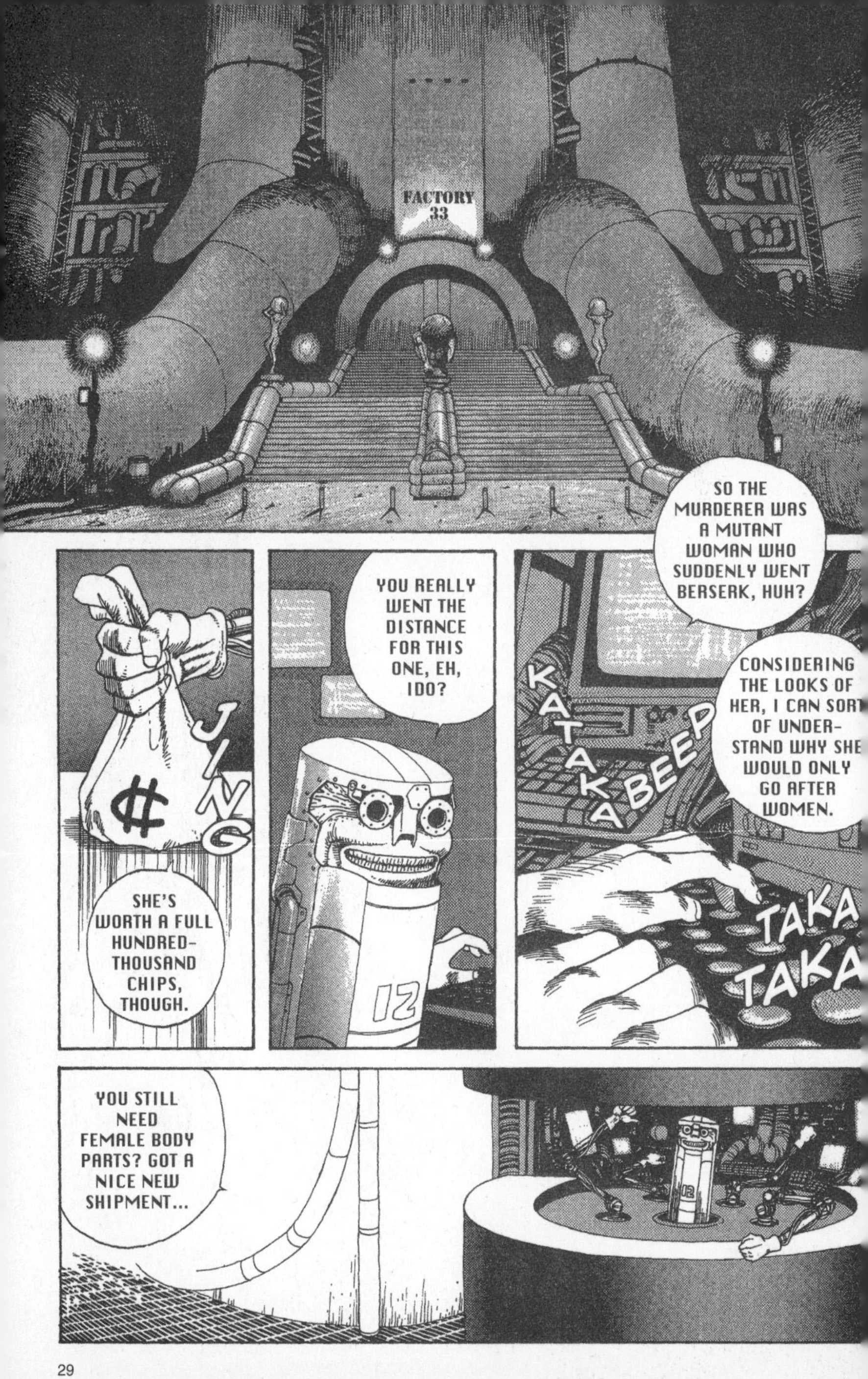
FACTORY 33
SO THE MURDERER WAS A MUTANT WOMAN WHO SUDDENLY WENT BERSERK, HUH?
CONSIDERING THE LOOKS OF HER, I CAN SORT OF UNDER-STAND WHY SHE WOULD ONLY GO AFTER WOMEN.
KATAKA
BEEP
TAKA TAKA
YOU REALLY WENT THE DISTANCE FOR THIS ONE, EH, IDO?
12
JING
SHE'S WORTH A FULL HUNDRED-THOUSAND CHIPS, THOUGH.
YOU STILL NEED FEMALE BODY PARTS? GOT A NICE NEW SHIPMENT...

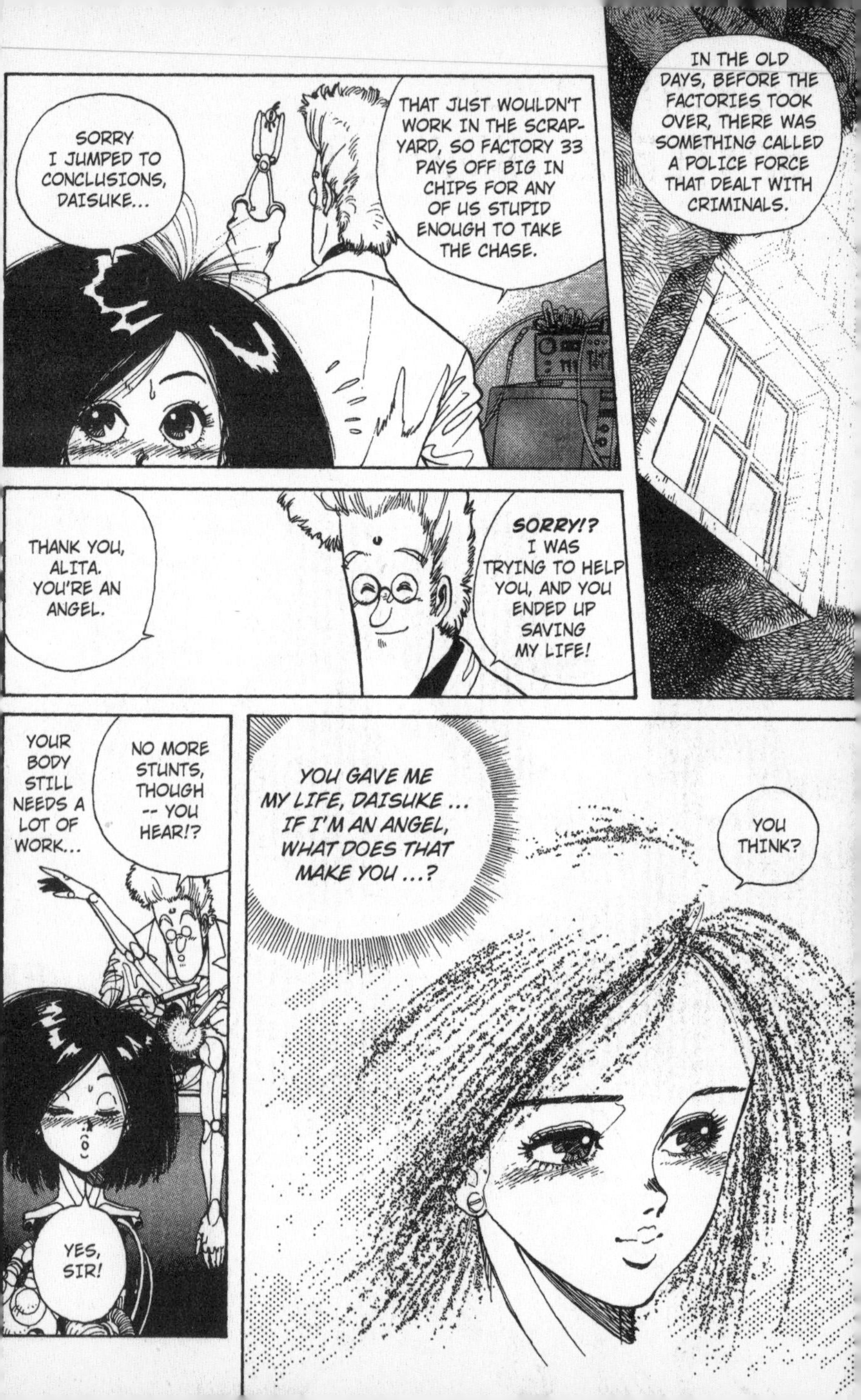

IN THE OLD DAYS, BEFORE THE FACTORIES TOOK OVER, THERE WAS SOMETHING CALLED A POLICE FORCE THAT DEALT WITH CRIMINALS.
THAT JUST WOULDN'T WORK IN THE SCRAP-YARD, SO FACTORY 33 PAYS OFF BIG IN CHIPS FOR ANY OF US STUPID ENOUGH TO TAKE THE CHASE.
SORRY I JUMPED TO CONCLUSIONS, DAISUKE...
SORRY!? I WAS TRYING TO HELP YOU, AND YOU ENDED UP SAVING MY LIFE!
THANK YOU, ALITA. YOU'RE AN ANGEL.
YOU THINK?
YOU GAVE ME MY LIFE, DAISUKE ... IF I'M AN ANGEL, WHAT DOES THAT MAKE YOU ...?
NO MORE STUNTS, THOUGH -- YOU HEAR!?
YOUR BODY STILL NEEDS A LOT OF WORK...
YES, SIR!

FIGHTING BLOOD
BATTLE 2: AWAKENING

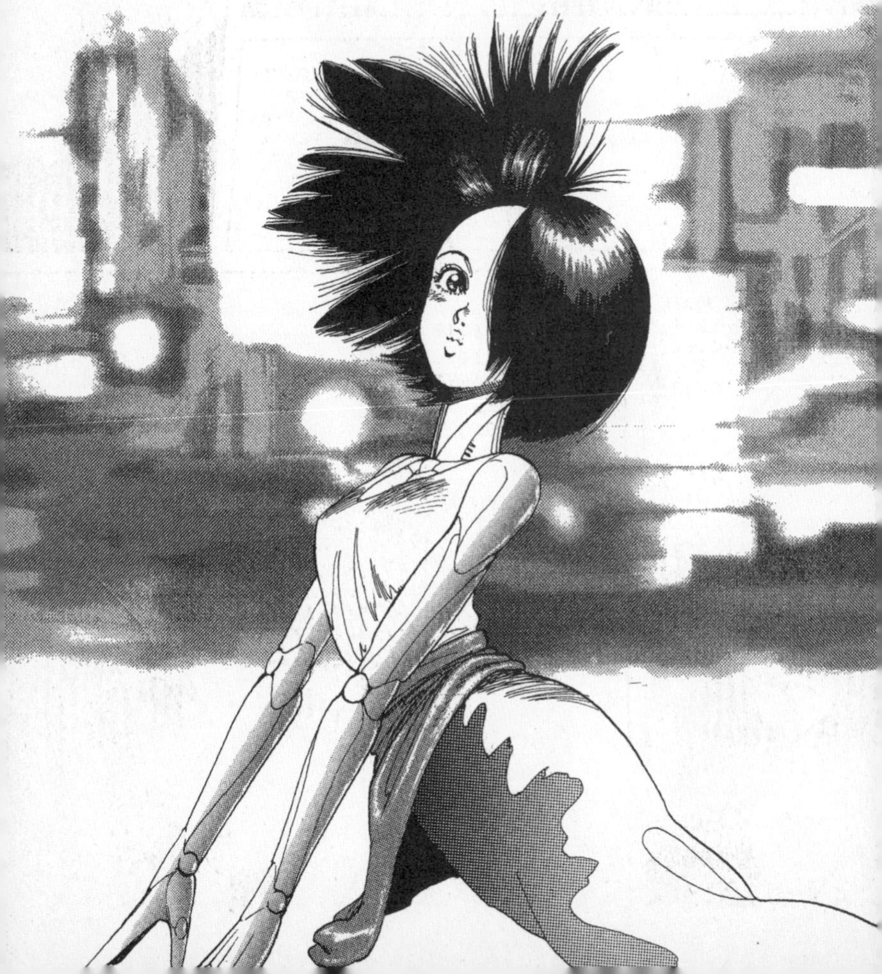

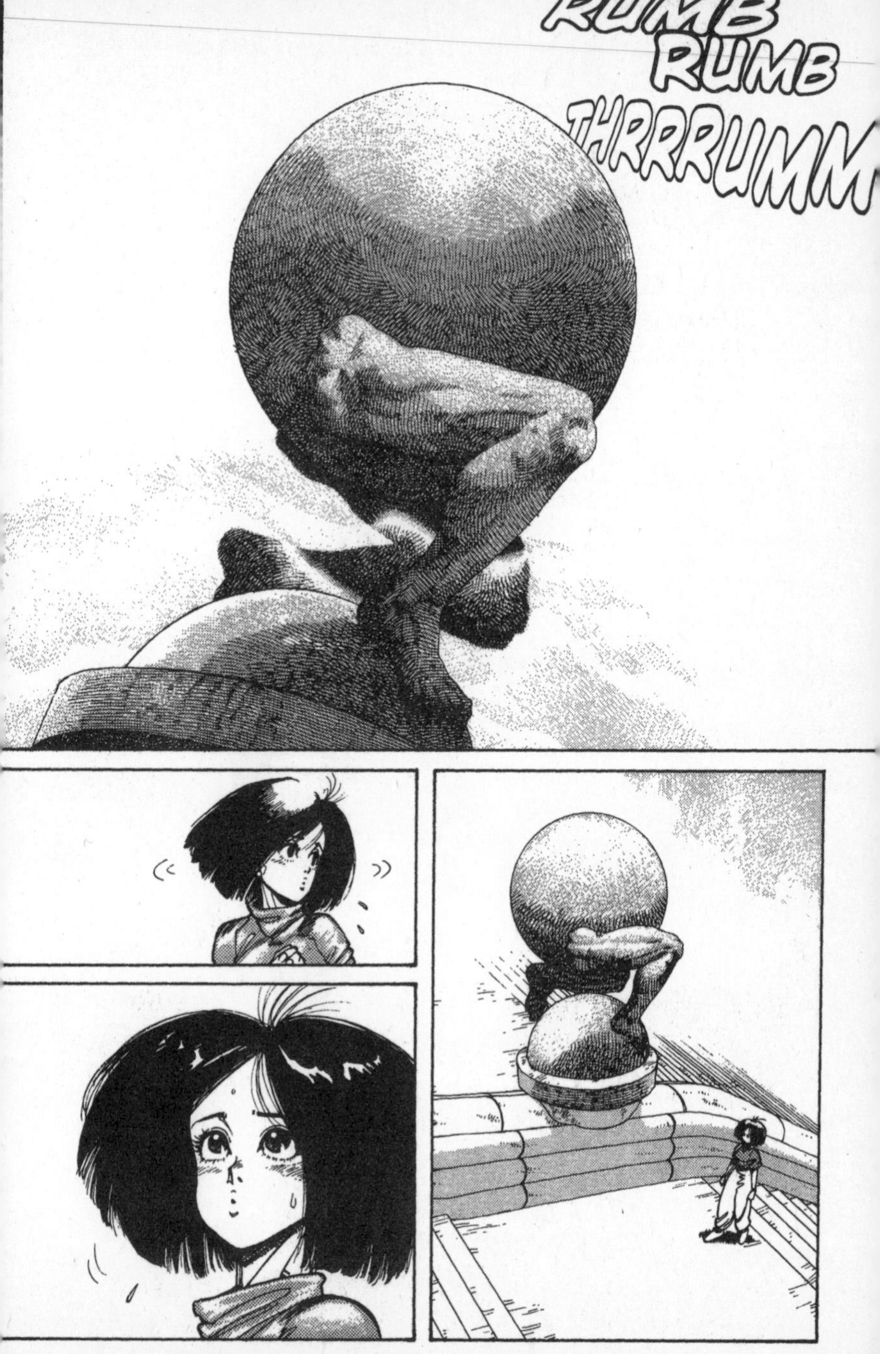
RUMB
RUMB
THRRRUMM

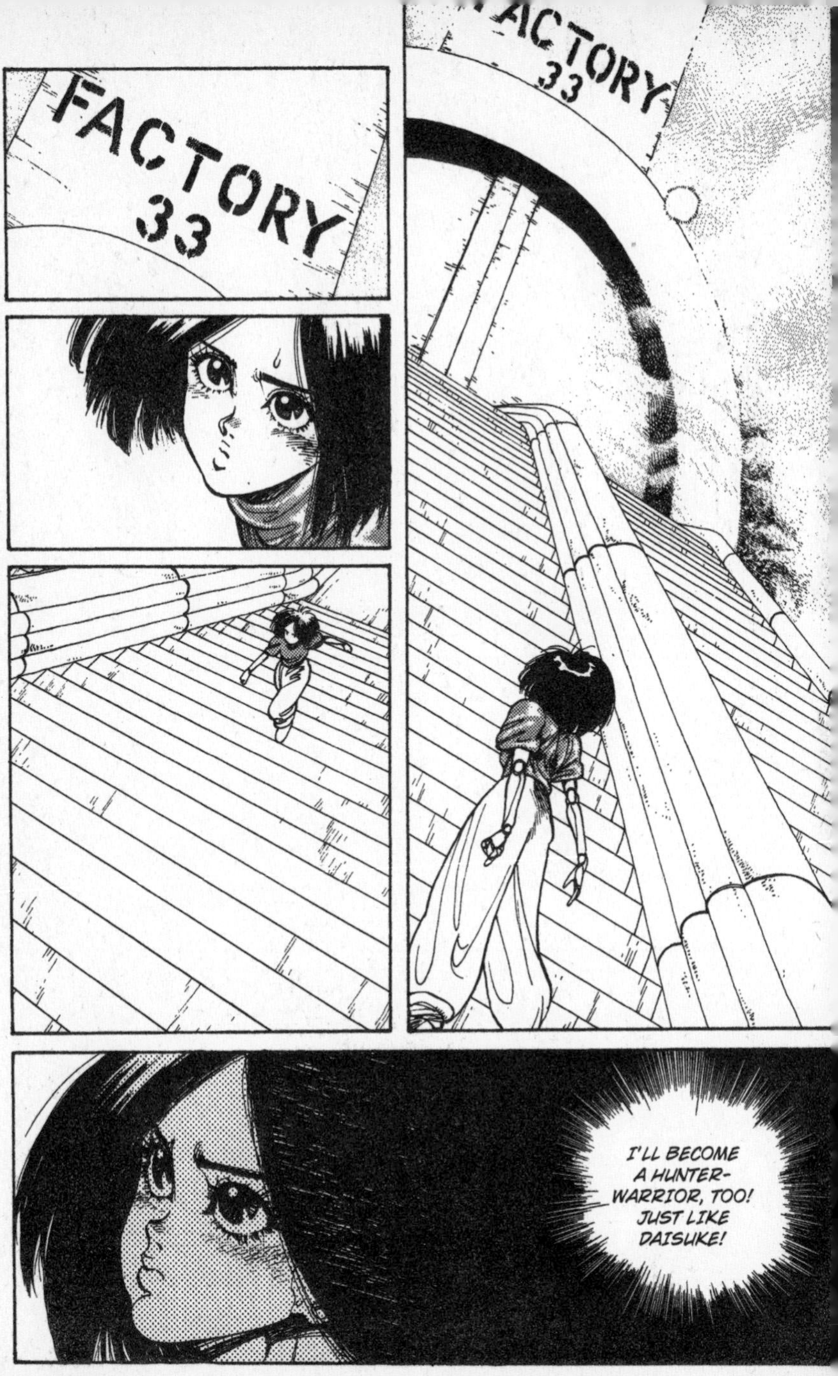
FACTORY 33
FACTORY 33
I'LL BECOME A HUNTER-WARRIOR, TOO! JUST LIKE DAISUKE!

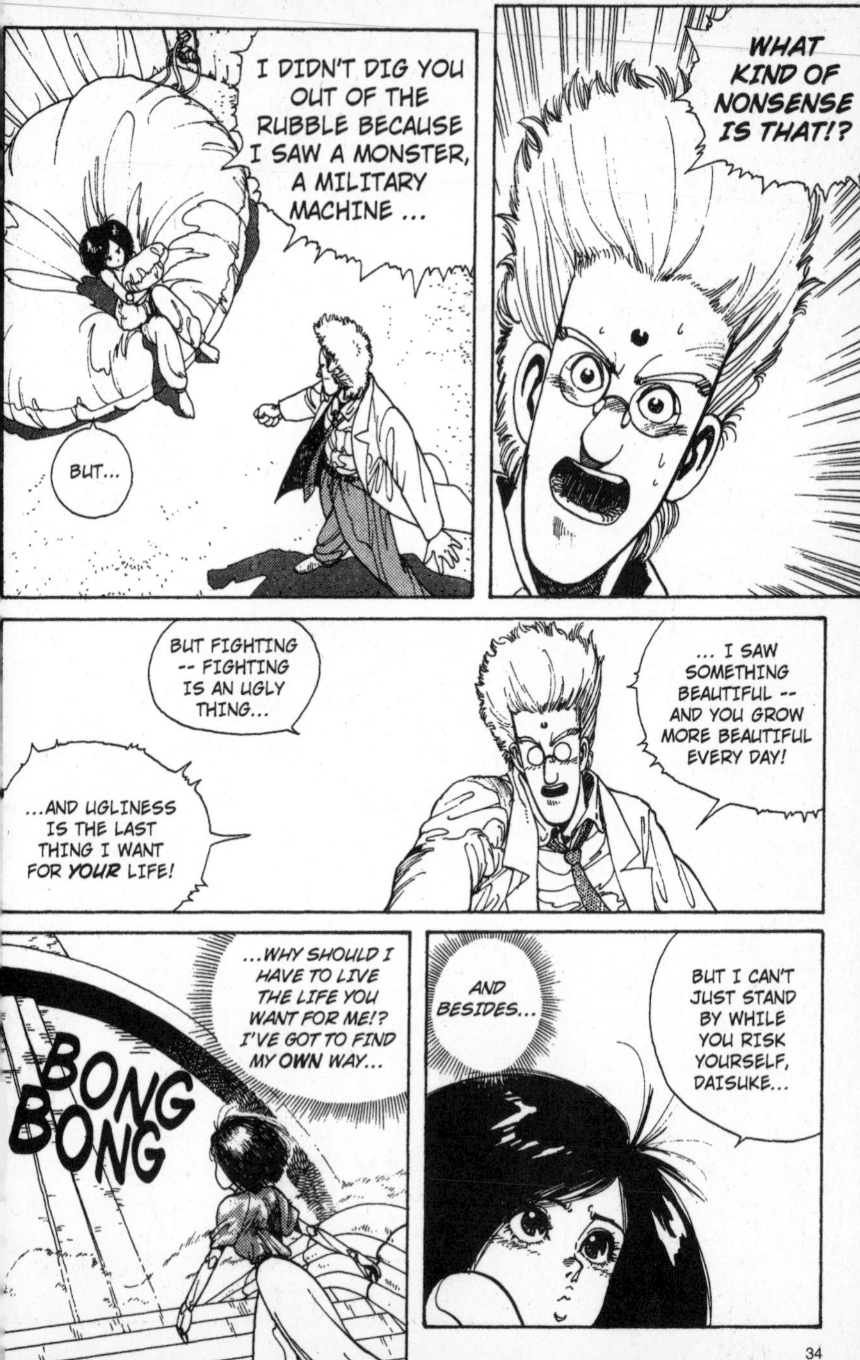

WHAT KIND OF NONSENSE IS THAT!?
I DIDN'T DIG YOU OUT OF THE RUBBLE BECAUSE I SAW A MONSTER, A MILITARY MACHINE ...
BUT...
... I SAW SOMETHING BEAUTIFUL -- AND YOU GROW MORE BEAUTIFUL EVERY DAY!
BUT FIGHTING -- FIGHTING IS AN UGLY THING...
...AND UGLINESS IS THE LAST THING I WANT FOR *YOUR* LIFE!
BUT I CAN'T JUST STAND BY WHILE YOU RISK YOURSELF, DAISUKE...
AND BESIDES...
...WHY SHOULD I HAVE TO LIVE THE LIFE YOU WANT FOR ME!? I'VE GOT TO FIND MY **OWN** WAY...
BONG BONG

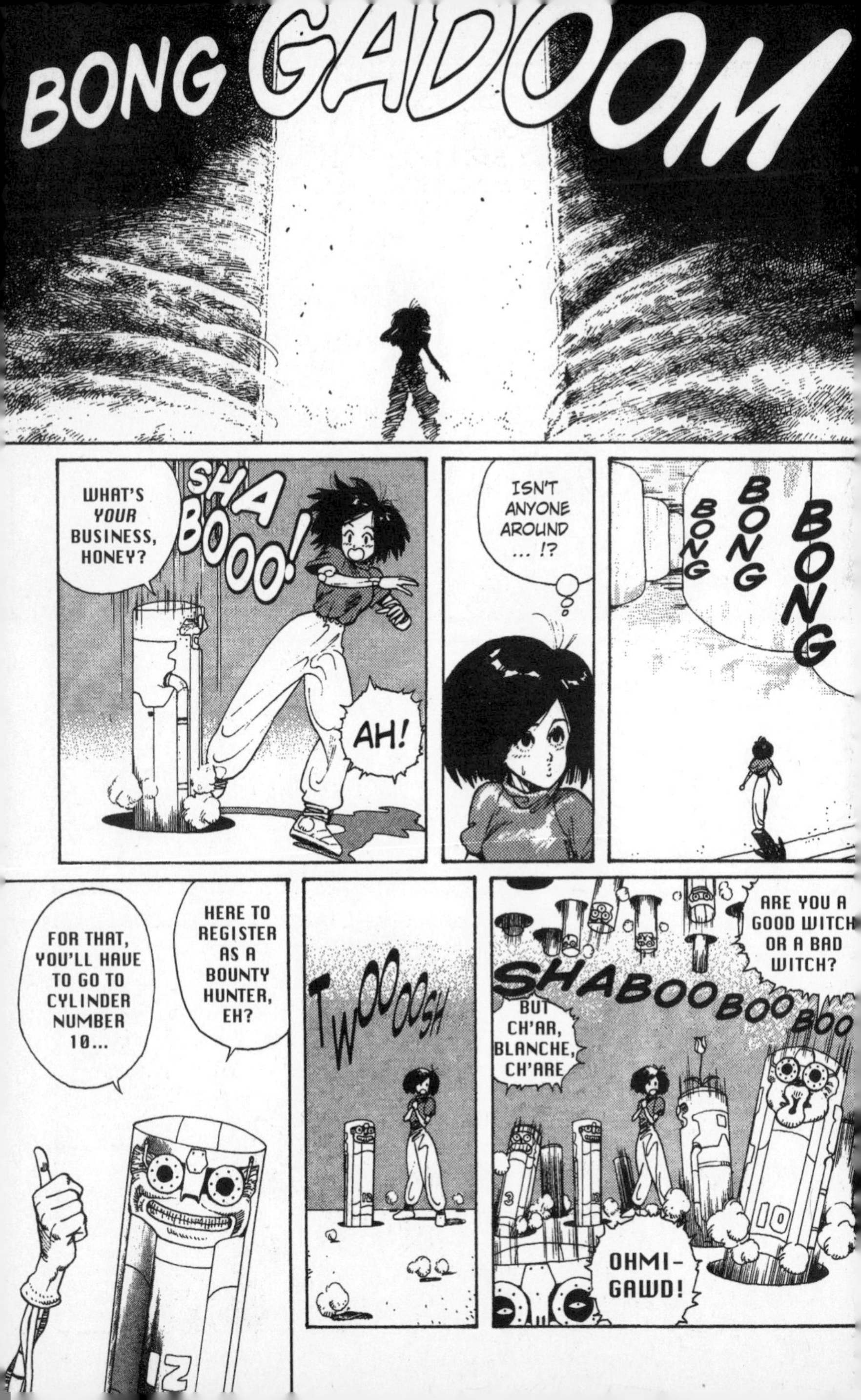
BONG GADOOOM
BONG BONG BONG
ISN'T ANYONE AROUND ...!?
SHABOOO!
WHAT'S *YOUR* BUSINESS, HONEY?
AH!
ARE YOU A GOOD WITCH OR A BAD WITCH?
SHABOOBOOBOO
BUT CH'AR, BLANCHE, CH'ARE
OHMI-GAWD!
TWOOOOSH
HERE TO REGISTER AS A BOUNTY HUNTER, EH?
FOR THAT, YOU'LL HAVE TO GO TO CYLINDER NUMBER 10...

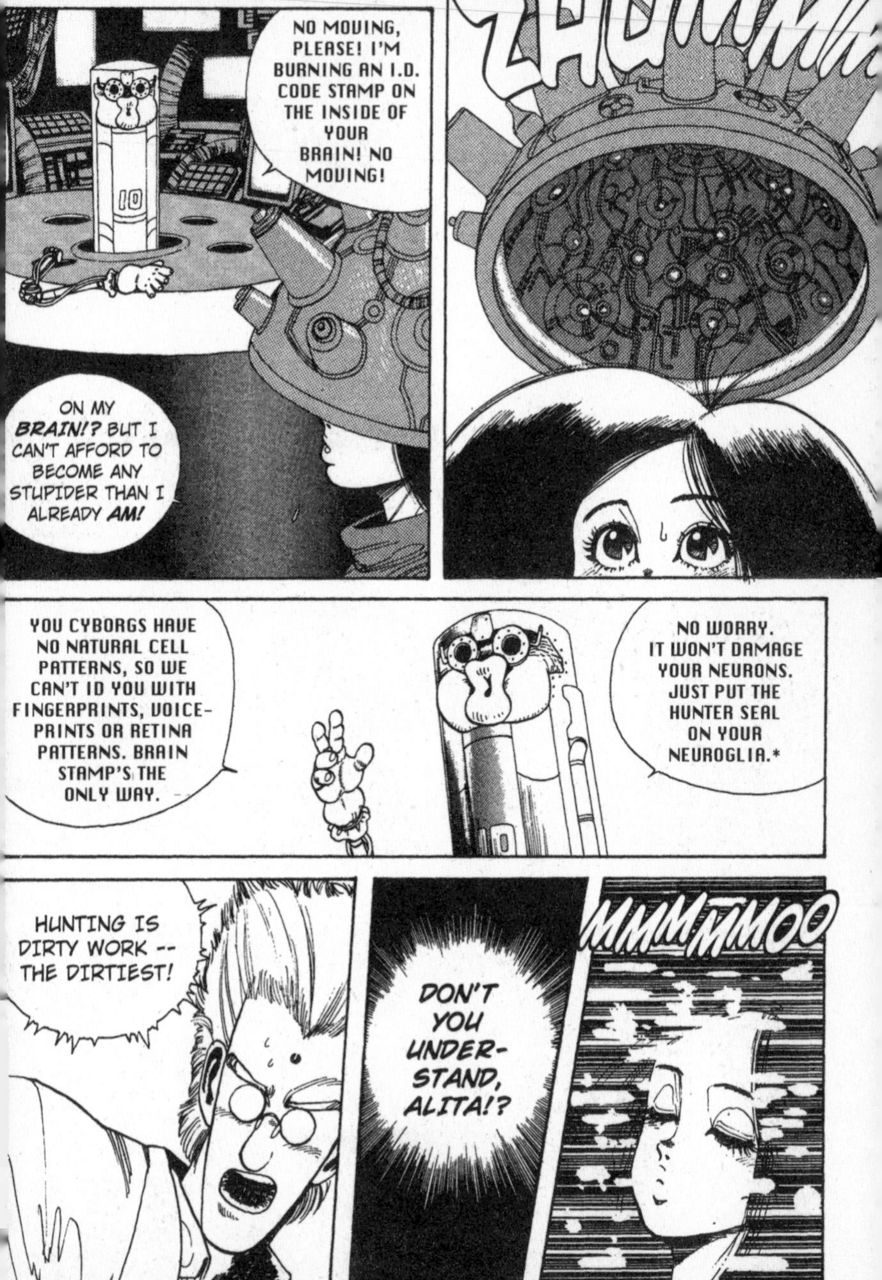
ZHUMMM
NO MOVING, PLEASE! I'M BURNING AN I.D. CODE STAMP ON THE INSIDE OF YOUR BRAIN! NO MOVING!
ON MY *BRAIN!?* BUT I CAN'T AFFORD TO BECOME ANY STUPIDER THAN I ALREADY *AM!*
NO WORRY. IT WON'T DAMAGE YOUR NEURONS. JUST PUT THE HUNTER SEAL ON YOUR NEUROGLIA.*
YOU CYBORGS HAVE NO NATURAL CELL PATTERNS, SO WE CAN'T ID YOU WITH FINGERPRINTS, VOICE-PRINTS OR RETINA PATTERNS. BRAIN STAMP'S THE ONLY WAY.
MMMMMMOO
DON'T YOU UNDER-STAND, ALITA!?
HUNTING IS DIRTY WORK -- THE DIRTIEST!

NEUROGLIA: OF THE TWO TYPES OF CELLS THAT MAKE UP THE BRAIN, NEURONS OCCUPY A MERE 85% OF THE VOLUME, WITH THE GREATER PART BEING FILLED BY THE GLUE-LIKE NEUROGLIA.

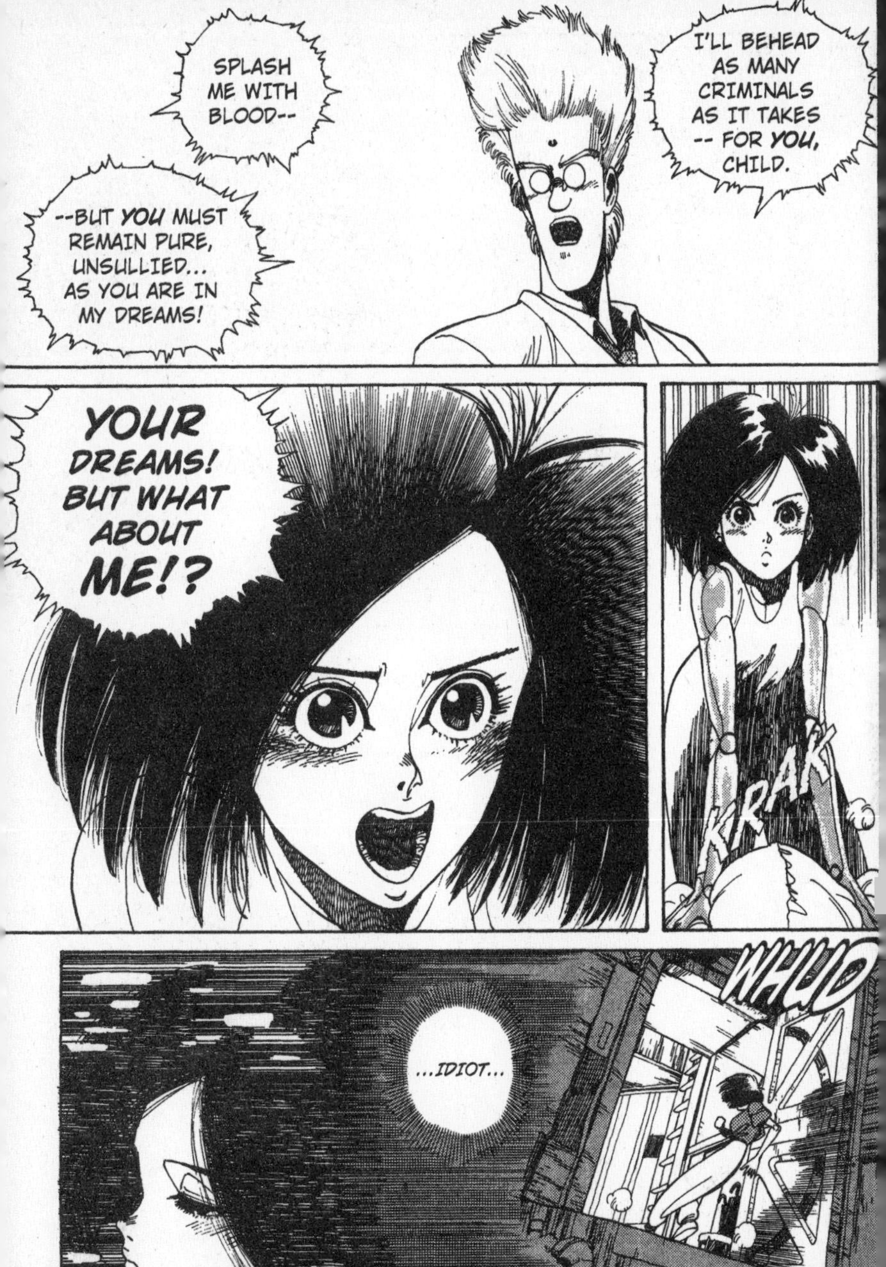
I'LL BEHEAD AS MANY CRIMINALS AS IT TAKES -- FOR YOU, CHILD.
SPLASH ME WITH BLOOD--
--BUT YOU MUST REMAIN PURE, UNSULLIED... AS YOU ARE IN MY DREAMS!
KRAK
YOUR DREAMS! BUT WHAT ABOUT ME!?
WHUD
...IDIOT...

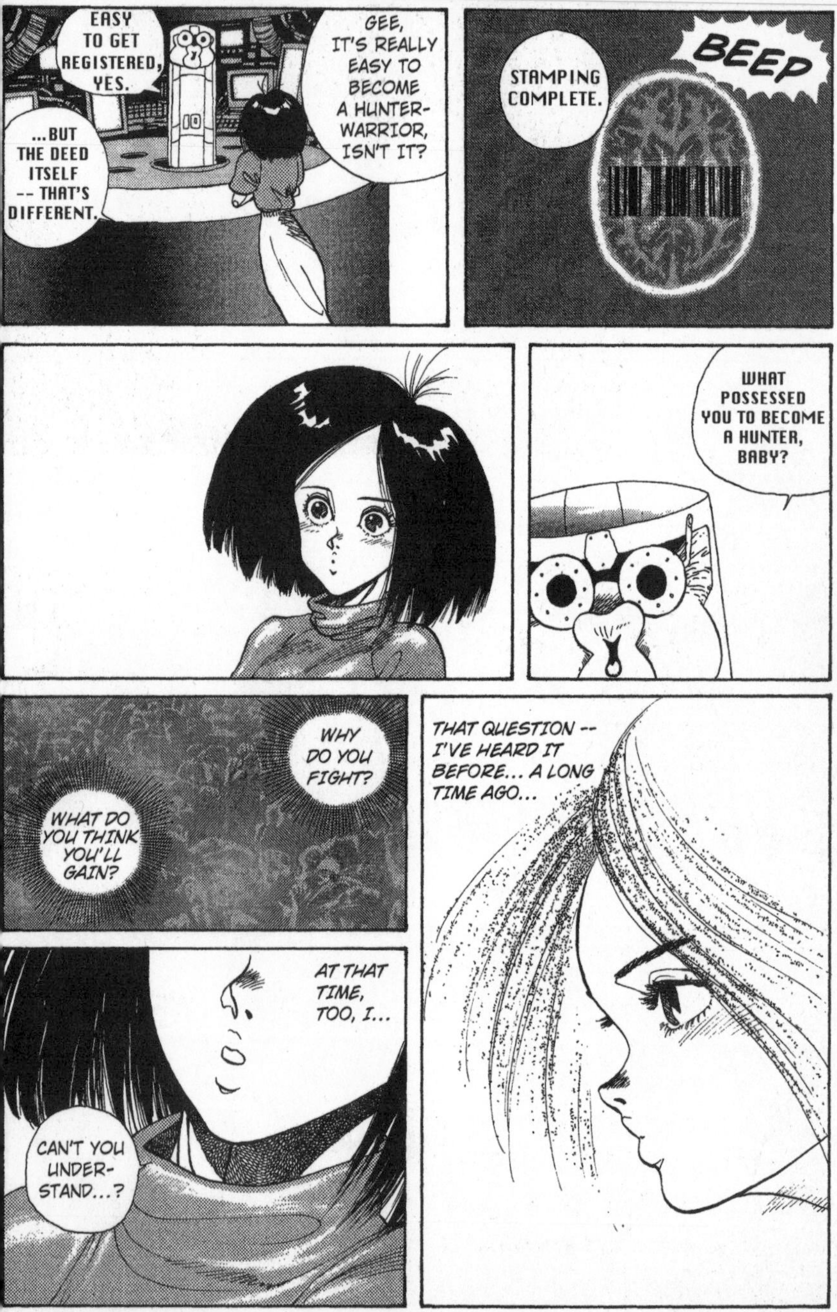
BEEP
STAMPING COMPLETE.
GEE, IT'S REALLY EASY TO BECOME A HUNTER-WARRIOR, ISN'T IT?
EASY TO GET REGISTERED, YES.
...BUT THE DEED ITSELF -- THAT'S DIFFERENT.
WHAT POSSESSED YOU TO BECOME A HUNTER, BABY?
THAT QUESTION -- I'VE HEARD IT BEFORE... A LONG TIME AGO...
WHY DO YOU FIGHT?
WHAT DO YOU THINK YOU'LL GAIN?
AT THAT TIME, TOO, I...
CAN'T YOU UNDER-STAND...?

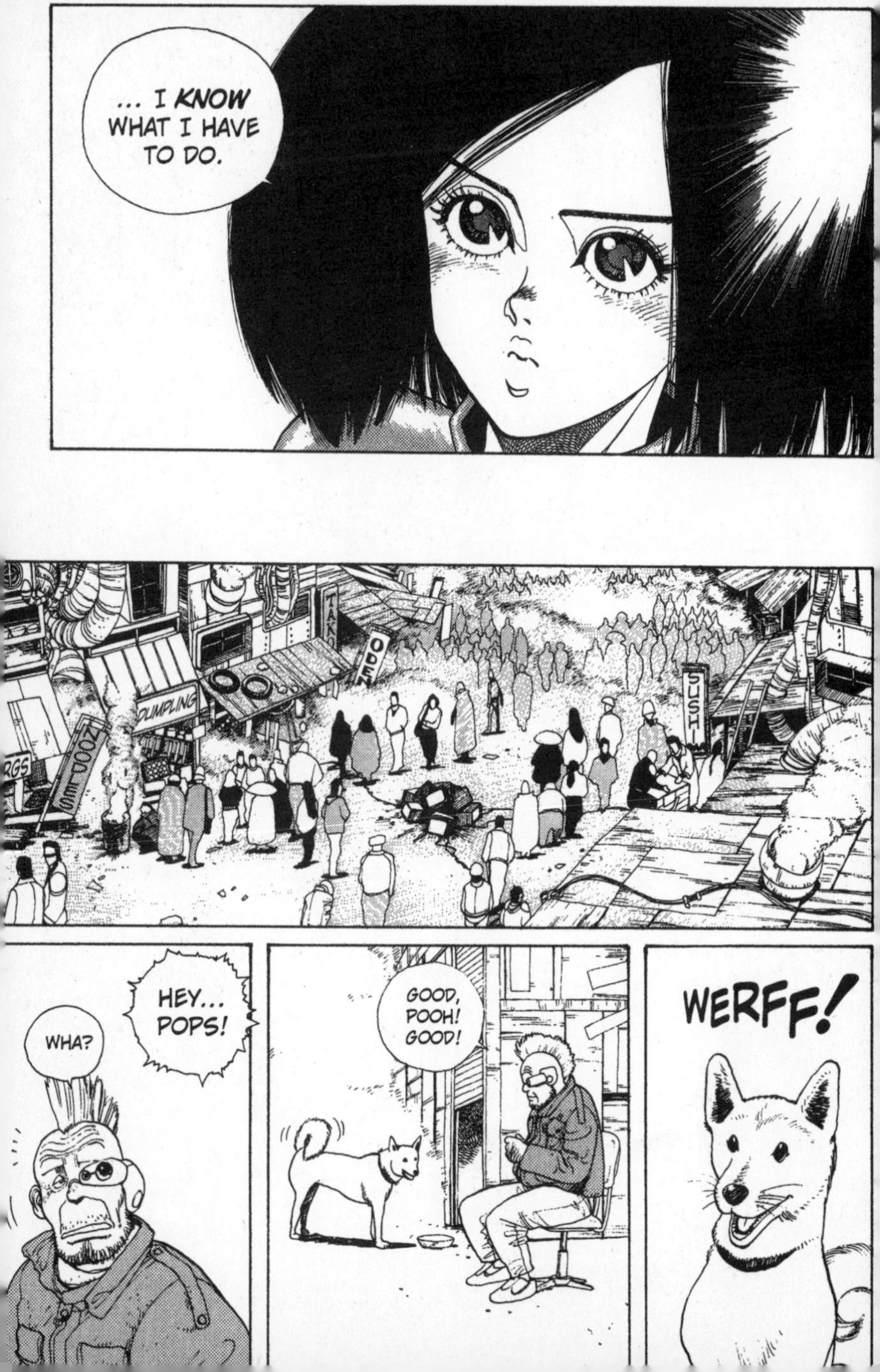
... I KNOW WHAT I HAVE TO DO.
SUSHI
ODEN
TAKO
DUMPLING
NOODLES
WERFF!
GOOD, POOH! GOOD!
HEY... POPS!
WHA?

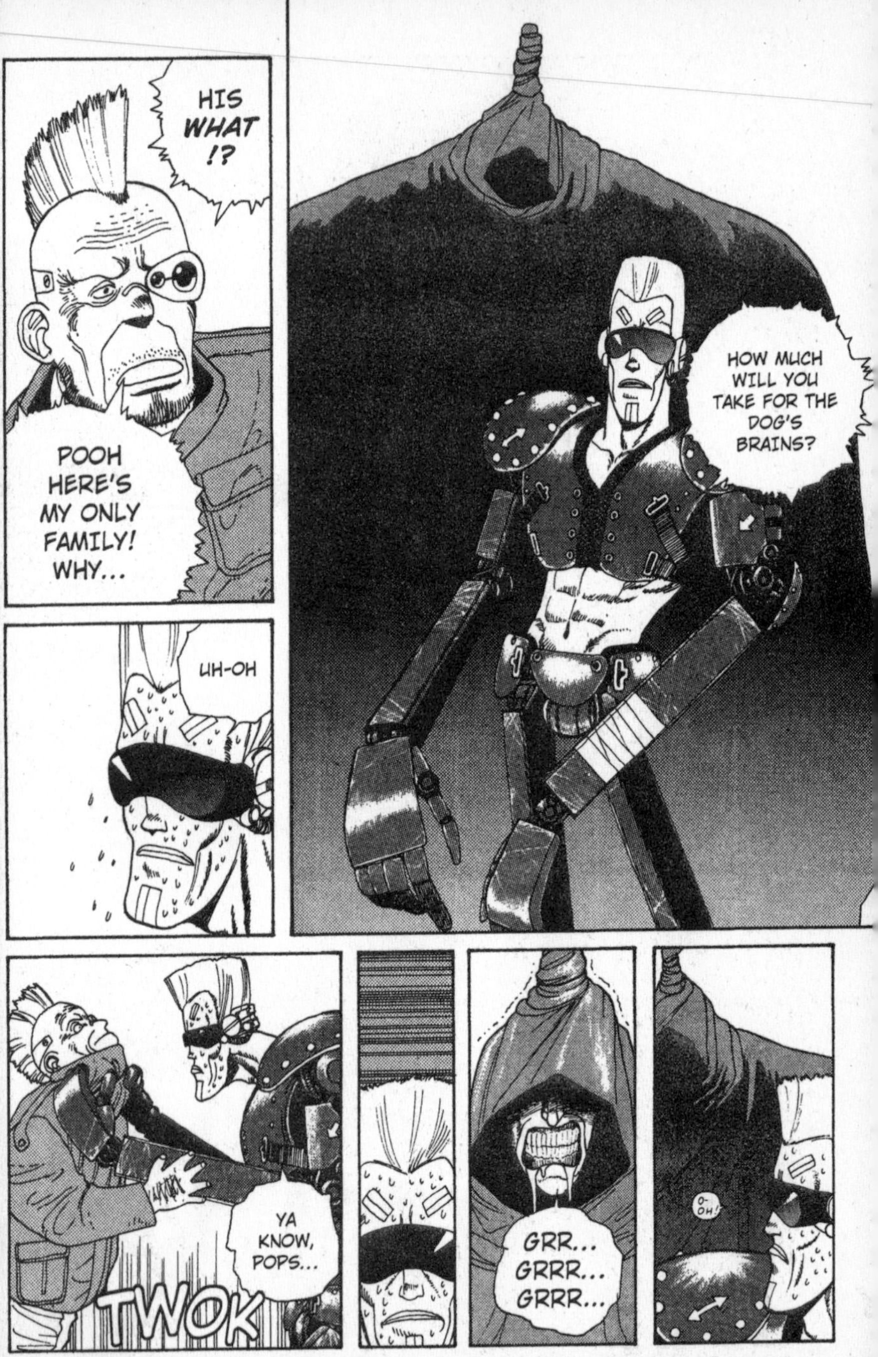
HOW MUCH WILL YOU TAKE FOR THE DOG'S BRAINS?
HIS WHAT !?
POOH HERE'S MY ONLY FAMILY! WHY...
UH-OH
O-OH!
GRR... GRRR... GRRR...
YA KNOW, POPS...
TWOK

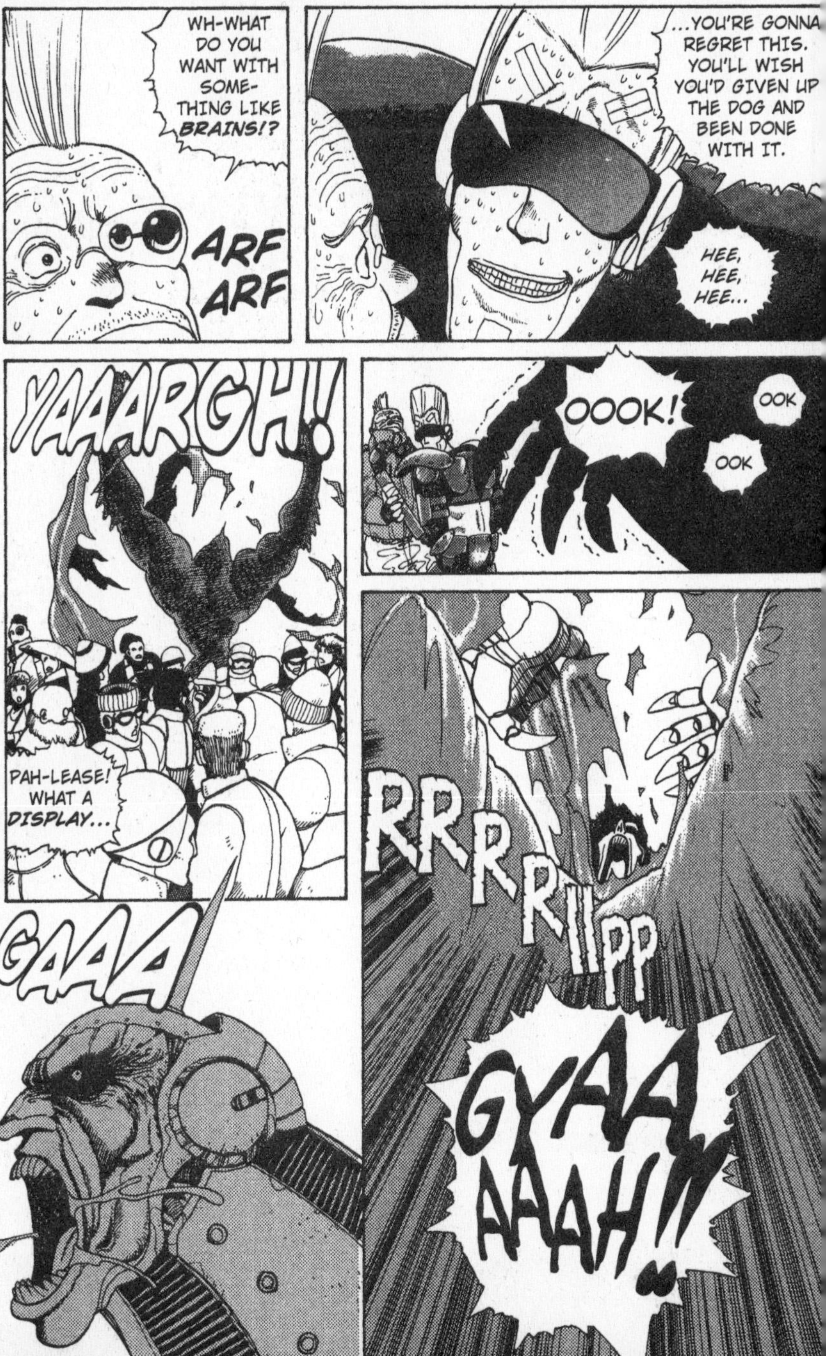
...YOU'RE GONNA REGRET THIS. YOU'LL WISH YOU'D GIVEN UP THE DOG AND BEEN DONE WITH IT.
HEE, HEE, HEE...
WH-WHAT DO YOU WANT WITH SOME-THING LIKE BRAINS!?
ARF ARF
OOOK!
OOK
OOK
RRRRIIPP
GYAAAAAH!!
YAAARGH!!
PAH-LEASE! WHAT A DISPLAY...
GAAA

HA, HEH, HEH. IT'S STARTED, AND THERE AIN'T NO TURNING BACK!

BOOSH

PLORFSH

EE EEE EEE!

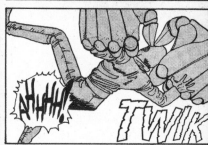

AHHHH!

TWIK

OH, YUCK! I DON'T BELIEVE IT...!

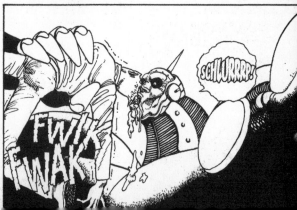

FWIK FWAK

SCHLURRRP!

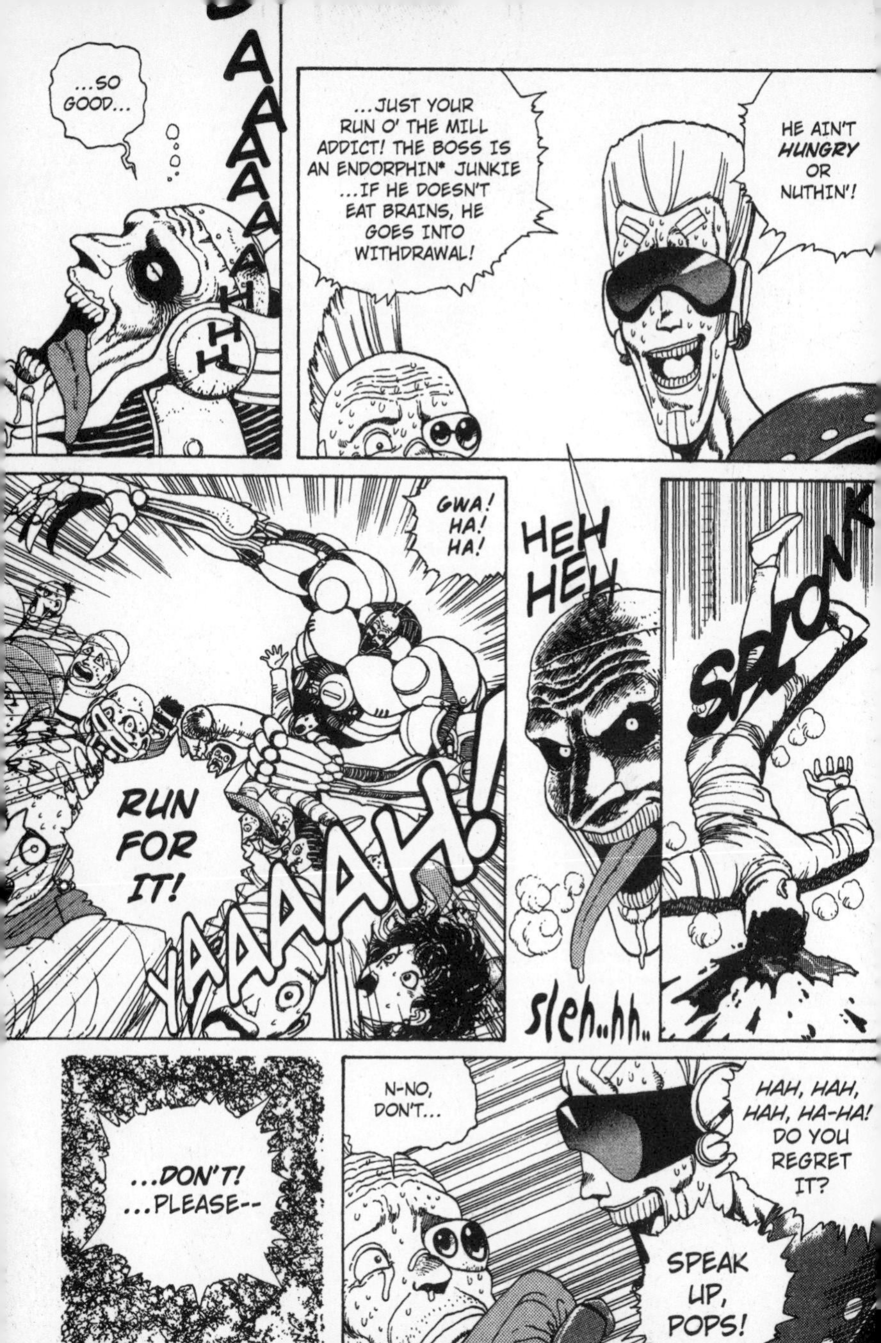
HE AIN'T *HUNGRY* OR NUTHIN'!
...JUST YOUR RUN O' THE MILL ADDICT! THE BOSS IS AN ENDORPHIN* JUNKIE ...IF HE DOESN'T EAT BRAINS, HE GOES INTO WITHDRAWAL!
...SO GOOD...
AAAAAAHHHH
SPLONK
HEH HEH
sleh..hh..
GWA! HA! HA!
RUN FOR IT!
YAAAAH!
HAH, HAH, HAH, HA-HA! DO YOU REGRET IT?
N-NO, DON'T...
SPEAK UP, POPS!
...DON'T! ...PLEASE--

**ENDORPHIN: A NARCOTIC SUBSTANCE PRODUCED IN THE BRAIN. ENDORPHIN MEANS LITERALLY "MORPHINE MADE INSIDE THE BODY." BETA-ENDORPHINS HAVE A PAIN-RELIEVING EFFECT 6.5 TIMES THAT OF MORPHINE.*

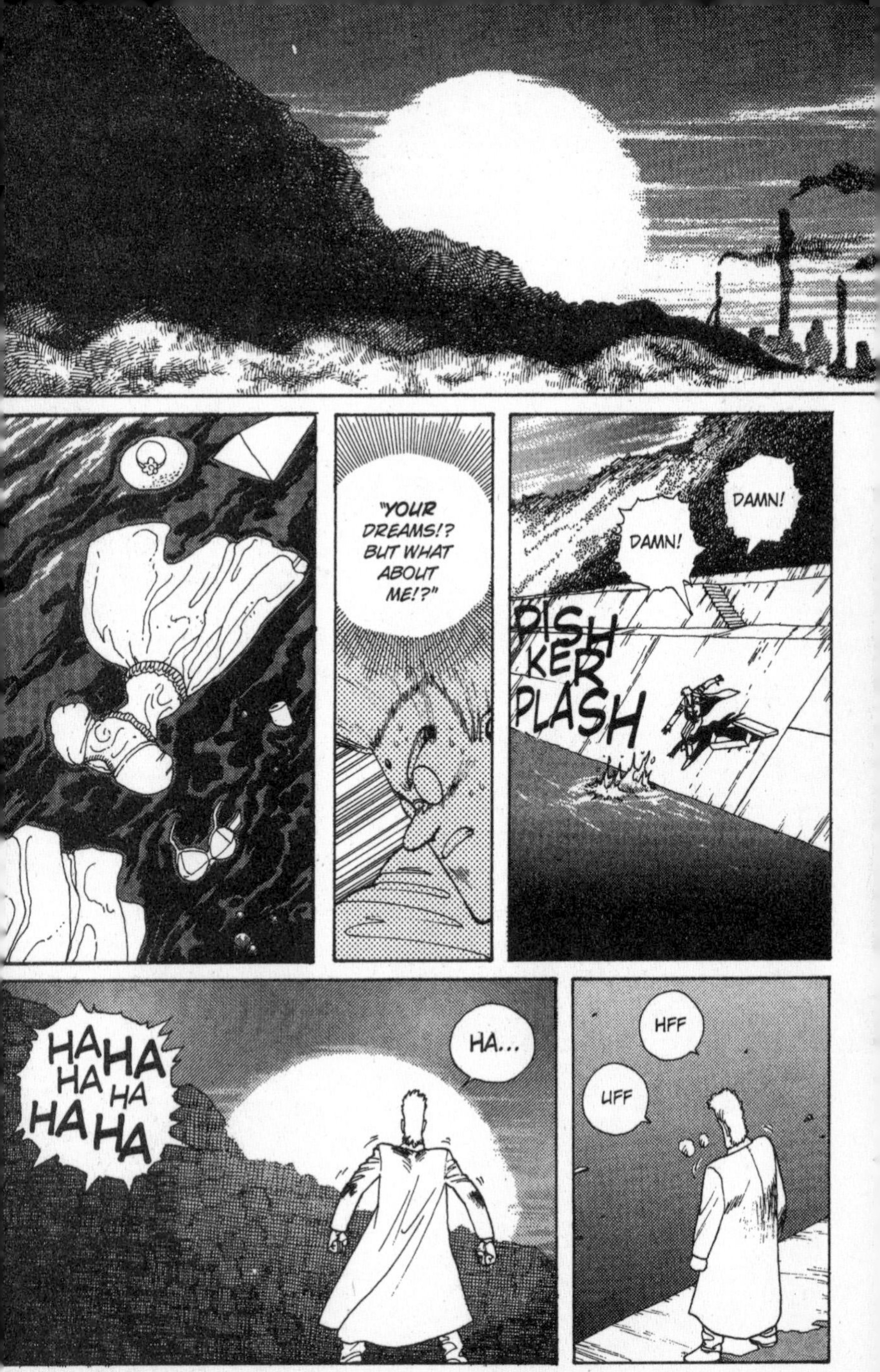
DAMN!
DAMN!
DISH KER PLASH
"YOUR DREAMS!? BUT WHAT ABOUT ME!?"
HFF
UFF
HA...
HAHA HA HA HAHA

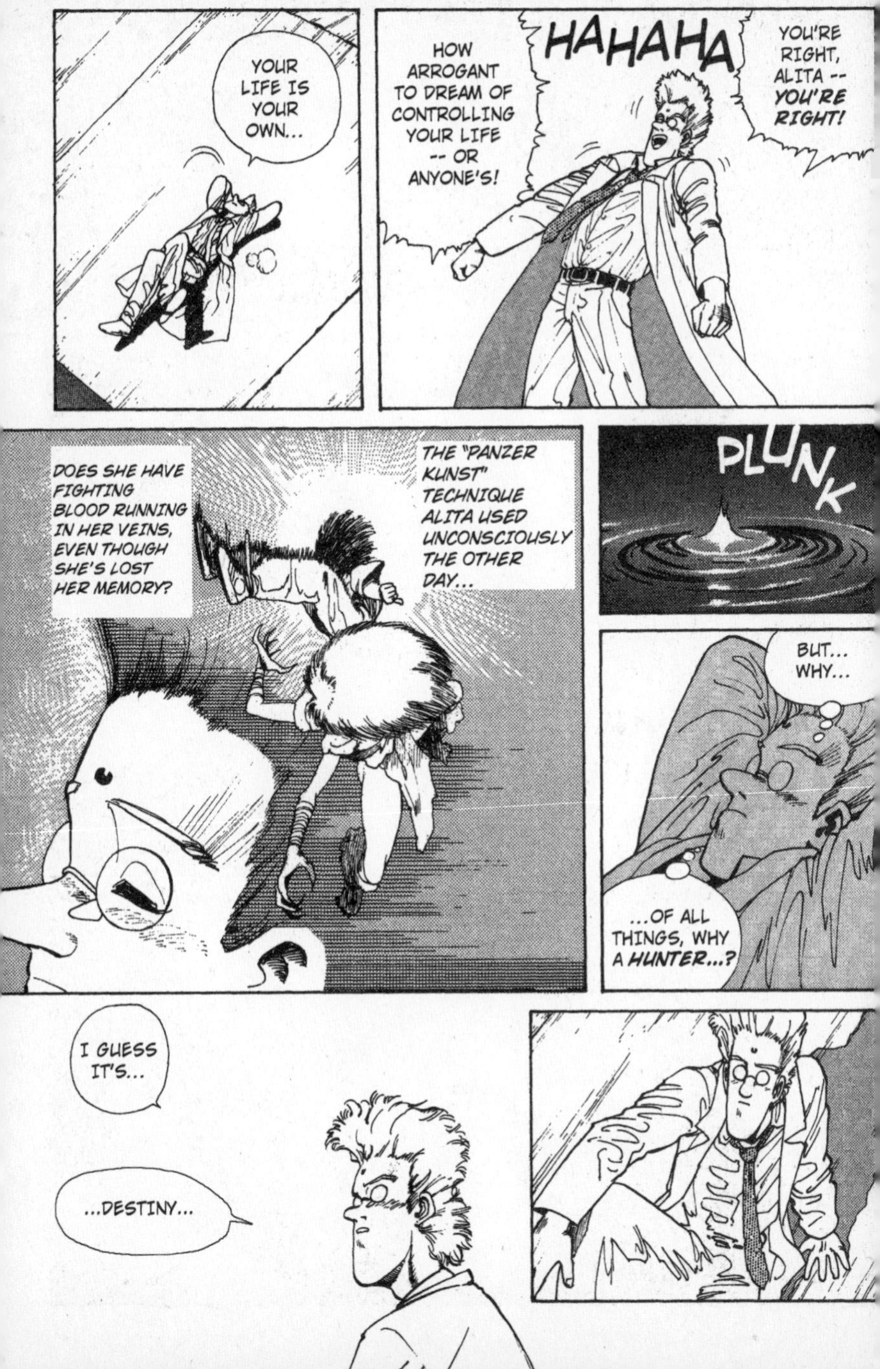
YOU'RE RIGHT, ALITA -- **YOU'RE RIGHT!**
HAHAHA
HOW ARROGANT TO DREAM OF CONTROLLING YOUR LIFE -- OR ANYONE'S!
YOUR LIFE IS YOUR OWN...
PLUNK
BUT... WHY...
...OF ALL THINGS, WHY A **HUNTER...?**
THE "PANZER KUNST" TECHNIQUE ALITA USED UNCONSCIOUSLY THE OTHER DAY...
DOES SHE HAVE FIGHTING BLOOD RUNNING IN HER VEINS, EVEN THOUGH SHE'S LOST HER MEMORY?
I GUESS IT'S...
...DESTINY...

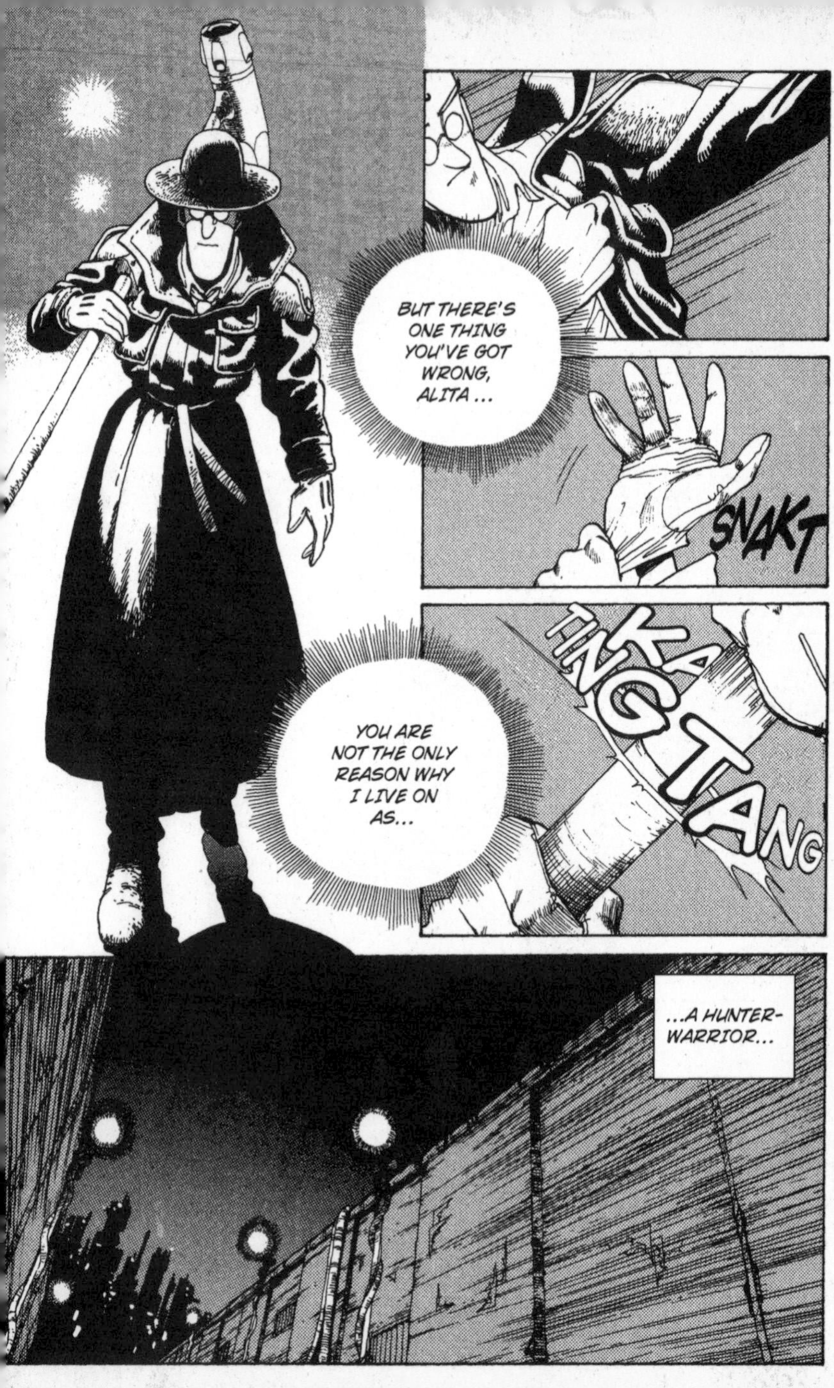
BUT THERE'S ONE THING YOU'VE GOT WRONG, ALITA ...
SNAKT
YOU ARE NOT THE ONLY REASON WHY I LIVE ON AS...
KATING TITANG
...A HUNTER-WARRIOR...

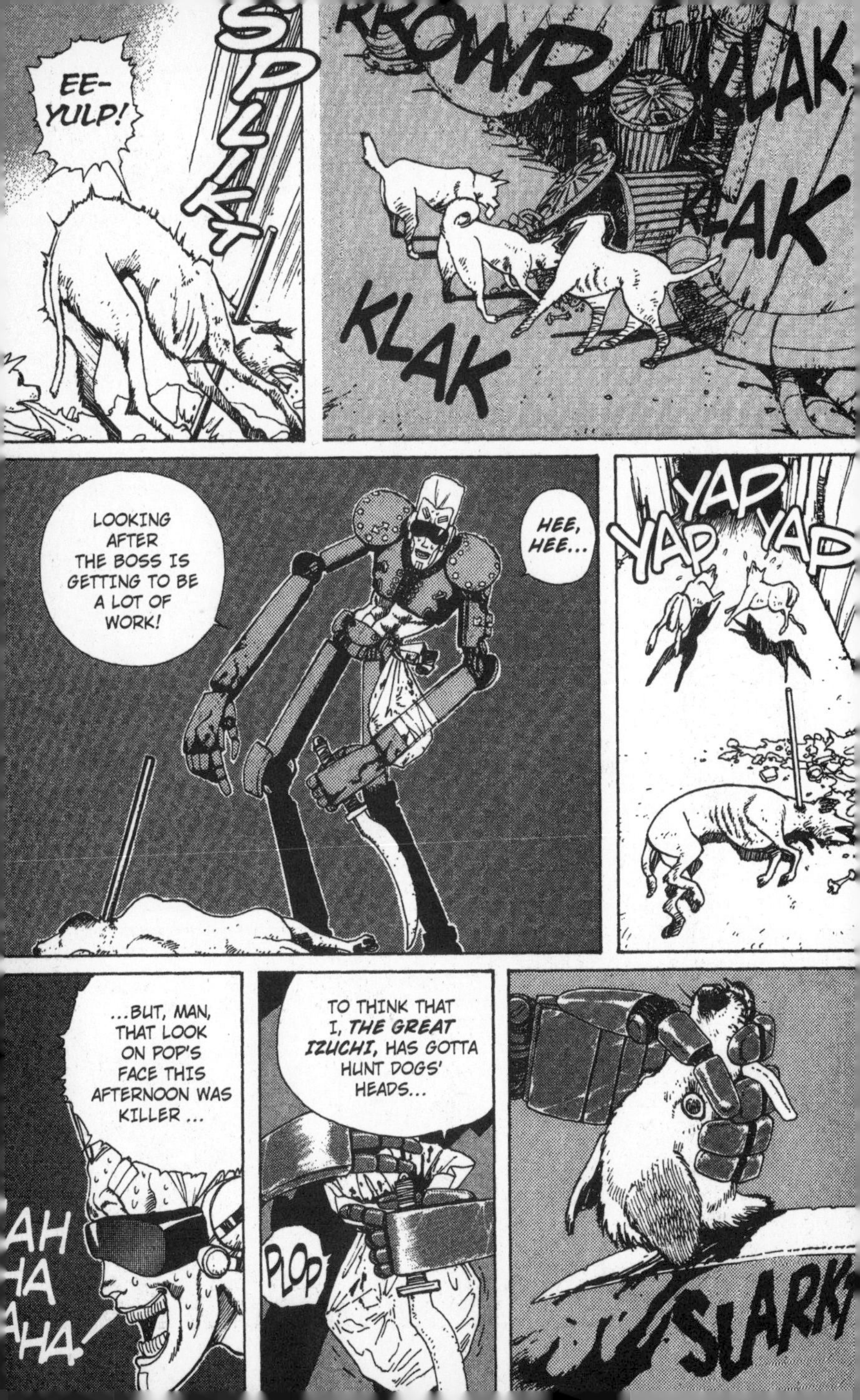
KROWR
KLAK
KLAK
KLAK
EE-YULP!
SPLIKT
YAP YAP YAP YAP
HEE, HEE...
LOOKING AFTER THE BOSS IS GETTING TO BE A LOT OF WORK!
SLARKT
TO THINK THAT I, ***THE GREAT IZUCHI***, HAS GOTTA HUNT DOGS' HEADS...
PLOP
...BUT, MAN, THAT LOOK ON POP'S FACE THIS AFTERNOON WAS KILLER ...
AH HA HAHA

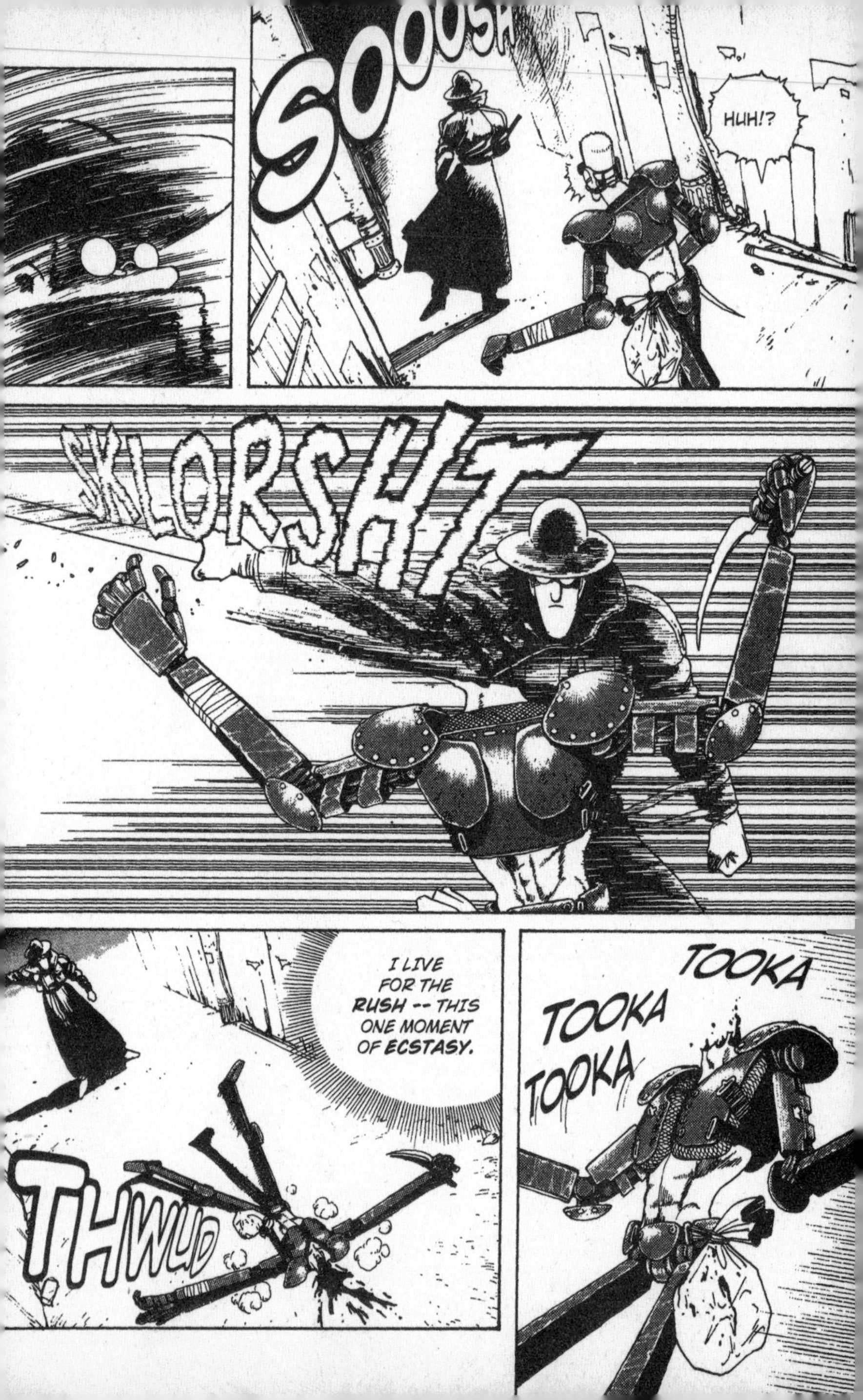
HUH!?
SOOOSH
SKLORSHT
TOOKA
TOOKA
TOOKA
I LIVE FOR THE RUSH -- THIS ONE MOMENT OF ECSTASY.
THWUD

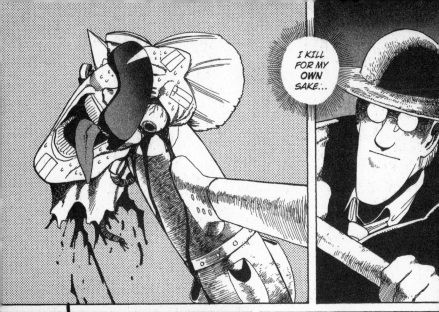

I KILL FOR MY OWN SAKE...

WASH

...NOTHING MORE, NOTHING LESS...

TWUFF

I DIDN'T WANT YOU TO SEE THIS SIDE OF ME...

...DIDN'T WANT YOUR LIFE TO TURN TOWARD THE SHADOWS...

OH, ALITA...

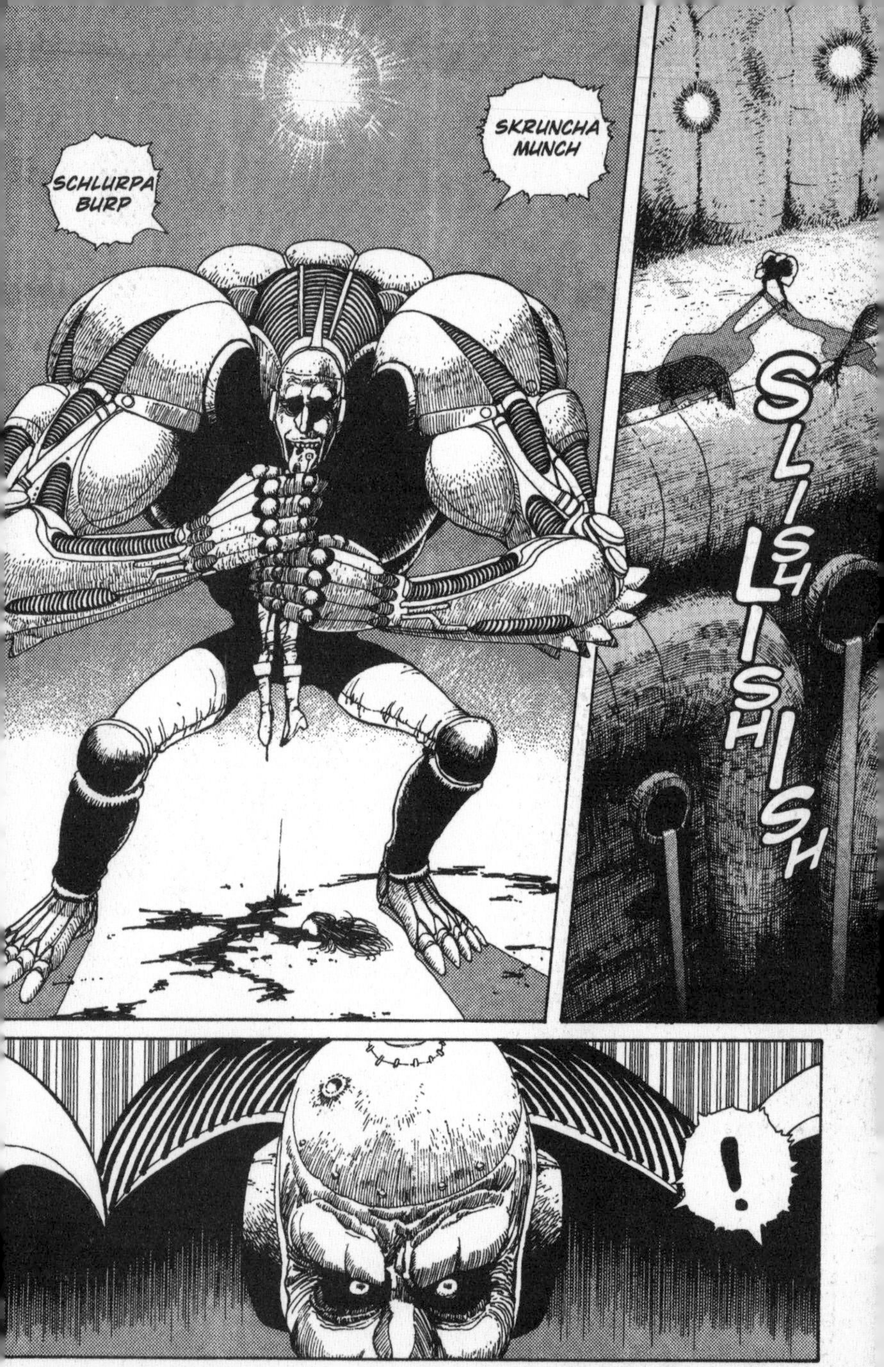
SLISH LISH ISH
SKRUNCHA MUNCH
SCHLURPA BURP
!

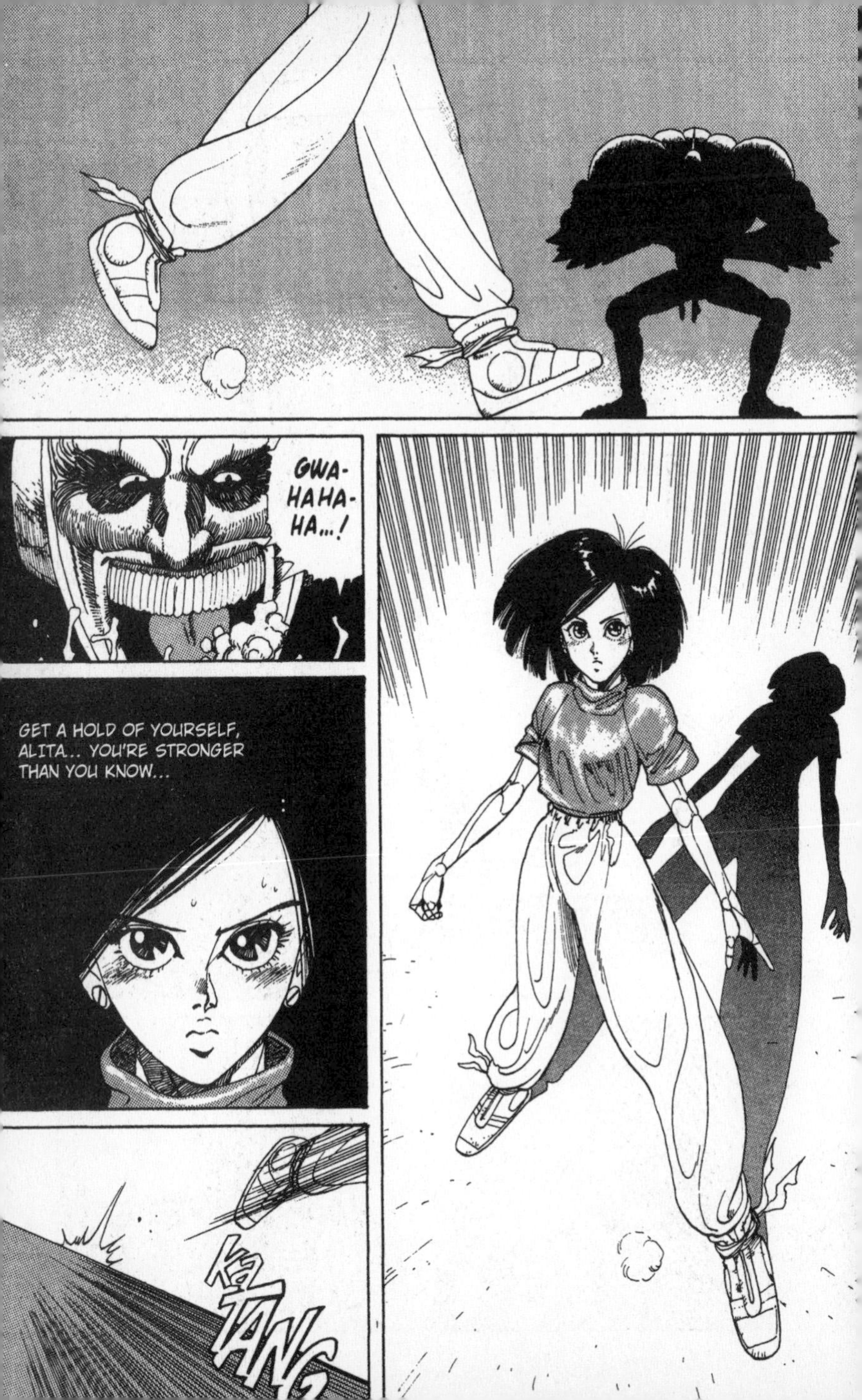
GWA-HAHAHA-HA...!
GET A HOLD OF YOURSELF, ALITA... YOU'RE STRONGER THAN YOU KNOW...
KaTANG

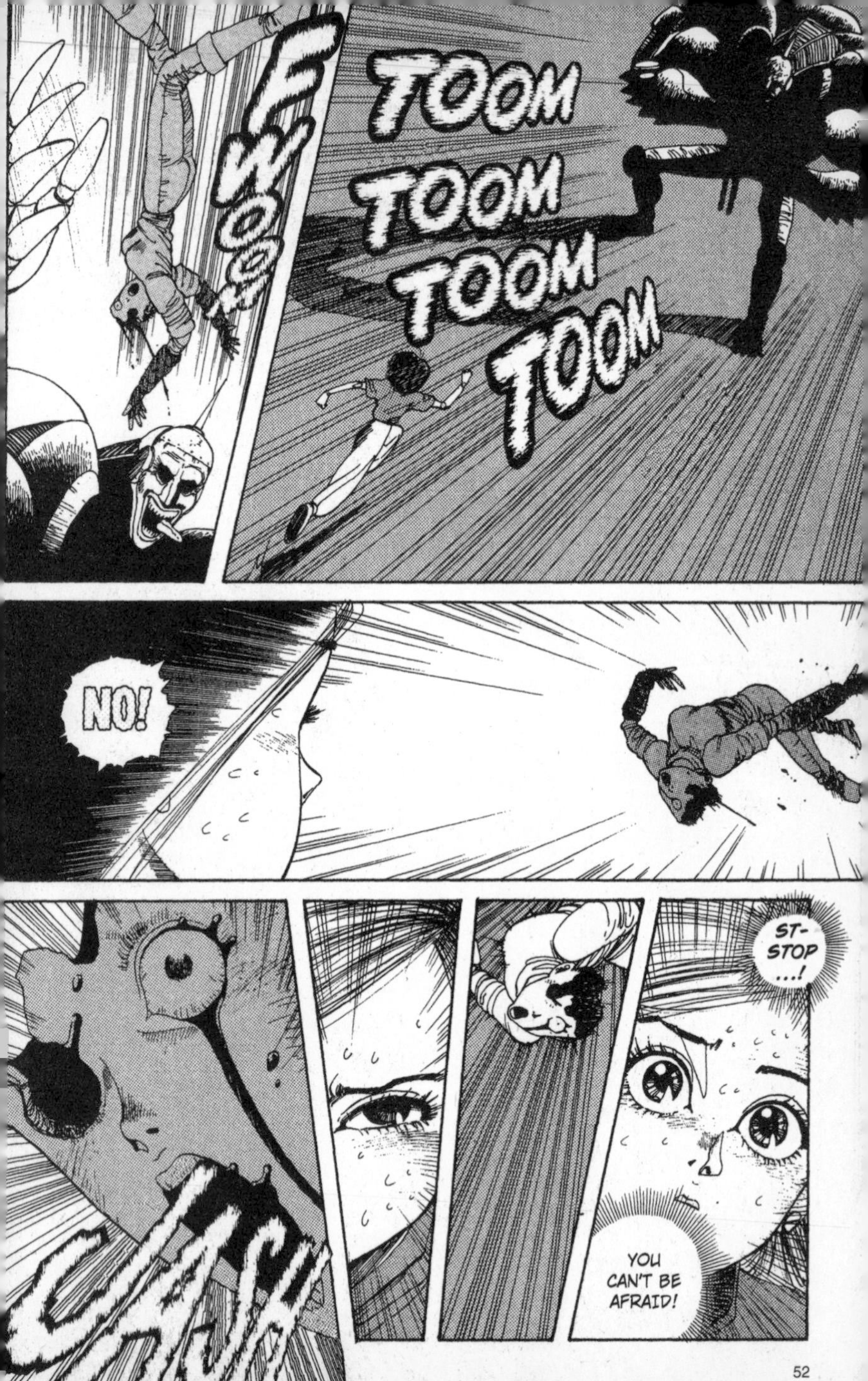
TOOM TOOM TOOM TOOM
FWOOSH
NO!
ST-STOP ...!
YOU CAN'T BE AFRAID!

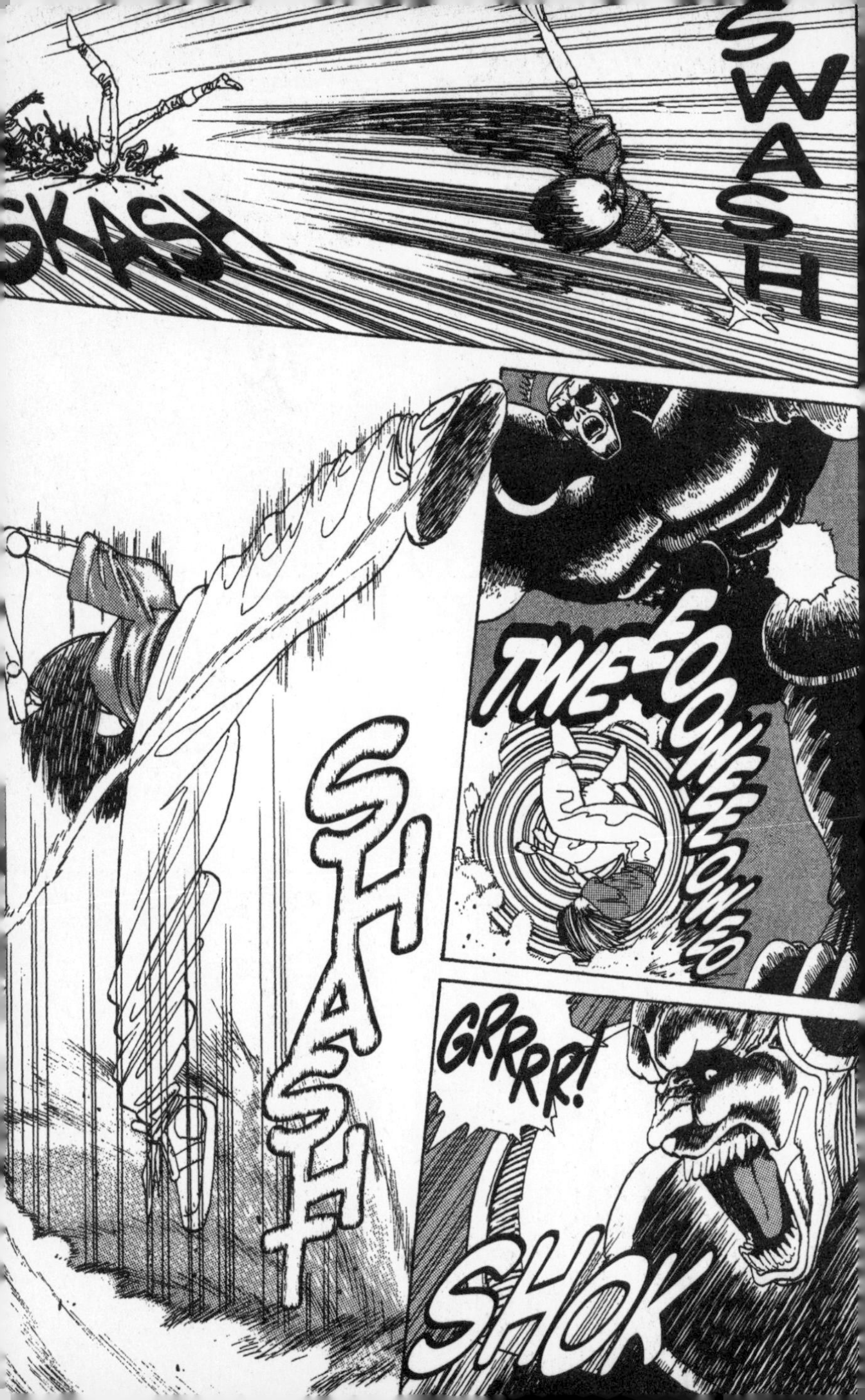
SWASH
SKASH
GRRRR!
SHOK
SHASH

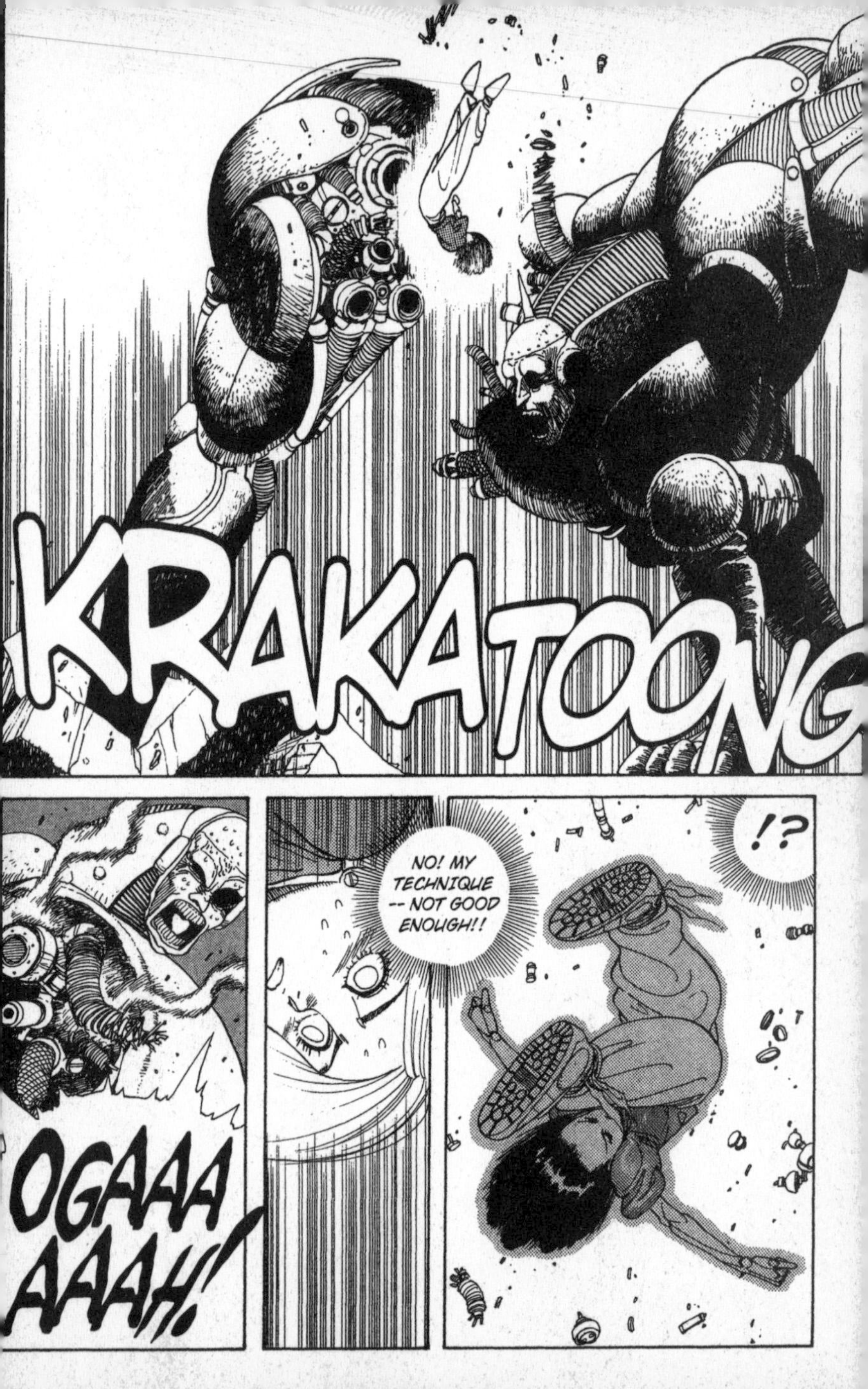
KRAKATOONG
!?
NO! MY TECHNIQUE -- NOT GOOD ENOUGH!!
OGAAA AAAH!

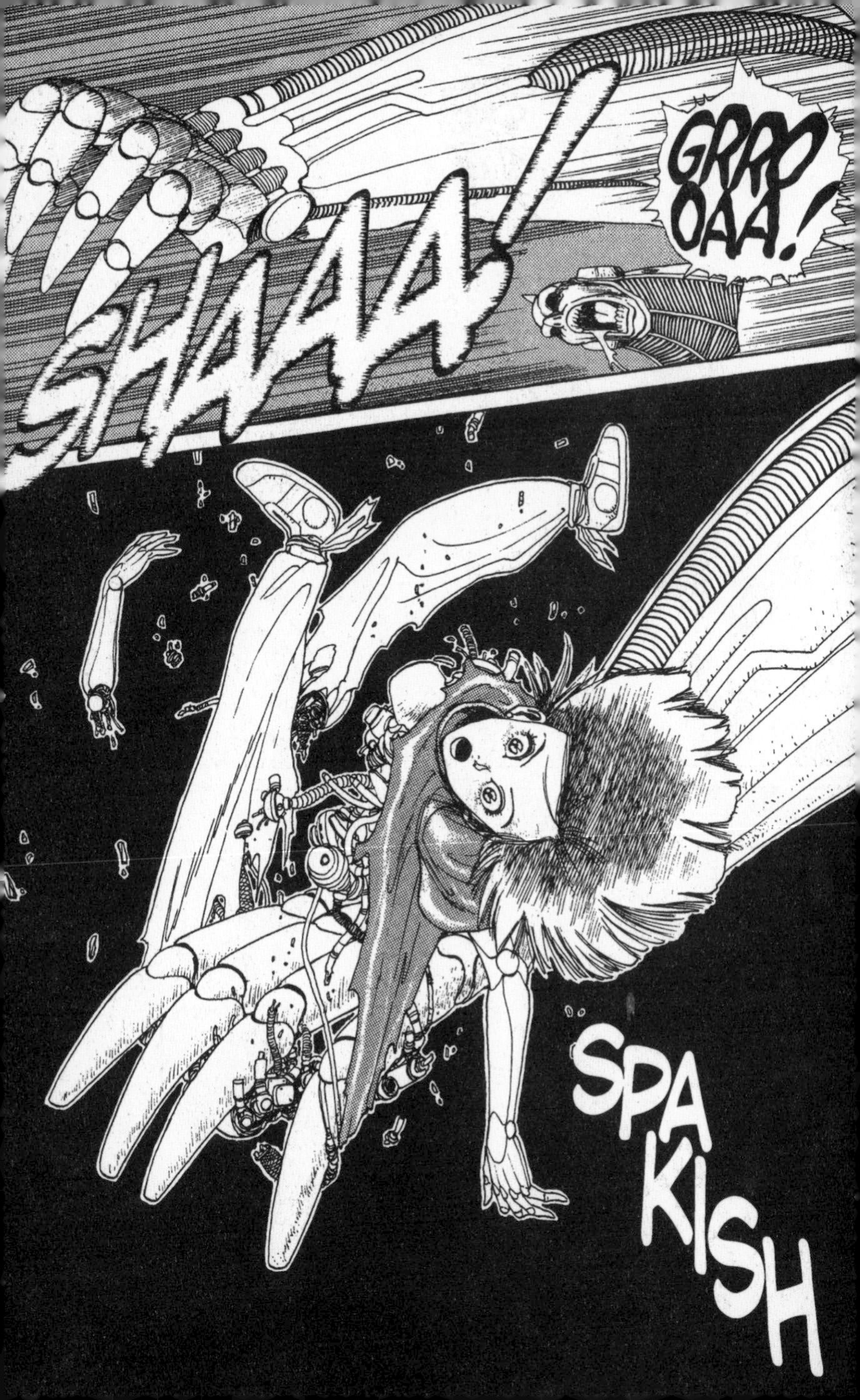
GRRO OAA!
SHAAA!
SPA KISH

TORN ASUNDER
BATTLE 3: VALUES

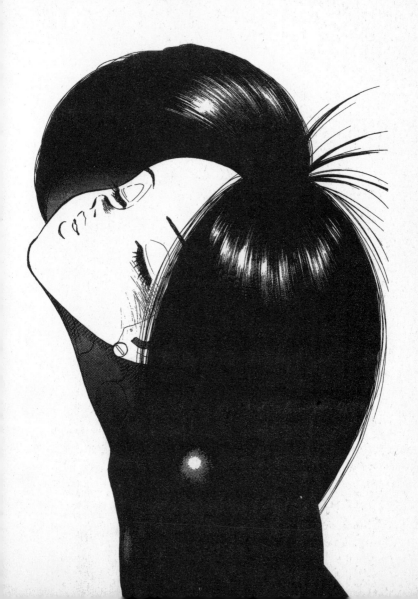

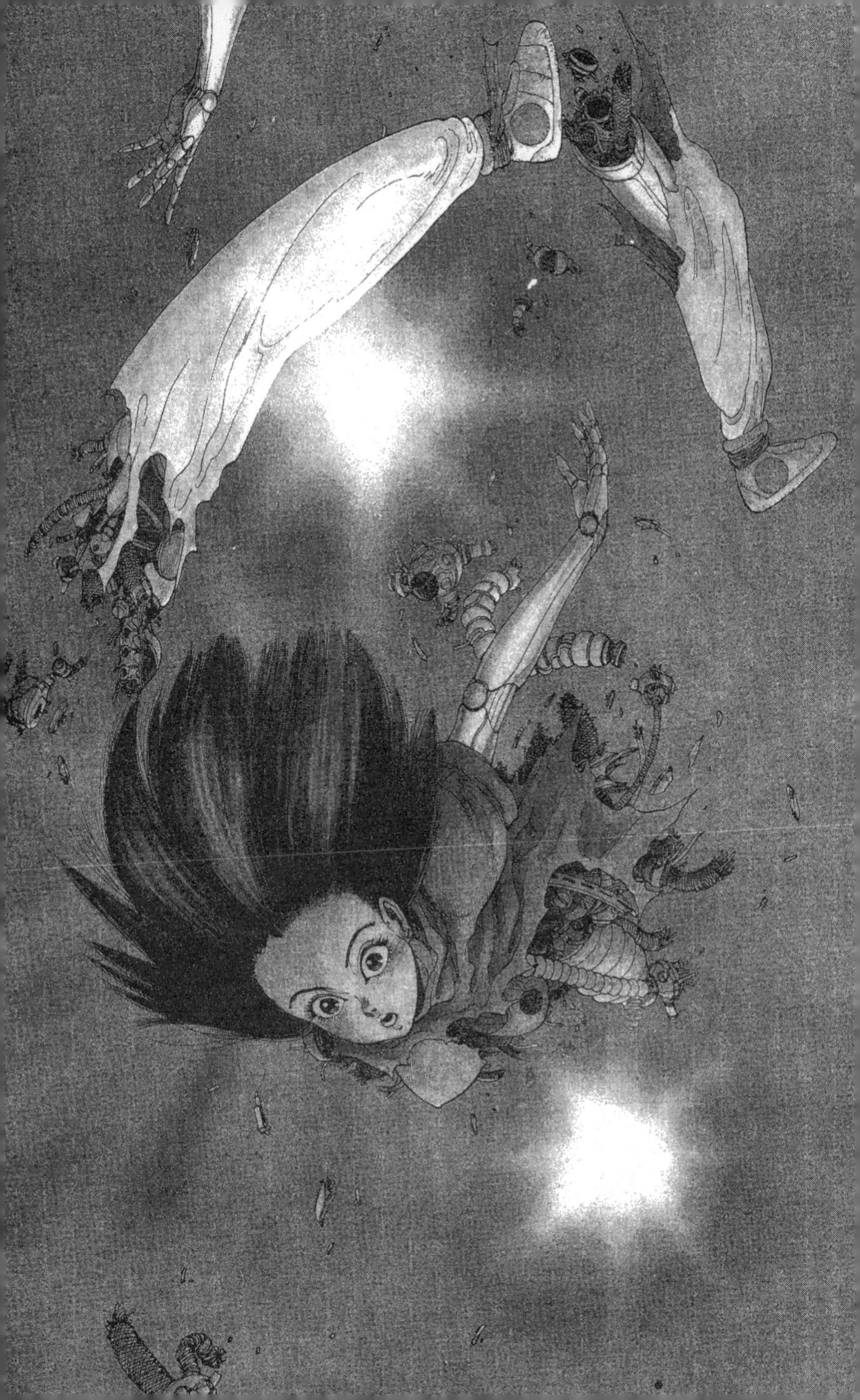

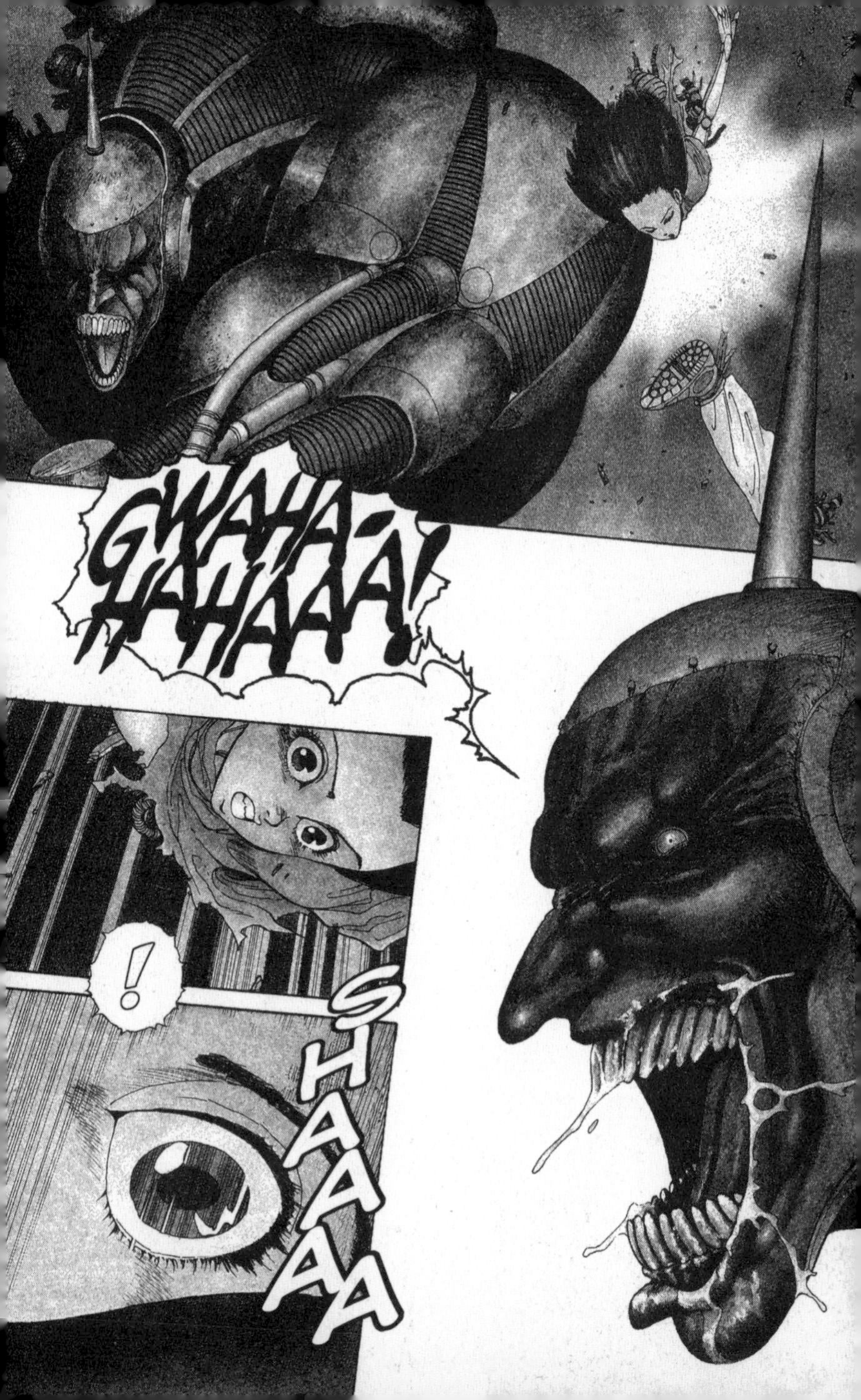
GWAHA-HAHAHAA!
!
SHAAAAAA

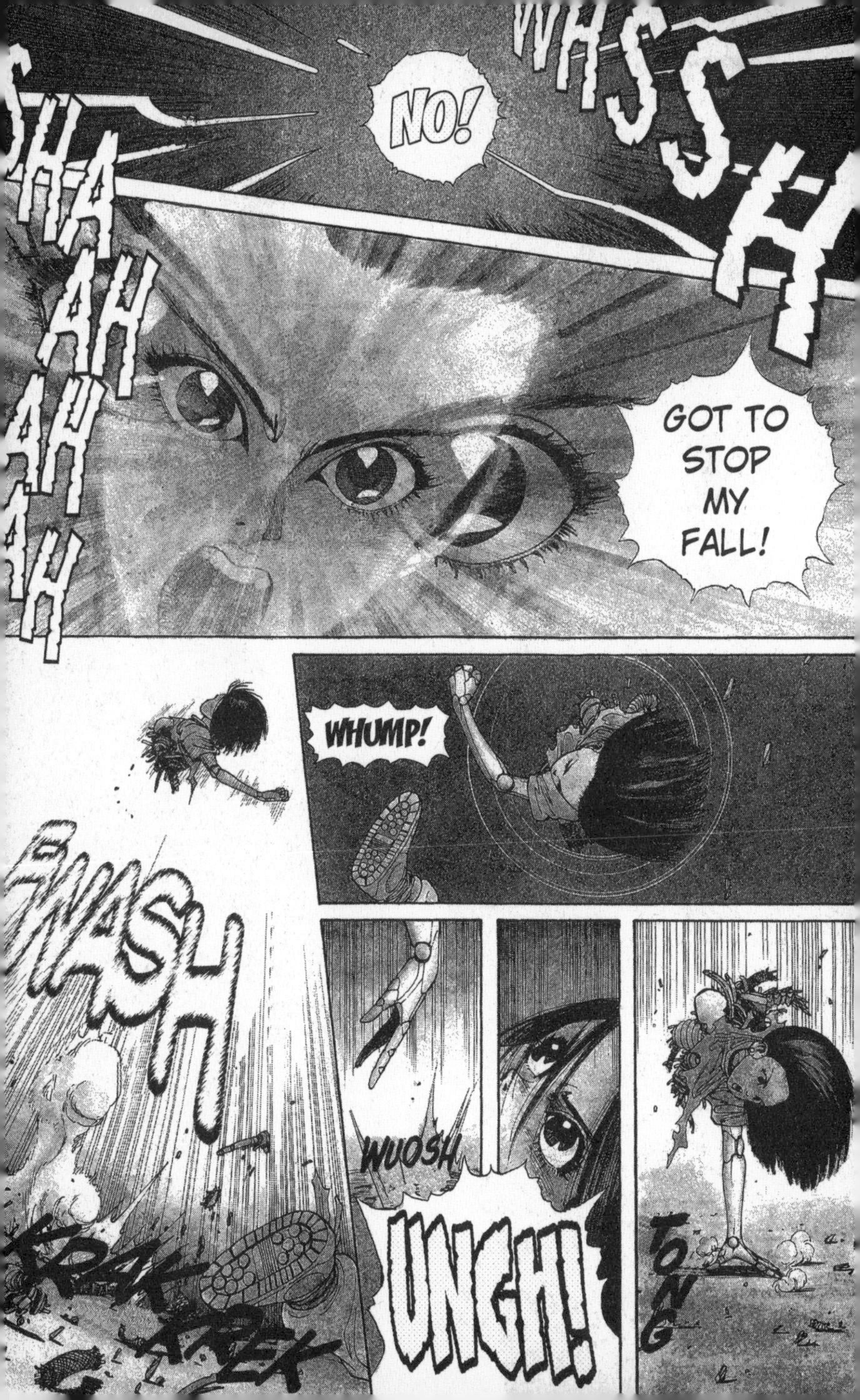
NO!
GOT TO STOP MY FALL!
WHUMP!
TONG
UNGH!
WUOSH

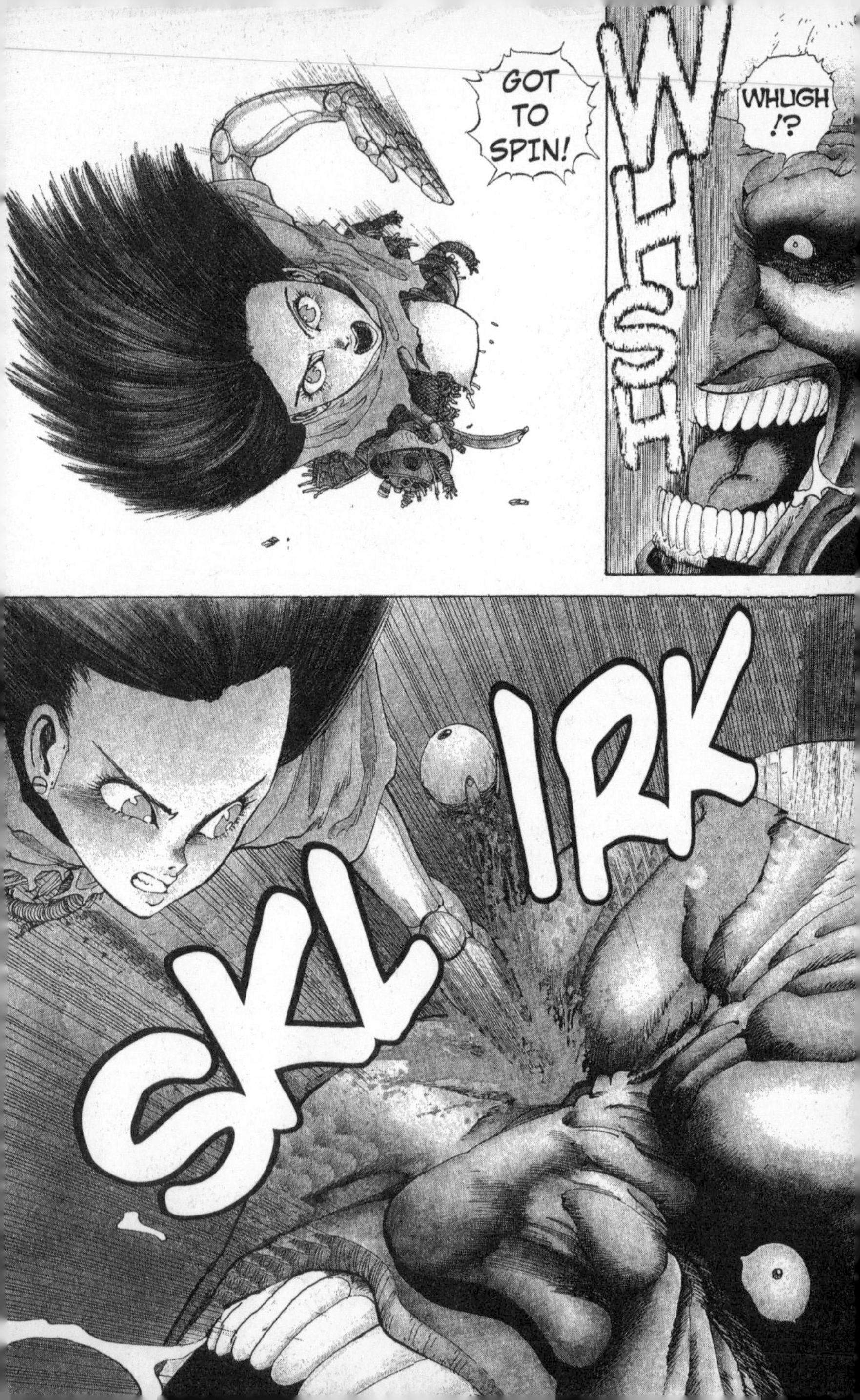
WHUGH !?
WHSH
GOT TO SPIN!
SKL IRK

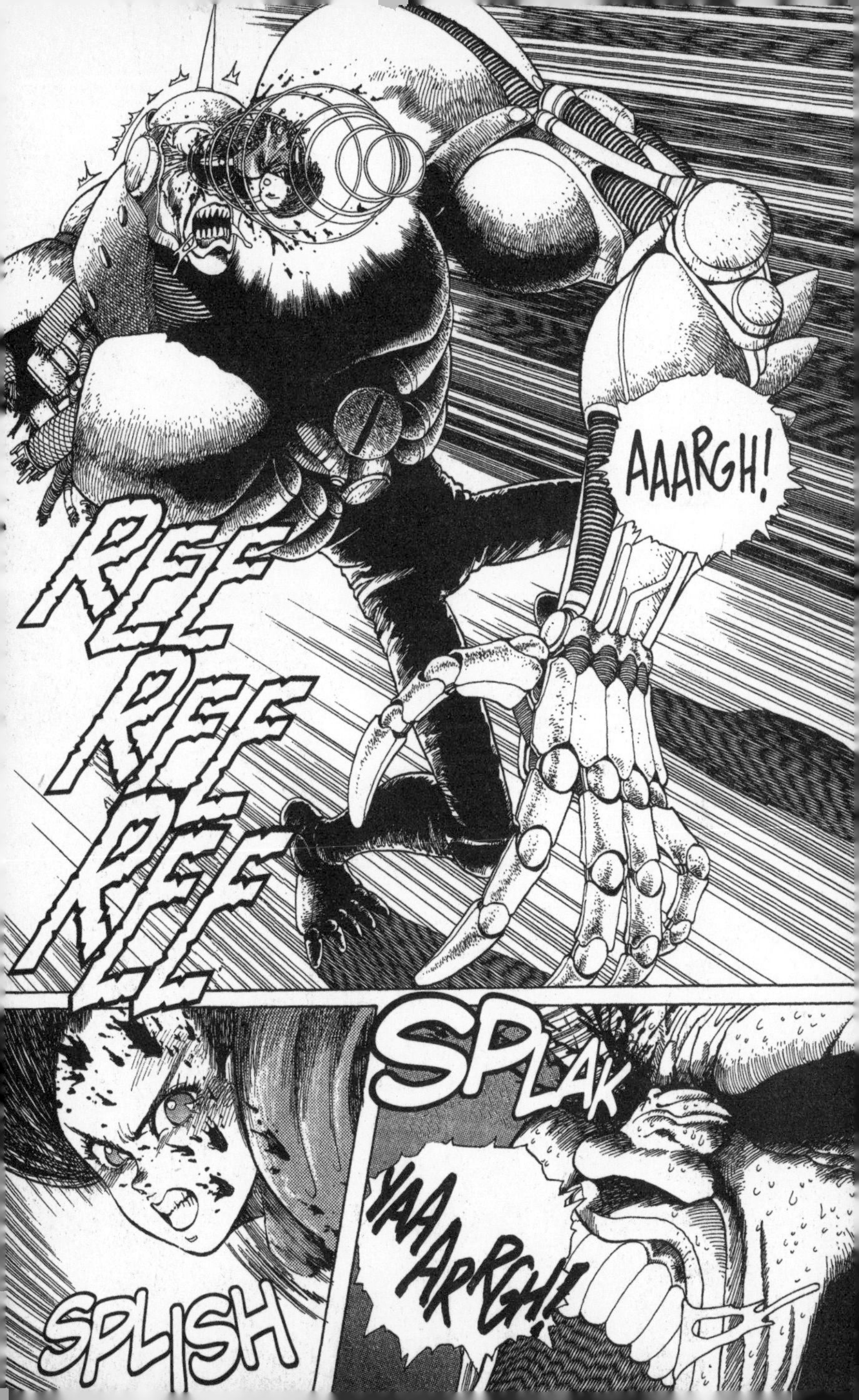
AAARGH!
SPLAK
YAAARRGH!
SPLISH

A-ALITA!

!

GAAA RHR!

SPLORT

UNG

UNH

REEREEREE

SPLORP

THAK TWAK

OWHHH!

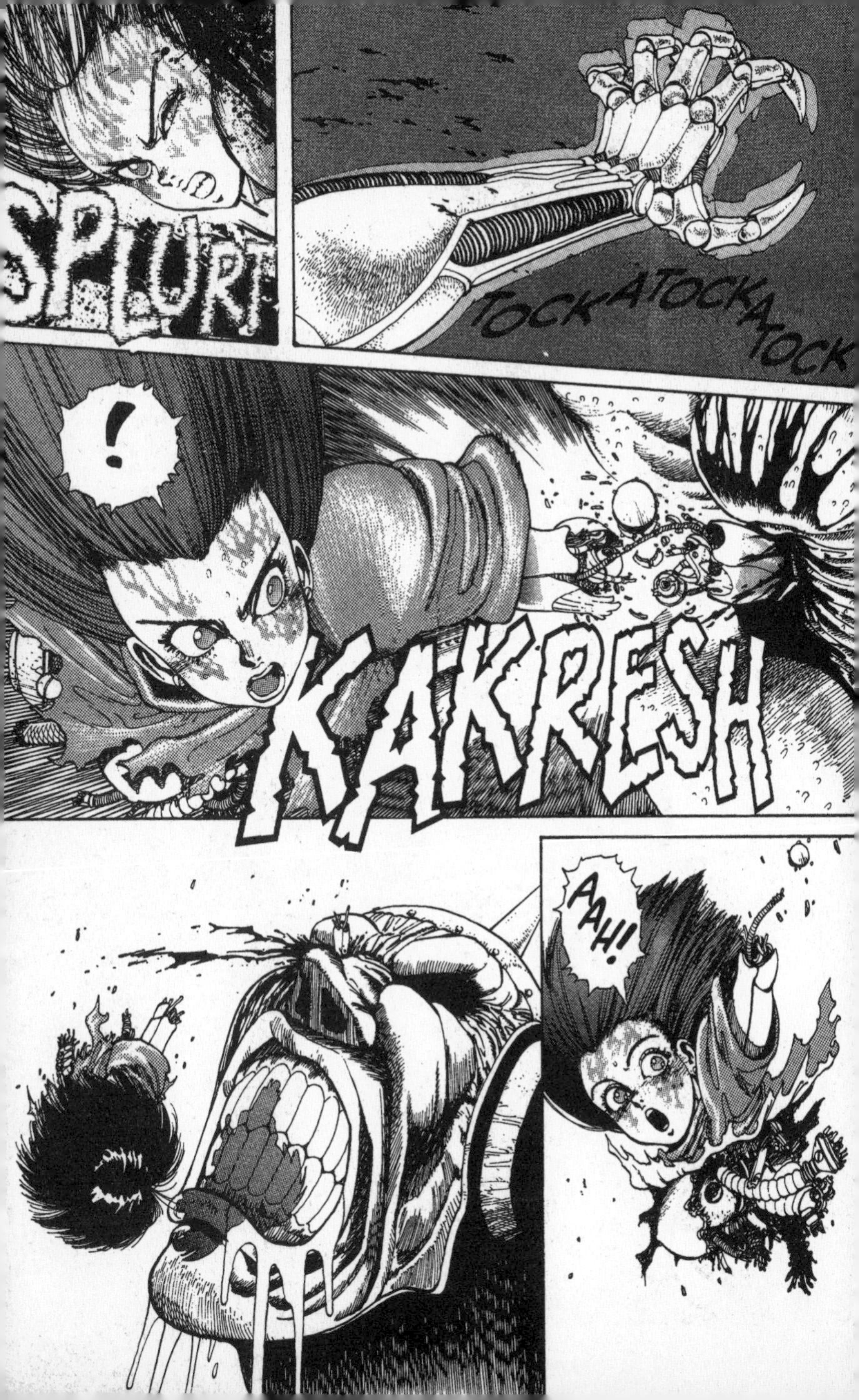
TOCK-A-TOCK-A-TOCK
SPLURT
!
KAKRESH
AAH!

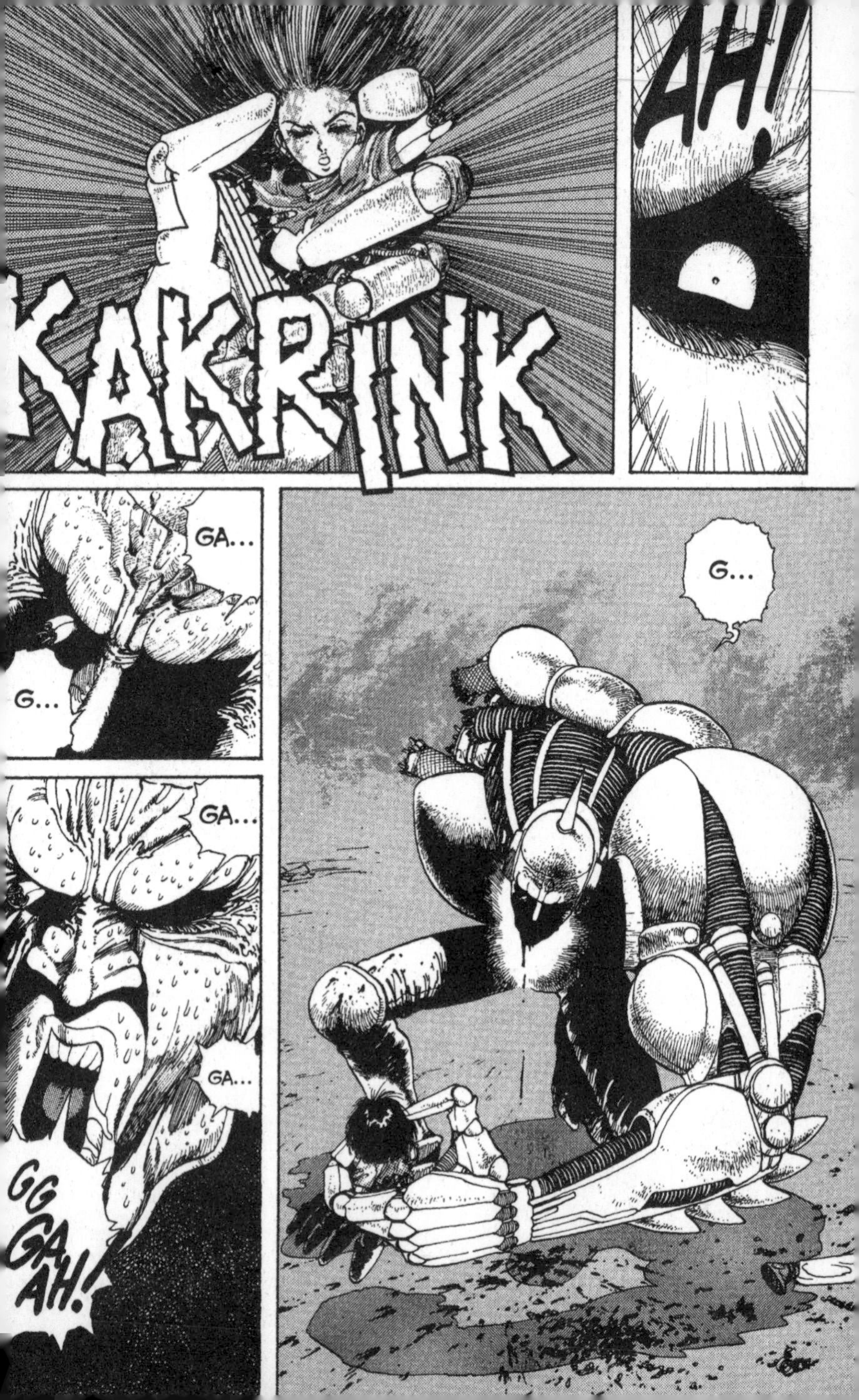
AH!
KAKRINK
G...
GA...
G...
GA...
GA...
GGGAAH!

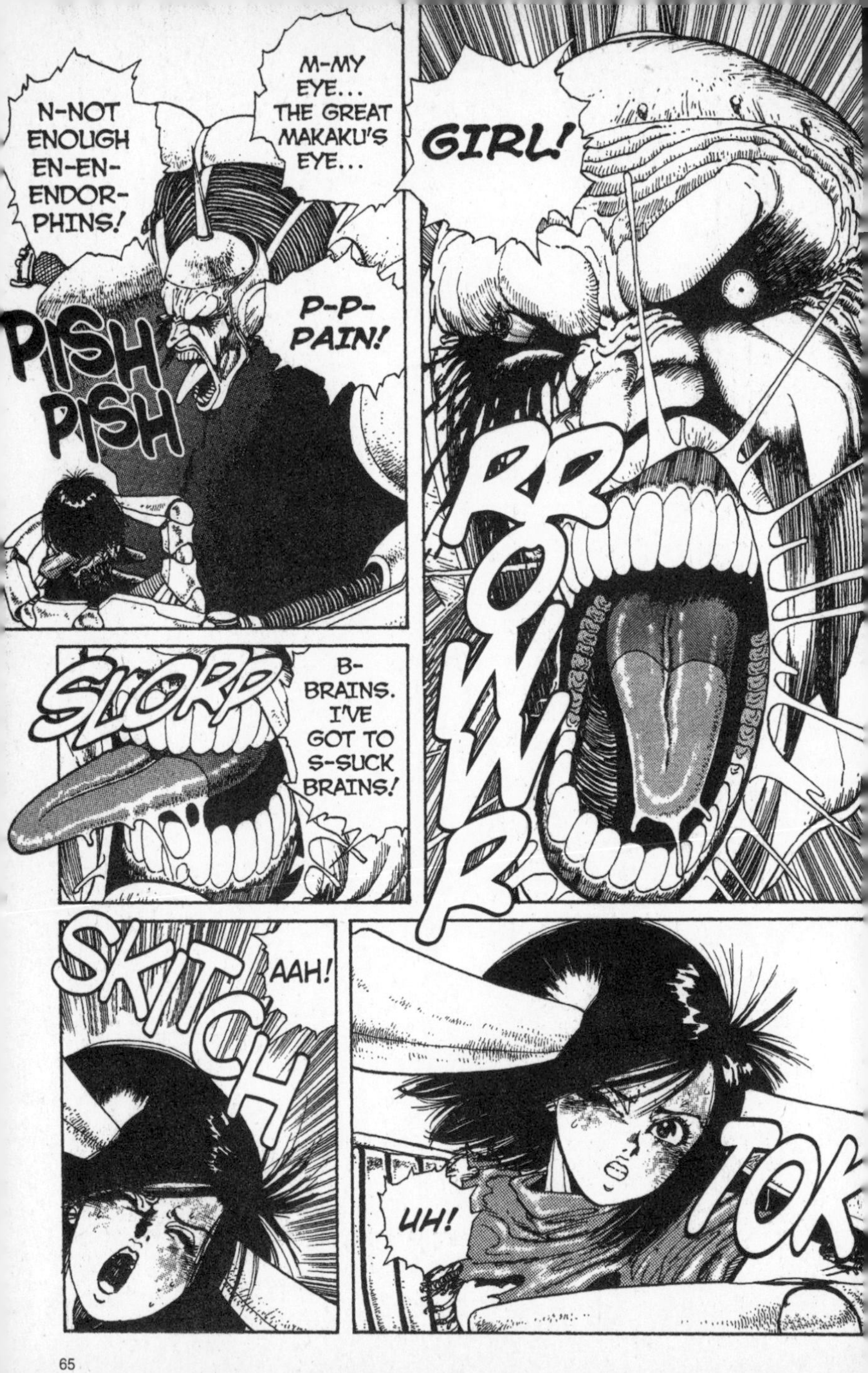
GIRL!
RROWWR
M-MY EYE... THE GREAT MAKAKU'S EYE...
N-NOT ENOUGH EN-EN-ENDOR-PHINS!
P-P-PAIN!
PISH PISH
B-BRAINS. I'VE GOT TO S-SUCK BRAINS!
SLORP
TOK
UH!
SKITCH
AAH!

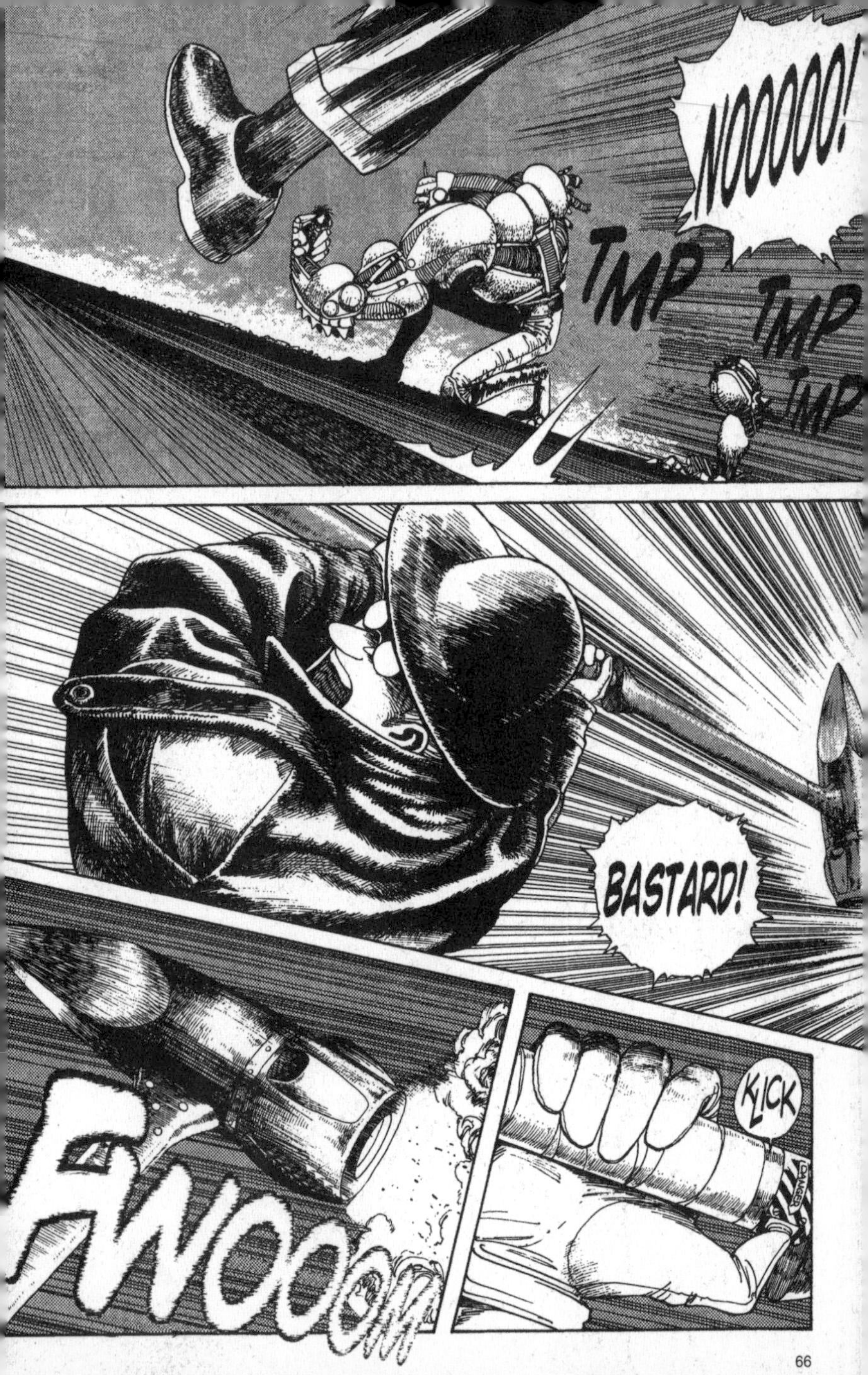
NOOOOO!
TMP
TMP
TMP
BASTARD!
KLICK
DANGER
FWOOOM

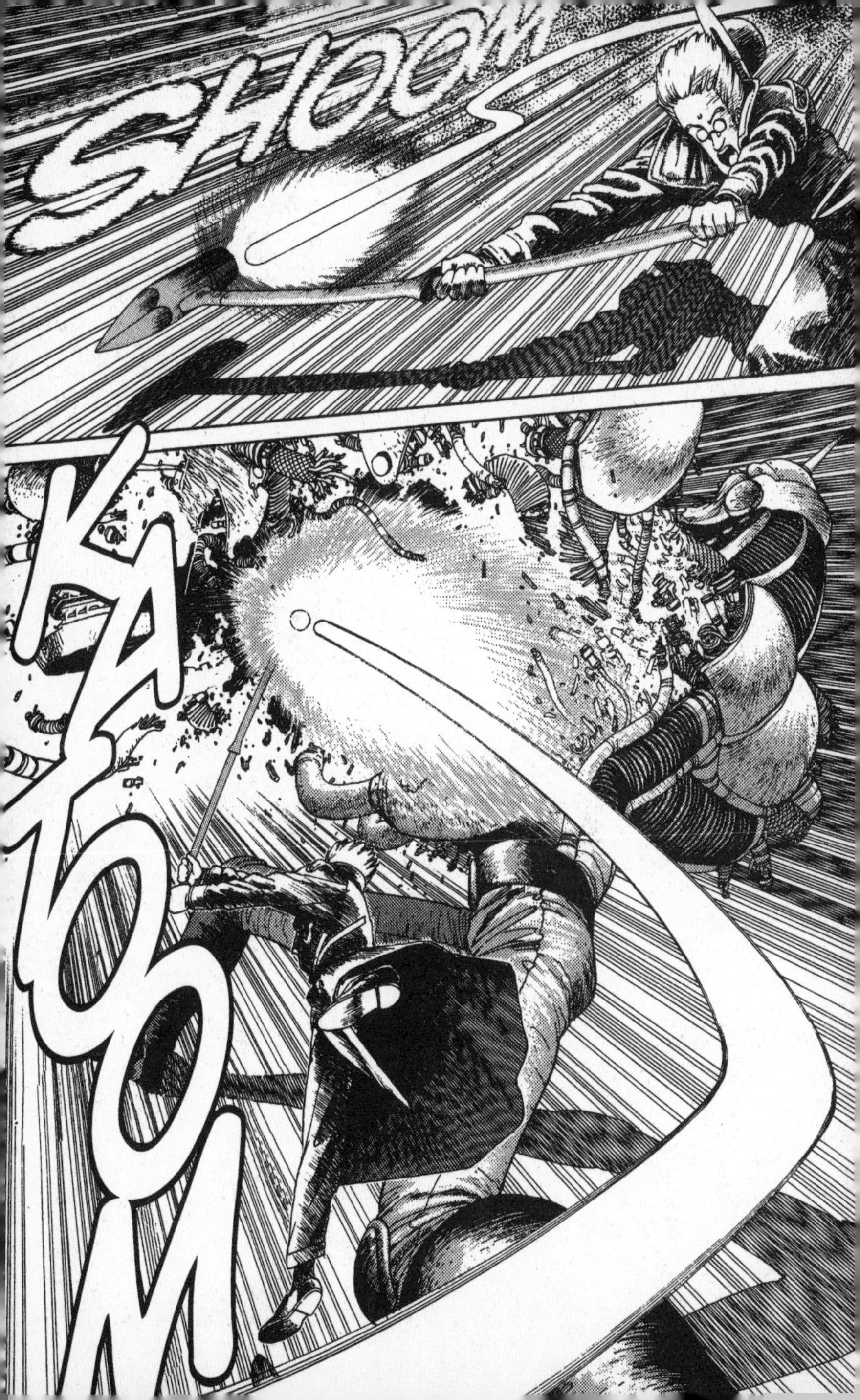
SHOOM
KA-BOOM

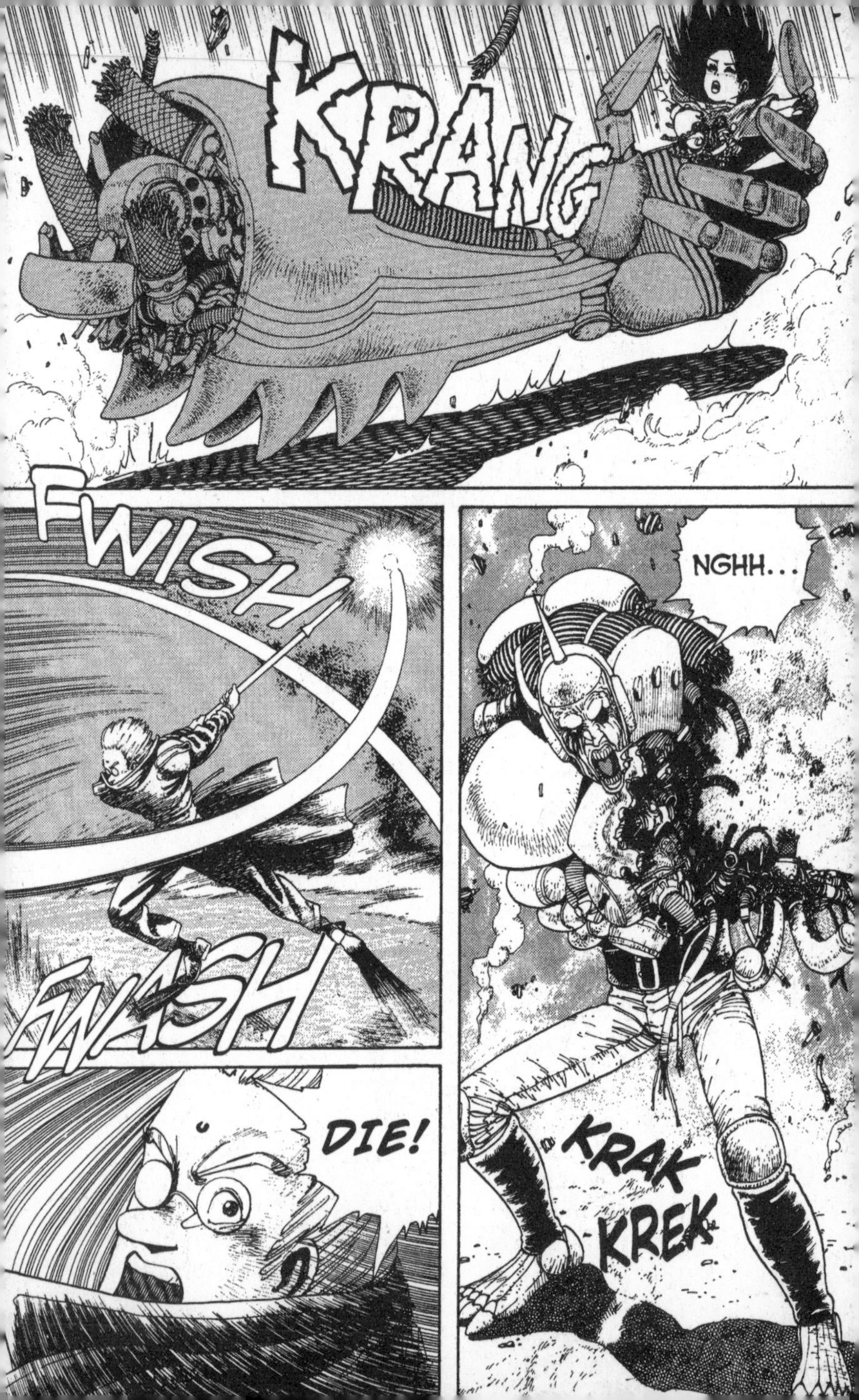
KRANG
NGHH...
KRAK
KREK
FWISH
FWASH
DIE!

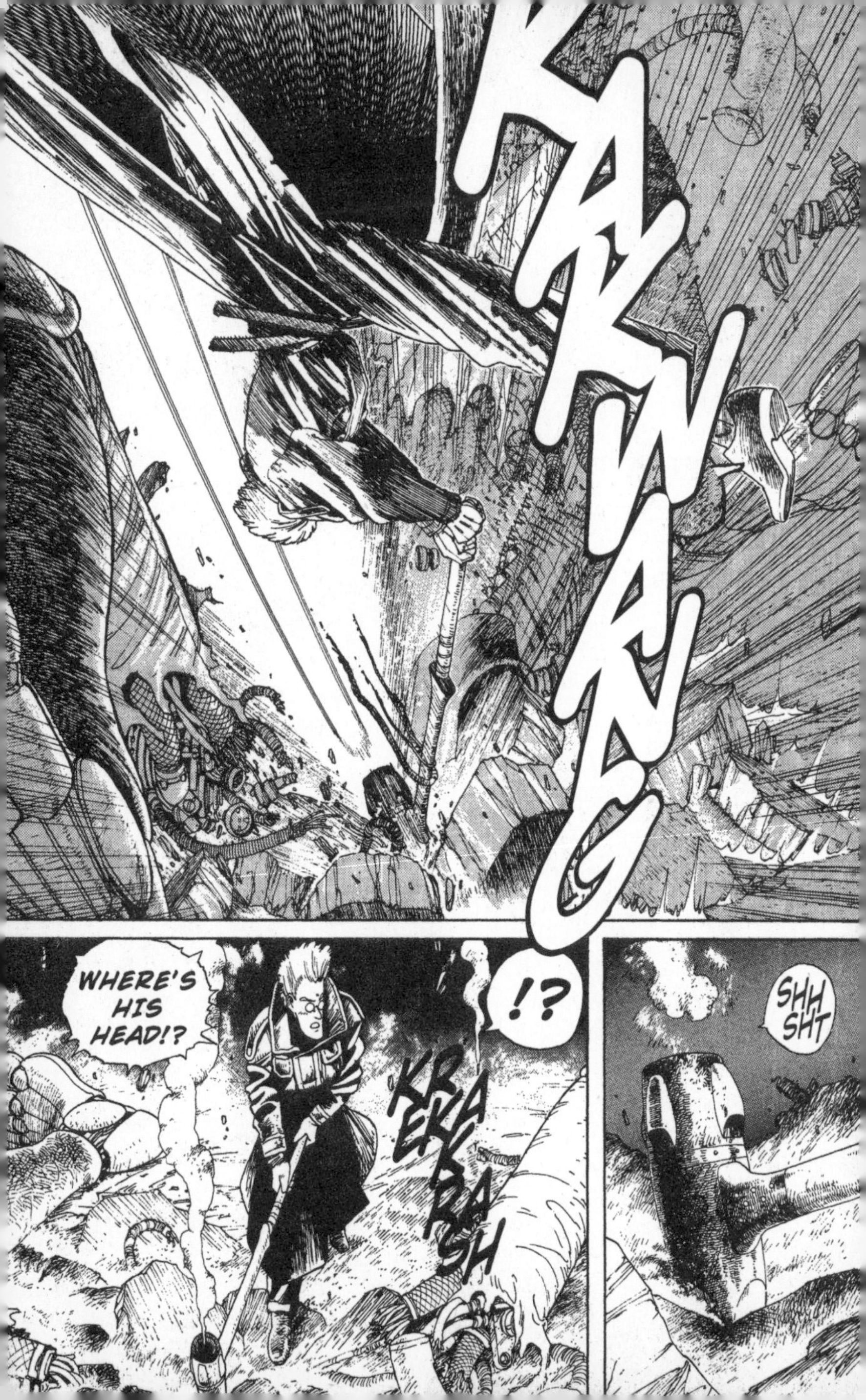
SHH SHT
!?
WHERE'S HIS HEAD!?

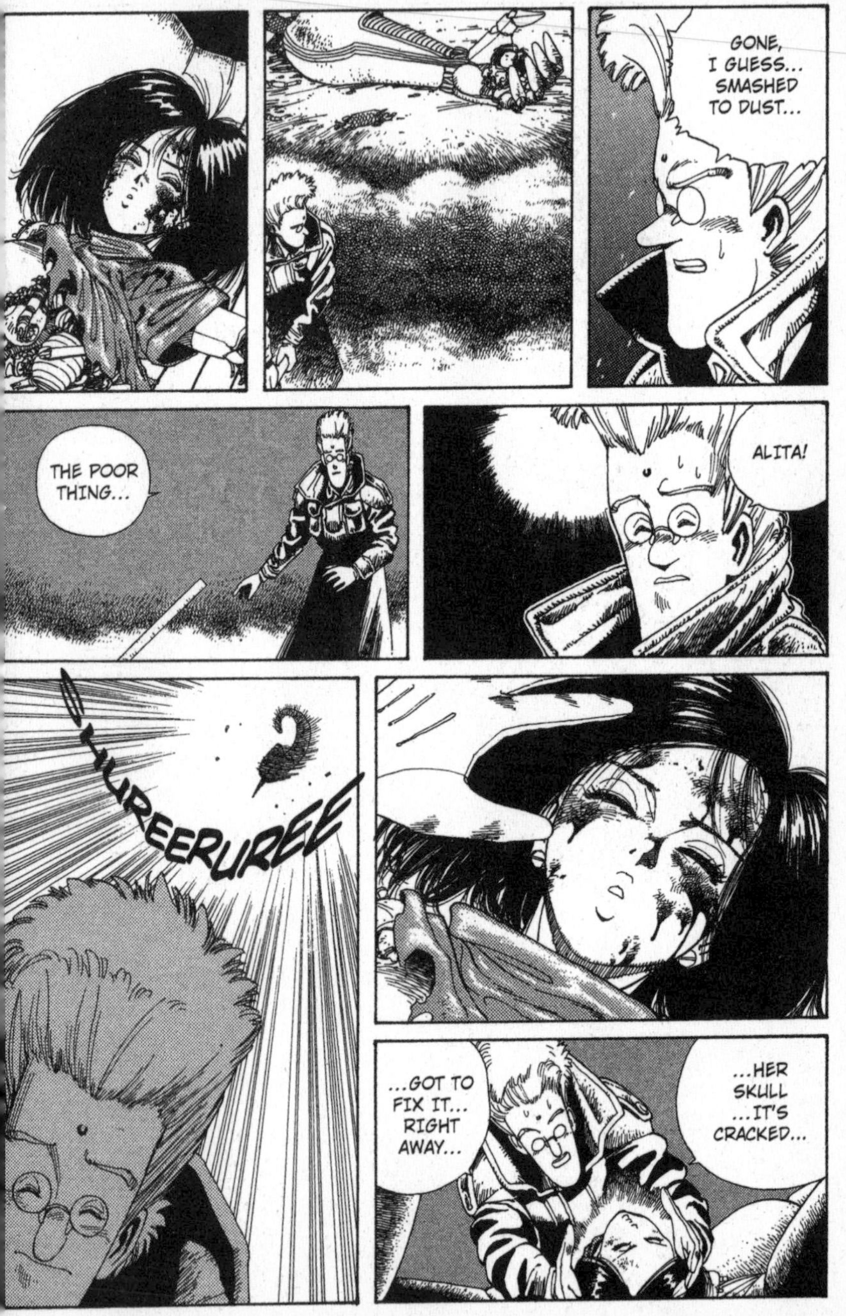
GONE, I GUESS... SMASHED TO DUST...
ALITA!
THE POOR THING...
...HER SKULL ...IT'S CRACKED...
...GOT TO FIX IT... RIGHT AWAY...
CHUREERUREE

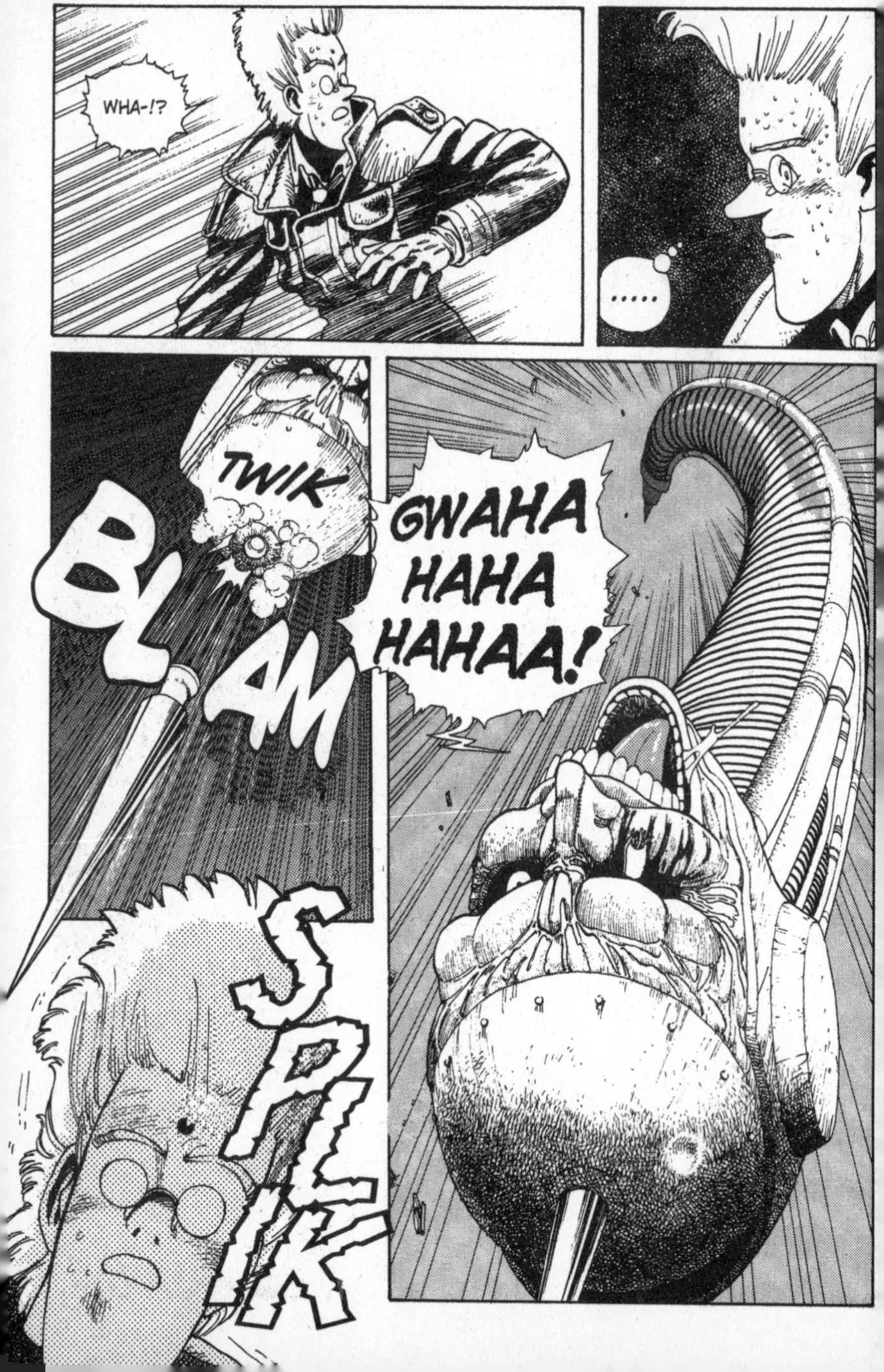
.....
WHA-!?
GWAHA HAHA HAHAA!
TWIK
BLAM
SPLIK

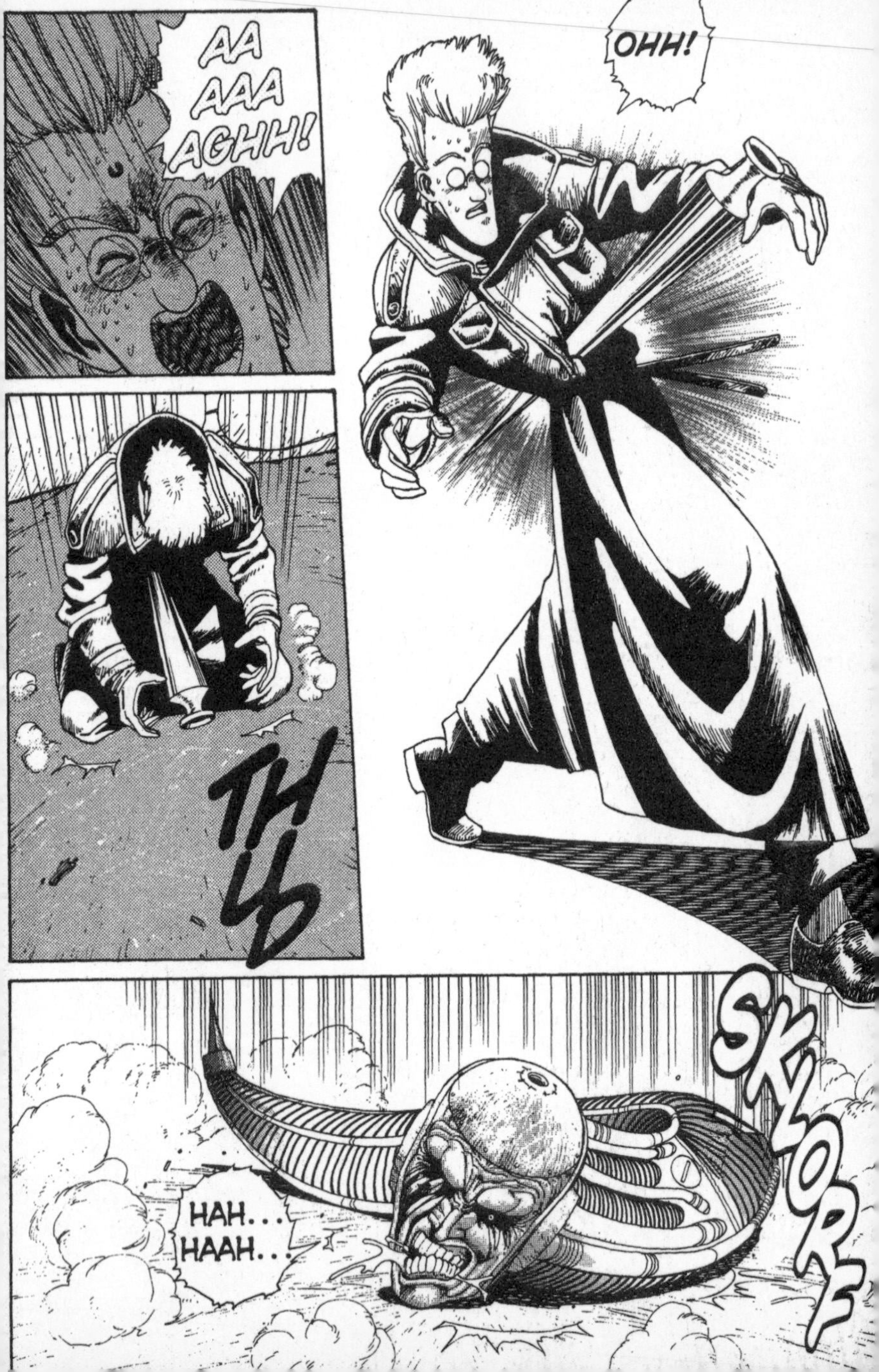
OHH!
AA AAA AGHH!
THUD
SKWORF
HAH... HAAH...

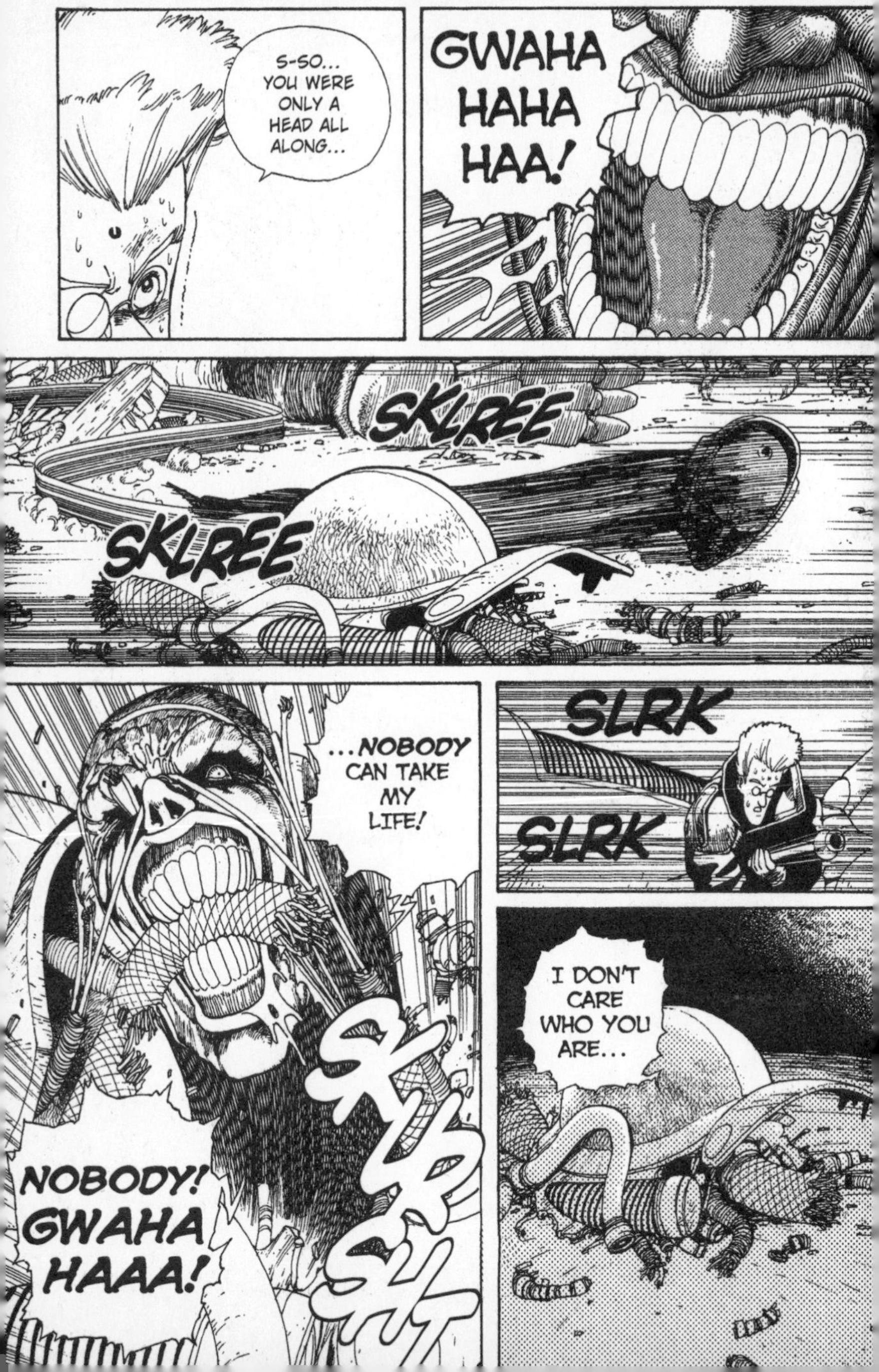
GWAHA HAHA HAA!
S-SO... YOU WERE ONLY A HEAD ALL ALONG...
SKLREE
SKLREE
SLRK
SLRK
I DON'T CARE WHO YOU ARE...
...NOBODY CAN TAKE MY LIFE!
NOBODY! GWAHA HAAAA!

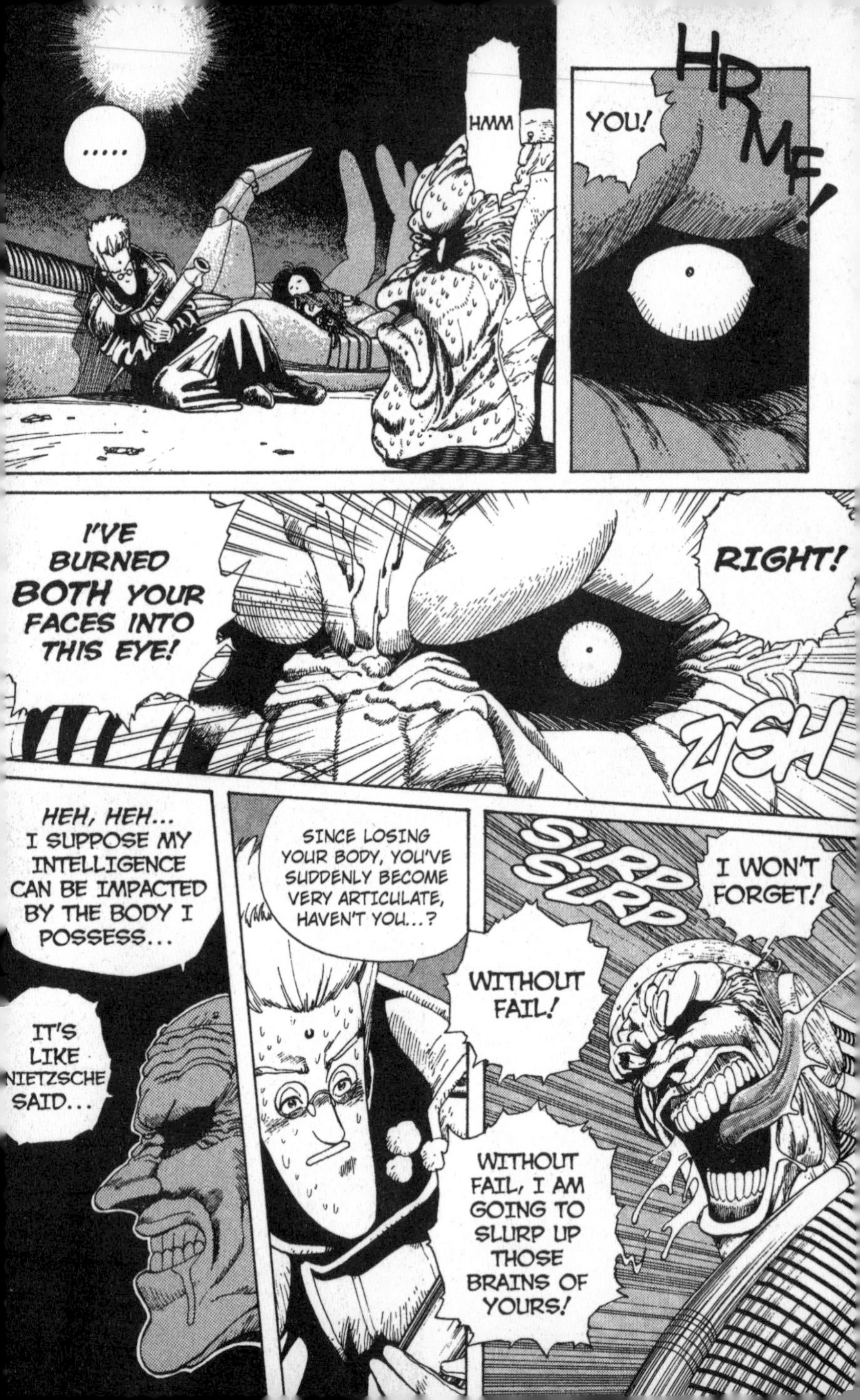
YOU!
HRMF!
HMM
......
RIGHT!
I'VE BURNED BOTH YOUR FACES INTO THIS EYE!
ZISH
SLRP SLRP
I WON'T FORGET!
WITHOUT FAIL!
WITHOUT FAIL, I AM GOING TO SLURP UP THOSE BRAINS OF YOURS!
SINCE LOSING YOUR BODY, YOU'VE SUDDENLY BECOME VERY ARTICULATE, HAVEN'T YOU...?
HEH, HEH... I SUPPOSE MY INTELLIGENCE CAN BE IMPACTED BY THE BODY I POSSESS...
IT'S LIKE NIETZSCHE SAID...

THE MIND IS NOTHING BUT A PLAYTHING OF THE BODY!

GWAHA HA HA HAA!

SKLRT

HFF

UFF

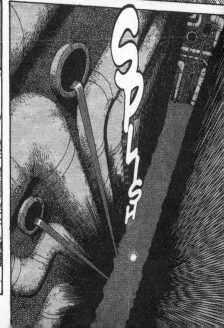

SPLSH

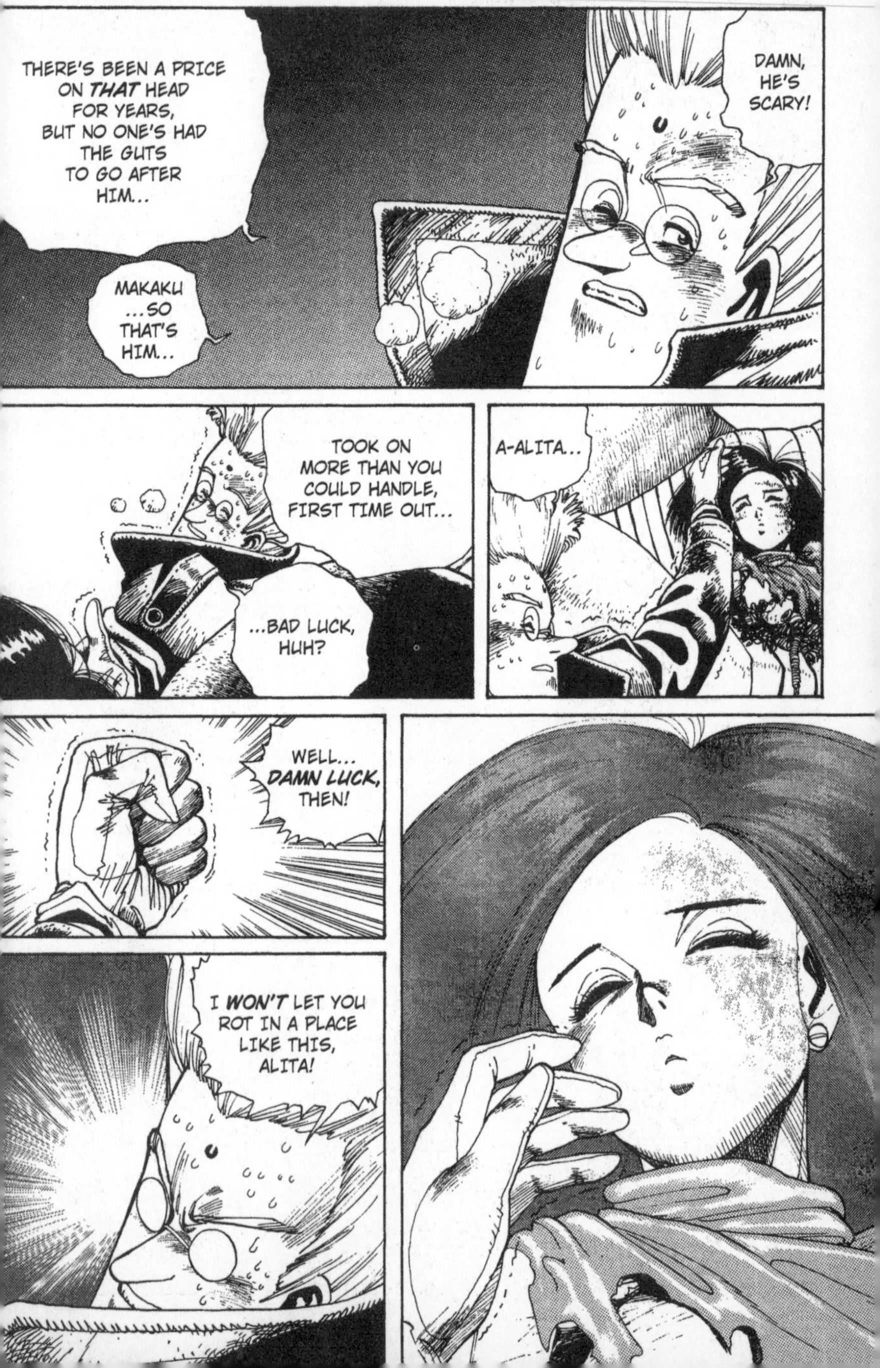
DAMN, HE'S SCARY!
THERE'S BEEN A PRICE ON *THAT* HEAD FOR YEARS, BUT NO ONE'S HAD THE GUTS TO GO AFTER HIM...
MAKAKU ...SO THAT'S HIM...
A-ALITA...
TOOK ON MORE THAN YOU COULD HANDLE, FIRST TIME OUT...
...BAD LUCK, HUH?
WELL... *DAMN LUCK,* THEN!
I *WON'T* LET YOU ROT IN A PLACE LIKE THIS, ALITA!

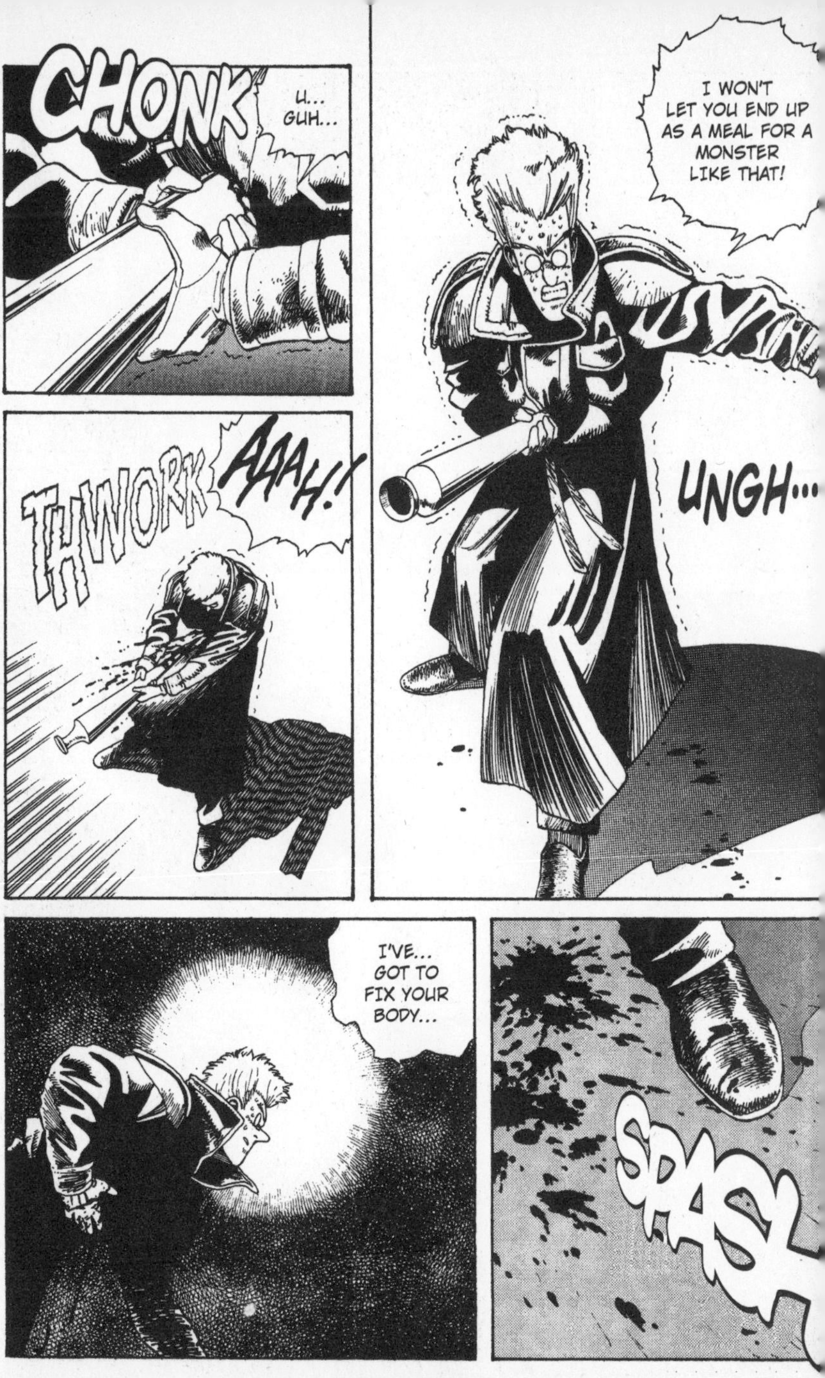
CHONK
U... GUH...
THWORK
AAAH!!
I WON'T LET YOU END UP AS A MEAL FOR A MONSTER LIKE THAT!
UNGH...
I'VE... GOT TO FIX YOUR BODY...
SPASH

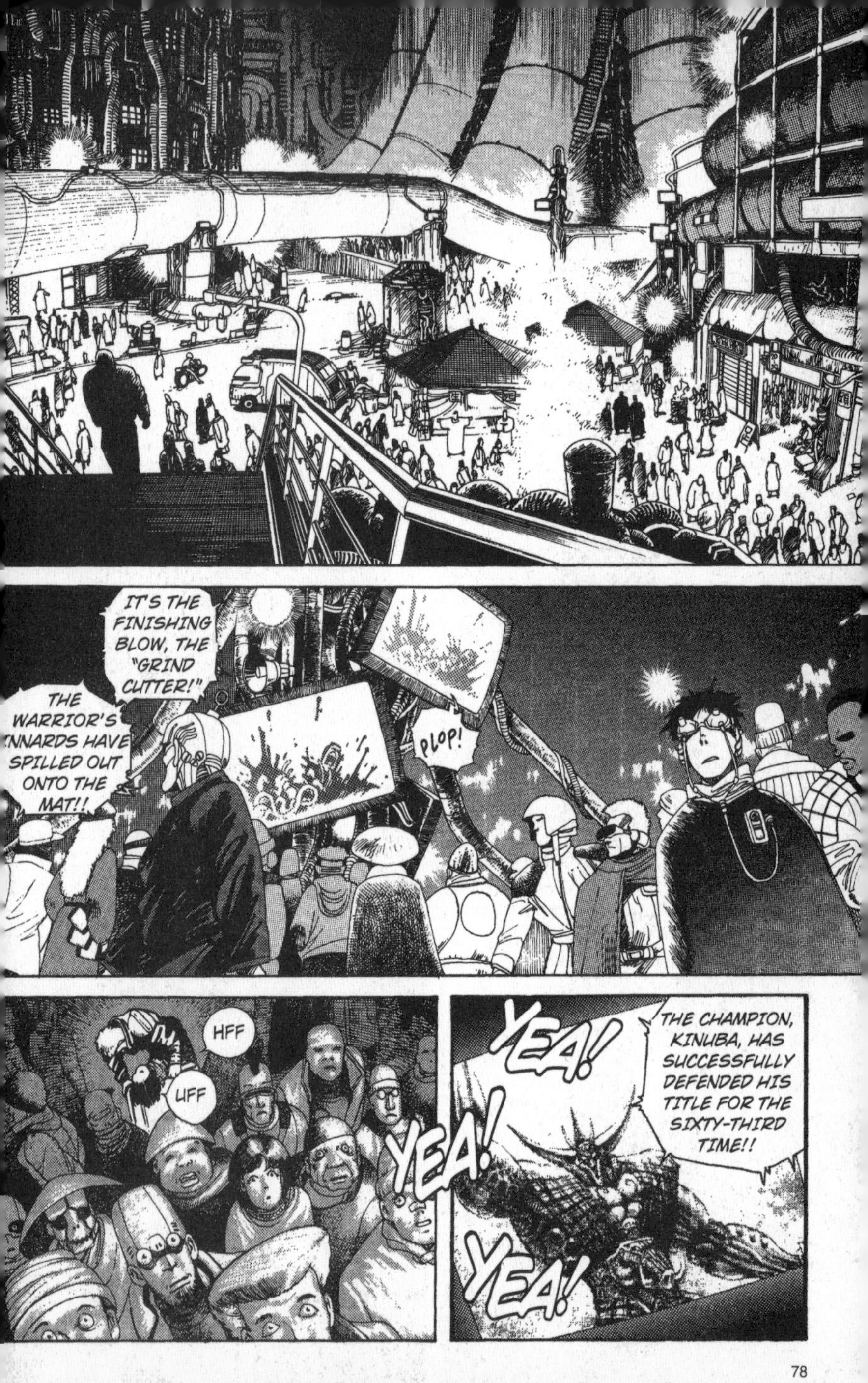
IT'S THE FINISHING BLOW, THE "GRIND CUTTER!"
PLOP!
THE WARRIOR'S INNARDS HAVE SPILLED OUT ONTO THE MAT!!
THE CHAMPION, KINUBA, HAS SUCCESSFULLY DEFENDED HIS TITLE FOR THE SIXTY-THIRD TIME!!
YEA!
YEA!
YEA!
HFF
UFF

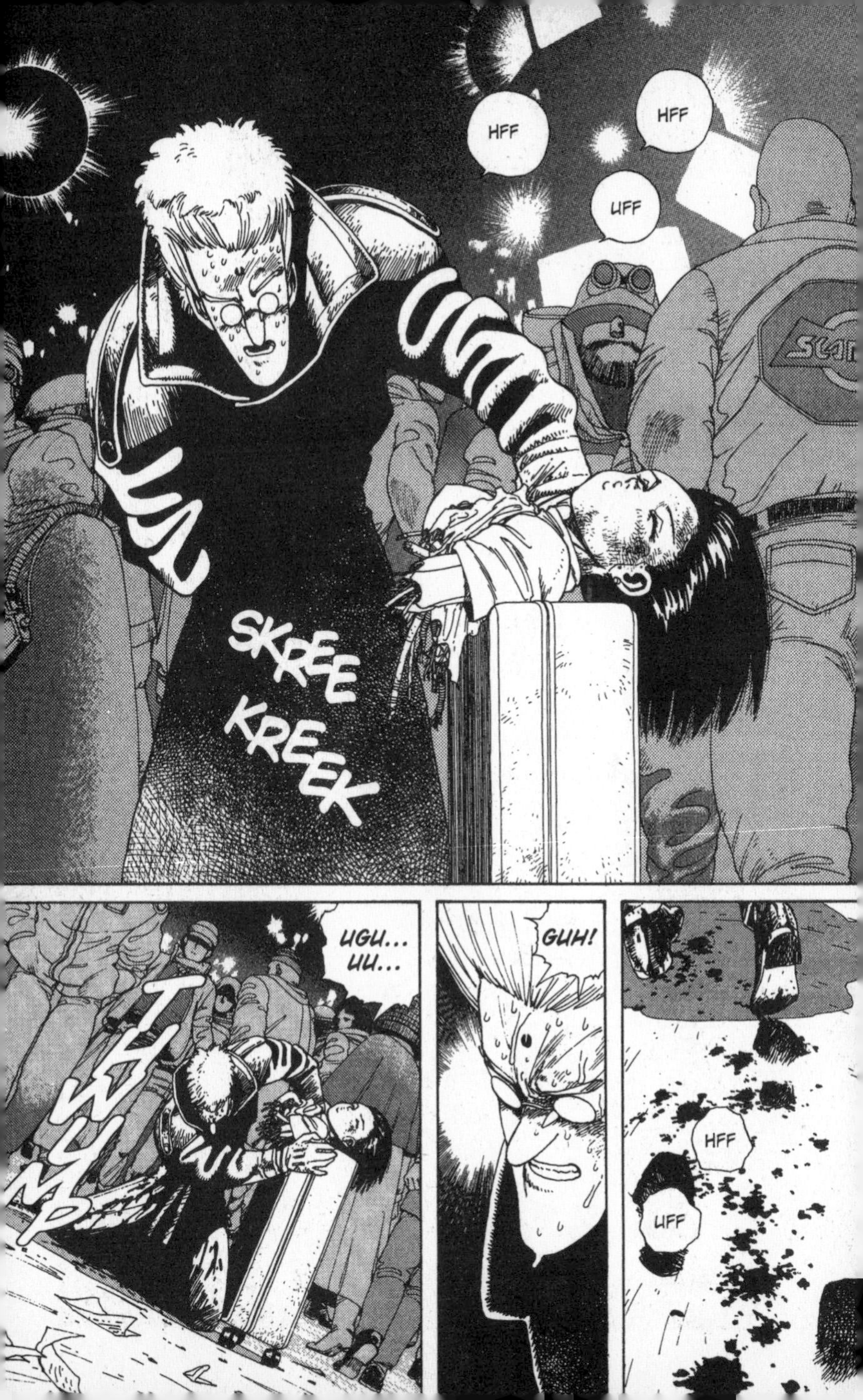
HFF
HFF
UFF
SKREE
KREEK
HFF
UFF
GUH!
UGU... UU...
THWUMP

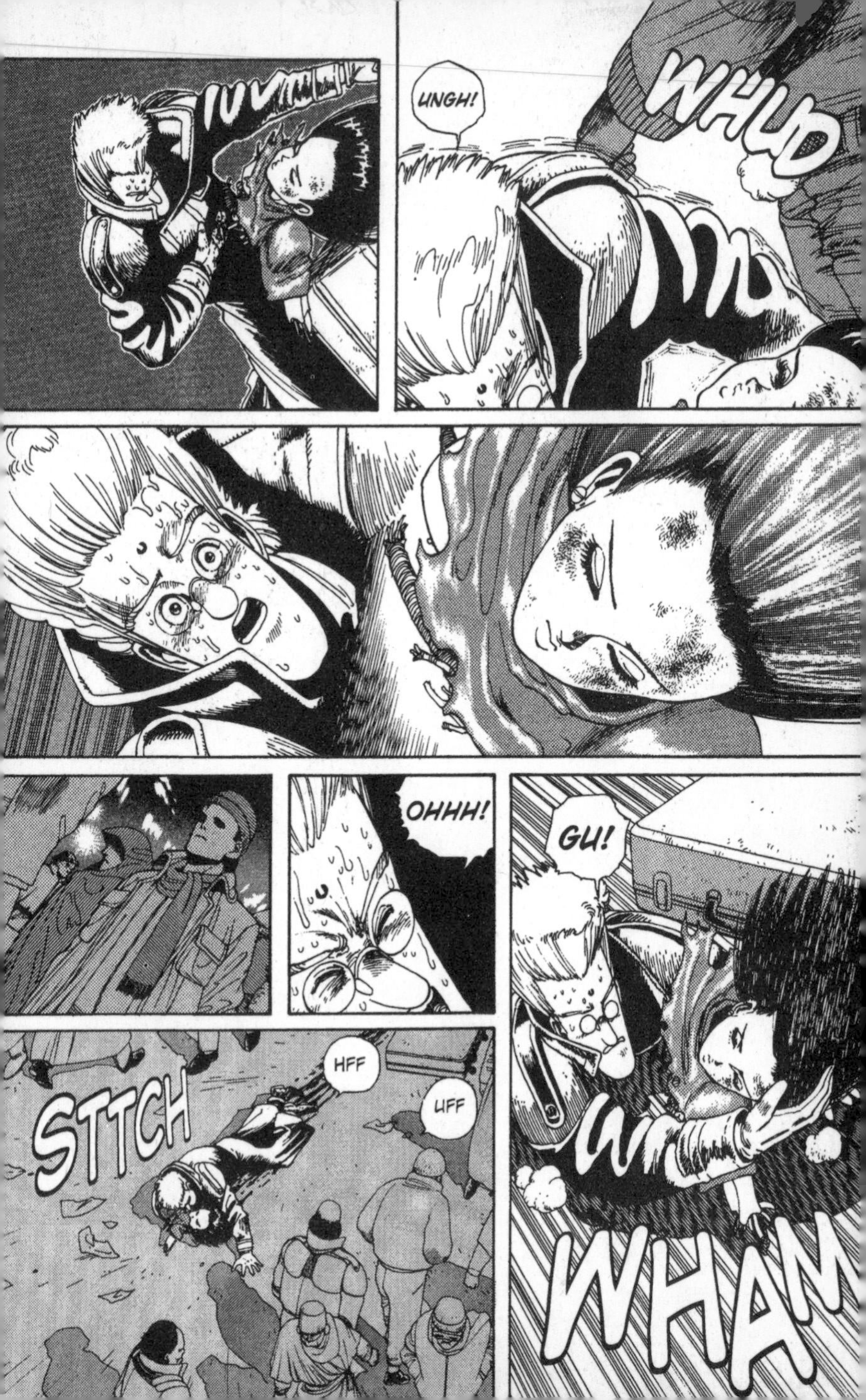
UNGH!
WHUD
GU!
WHAM
OHHH!
HFF
UFF
STTCH

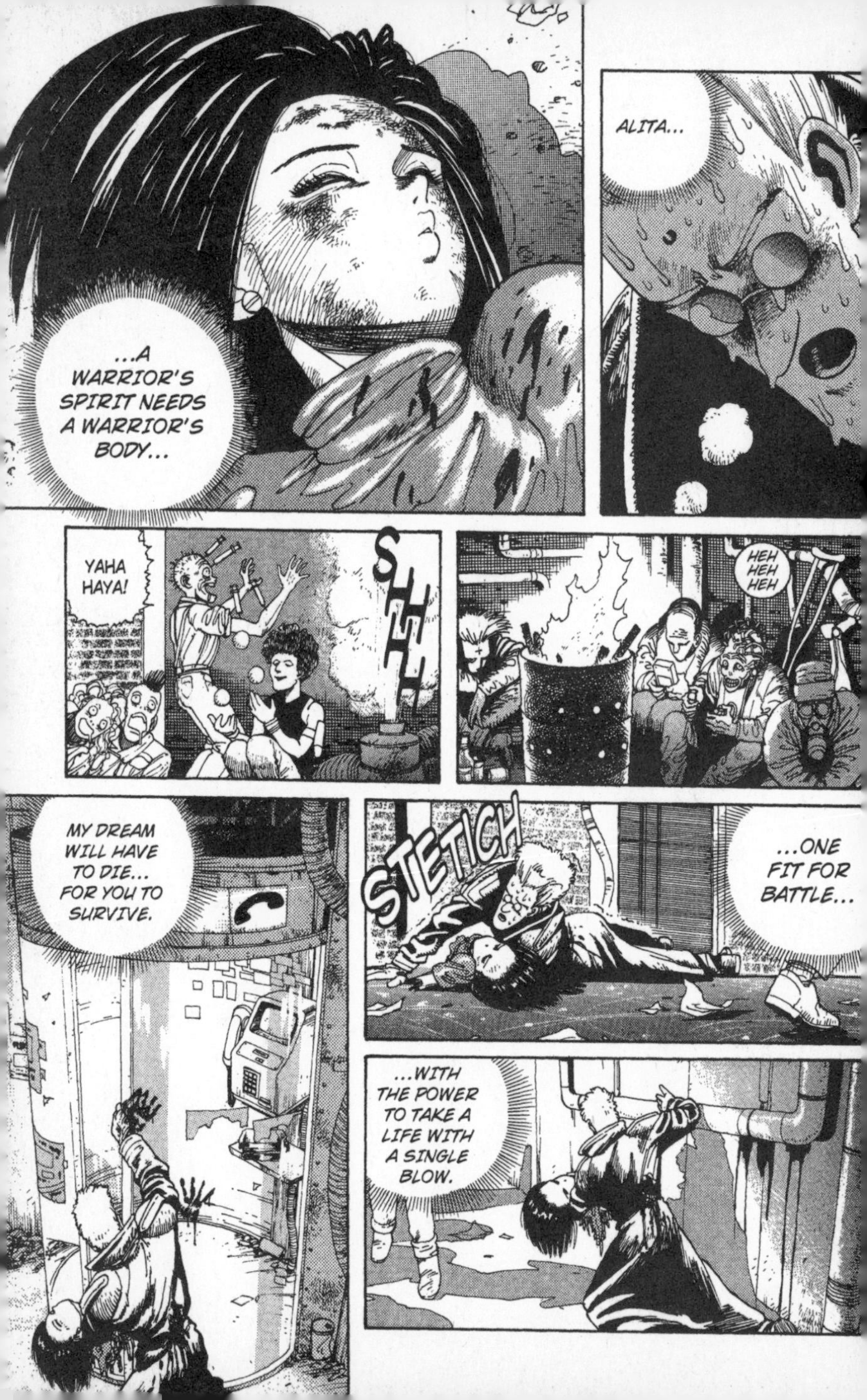
ALITA...
...A WARRIOR'S SPIRIT NEEDS A WARRIOR'S BODY...
HEH HEH HEH
SHHHH
YAHA HAYA!
STETCH
...ONE FIT FOR BATTLE...
...WITH THE POWER TO TAKE A LIFE WITH A SINGLE BLOW.
MY DREAM WILL HAVE TO DIE... FOR YOU TO SURVIVE.

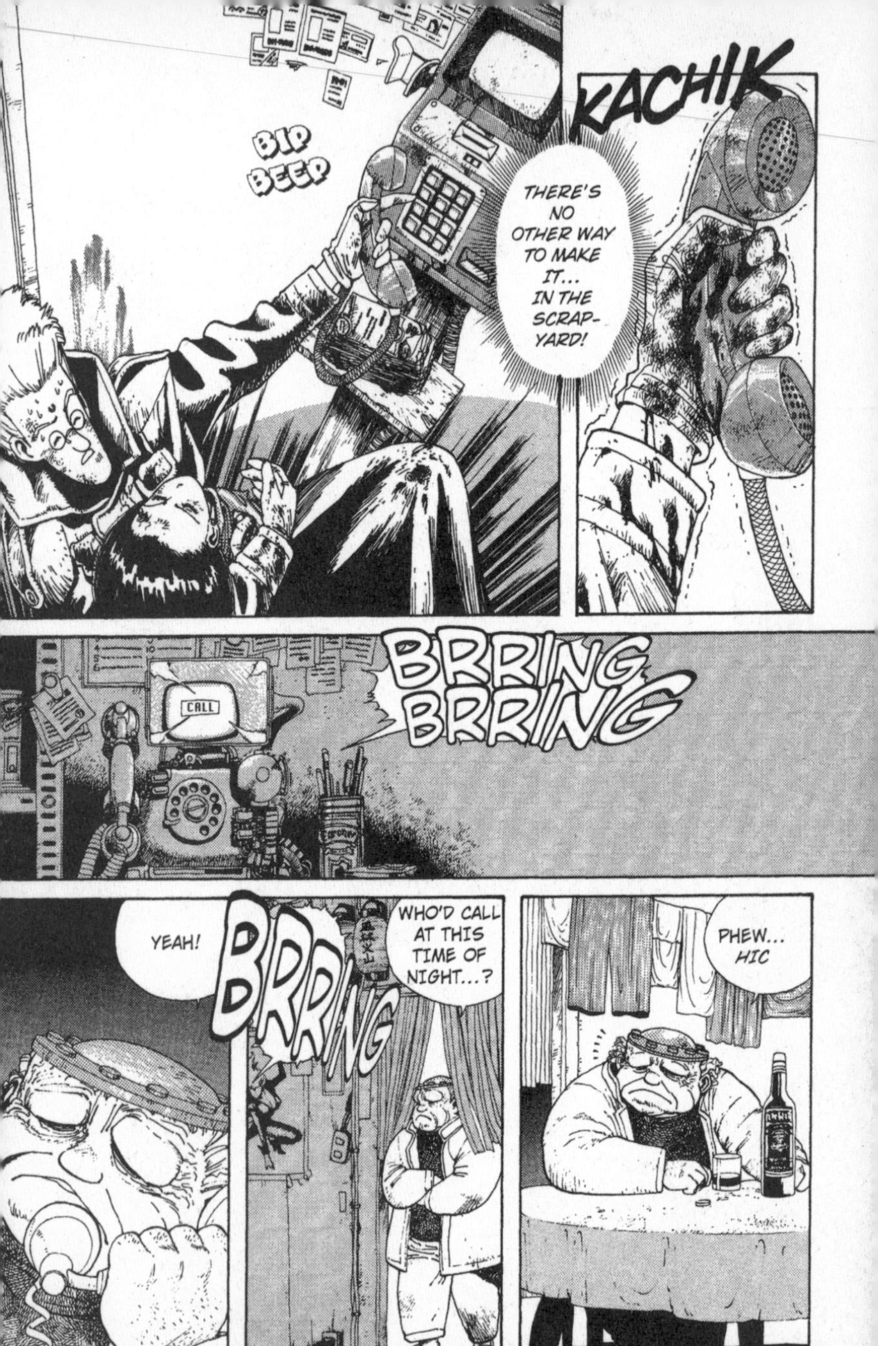
KACHIK
THERE'S NO OTHER WAY TO MAKE IT... IN THE SCRAP-YARD!
BIP BEEP
BRRING BRRING
CALL
PHEW... HIC
WHO'D CALL AT THIS TIME OF NIGHT...?
BRRING
YEAH!

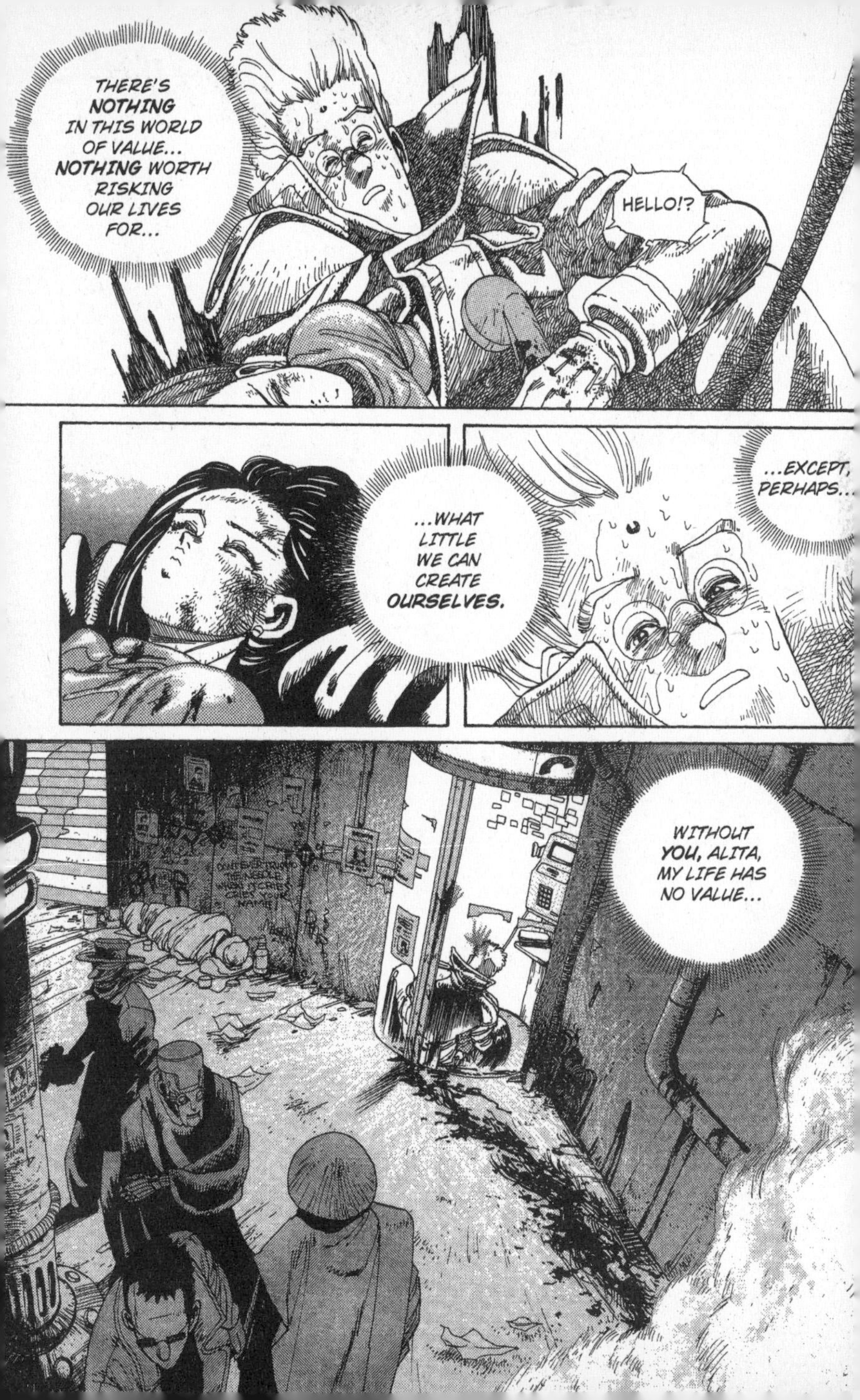
THERE'S NOTHING IN THIS WORLD OF VALUE... NOTHING WORTH RISKING OUR LIVES FOR...
HELLO!?
...EXCEPT, PERHAPS...
...WHAT LITTLE WE CAN CREATE OURSELVES.
WITHOUT YOU, ALITA, MY LIFE HAS NO VALUE...

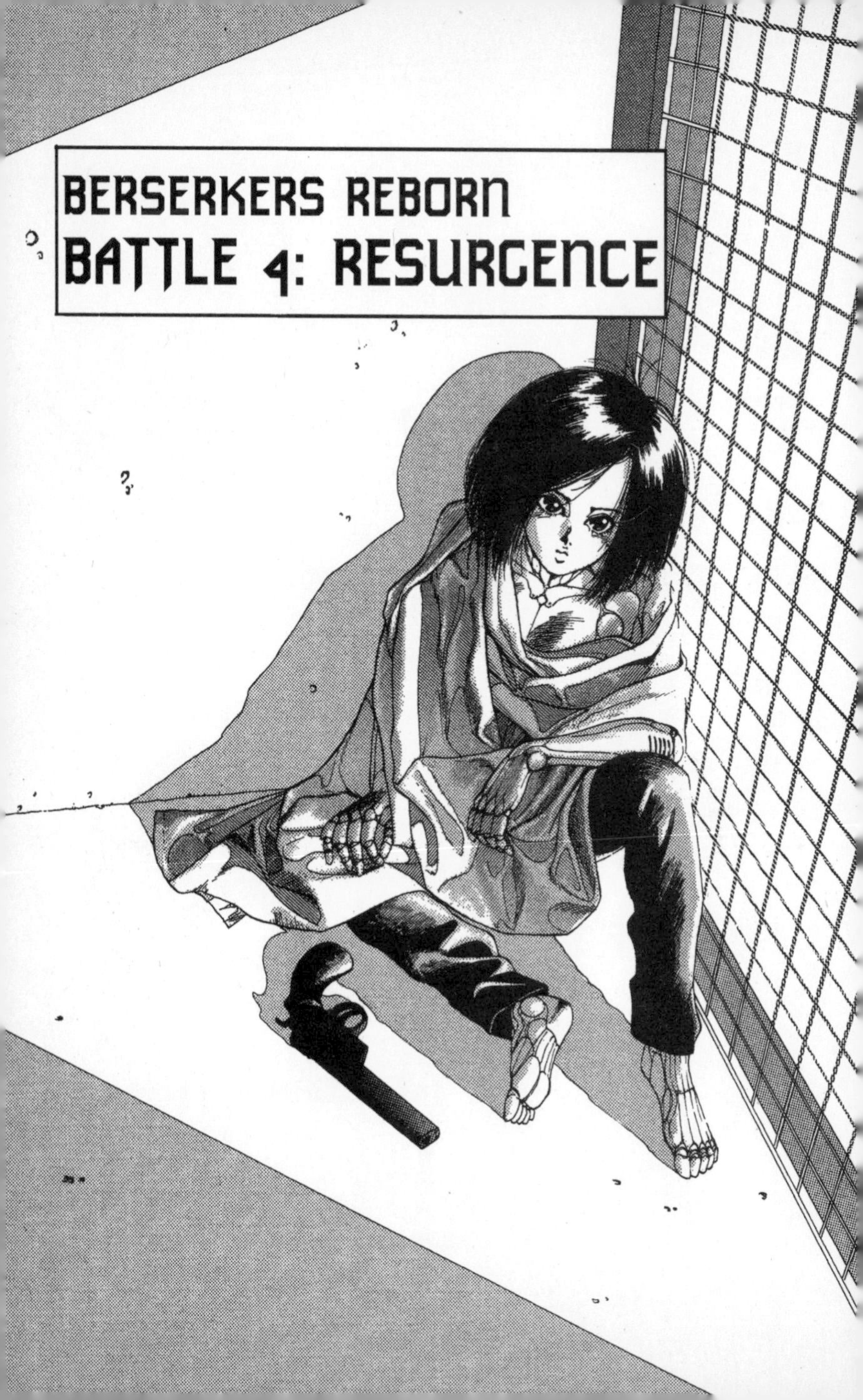
BERSERKERS REBORN
BATTLE 4: RESURGENCE

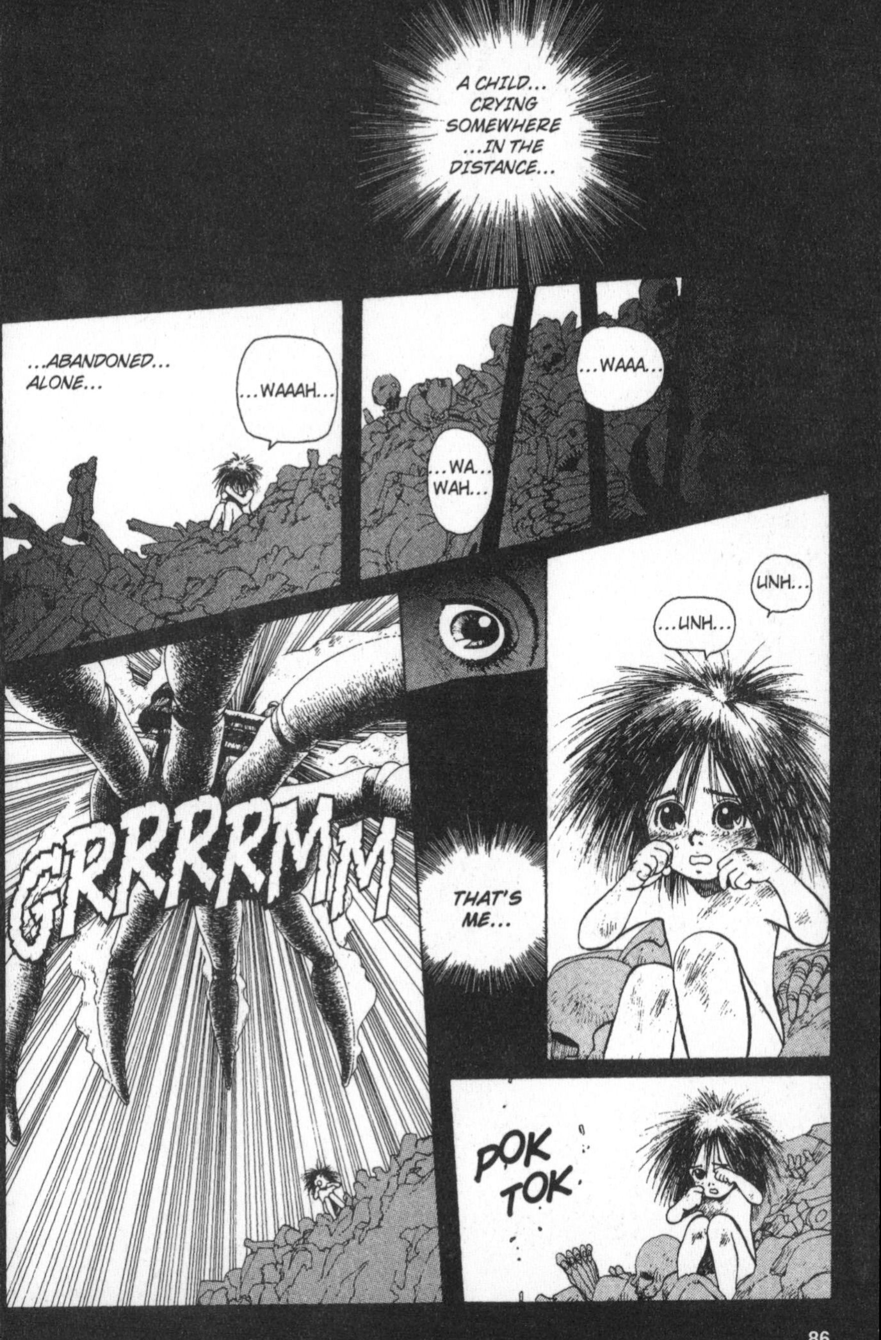

A CHILD... CRYING SOMEWHERE ...IN THE DISTANCE...
...WAAA...
...WA... WAH...
...ABANDONED... ALONE...
...WAAAH...
UNH...
...UNH...
THAT'S ME...
GRRRRMM
POK TOK

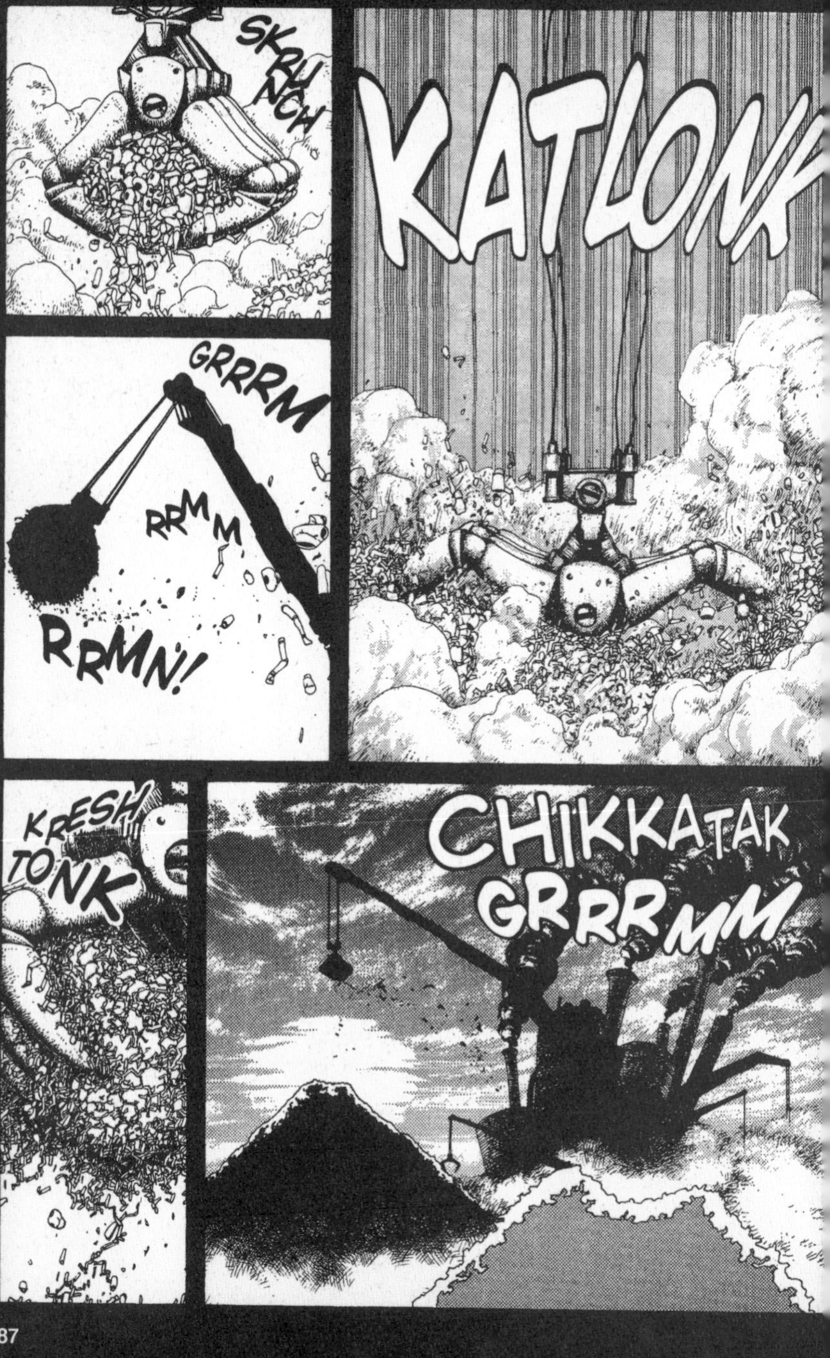
KATLONK
SKRUNCH
GRRRM
RRMM
RRMN!
CHIKKATAK
GRRRMM
KRESH
TONK

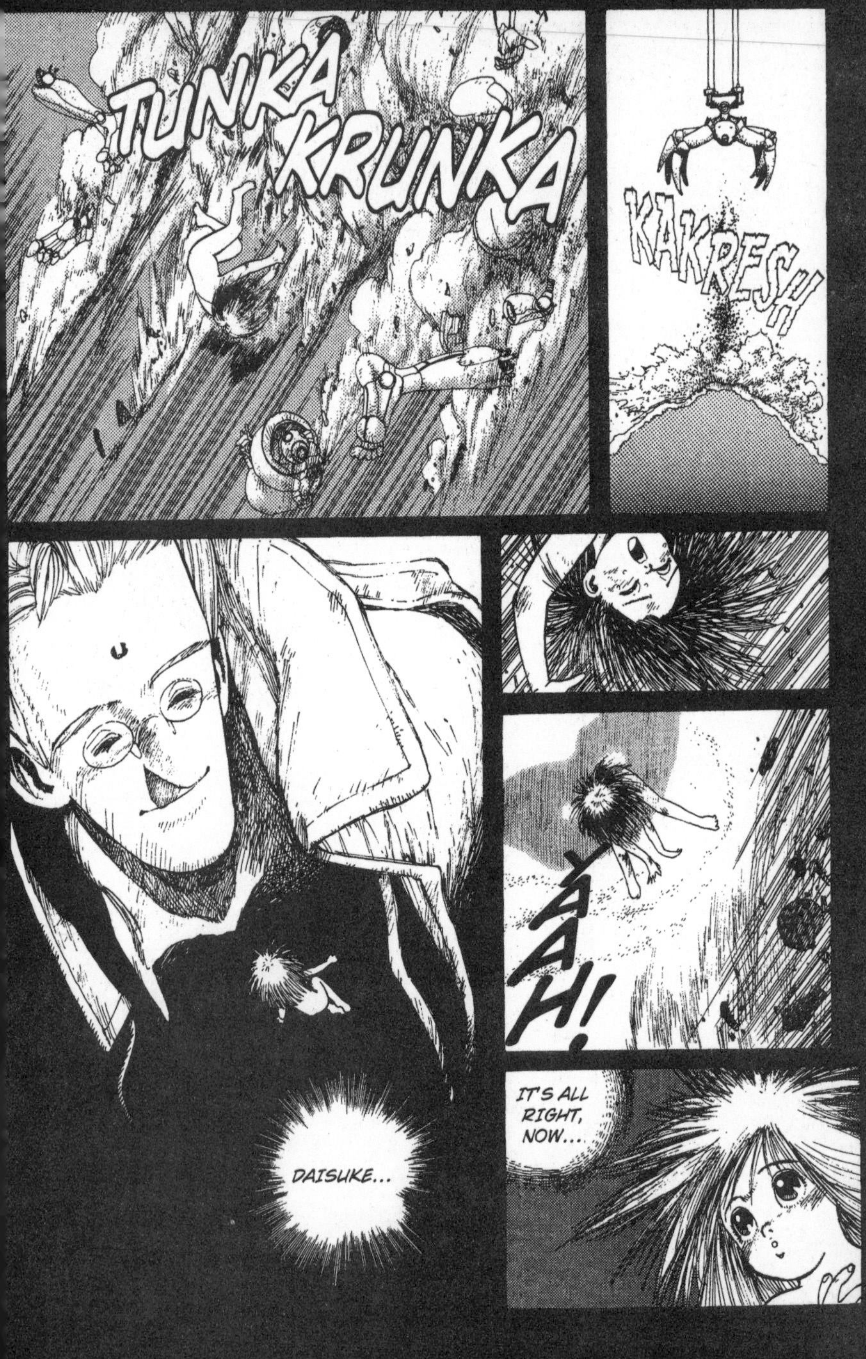
KAKRESH
TUNKA
KRUNKA
AAH!
IT'S ALL RIGHT, NOW...
DAISUKE...

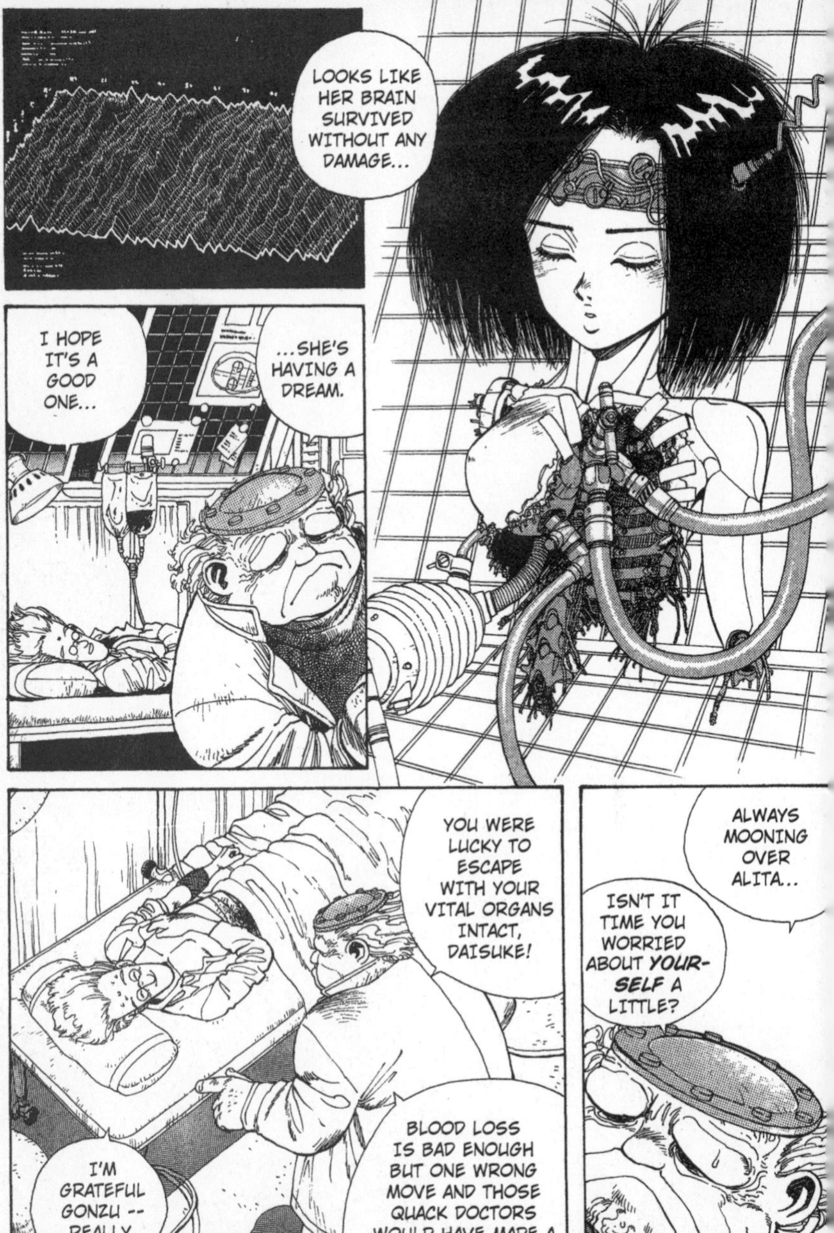
LOOKS LIKE HER BRAIN SURVIVED WITHOUT ANY DAMAGE...
...SHE'S HAVING A DREAM.
I HOPE IT'S A GOOD ONE...
ALWAYS MOONING OVER ALITA...
ISN'T IT TIME YOU WORRIED ABOUT ***YOUR-SELF*** A LITTLE?
YOU WERE LUCKY TO ESCAPE WITH YOUR VITAL ORGANS INTACT, DAISUKE!
BLOOD LOSS IS BAD ENOUGH BUT ONE WRONG MOVE AND THOSE QUACK DOCTORS WOULD HAVE MADE A CYBORG OUT OF YOU!
I'M GRATEFUL GONZU -- REALLY.

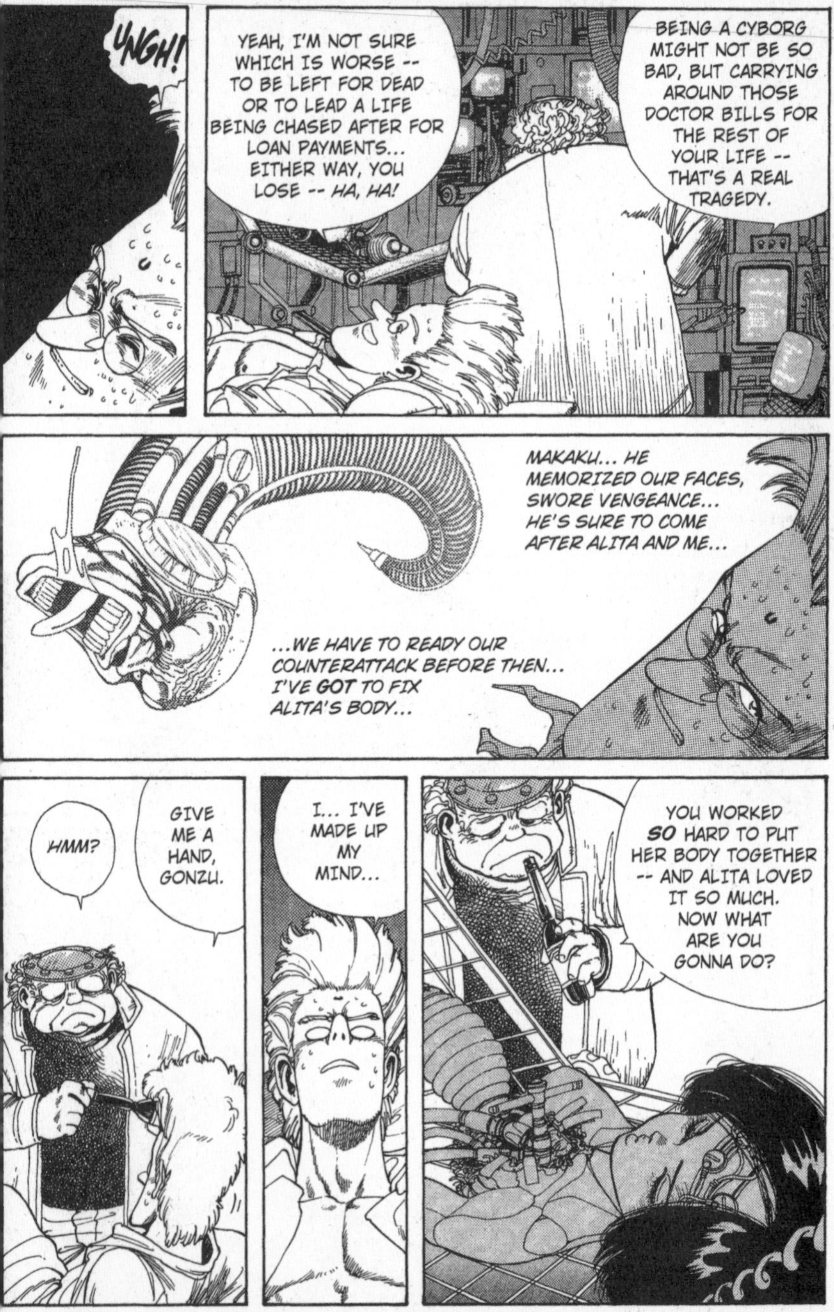
BEING A CYBORG MIGHT NOT BE SO BAD, BUT CARRYING AROUND THOSE DOCTOR BILLS FOR THE REST OF YOUR LIFE -- THAT'S A REAL TRAGEDY.
YEAH, I'M NOT SURE WHICH IS WORSE -- TO BE LEFT FOR DEAD OR TO LEAD A LIFE BEING CHASED AFTER FOR LOAN PAYMENTS... EITHER WAY, YOU LOSE -- *HA, HA!*
UNGH!
MAKAKU... HE MEMORIZED OUR FACES, SWORE VENGEANCE... HE'S SURE TO COME AFTER ALITA AND ME...
...WE HAVE TO READY OUR COUNTERATTACK BEFORE THEN... I'VE ***GOT*** *TO FIX ALITA'S BODY...*
YOU WORKED **SO** HARD TO PUT HER BODY TOGETHER -- AND ALITA LOVED IT SO MUCH. NOW WHAT ARE YOU GONNA DO?
I... I'VE MADE UP MY MIND...
GIVE ME A HAND, GONZU.
HMM?

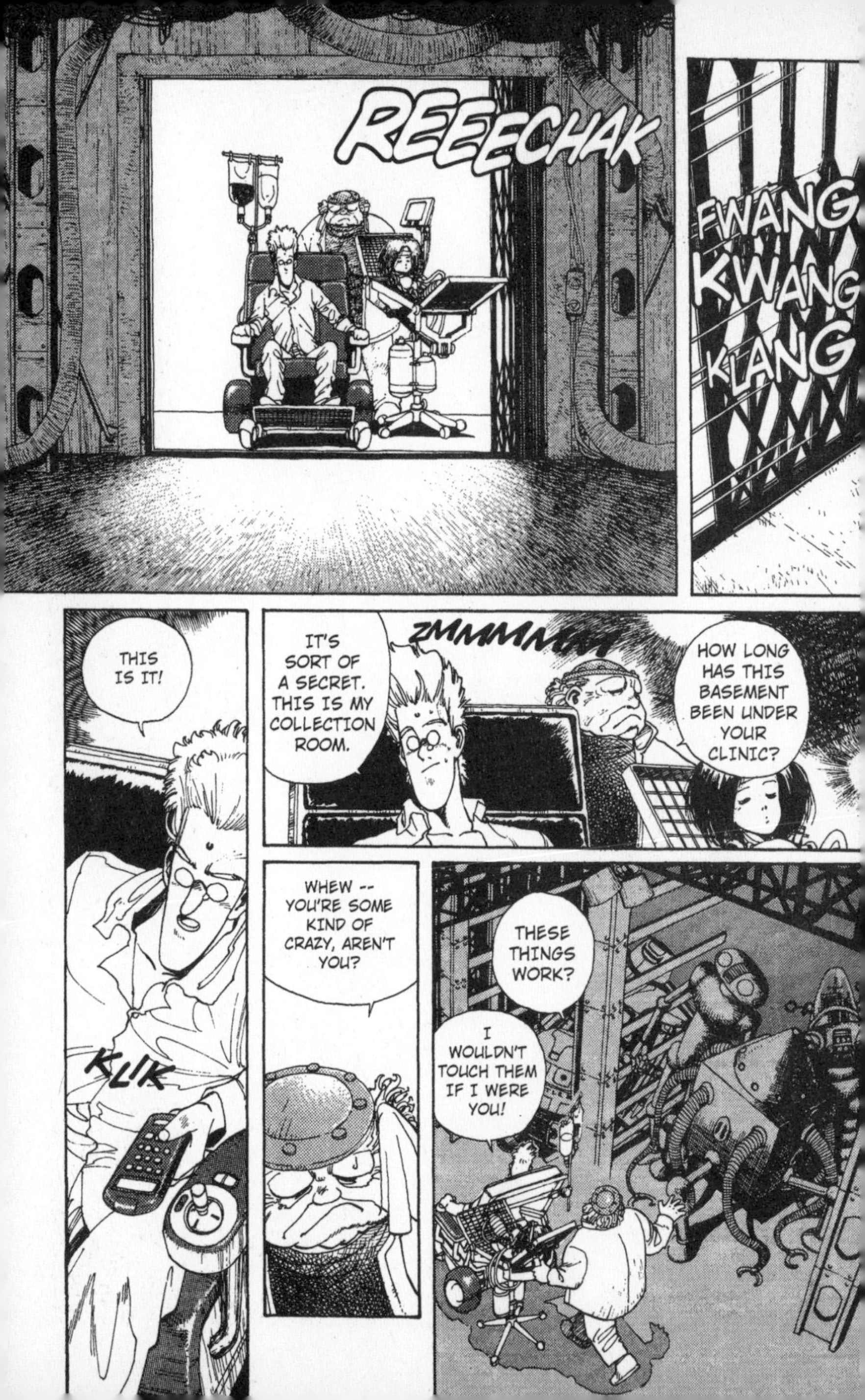
FWANG
KWANG
KLANG
REEECHAK
HOW LONG HAS THIS BASEMENT BEEN UNDER YOUR CLINIC?
IT'S SORT OF A SECRET. THIS IS MY COLLECTION ROOM.
THESE THINGS WORK?
I WOULDN'T TOUCH THEM IF I WERE YOU!
WHEW -- YOU'RE SOME KIND OF CRAZY, AREN'T YOU?
THIS IS IT!
KLIK

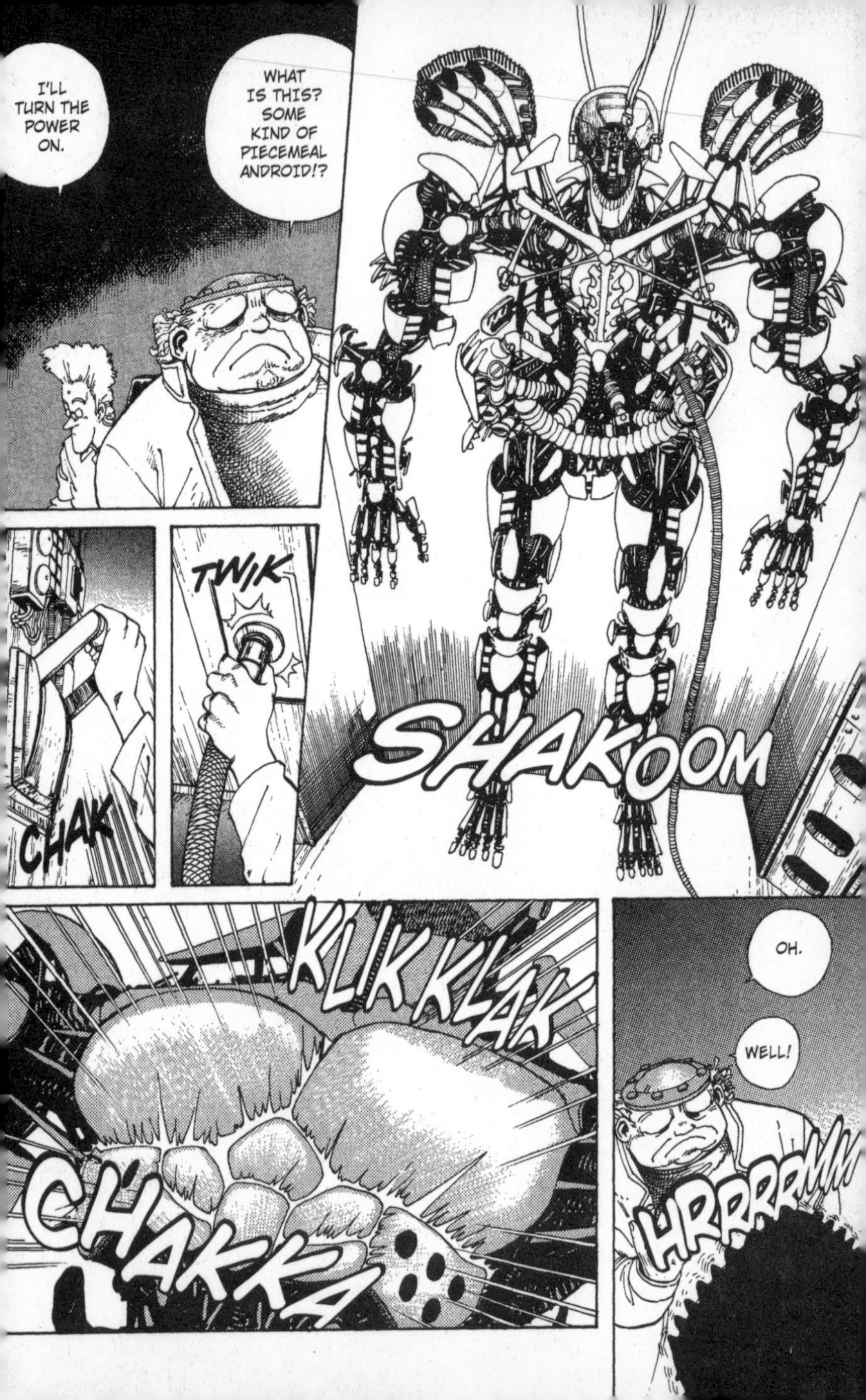
SHAKOOM
WHAT IS THIS? SOME KIND OF PIECEMEAL ANDROID!?
I'LL TURN THE POWER ON.
TWIK
CHAK
OH.
WELL!
HRRRMM
KLIK KLAK
CHAKKA

OHHHHH!

THAKK
CHICKA

TACK
TICK
TOCK

TIKKA

TAKK

CHAKKA

KLINK

THWAKA

CREEPY...
THIS
BODY'S
ALIVE!

THWITCH

KASHOOM

IT -- IT'S
MAGNIFICENT...
WHY DIDN'T YOU
ATTACH IT TO ALITA
IN THE FIRST
PLACE?

WELL,
GONZU...

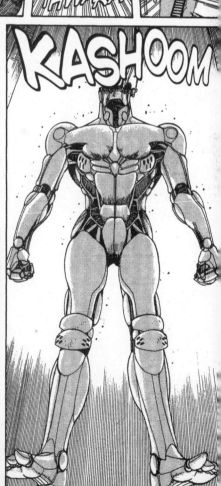

NOTHING'S
EVER SIMPLE.
THIS IS THE
BODY OF A
"BERSERKER."

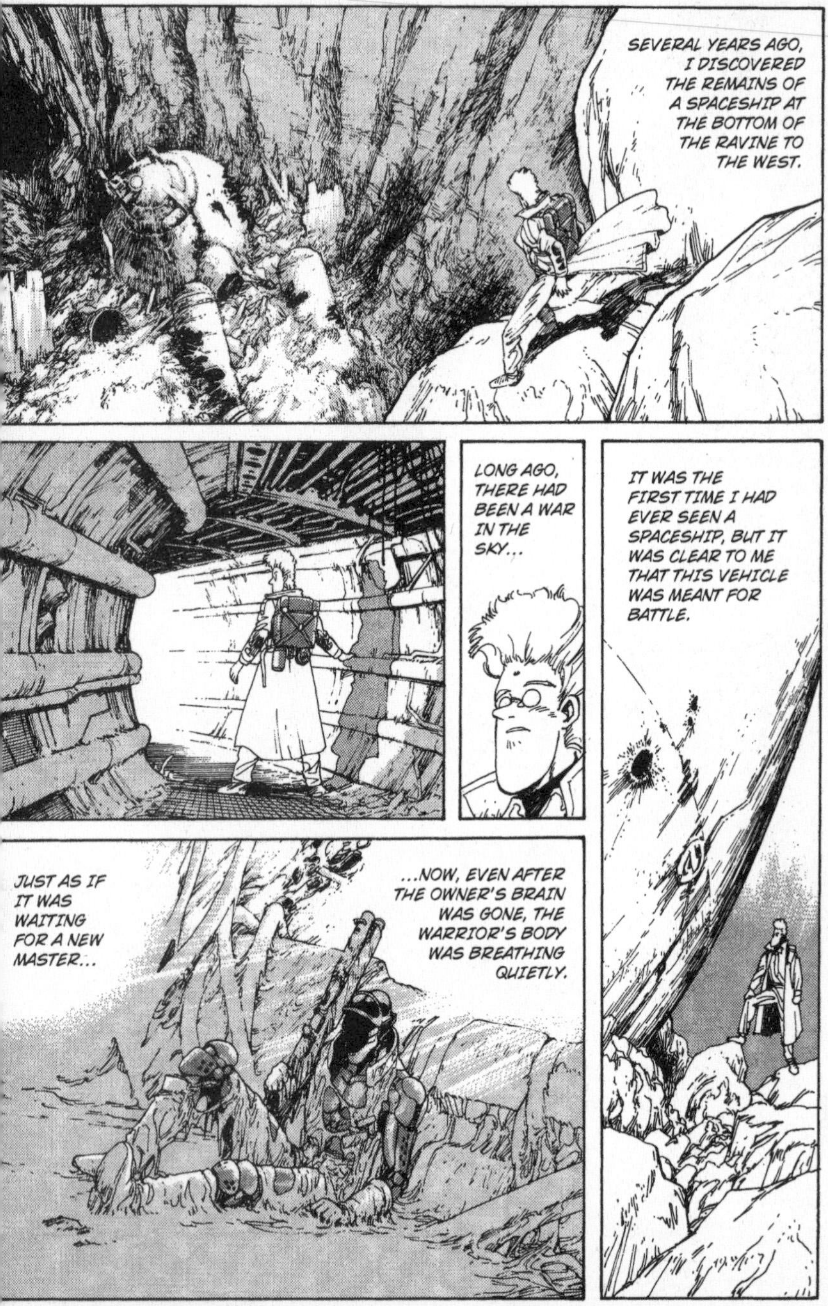
SEVERAL YEARS AGO, I DISCOVERED THE REMAINS OF A SPACESHIP AT THE BOTTOM OF THE RAVINE TO THE WEST.
IT WAS THE FIRST TIME I HAD EVER SEEN A SPACESHIP, BUT IT WAS CLEAR TO ME THAT THIS VEHICLE WAS MEANT FOR BATTLE.
LONG AGO, THERE HAD BEEN A WAR IN THE SKY...
...NOW, EVEN AFTER THE OWNER'S BRAIN WAS GONE, THE WARRIOR'S BODY WAS BREATHING QUIETLY.
JUST AS IF IT WAS WAITING FOR A NEW MASTER...

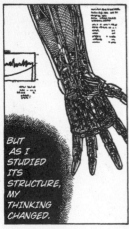

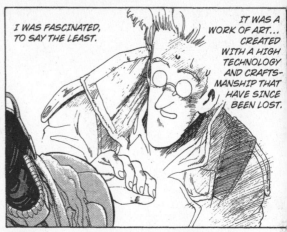

IT WAS A WORK OF ART... CREATED WITH A HIGH TECHNOLOGY AND CRAFTS-MANSHIP THAT HAVE SINCE BEEN LOST.
I WAS FASCINATED, TO SAY THE LEAST.
BUT AS I STUDIED ITS STRUCTURE, MY THINKING CHANGED.
THIS MACHINE -- IT'S A MURDER WEAPON! THE DESIGN MAKES IT GOOD FOR ONLY ONE THING!
ITS CREATORS WANTED TO MAKE A HUMAN BEING INTO AN EFFICIENT WEAPON!
THEY SAY THAT IN OLDEN TIMES, ABLE-BODIED SOLDIERS WERE MADE OVER AND SENT TO WAR -- AS "BERSERKERS."
THIS DISCOVERY WAS MY FIRST TASTE OF THE TRUE MADNESS OF WAR...
TO THINK OF HUMAN BEINGS AS NOTHING BUT TOOLS ...UNFOR-GIVABLE...
AND SO I LOCKED THE BERSERKER BODY DOWN HERE...
KASHANG

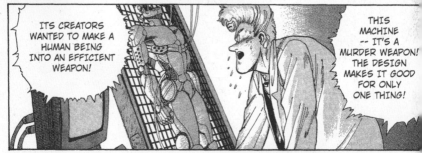

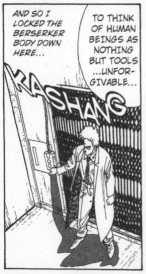

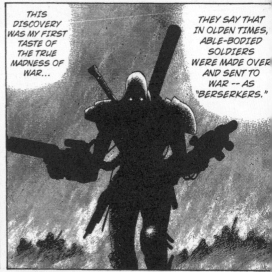

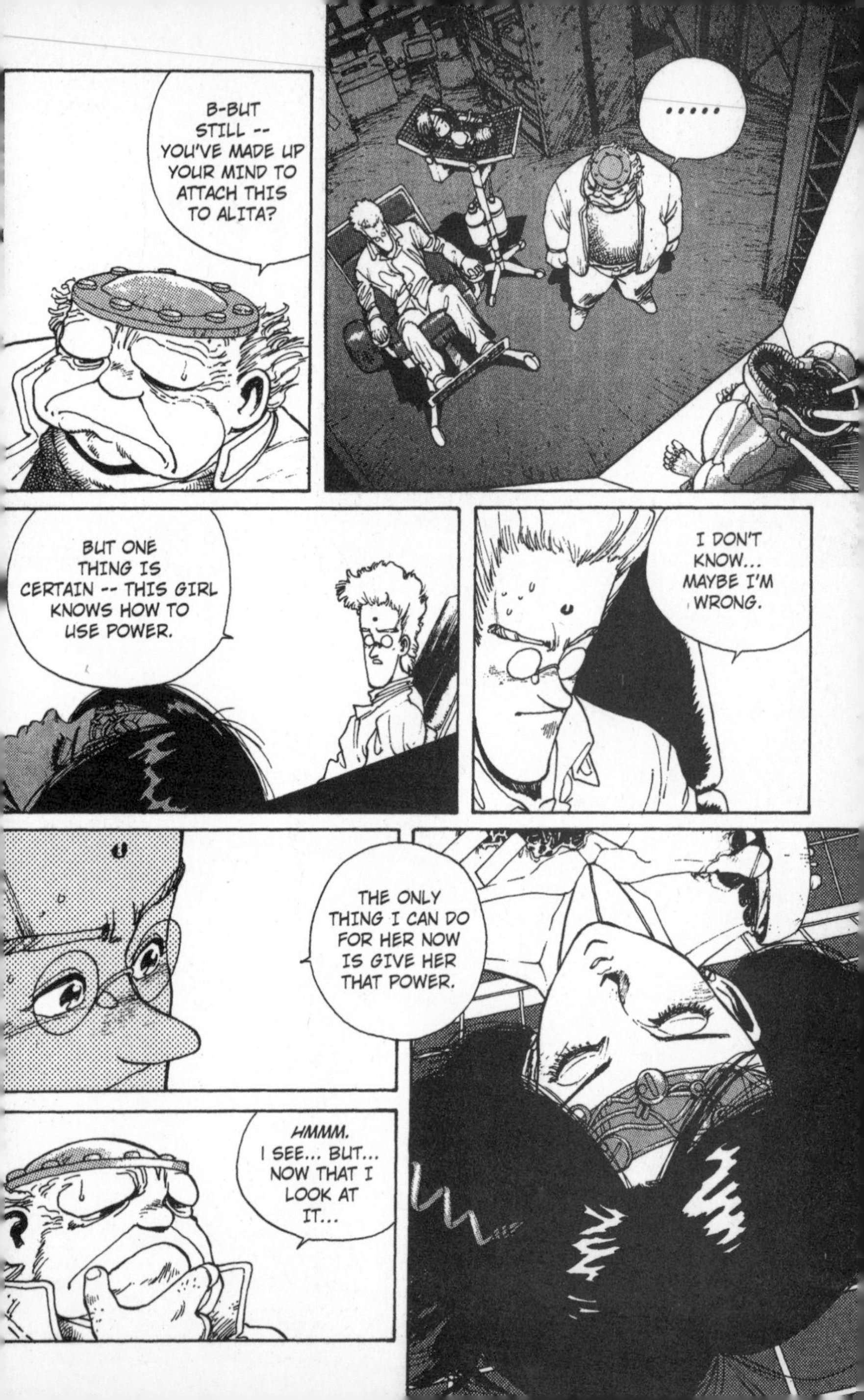
.....
B-BUT STILL -- YOU'VE MADE UP YOUR MIND TO ATTACH THIS TO ALITA?
I DON'T KNOW... MAYBE I'M WRONG.
BUT ONE THING IS CERTAIN -- THIS GIRL KNOWS HOW TO USE POWER.
THE ONLY THING I CAN DO FOR HER NOW IS GIVE HER THAT POWER.
HMMM. I SEE... BUT... NOW THAT I LOOK AT IT...

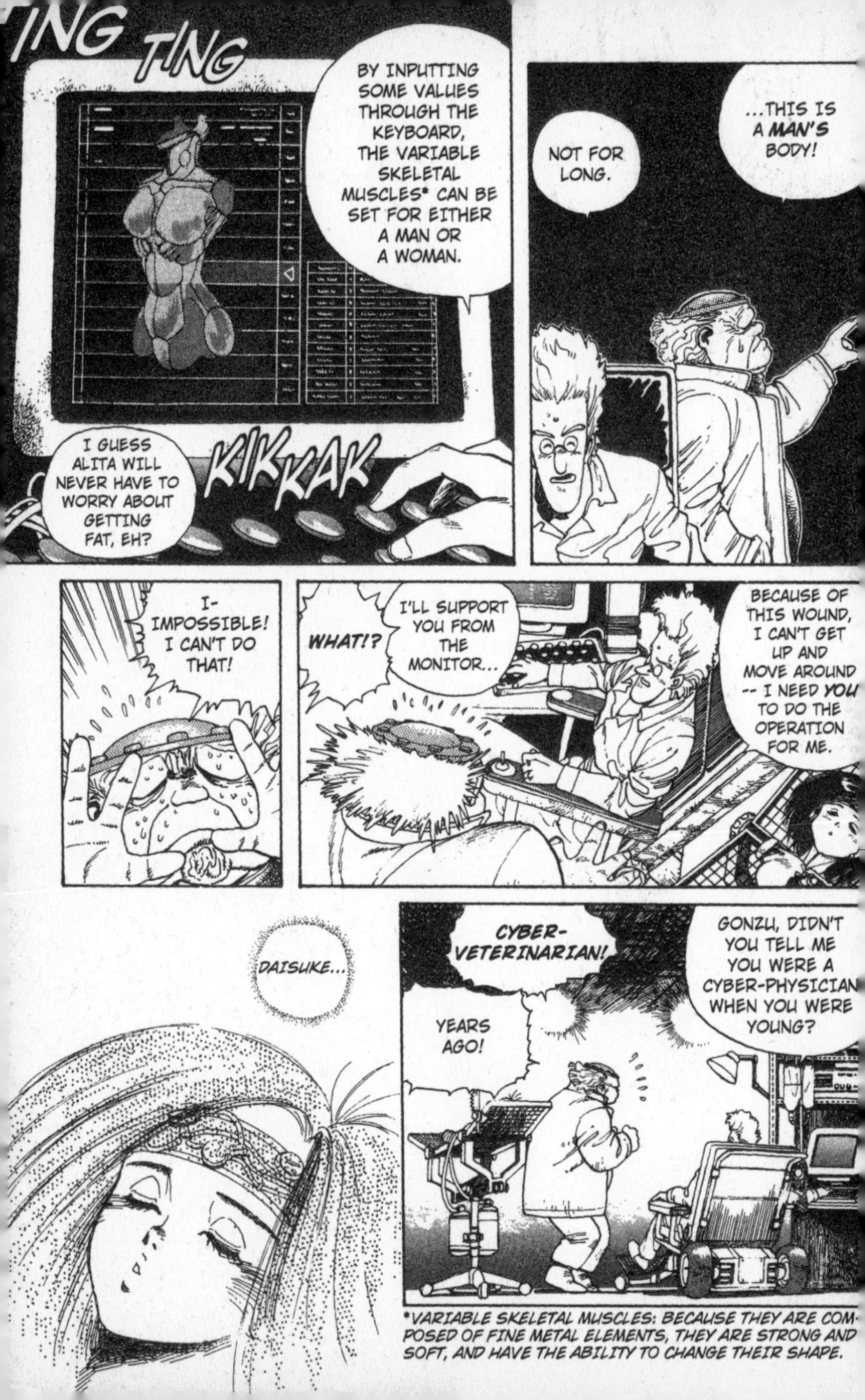

...THIS IS A *MAN'S* BODY!
NOT FOR LONG.
ING TING
BY INPUTTING SOME VALUES THROUGH THE KEYBOARD, THE VARIABLE SKELETAL MUSCLES* CAN BE SET FOR EITHER A MAN OR A WOMAN.
KIK KAK
I GUESS ALITA WILL NEVER HAVE TO WORRY ABOUT GETTING FAT, EH?
BECAUSE OF THIS WOUND, I CAN'T GET UP AND MOVE AROUND -- I NEED *YOU* TO DO THE OPERATION FOR ME.
I'LL SUPPORT YOU FROM THE MONITOR...
WHAT!?
I- IMPOSSIBLE! I CAN'T DO THAT!
GONZU, DIDN'T YOU TELL ME YOU WERE A CYBER-PHYSICIAN WHEN YOU WERE YOUNG?
CYBER-VETERINARIAN!
YEARS AGO!
DAISUKE...

**VARIABLE SKELETAL MUSCLES: BECAUSE THEY ARE COMPOSED OF FINE METAL ELEMENTS, THEY ARE STRONG AND SOFT, AND HAVE THE ABILITY TO CHANGE THEIR SHAPE.*

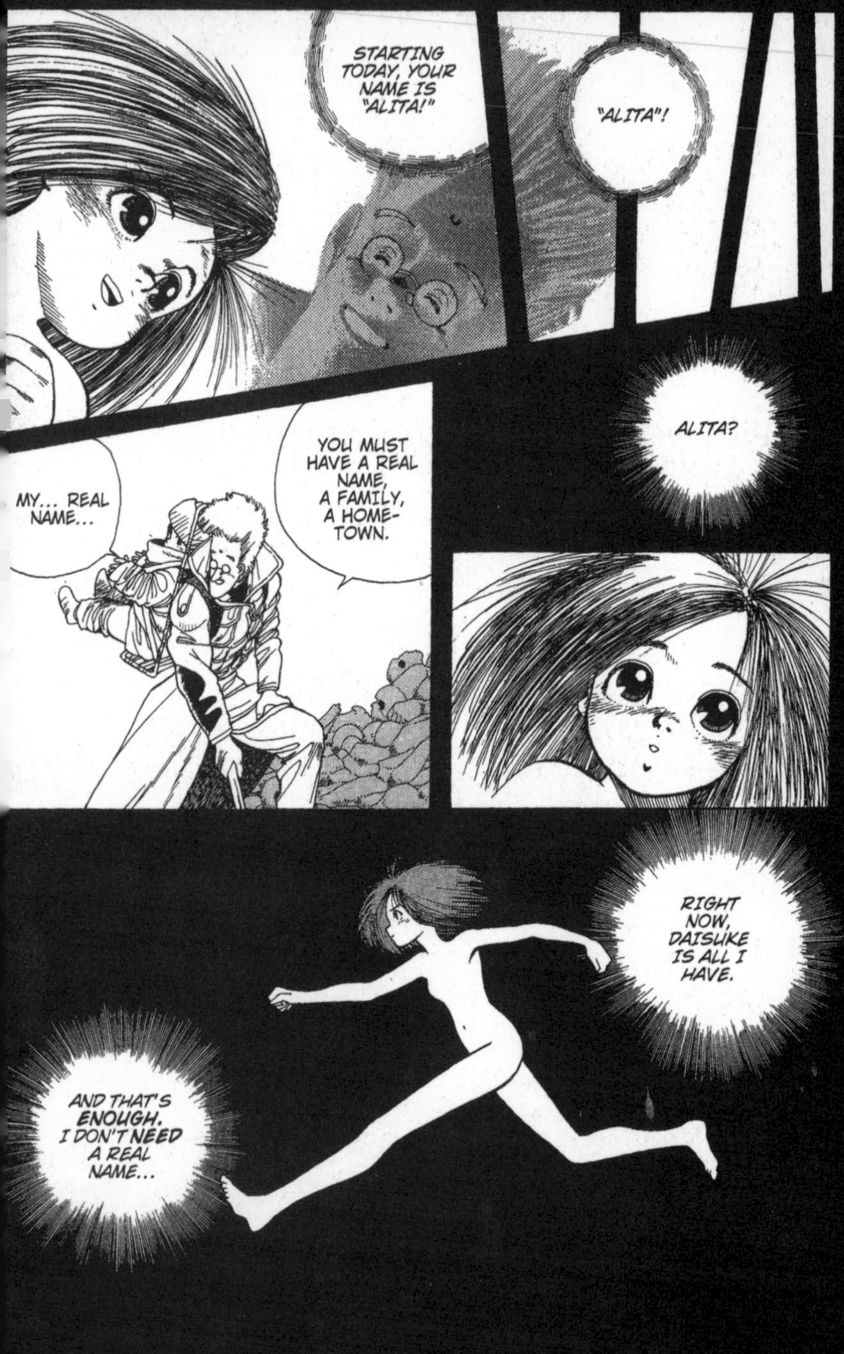
"ALITA"!
STARTING TODAY, YOUR NAME IS "ALITA!"
ALITA?
YOU MUST HAVE A REAL NAME, A FAMILY, A HOME-TOWN.
MY... REAL NAME...
RIGHT NOW, DAISUKE IS ALL I HAVE.
AND THAT'S **ENOUGH.** I DON'T **NEED** A REAL NAME...

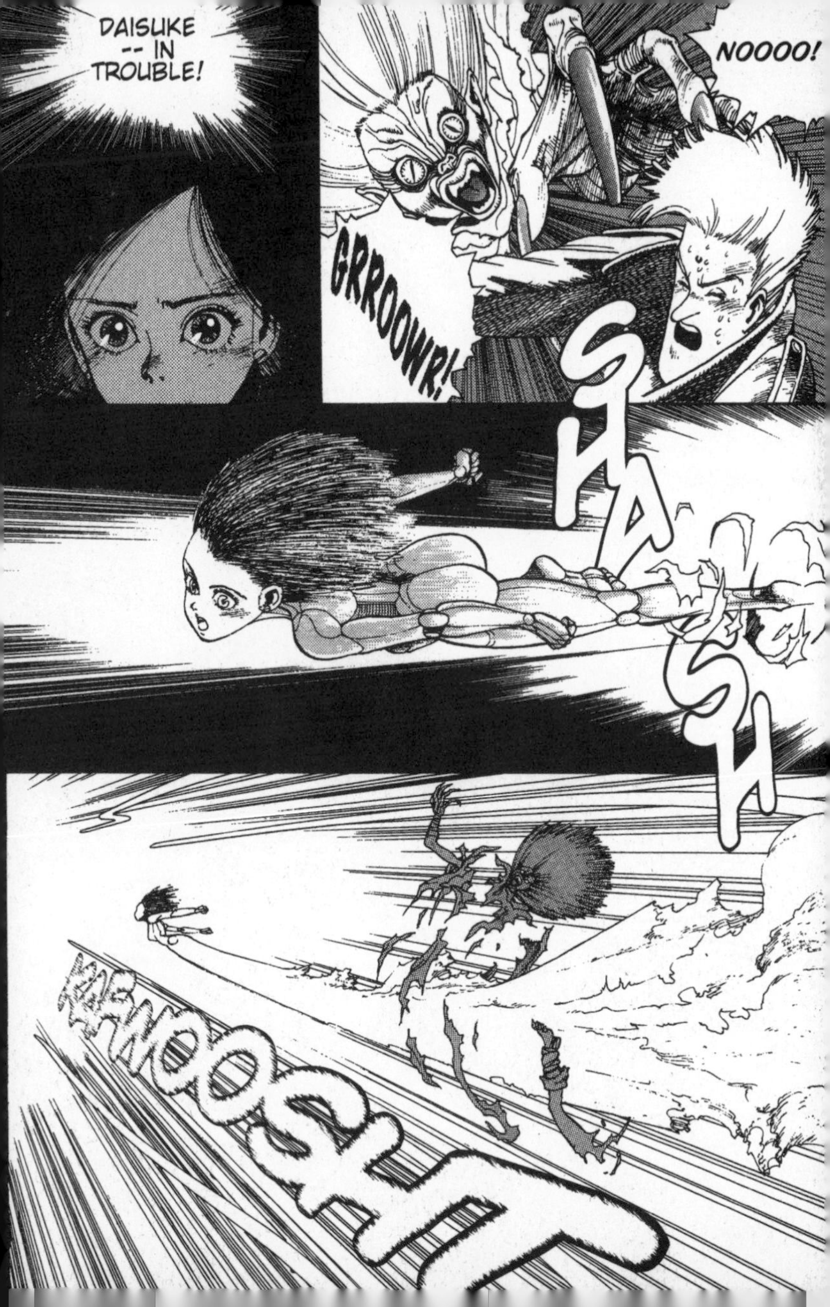
NOOOO!
GRROOWR!
DAISUKE -- IN TROUBLE!
SHASH

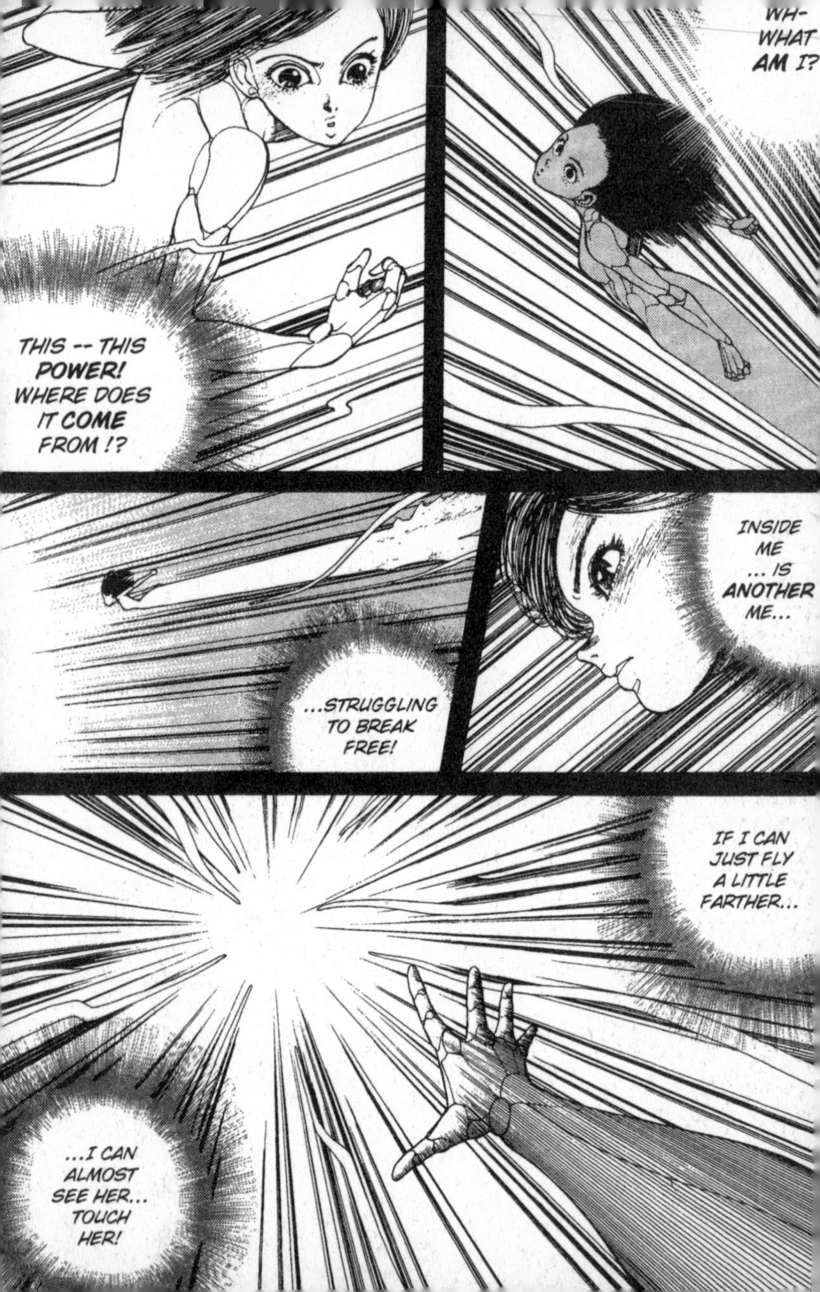
WH- WHAT AM I?
THIS -- THIS POWER! WHERE DOES IT COME FROM !?
INSIDE ME ... IS ANOTHER ME...
...STRUGGLING TO BREAK FREE!
IF I CAN JUST FLY A LITTLE FARTHER...
...I CAN ALMOST SEE HER... TOUCH HER!

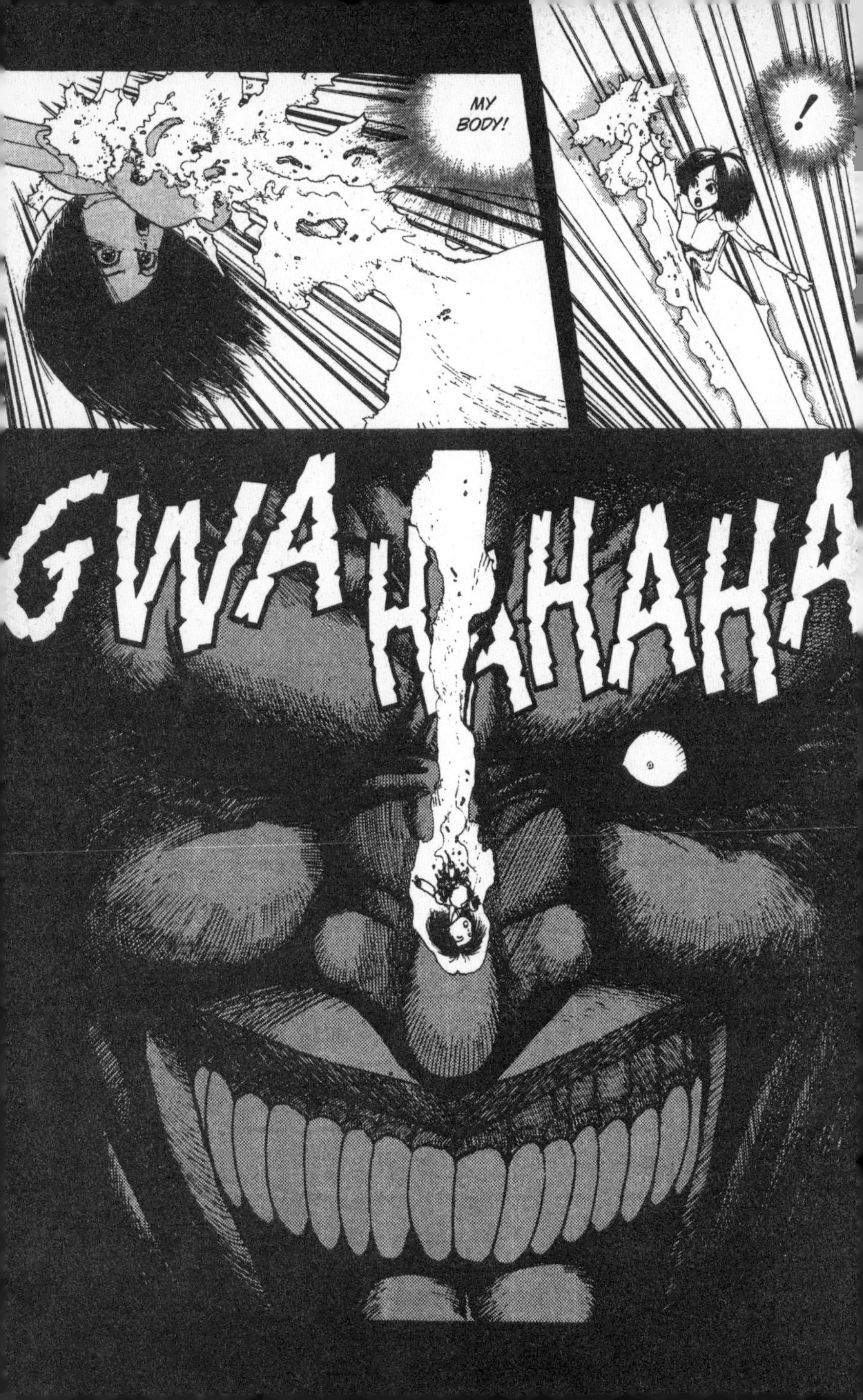
!
MY BODY!
GWAHAHAHA

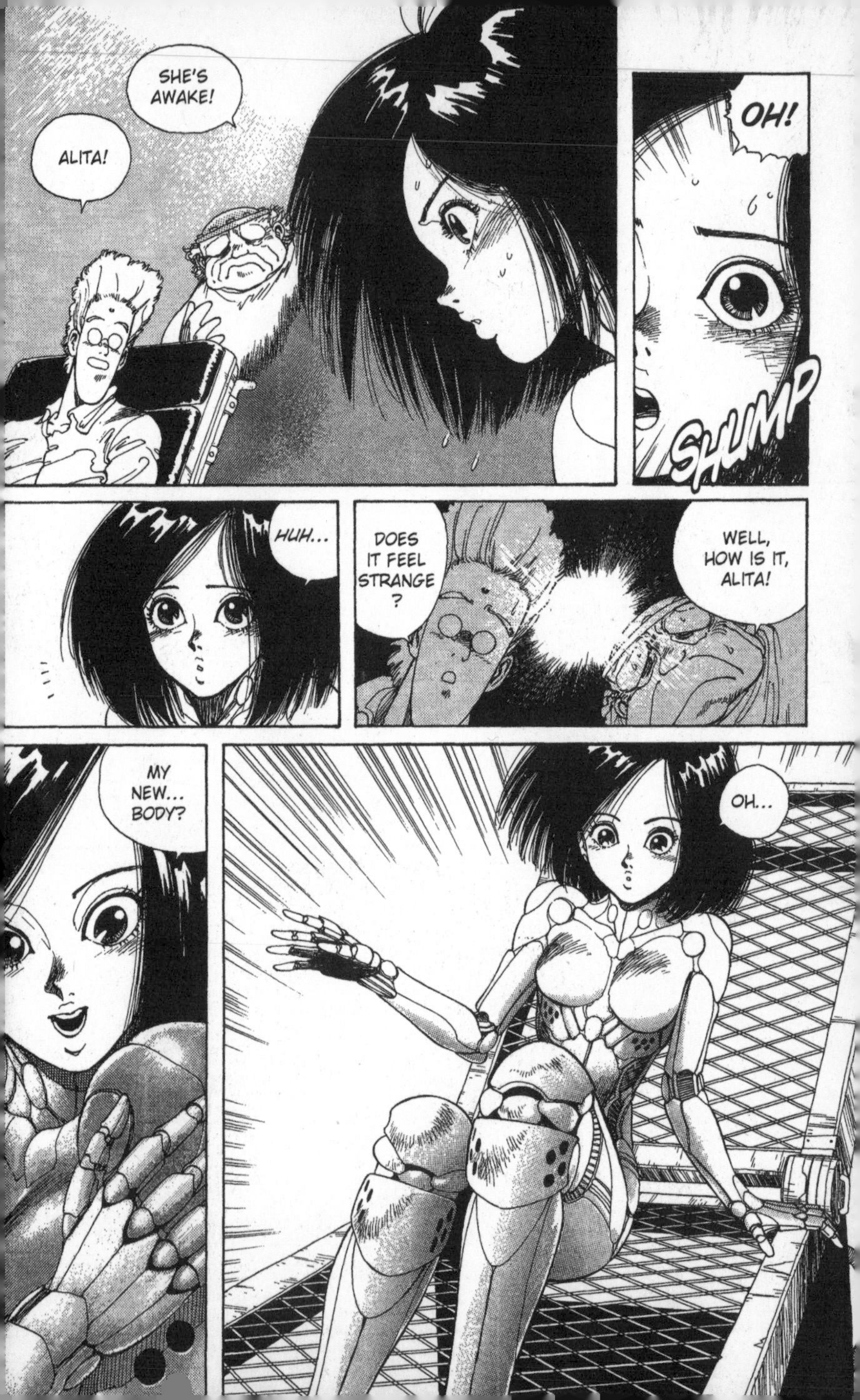
OH!
SHUMP
SHE'S AWAKE!
ALITA!
WELL, HOW IS IT, ALITA!
DOES IT FEEL STRANGE?
HUH...
OH...
MY NEW... BODY?

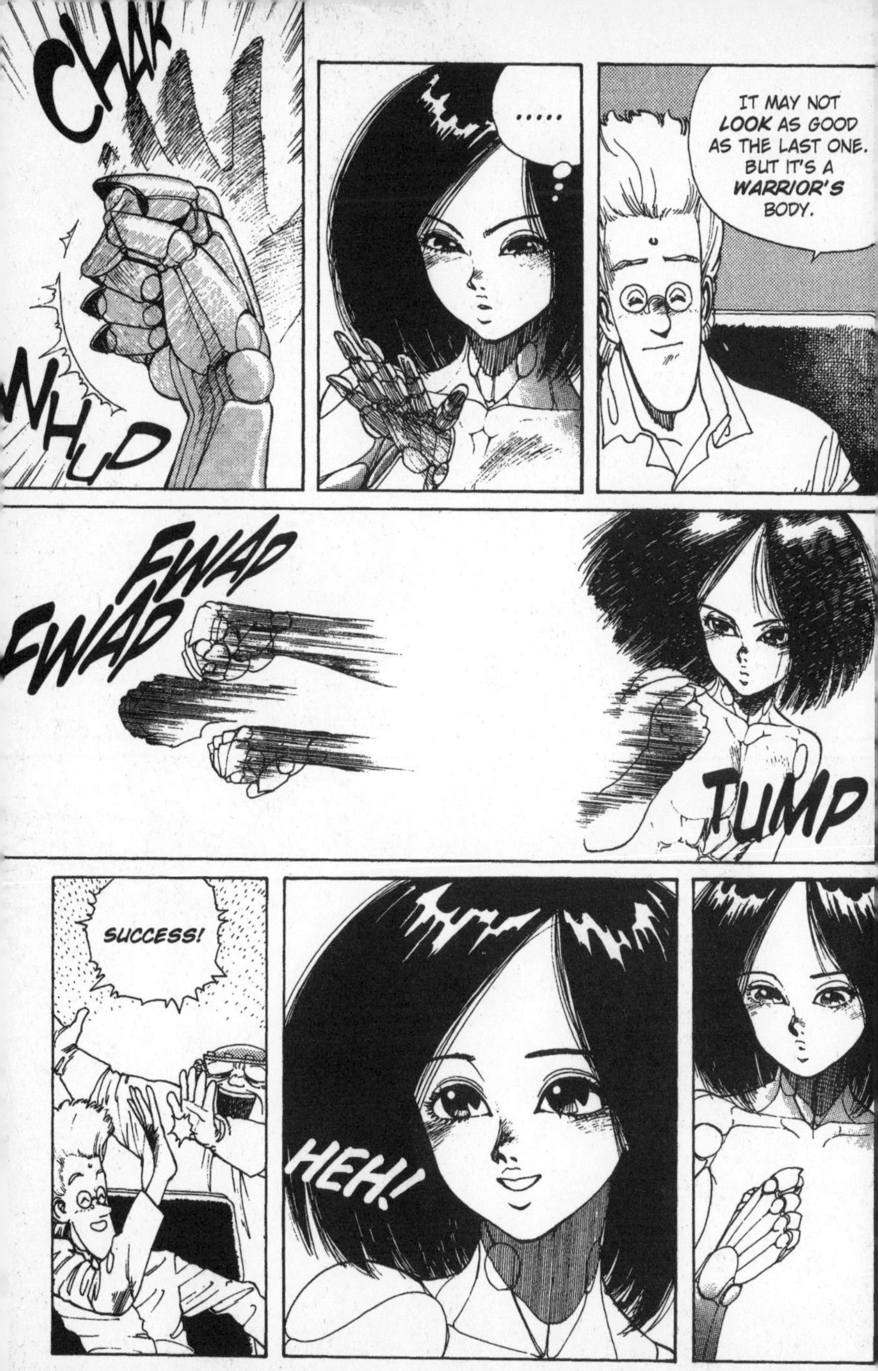
IT MAY NOT LOOK AS GOOD AS THE LAST ONE. BUT IT'S A WARRIOR'S BODY.
.....
CHAK
WHUD
FWAP
FWAP
TUMP
HEH!
SUCCESS!

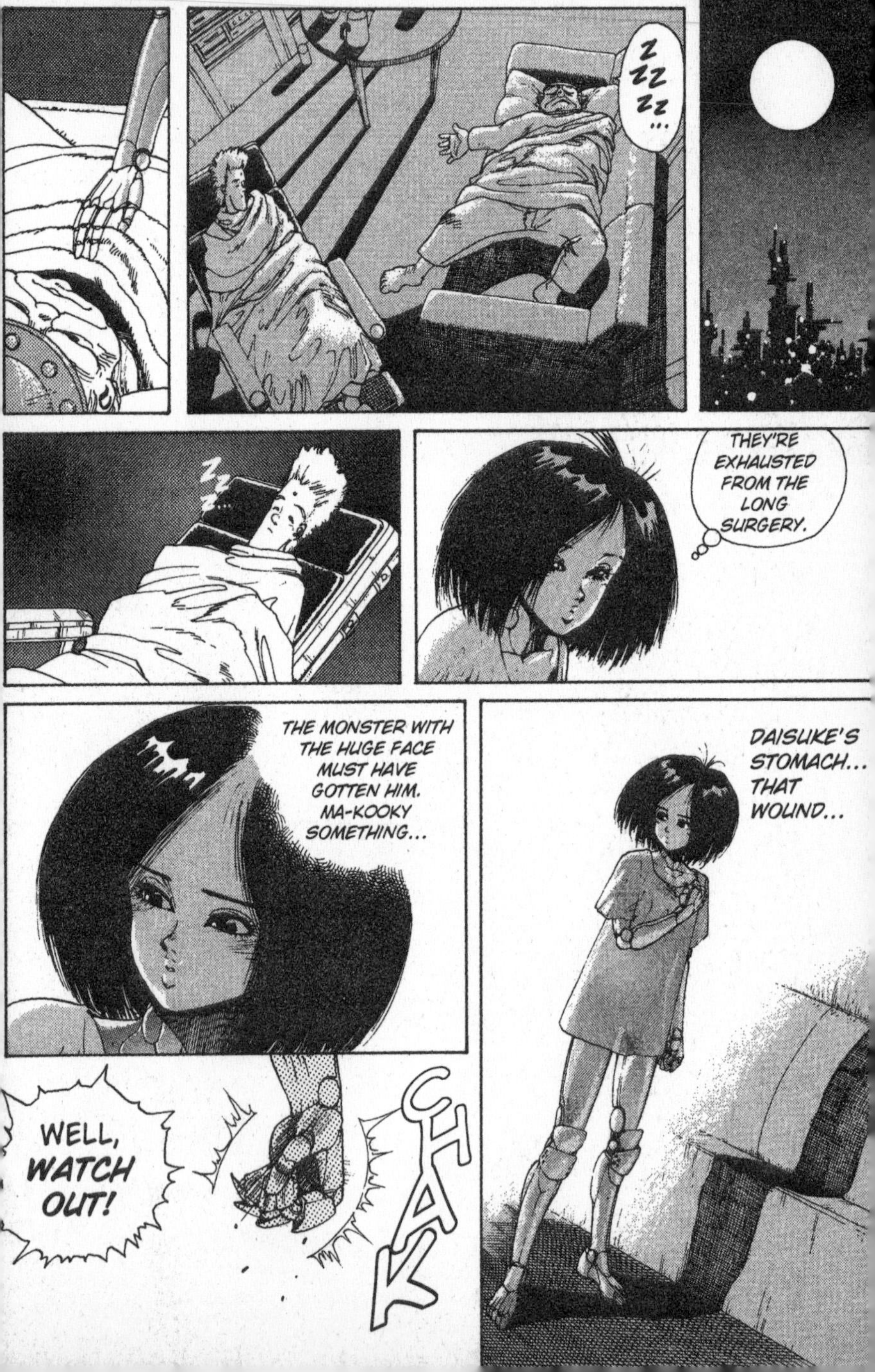
ZZZZZ...
THEY'RE EXHAUSTED FROM THE LONG SURGERY.
ZZ
DAISUKE'S STOMACH... THAT WOUND...
THE MONSTER WITH THE HUGE FACE MUST HAVE GOTTEN HIM. MA-KOOKY SOMETHING...
CHAK
WELL, WATCH OUT!

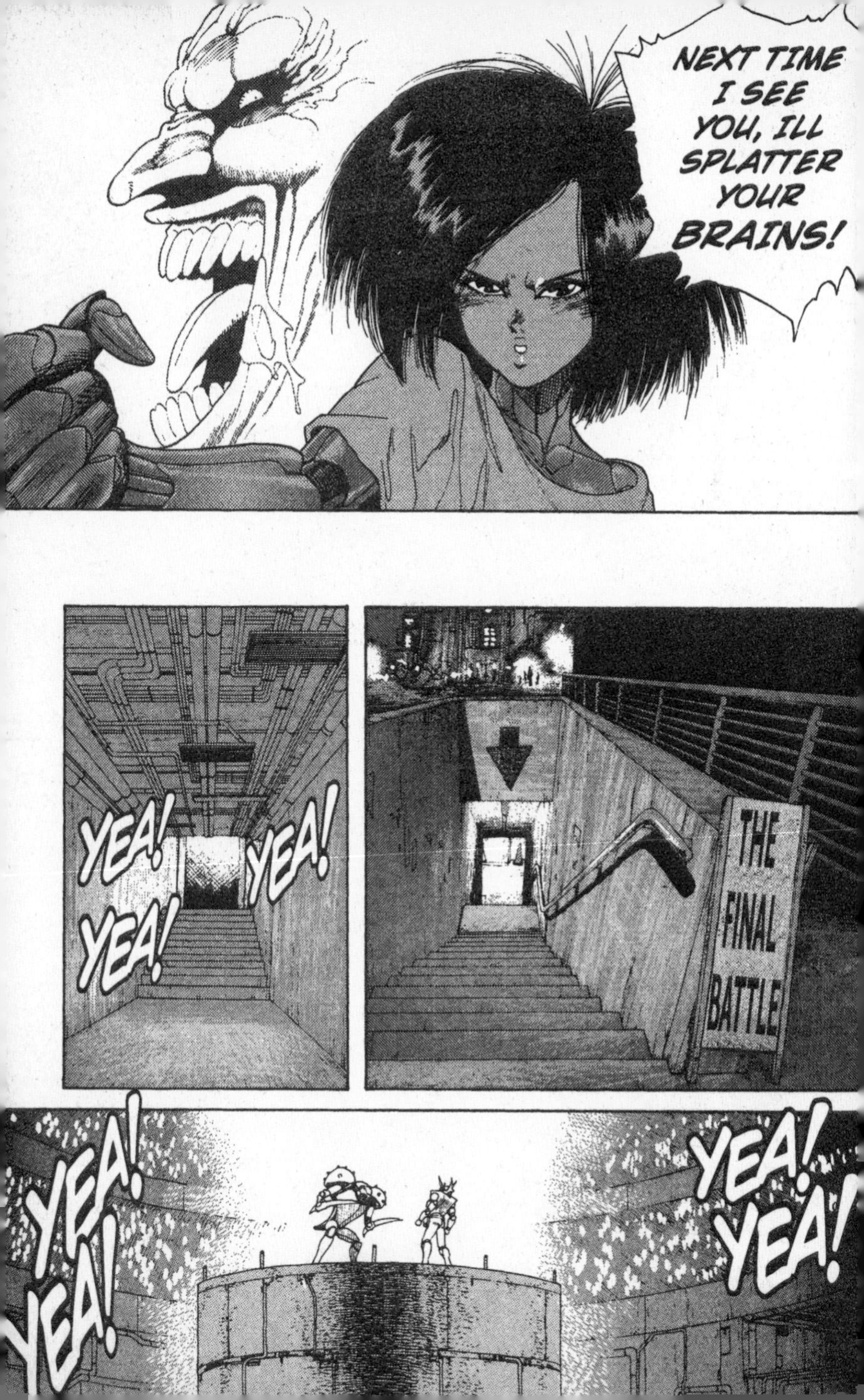
NEXT TIME I SEE YOU, ILL SPLATTER YOUR BRAINS!
THE FINAL BATTLE
YEA! YEA!
YEA!
YEA! YEA!
YEA! YEA!

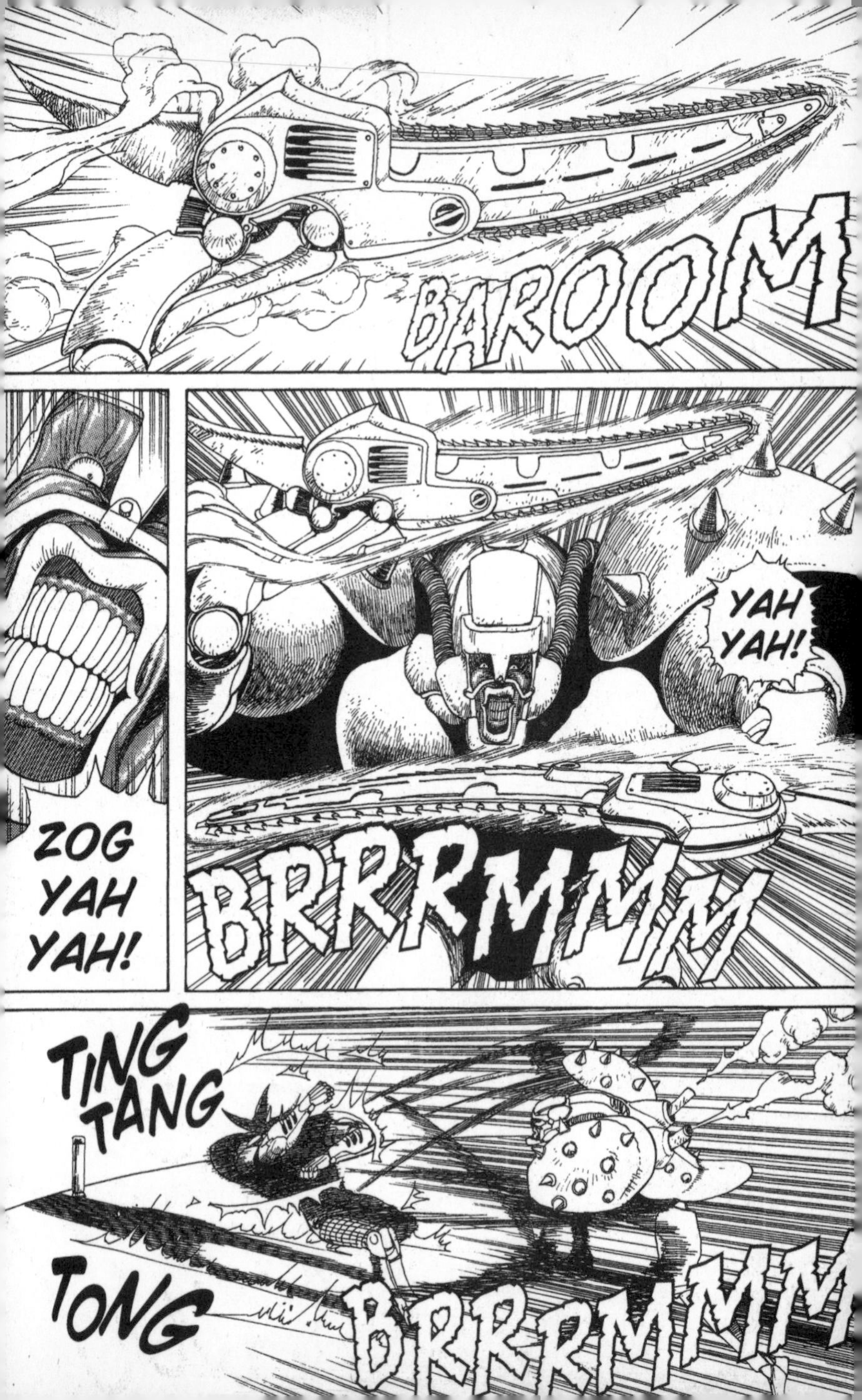
BAROOM
YAH YAH!
BRRRMMM
ZOG YAH YAH!
TING TANG
TONG
BRRRMMM

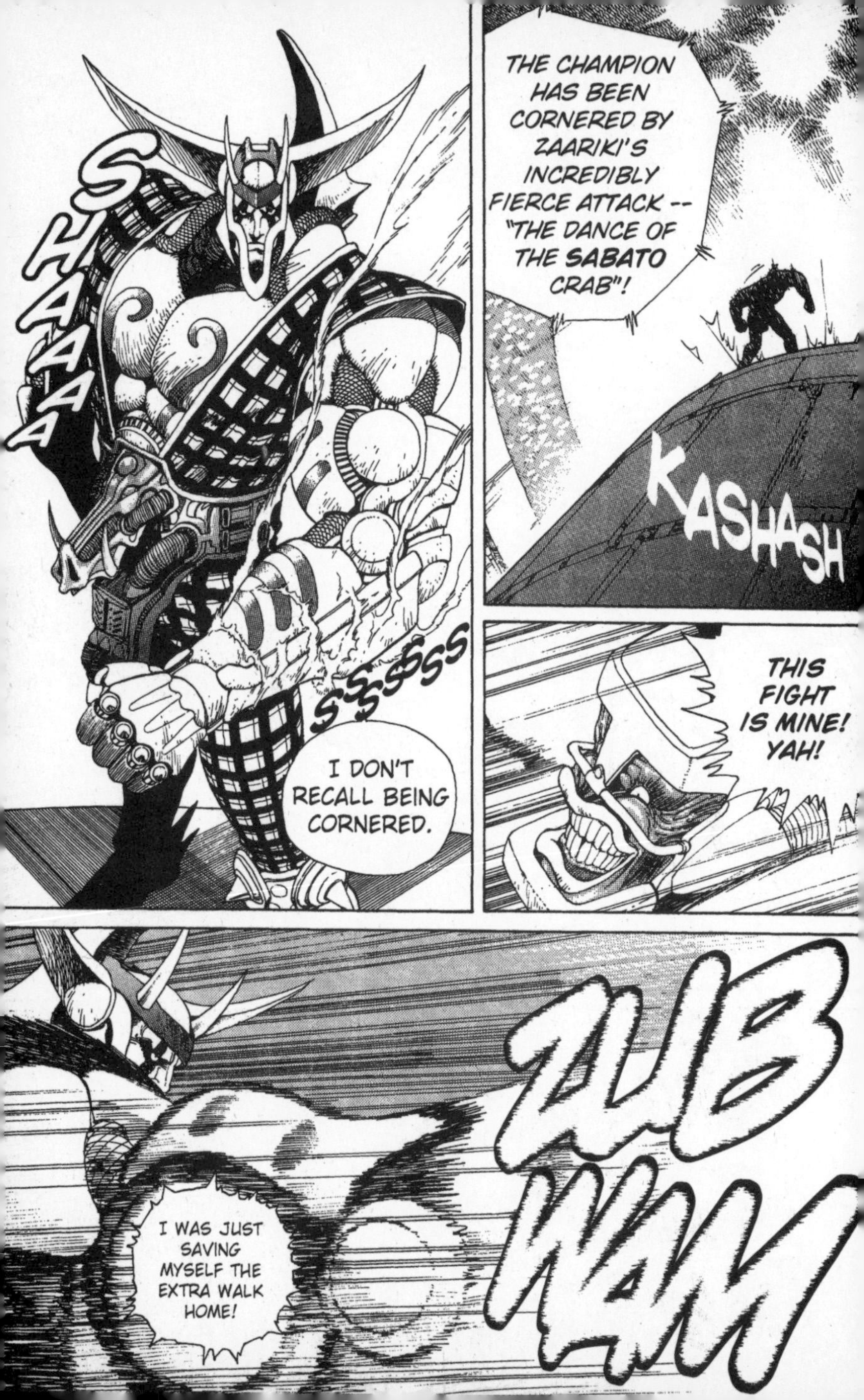
THE CHAMPION HAS BEEN CORNERED BY ZAARIKI'S INCREDIBLY FIERCE ATTACK -- "THE DANCE OF THE SABATO CRAB"!
KASHASH
THIS FIGHT IS MINE! YAH!
SHAHAAAA
SSSSSSS
I DON'T RECALL BEING CORNERED.
ZUB WAM
I WAS JUST SAVING MYSELF THE EXTRA WALK HOME!

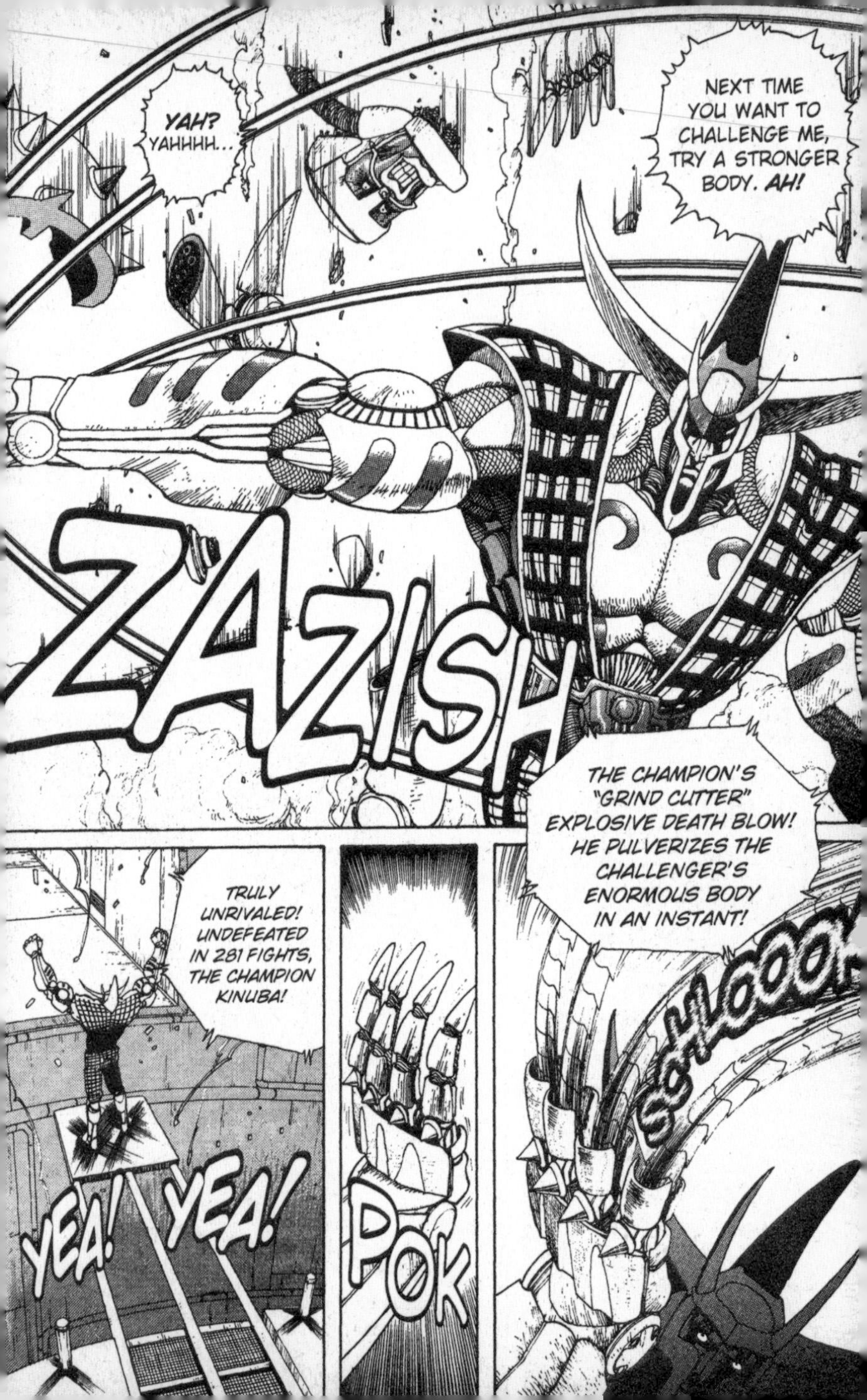

NEXT TIME YOU WANT TO CHALLENGE ME, TRY A STRONGER BODY. AH!
YAH? YAHHHH...
ZAZISH
THE CHAMPION'S "GRIND CUTTER" EXPLOSIVE DEATH BLOW! HE PULVERIZES THE CHALLENGER'S ENORMOUS BODY IN AN INSTANT!
SCHLOOOK
POK
TRULY UNRIVALED! UNDEFEATED IN 281 FIGHTS, THE CHAMPION KINUBA!
YEA! YEA!

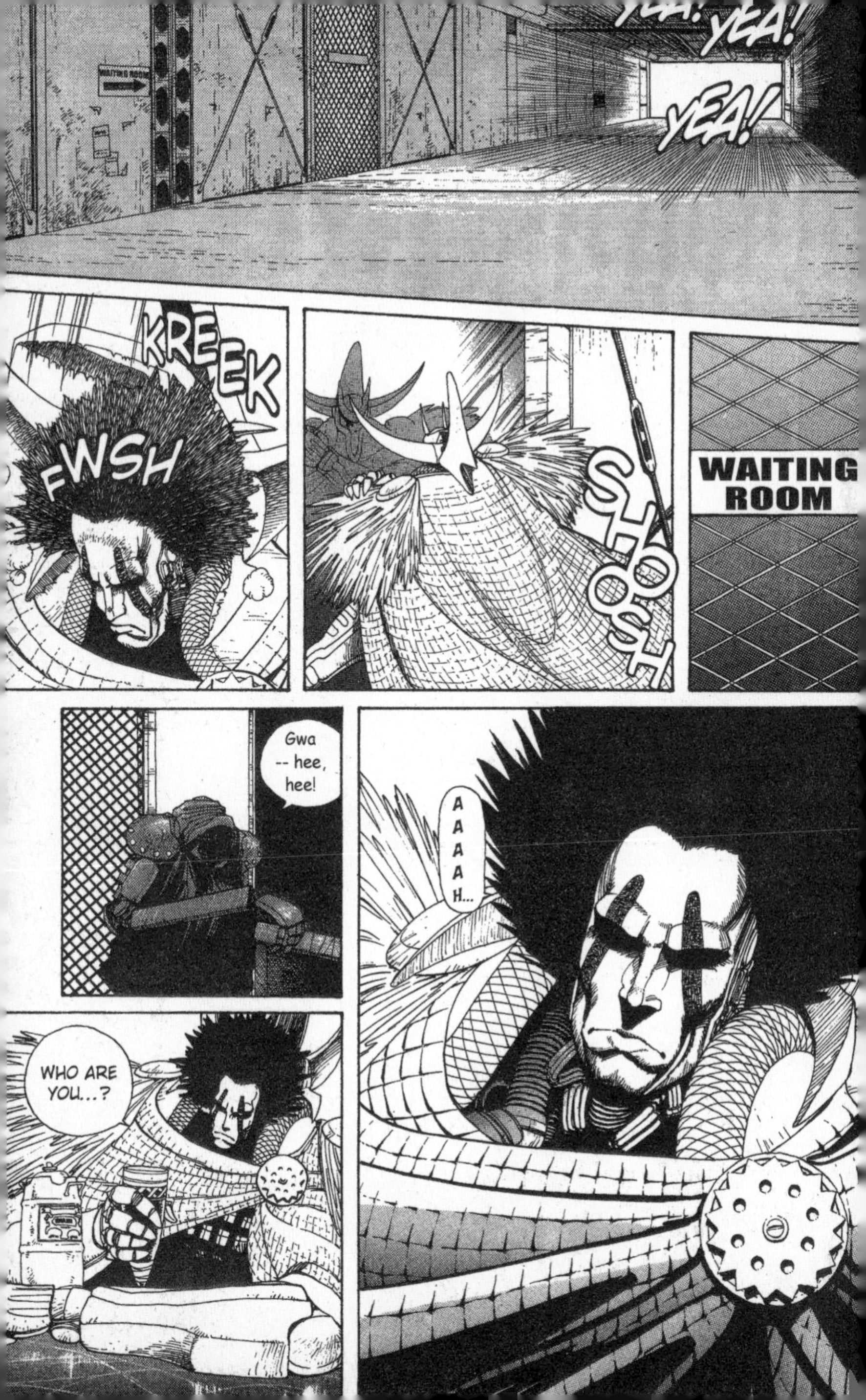
YEA!
YEA!
WAITING ROOM
SHOOSH
KREEK
FWSH
AAAAH...
Gwa -- hee, hee!
WHO ARE YOU...?

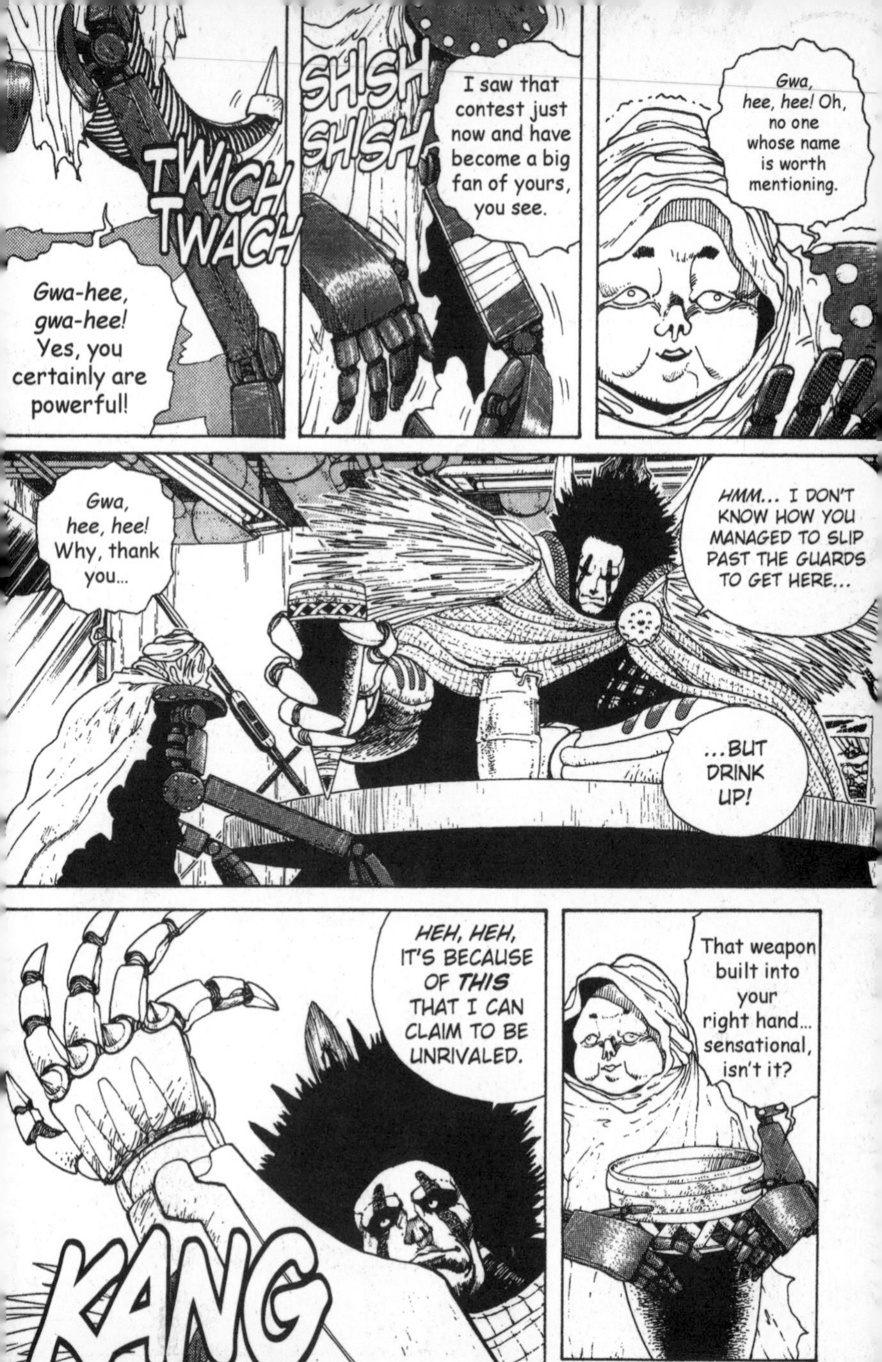
Gwa, hee, hee! Oh, no one whose name is worth mentioning.
SHISH SHISH
I saw that contest just now and have become a big fan of yours, you see.
TWICH TWACH
Gwa-hee, gwa-hee! Yes, you certainly are powerful!
HMM... I DON'T KNOW HOW YOU MANAGED TO SLIP PAST THE GUARDS TO GET HERE...
...BUT DRINK UP!
Gwa, hee, hee! Why, thank you...
That weapon built into your right hand... sensational, isn't it?
HEH, HEH, IT'S BECAUSE OF THIS THAT I CAN CLAIM TO BE UNRIVALED.
KANG

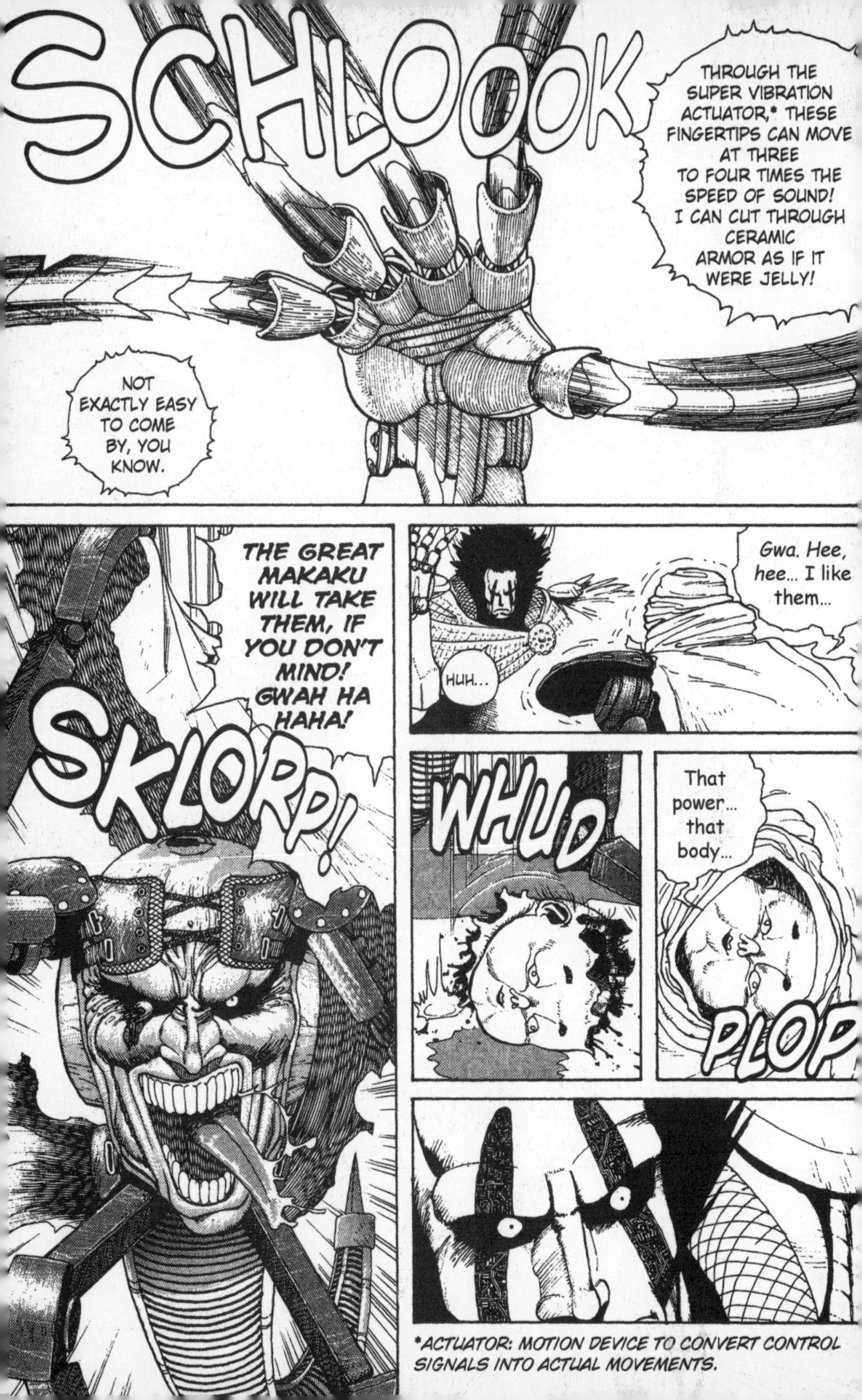
SCHLOOOK
THROUGH THE SUPER VIBRATION ACTUATOR,* THESE FINGERTIPS CAN MOVE AT THREE TO FOUR TIMES THE SPEED OF SOUND! I CAN CUT THROUGH CERAMIC ARMOR AS IF IT WERE JELLY!
NOT EXACTLY EASY TO COME BY, YOU KNOW.
Gwa. Hee, hee... I like them...
HUH...
That power... that body...
PLOP
WHUD
THE GREAT MAKAKU WILL TAKE THEM, IF YOU DON'T MIND! GWAH HA HAHA!
SKLORP!

*ACTUATOR: MOTION DEVICE TO CONVERT CONTROL SIGNALS INTO ACTUAL MOVEMENTS.

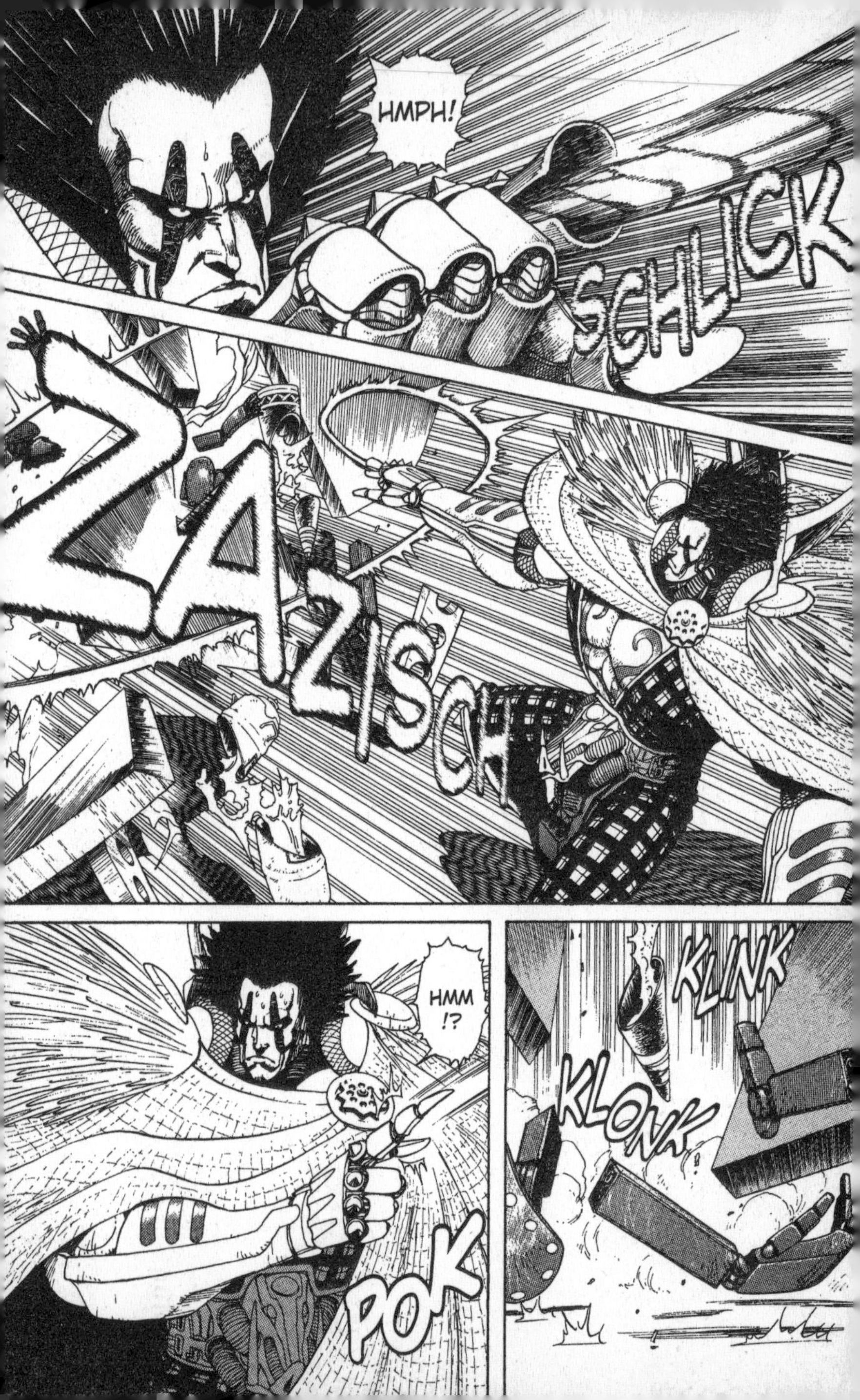
HMPH!
SCHLICK
ZAZISCH
KLINK
KLONK
HMM !?
POK

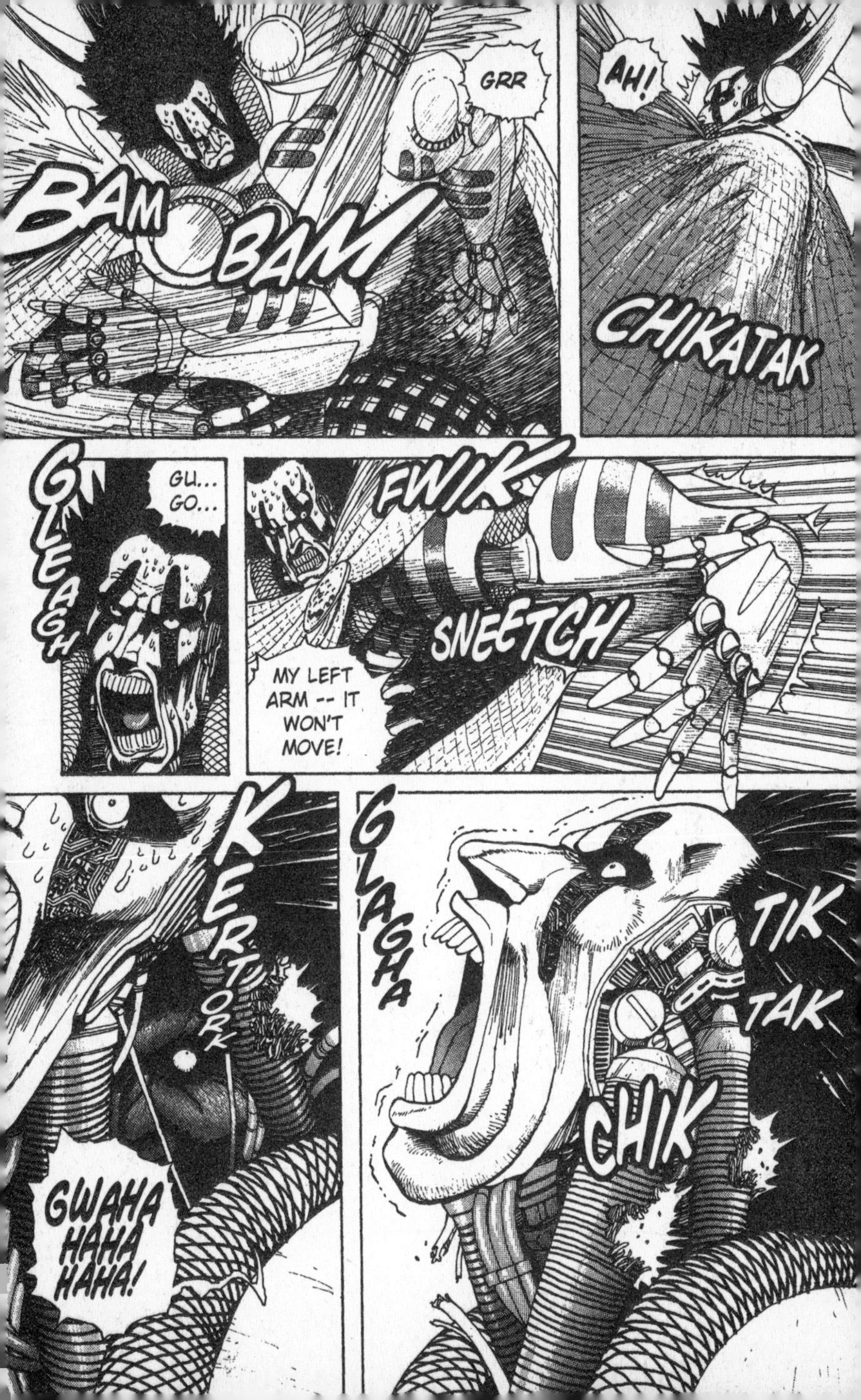
AH!
CHIKATAK
GRR
BAM
BAM
FWIK
SNEETCH
MY LEFT ARM -- IT WON'T MOVE!
GU... GO...
GLEAGH
TIK TAK
GLAGHA
CHIK
KERTORK
GWAHA HAHA HAHA!

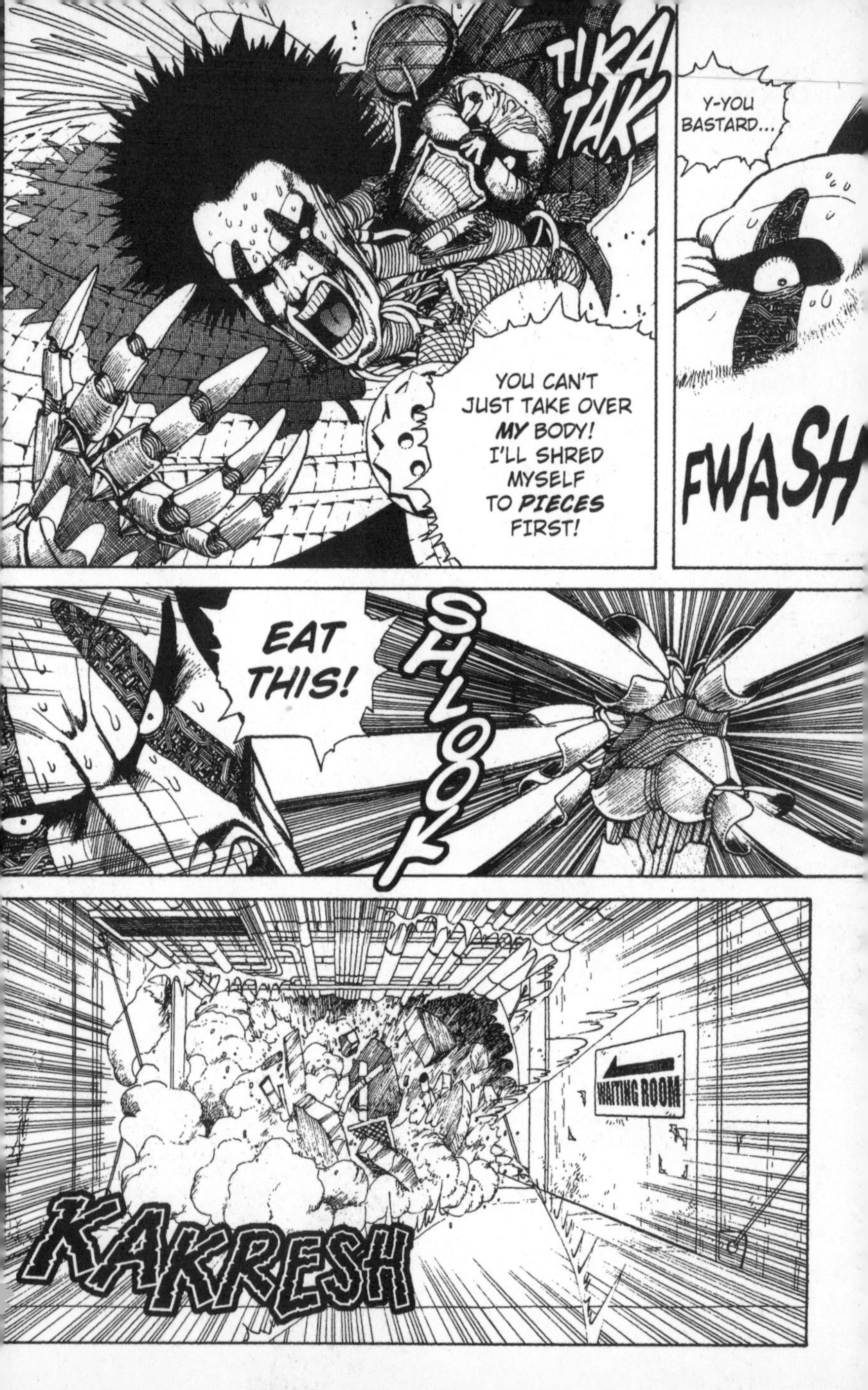
Y-YOU BASTARD...
FWASH
TIKA TAK
YOU CAN'T JUST TAKE OVER *MY* BODY! I'LL SHRED MYSELF TO *PIECES* FIRST!
SHLOOOK
EAT THIS!
WAITING ROOM
KAKRESH

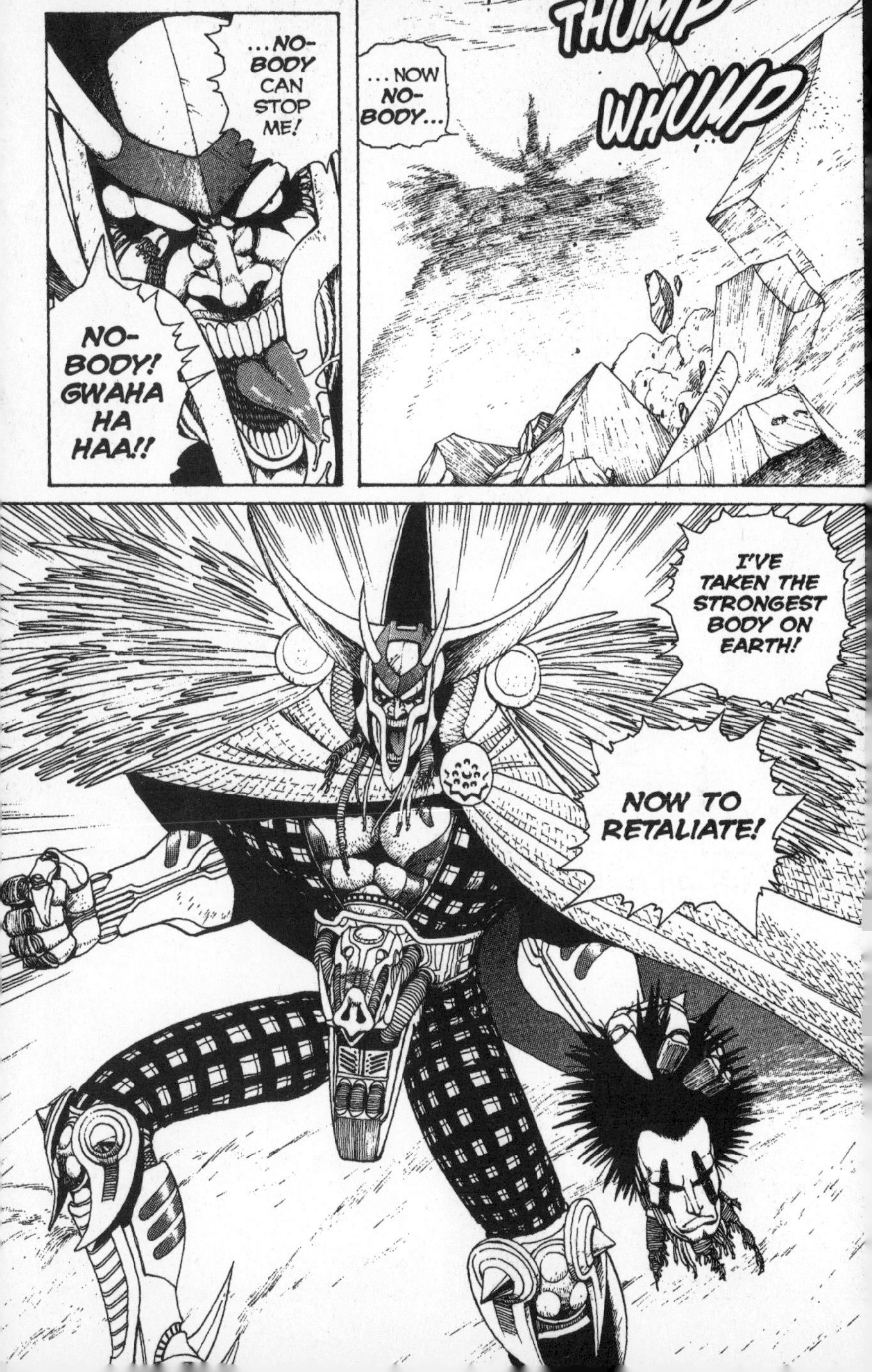
THUMP
WHUMP
...NOW NO-BODY...
...NO-BODY CAN STOP ME!
NO-BODY! GWAHA HA HAA!!
I'VE TAKEN THE STRONGEST BODY ON EARTH!
NOW TO RETALIATE!

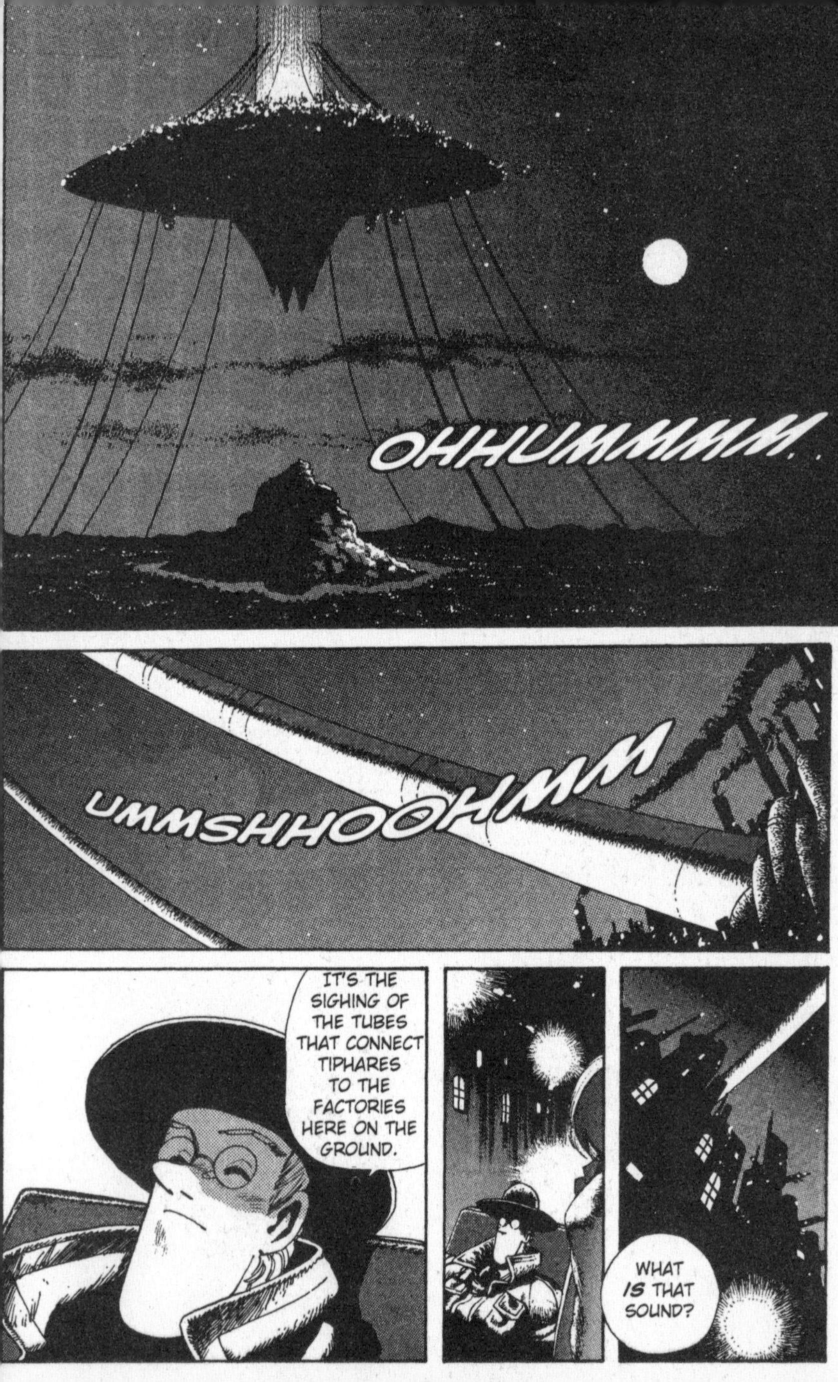
OHHUMMMMM...
UMMSHHOOHMMM
WHAT *IS* THAT SOUND?
IT'S THE SIGHING OF THE TUBES THAT CONNECT TIPHARES TO THE FACTORIES HERE ON THE GROUND.

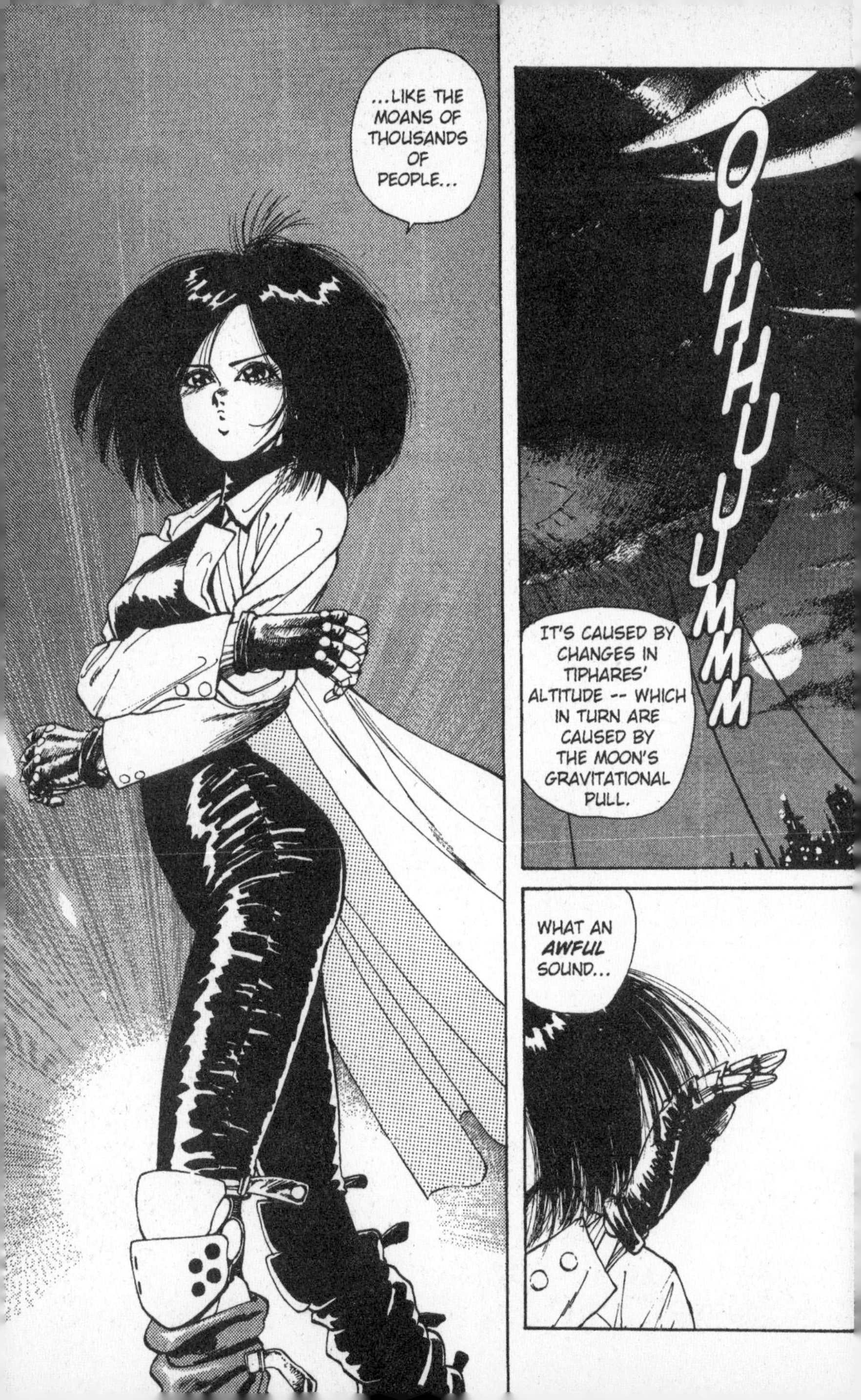
OHHHUUUMMM
IT'S CAUSED BY CHANGES IN TIPHARES' ALTITUDE -- WHICH IN TURN ARE CAUSED BY THE MOON'S GRAVITATIONAL PULL.
WHAT AN **AWFUL** SOUND...
...LIKE THE MOANS OF THOUSANDS OF PEOPLE...

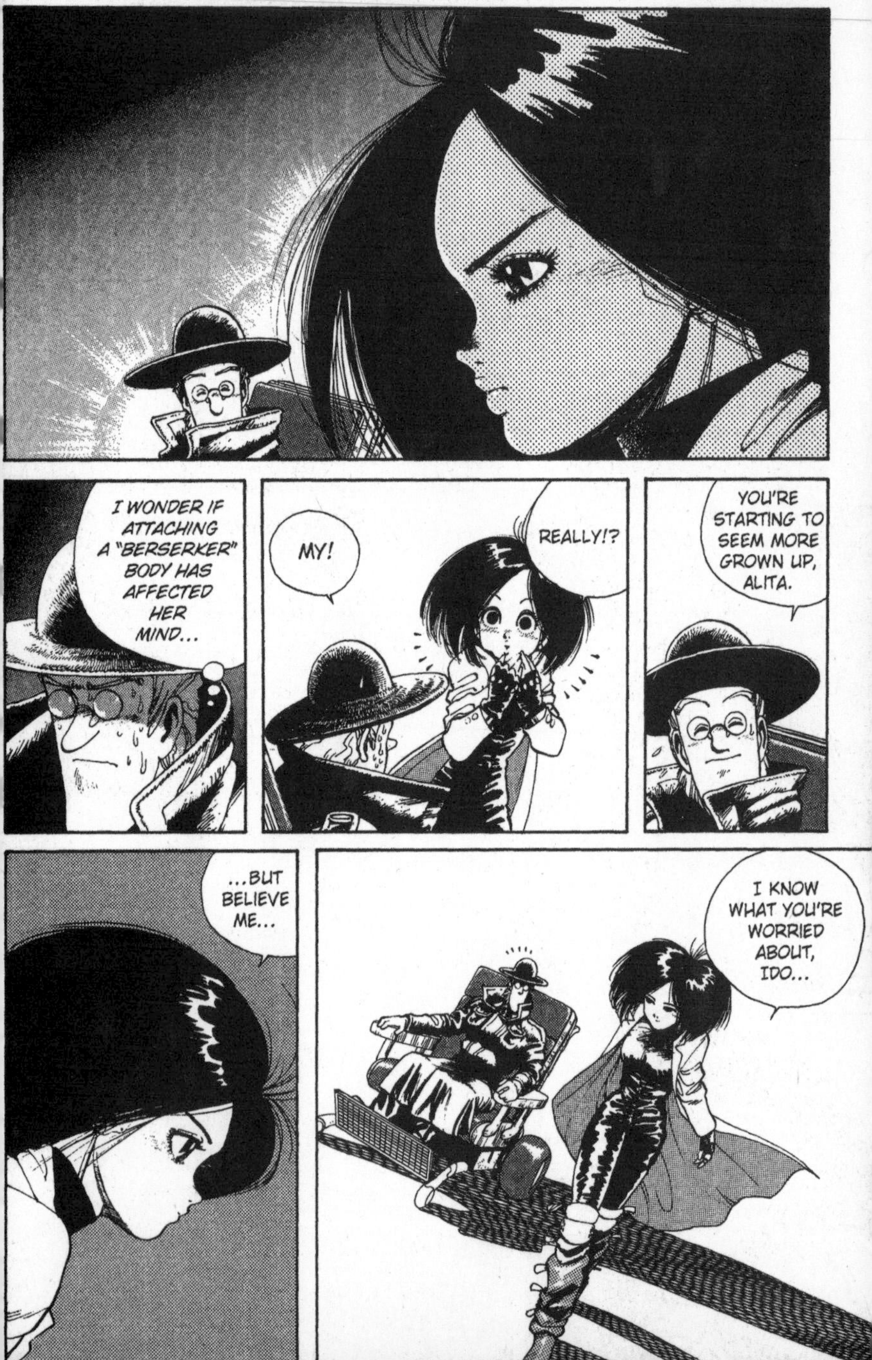
YOU'RE STARTING TO SEEM MORE GROWN UP, ALITA.
REALLY!?
MY!
I WONDER IF ATTACHING A "BERSERKER" BODY HAS AFFECTED HER MIND...
I KNOW WHAT YOU'RE WORRIED ABOUT, IDO...
...BUT BELIEVE ME...

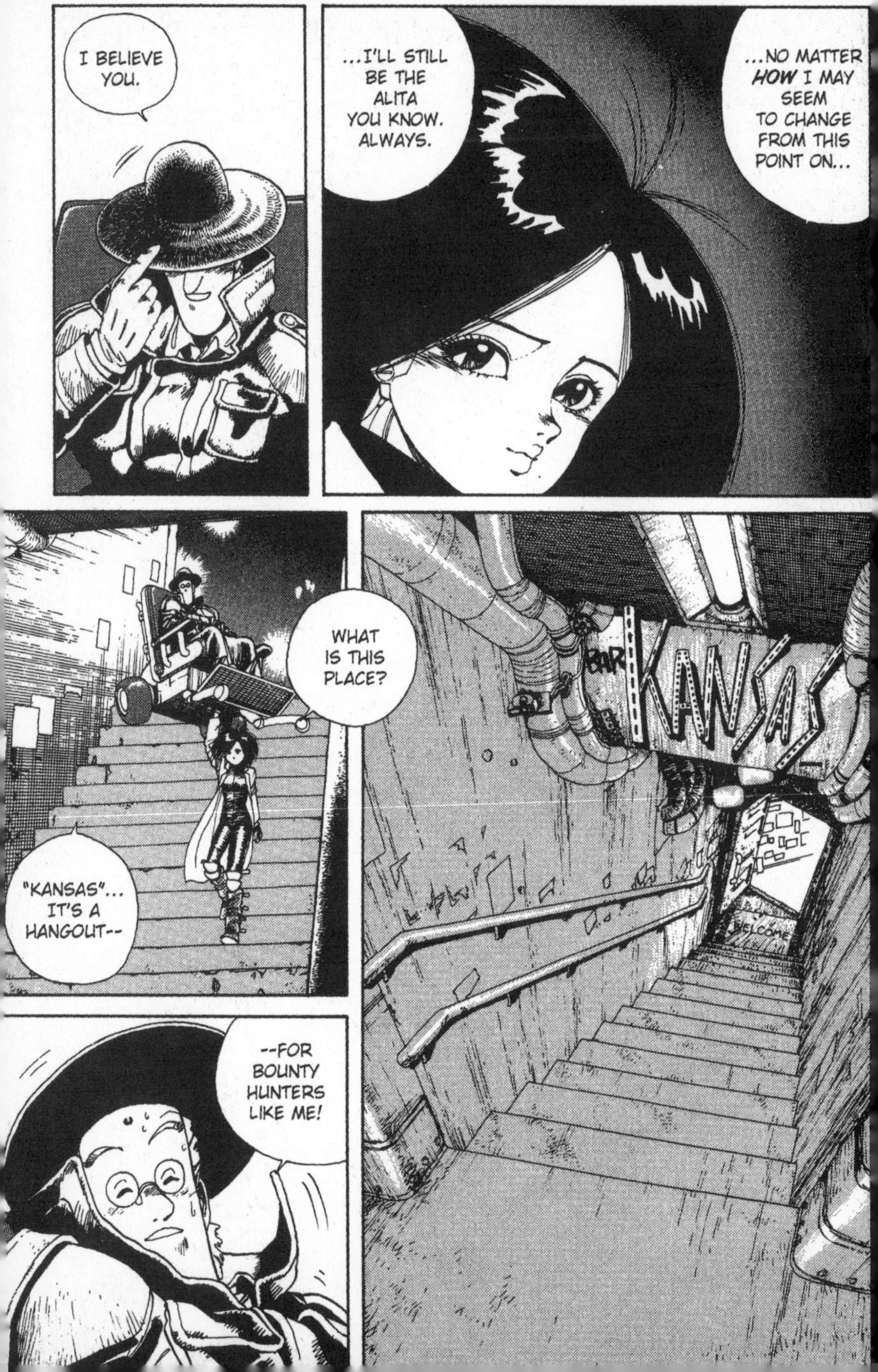
...NO MATTER *HOW* I MAY SEEM TO CHANGE FROM THIS POINT ON...
...I'LL STILL BE THE ALITA YOU KNOW. ALWAYS.
I BELIEVE YOU.
BAR
KANSAS
WELCOME
WHAT IS THIS PLACE?
"KANSAS"... IT'S A HANGOUT--
--FOR BOUNTY HUNTERS LIKE ME!

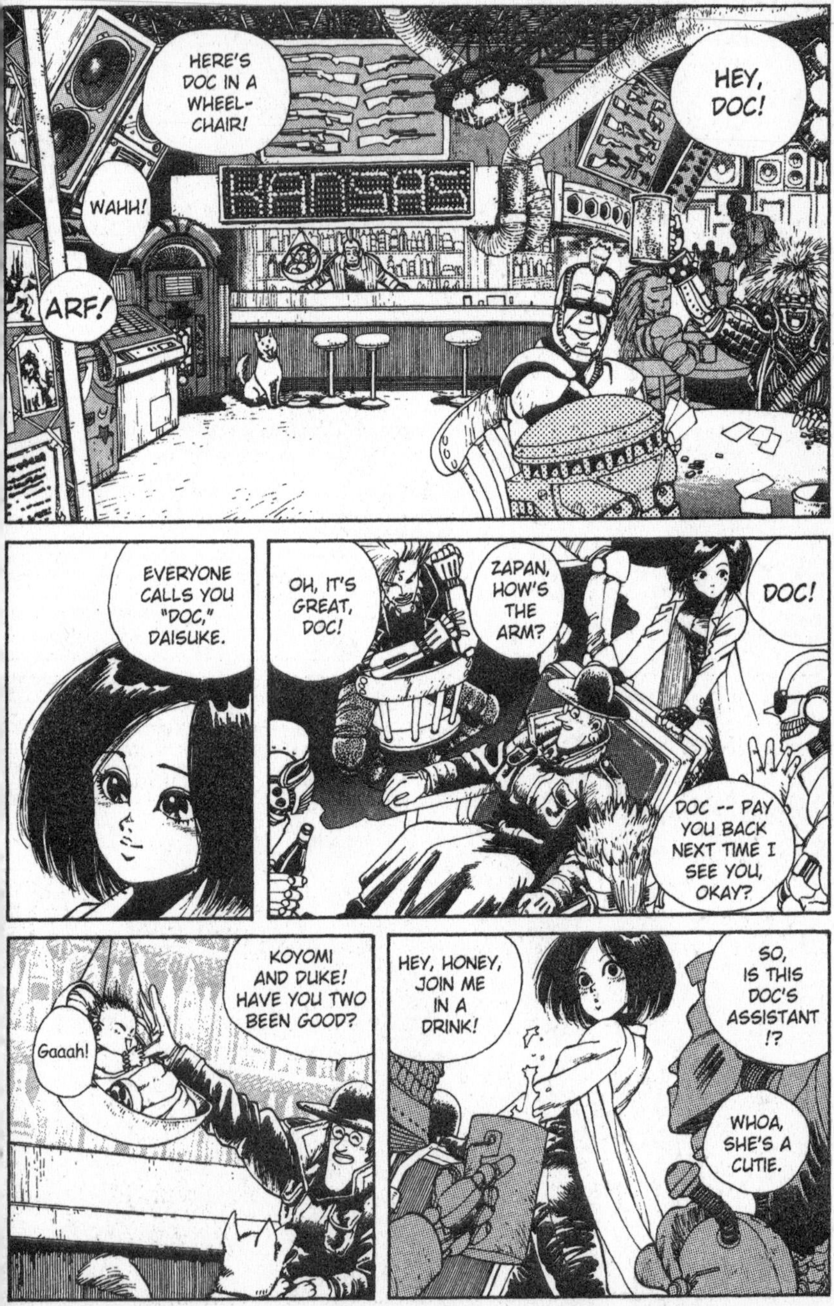
HEY, DOC!
HERE'S DOC IN A WHEEL-CHAIR!
WAHH!
ARF!
DOC!
ZAPAN, HOW'S THE ARM?
OH, IT'S GREAT, DOC!
DOC -- PAY YOU BACK NEXT TIME I SEE YOU, OKAY?
EVERYONE CALLS YOU "DOC," DAISUKE.
SO, IS THIS DOC'S ASSISTANT !?
HEY, HONEY, JOIN ME IN A DRINK!
WHOA, SHE'S A CUTIE.
KOYOMI AND DUKE! HAVE YOU TWO BEEN GOOD?
Gaaah!

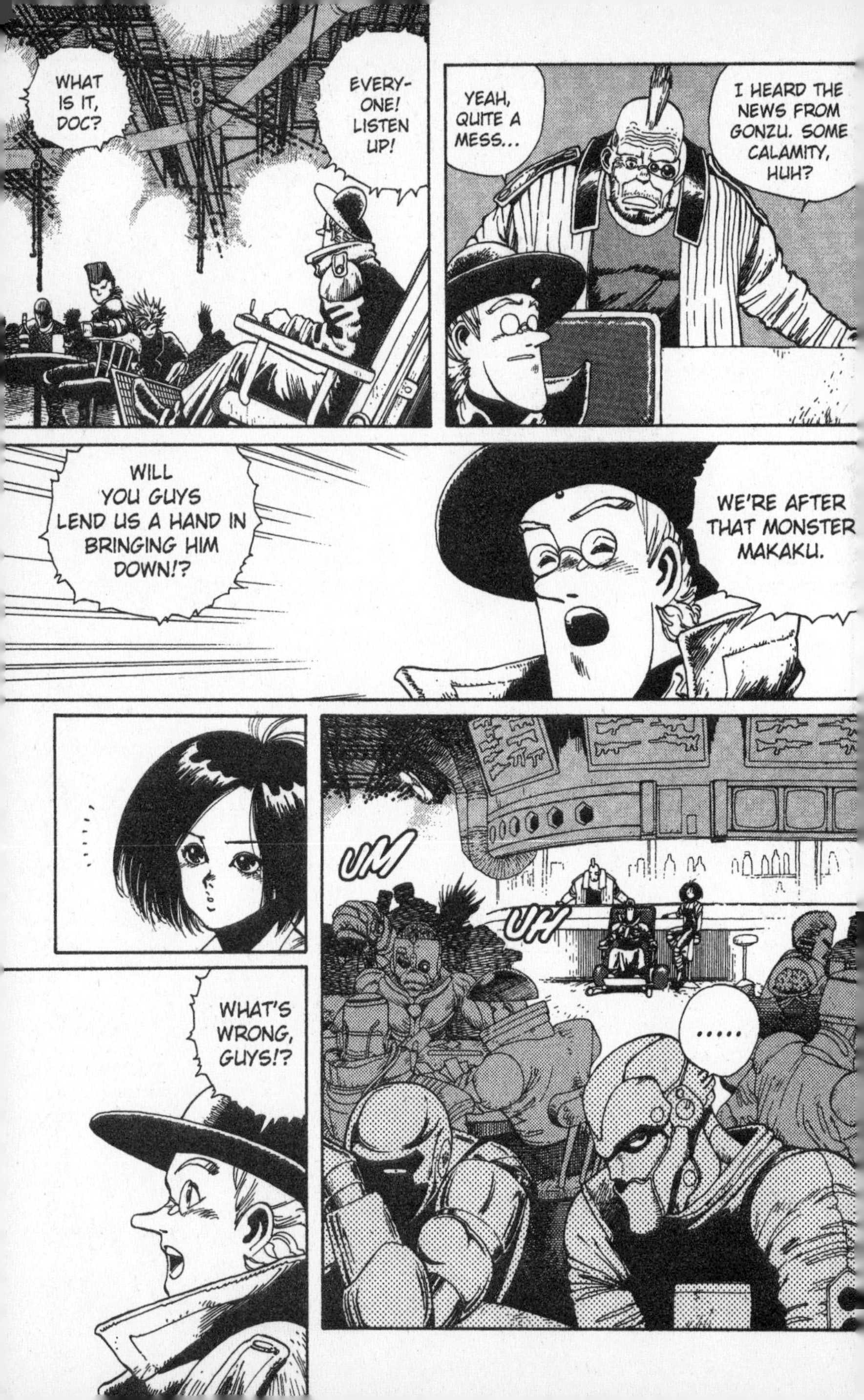
I HEARD THE NEWS FROM GONZU. SOME CALAMITY, HUH?
YEAH, QUITE A MESS...
EVERY-ONE! LISTEN UP!
WHAT IS IT, DOC?
WE'RE AFTER THAT MONSTER MAKAKU.
WILL YOU GUYS LEND US A HAND IN BRINGING HIM DOWN!?
UM
UH
.....
WHAT'S WRONG, GUYS!?

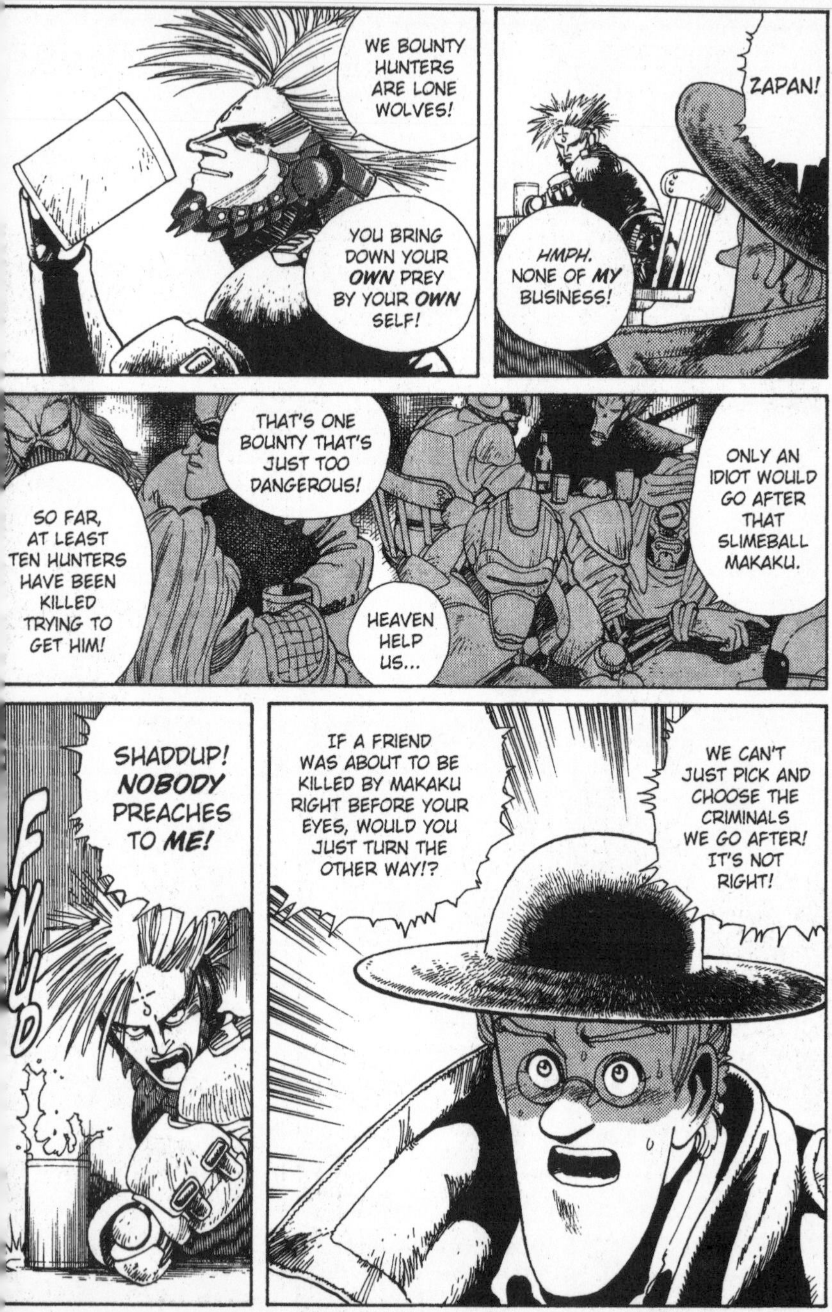
ZAPAN!
HMPH. NONE OF *MY* BUSINESS!
WE BOUNTY HUNTERS ARE LONE WOLVES!
YOU BRING DOWN YOUR *OWN* PREY BY YOUR *OWN* SELF!
ONLY AN IDIOT WOULD GO AFTER THAT SLIMEBALL MAKAKU.
THAT'S ONE BOUNTY THAT'S JUST TOO DANGEROUS!
HEAVEN HELP US...
SO FAR, AT LEAST TEN HUNTERS HAVE BEEN KILLED TRYING TO GET HIM!
WE CAN'T JUST PICK AND CHOOSE THE CRIMINALS WE GO AFTER! IT'S NOT RIGHT!
IF A FRIEND WAS ABOUT TO BE KILLED BY MAKAKU RIGHT BEFORE YOUR EYES, WOULD YOU JUST TURN THE OTHER WAY!?
SHADDUP! ***NOBODY*** PREACHES TO ***ME!***
FNUD

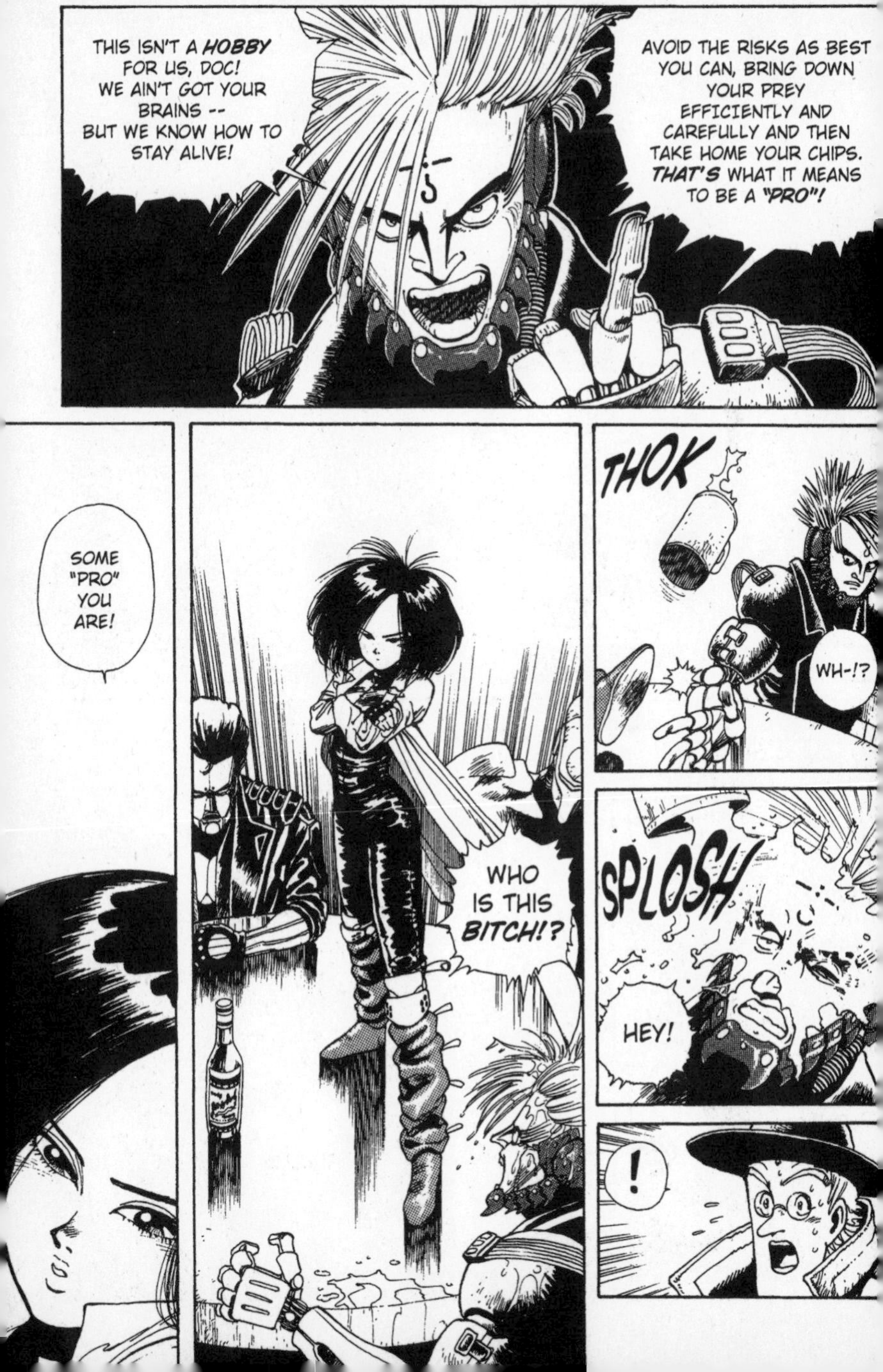
AVOID THE RISKS AS BEST YOU CAN, BRING DOWN YOUR PREY EFFICIENTLY AND CAREFULLY AND THEN TAKE HOME YOUR CHIPS. THAT'S WHAT IT MEANS TO BE A "PRO"!
THIS ISN'T A HOBBY FOR US, DOC! WE AIN'T GOT YOUR BRAINS -- BUT WE KNOW HOW TO STAY ALIVE!
THOK
WH-!?
SPLOSH
HEY!
!
WHO IS THIS BITCH!?
SOME "PRO" YOU ARE!

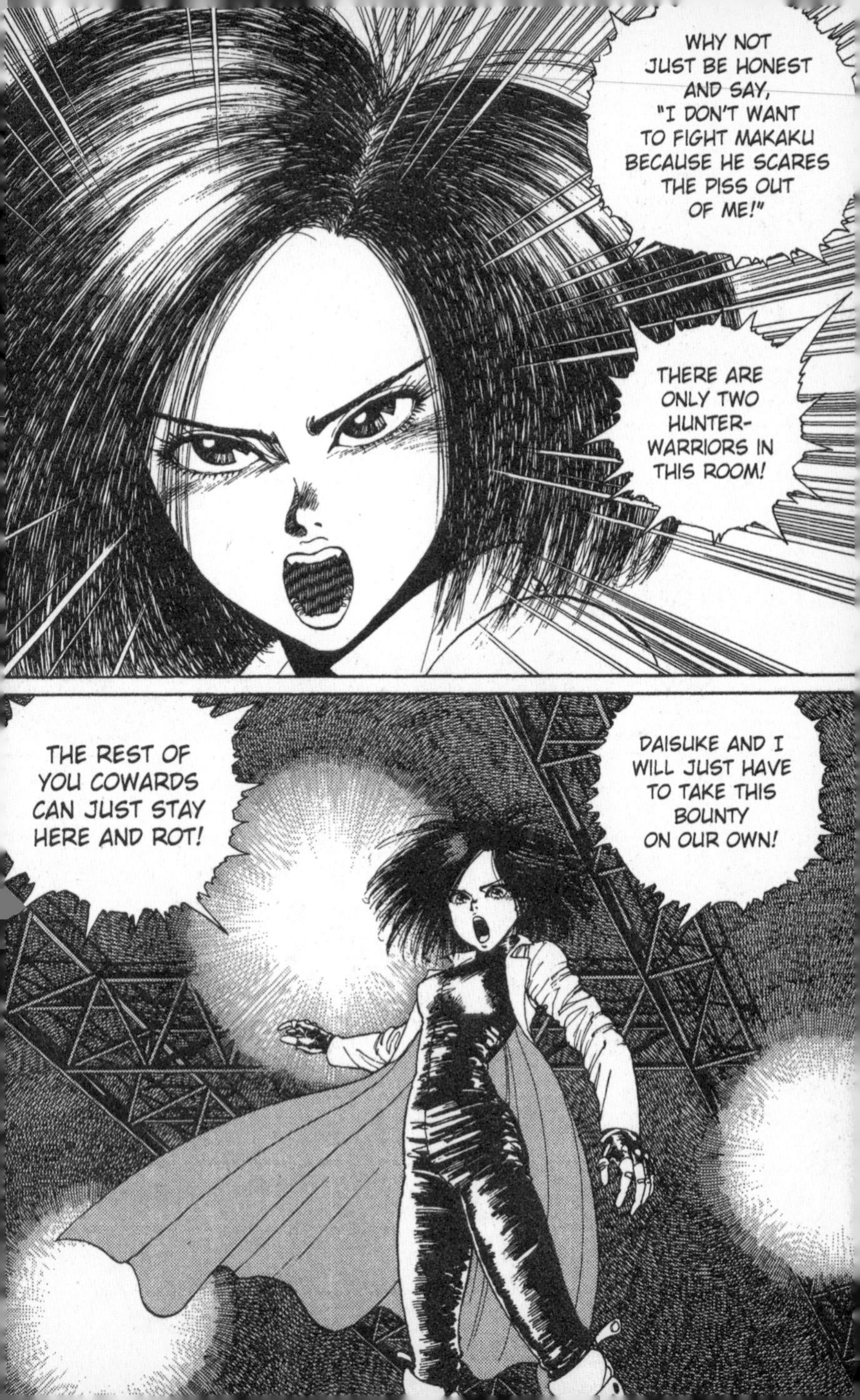
WHY NOT JUST BE HONEST AND SAY, "I DON'T WANT TO FIGHT MAKAKU BECAUSE HE SCARES THE PISS OUT OF ME!"
THERE ARE ONLY TWO HUNTER-WARRIORS IN THIS ROOM!
DAISUKE AND I WILL JUST HAVE TO TAKE THIS BOUNTY ON OUR OWN!
THE REST OF YOU COWARDS CAN JUST STAY HERE AND ROT!

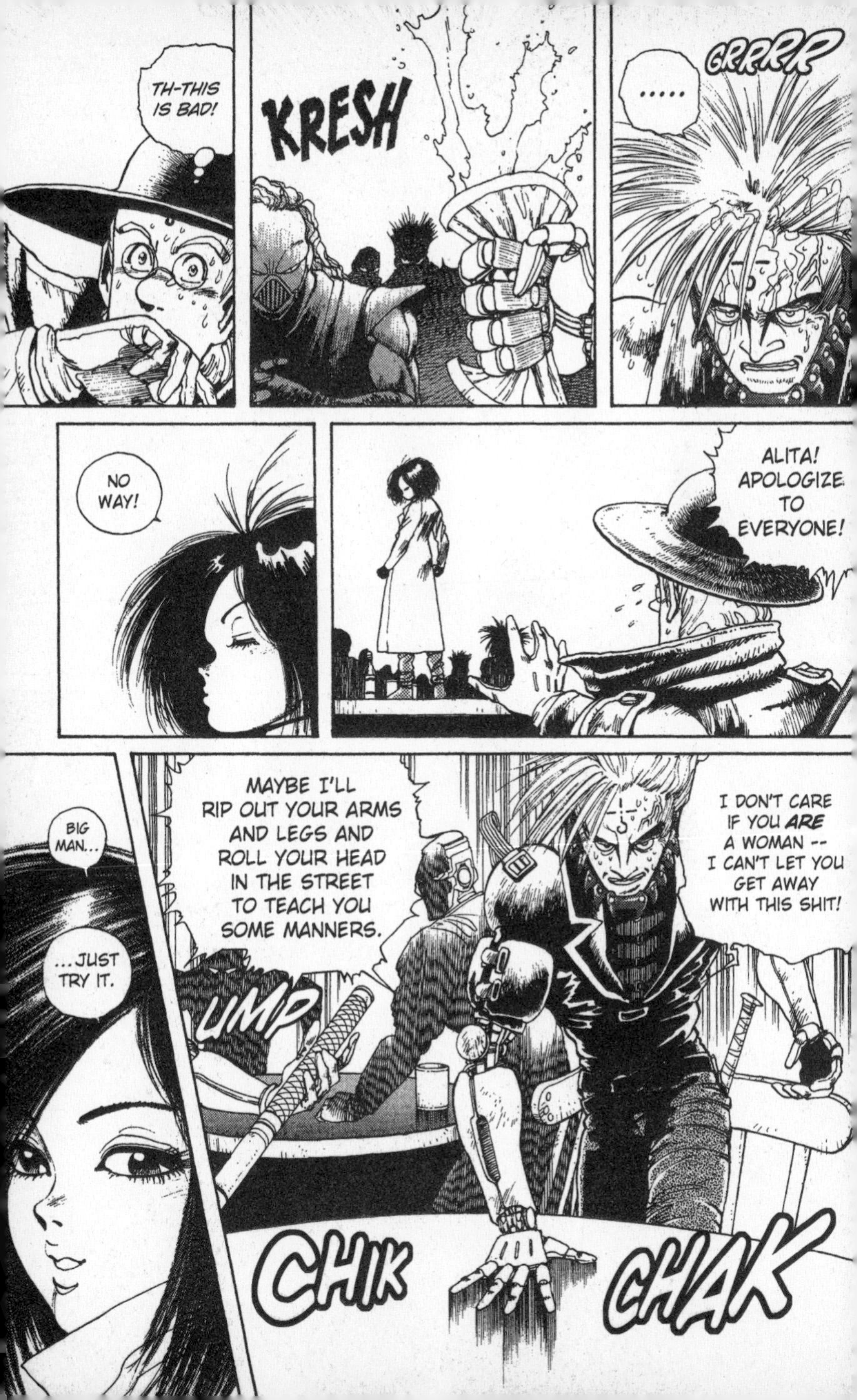
GRRRR
.....
KRESH
TH-THIS IS BAD!
ALITA! APOLOGIZE TO EVERYONE!
NO WAY!
I DON'T CARE IF YOU *ARE* A WOMAN -- I CAN'T LET YOU GET AWAY WITH THIS SHIT!
MAYBE I'LL RIP OUT YOUR ARMS AND LEGS AND ROLL YOUR HEAD IN THE STREET TO TEACH YOU SOME MANNERS.
UMP
CHIK CHAK
BIG MAN...
...JUST TRY IT.

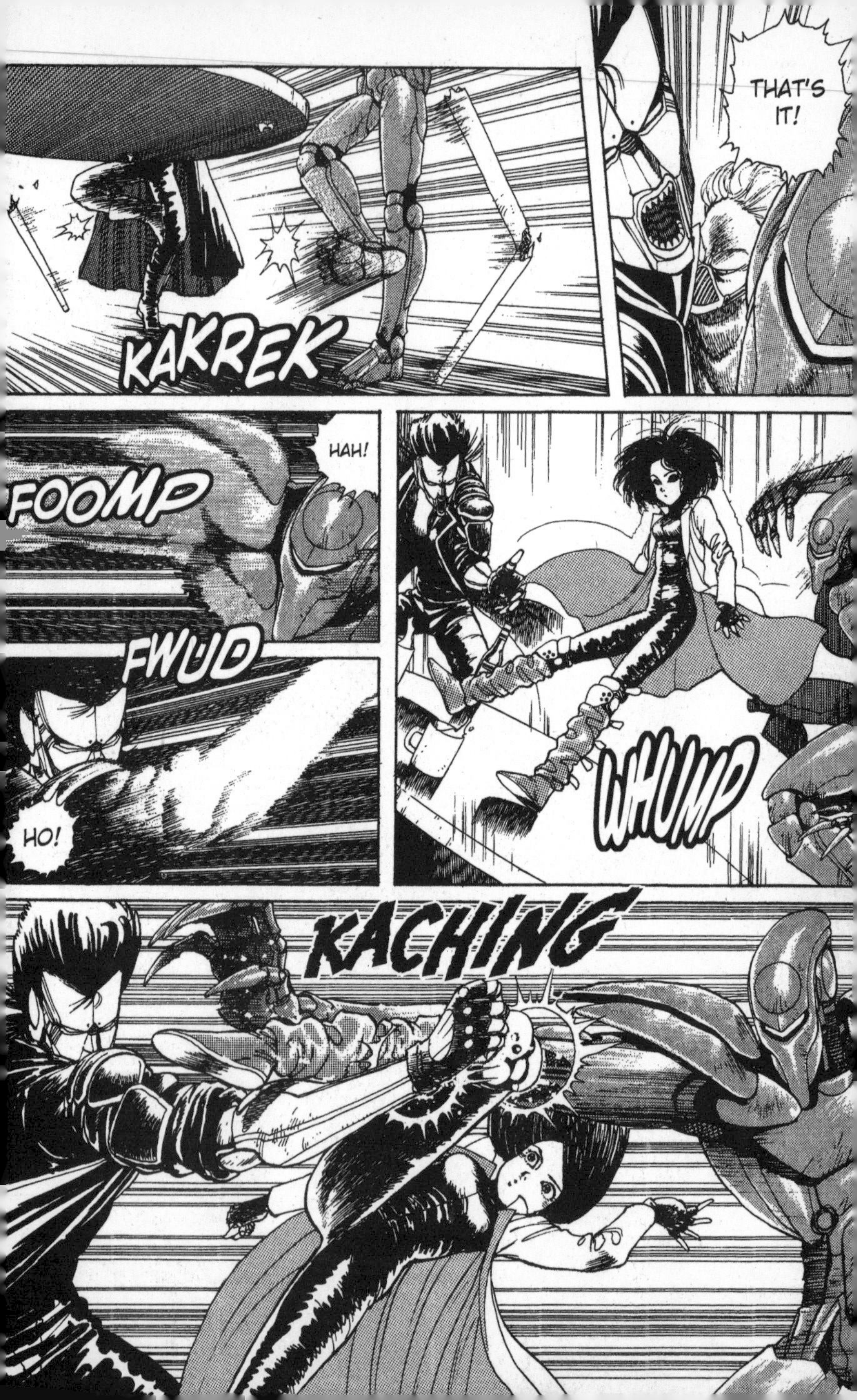
THAT'S IT!
KAKREK
WHUMP
HAH!
FOOMP
FWUD
HO!
KACHING

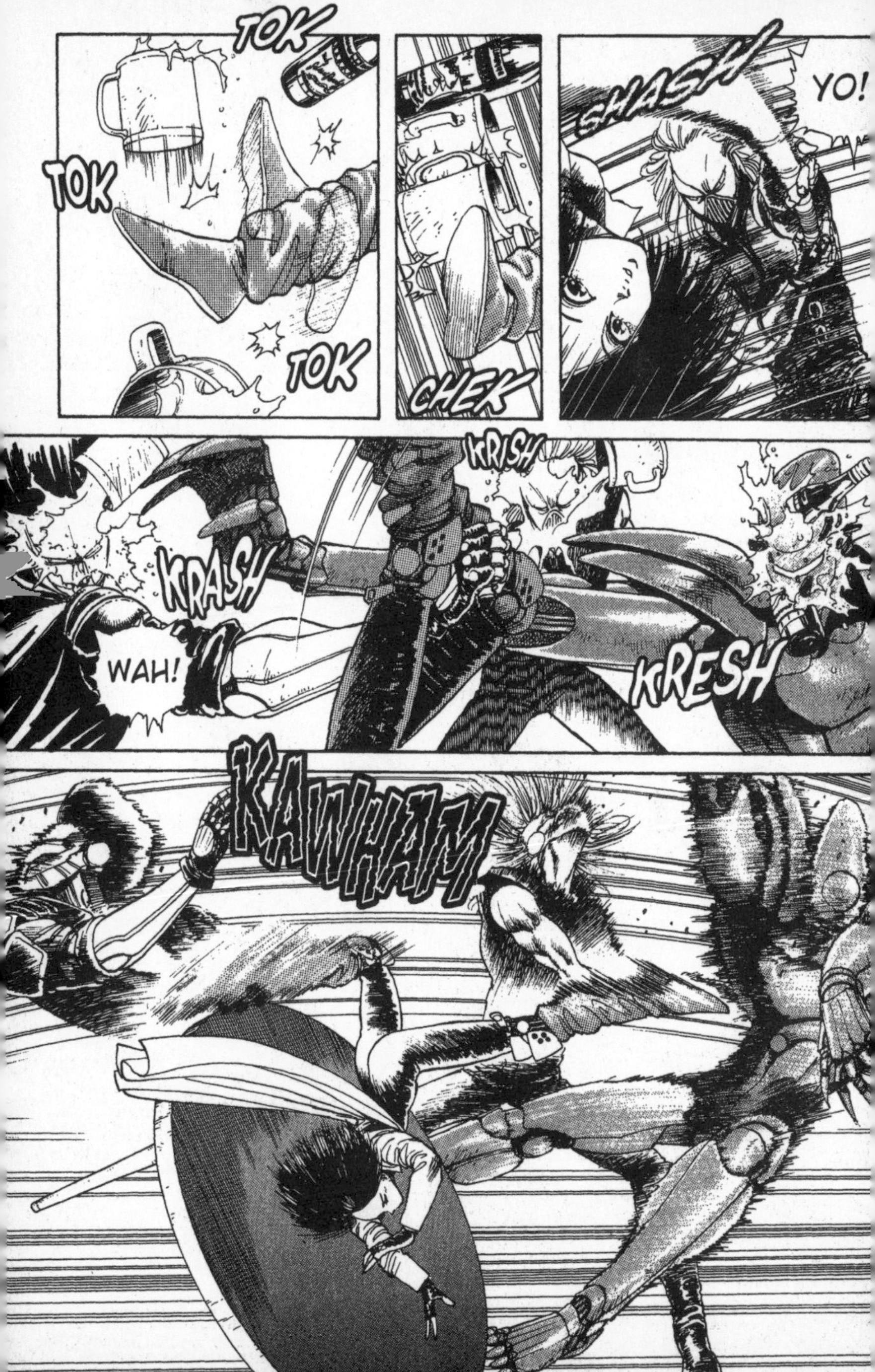
SHASH
YO!
CHEK
TOK
TOK
TOK
KRESH
KRISH
KRASH
WAH!
KAWHAM

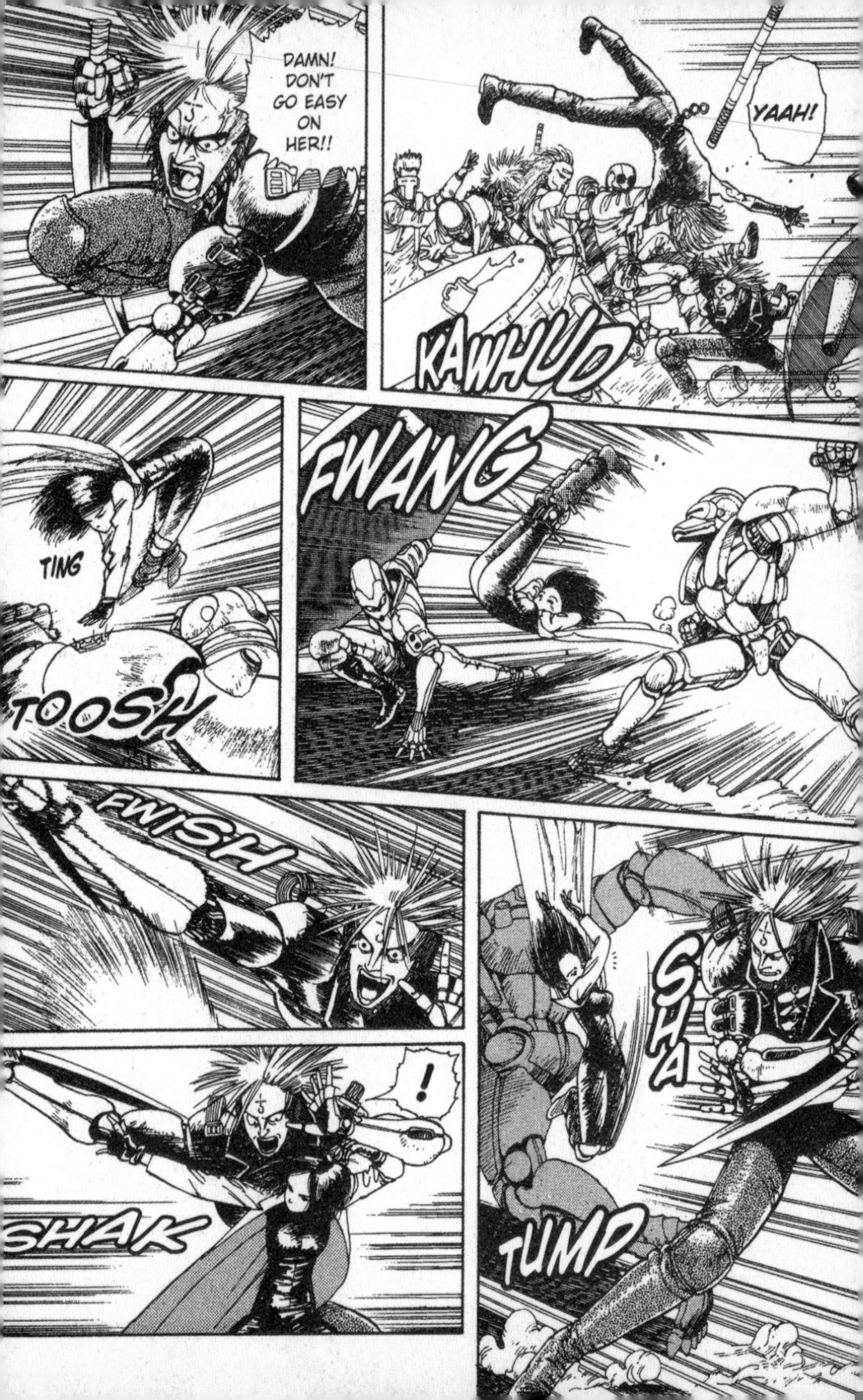
YAAH!
KAWHUD
DAMN! DON'T GO EASY ON HER!!
FWANG
TING
TOOSH
SHA
TUMP
FWISH
!
SHAK

OOPS! I-I'M SORRY!

SKRIK

GAH!

TOOMP

WHY, YOU--!

CHING

WAH!

KAFWHAM

AAAGH!

I-IT'S NOT ME! IT'S NOT ME!

SKRIK

SKRIK

SKRIK

HA! HA!

DAMMIT! WOULD YOU LET GO OF ME!

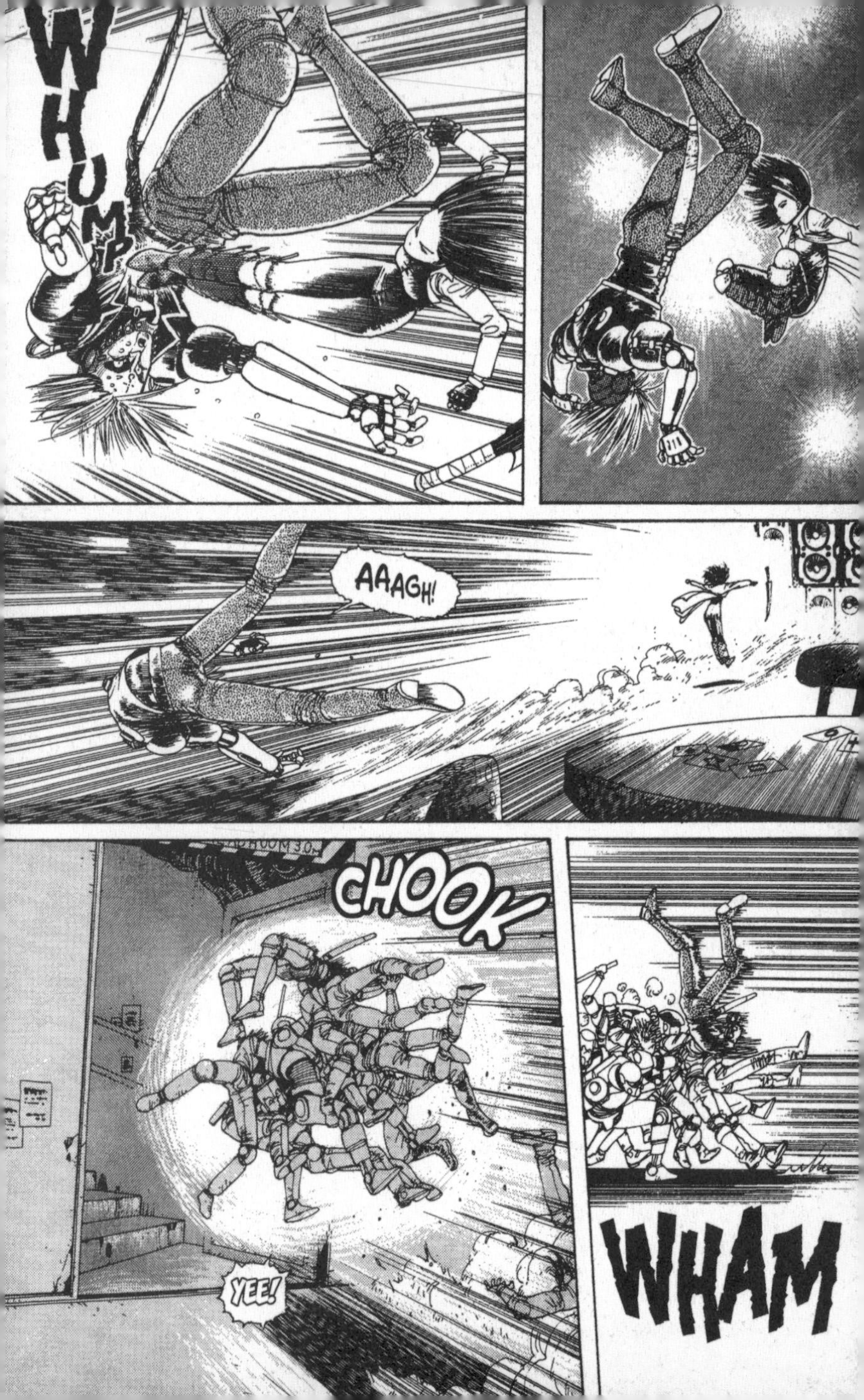
WHUMP
AAAGH!
WHAM
CHOOK
YEE!

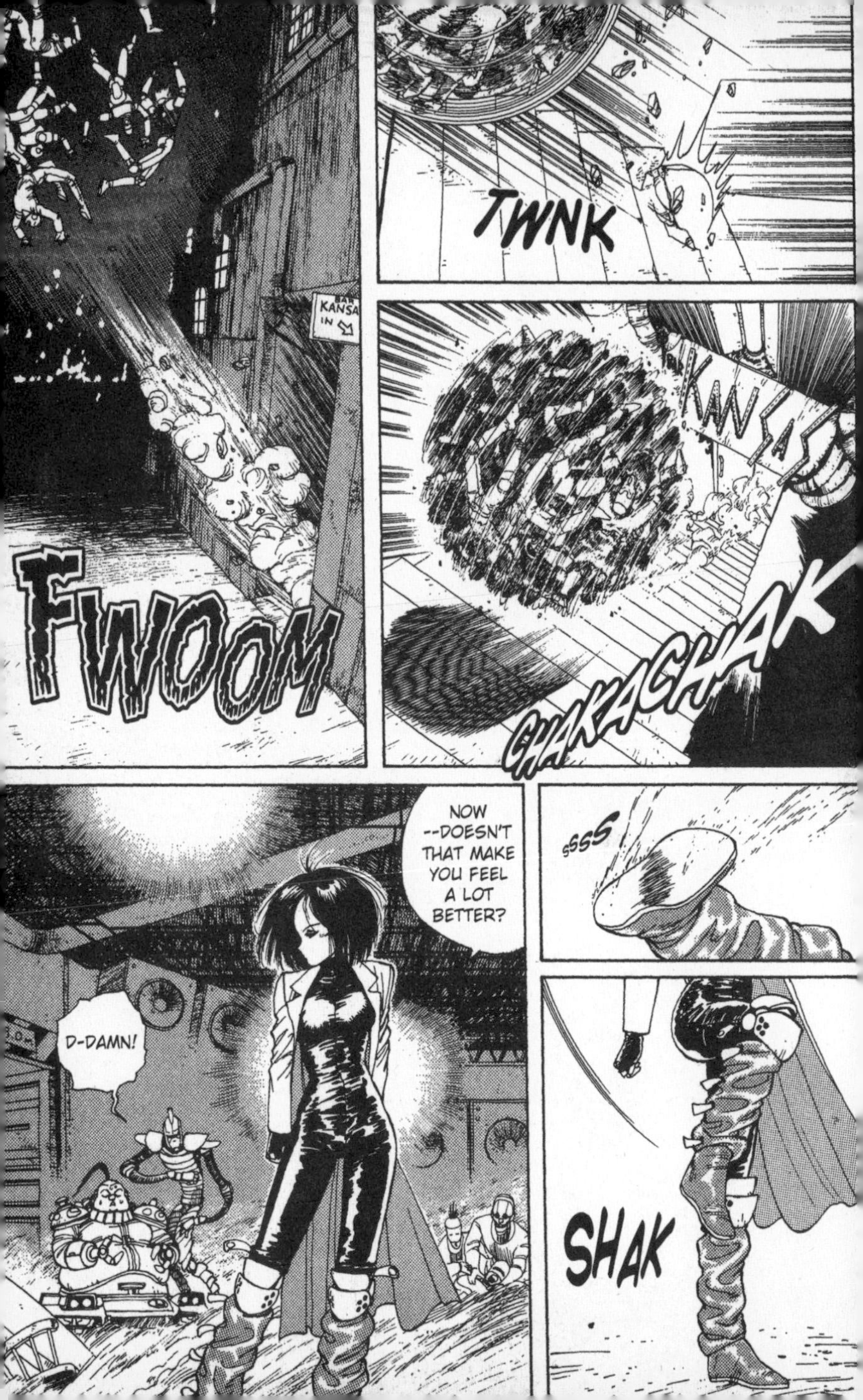

TWNK
CHAKACHAK
BAR KANSA IN
FWOOM
SSSS
SHAK
NOW --DOESN'T THAT MAKE YOU FEEL A LOT BETTER?
D-DAMN!

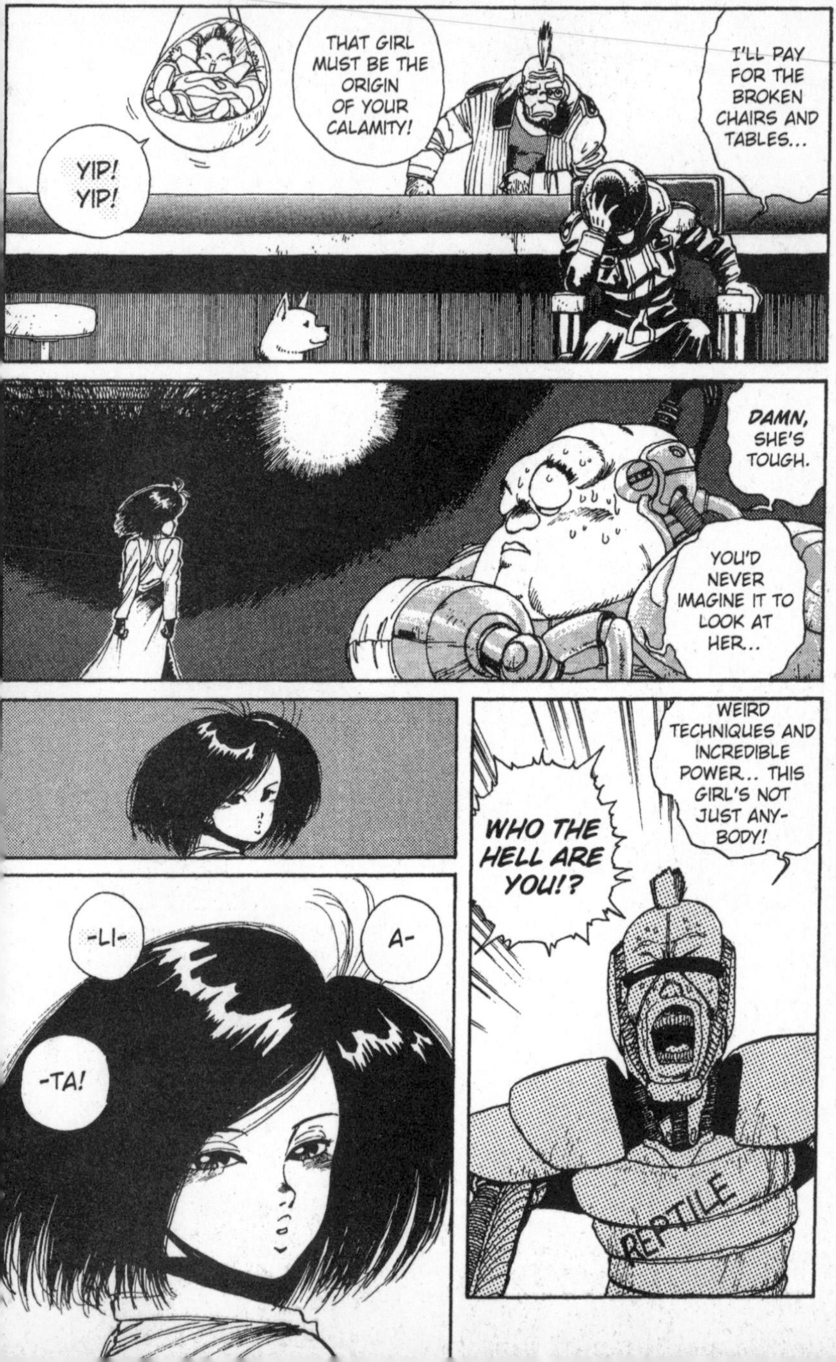
I'LL PAY FOR THE BROKEN CHAIRS AND TABLES...
THAT GIRL MUST BE THE ORIGIN OF YOUR CALAMITY!
YIP! YIP!
DAMN, SHE'S TOUGH.
YOU'D NEVER IMAGINE IT TO LOOK AT HER...
WEIRD TECHNIQUES AND INCREDIBLE POWER... THIS GIRL'S NOT JUST ANY-BODY!
WHO THE HELL ARE YOU!?
REPTILE
A-
-LI-
-TA!

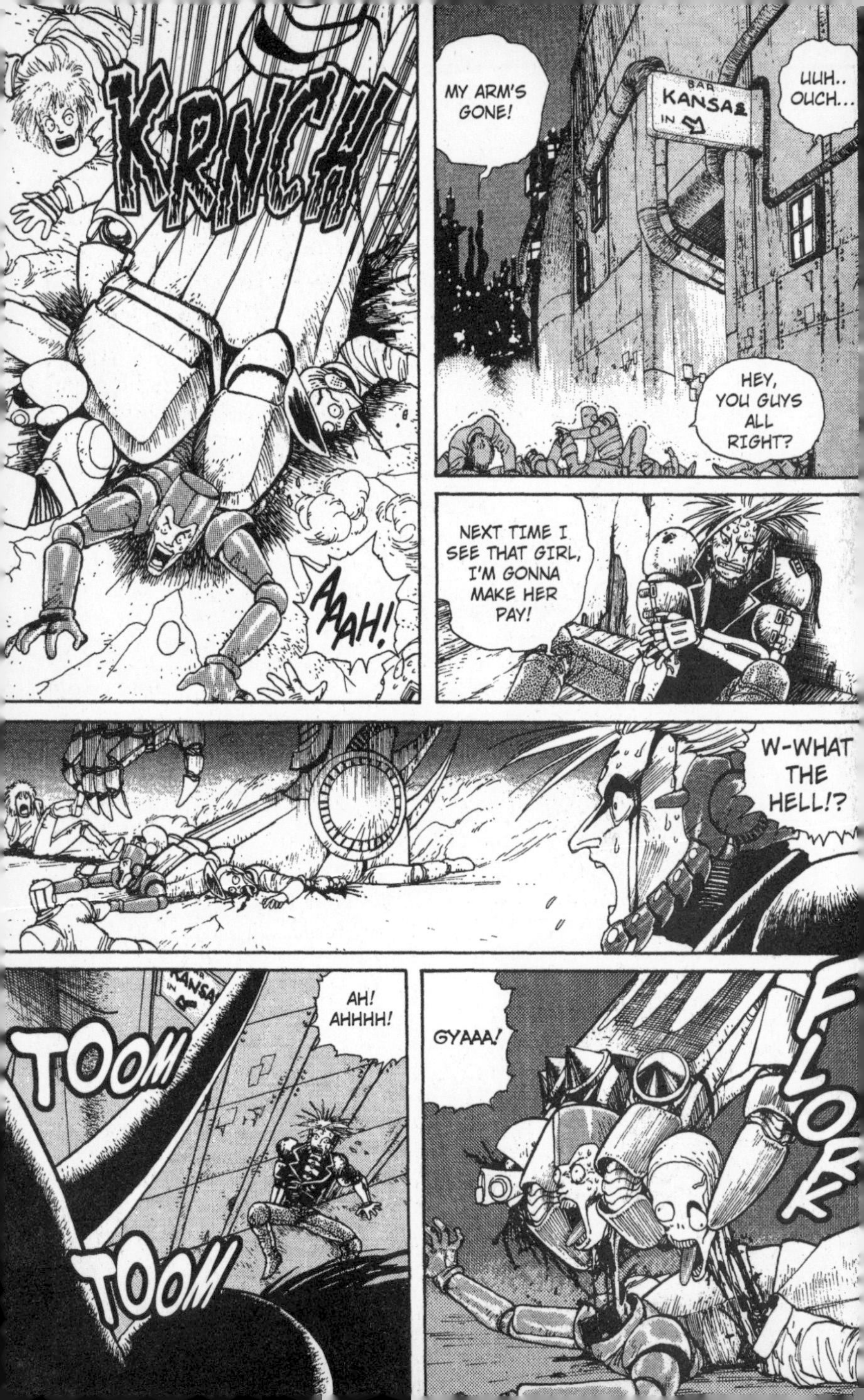
UUH.. OUCH...
BAR KANSAS IN
MY ARM'S GONE!
HEY, YOU GUYS ALL RIGHT?
NEXT TIME I SEE THAT GIRL, I'M GONNA MAKE HER PAY!
KRNCH
AAAH!
W-WHAT THE HELL!?
FLOKK
GYAAA!
AH! AHHHH!
TOOM
TOOM

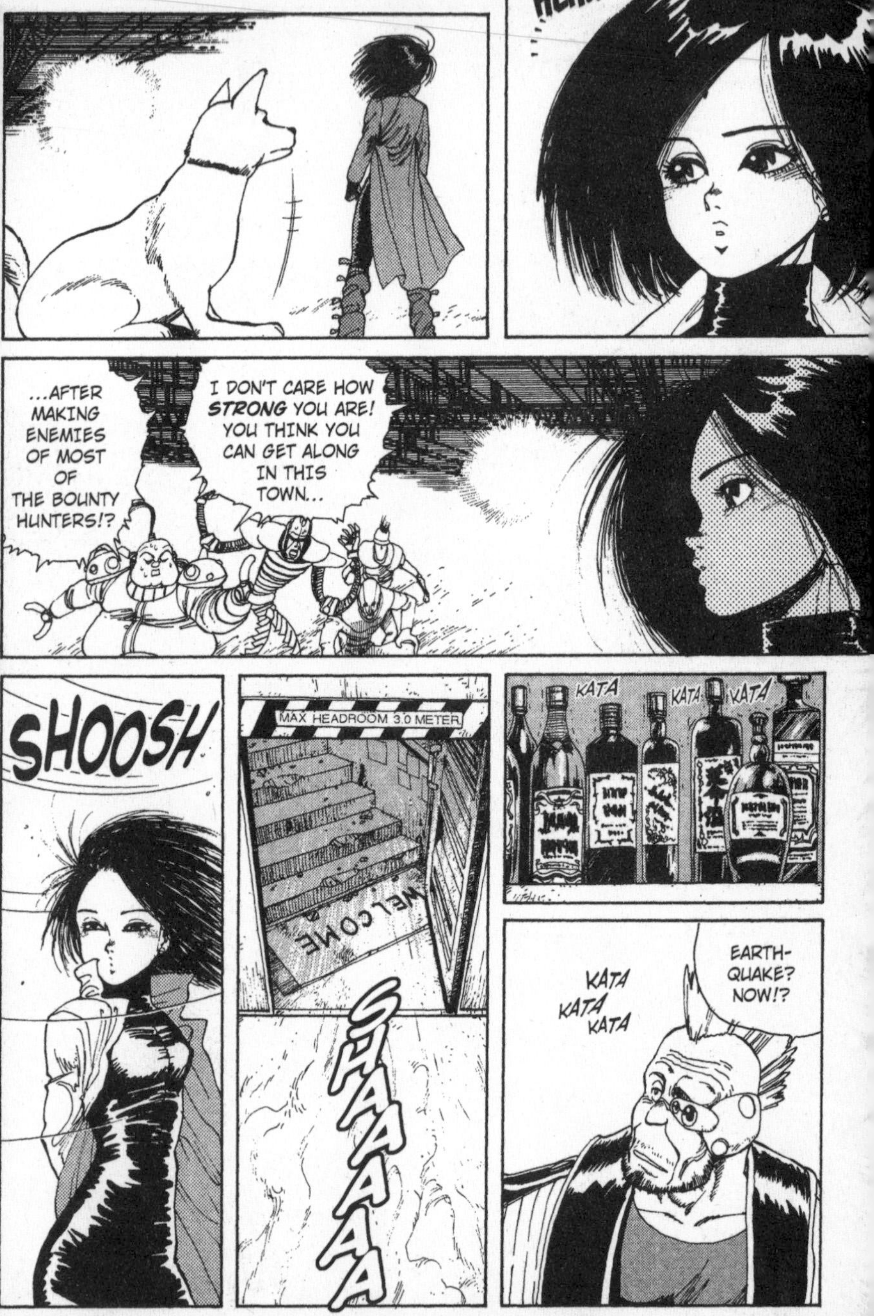
HEH!?
I DON'T CARE HOW STRONG YOU ARE! YOU THINK YOU CAN GET ALONG IN THIS TOWN...
...AFTER MAKING ENEMIES OF MOST OF THE BOUNTY HUNTERS!?
KATA
KATA
KATA
EARTH-QUAKE? NOW!?
KATA KATA KATA
MAX HEADROOM 3.0 METER
WELCOME
SHAAAAAA
SHOOSH

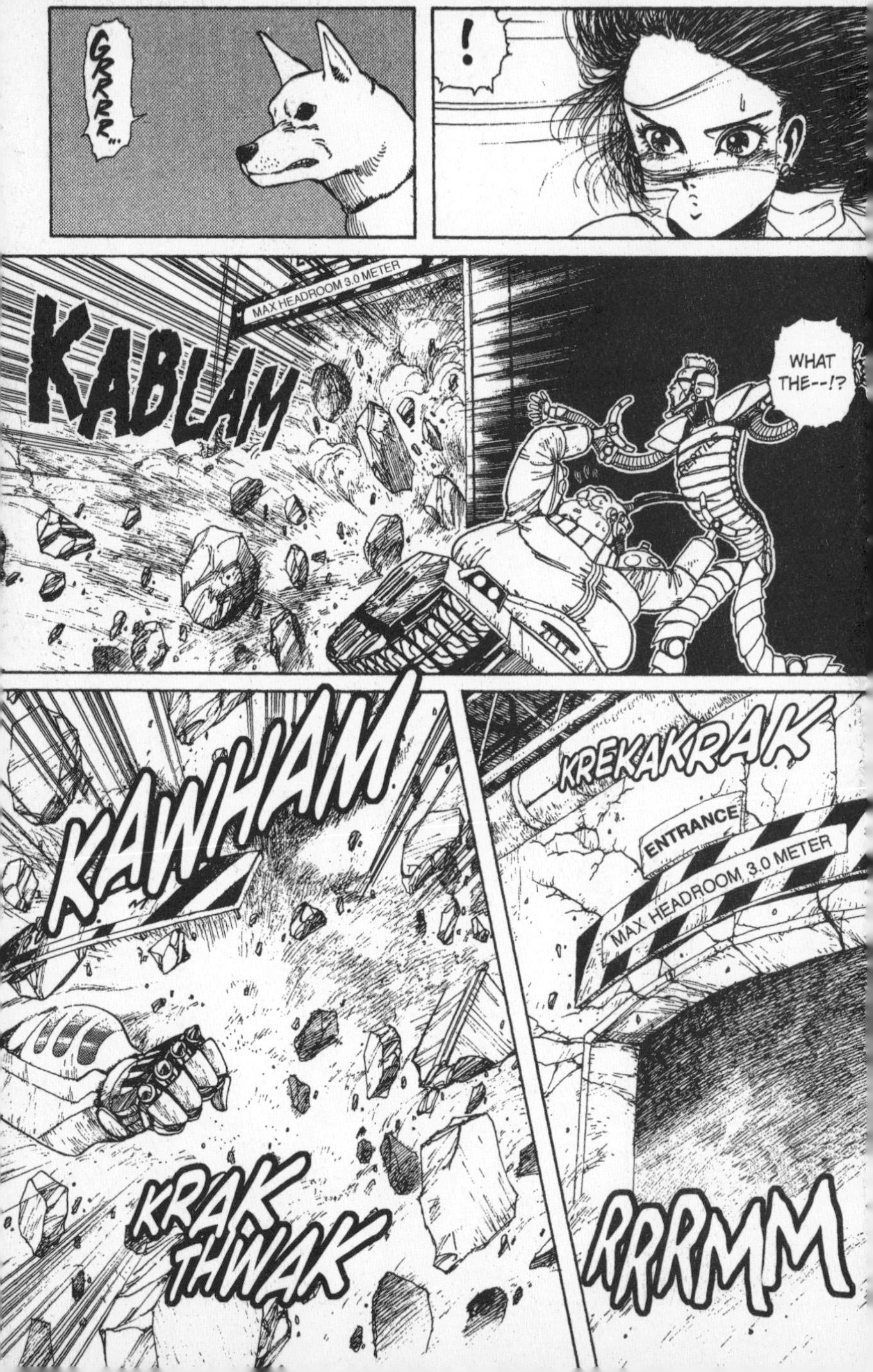
!
GRRRR..
WHAT THE--!?
MAX HEADROOM 3.0 METER
KABLAM
KREKAKRAK
ENTRANCE
MAX HEADROOM 3.0 METER
RRRMM
KAWHAM
KRAK THWAK

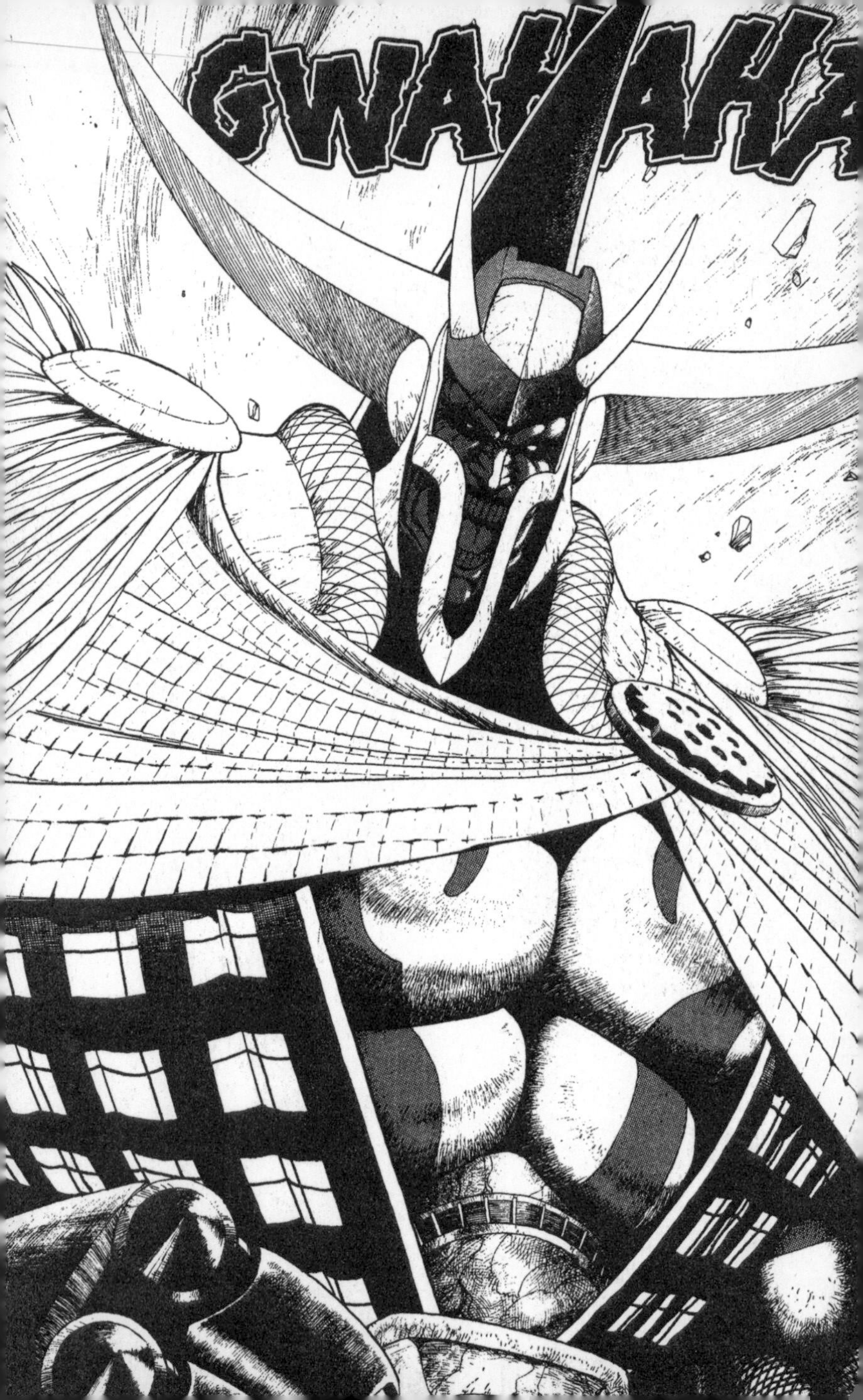
GWAHAHA

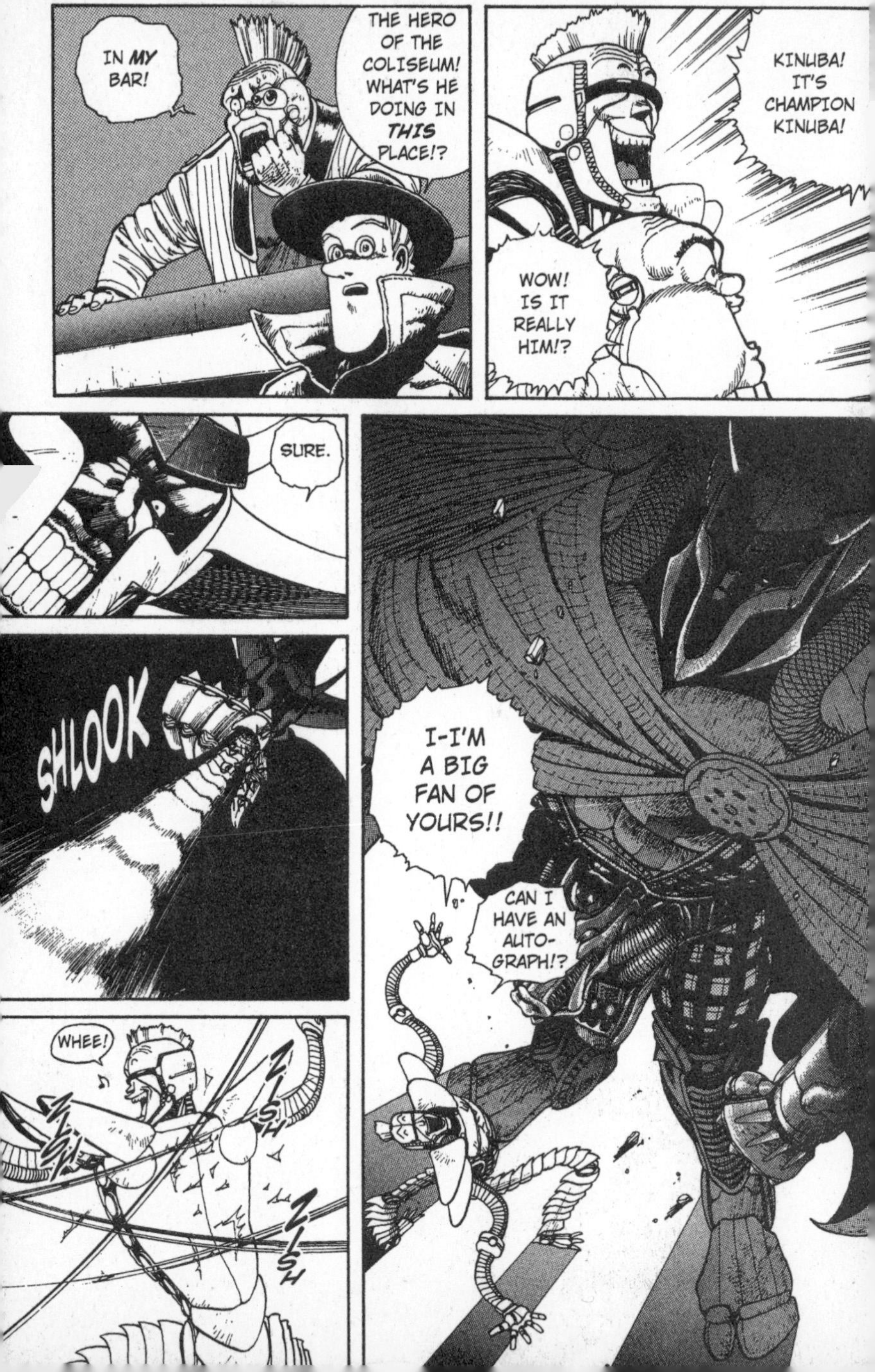
KINUBA! IT'S CHAMPION KINUBA!
WOW! IS IT REALLY HIM!?
THE HERO OF THE COLISEUM! WHAT'S HE DOING IN **THIS** PLACE!?
IN **MY** BAR!
I-I'M A BIG FAN OF YOURS!!
CAN I HAVE AN AUTO-GRAPH!?
SURE.
SHLOOK
WHEE!
ZISH
ZISH

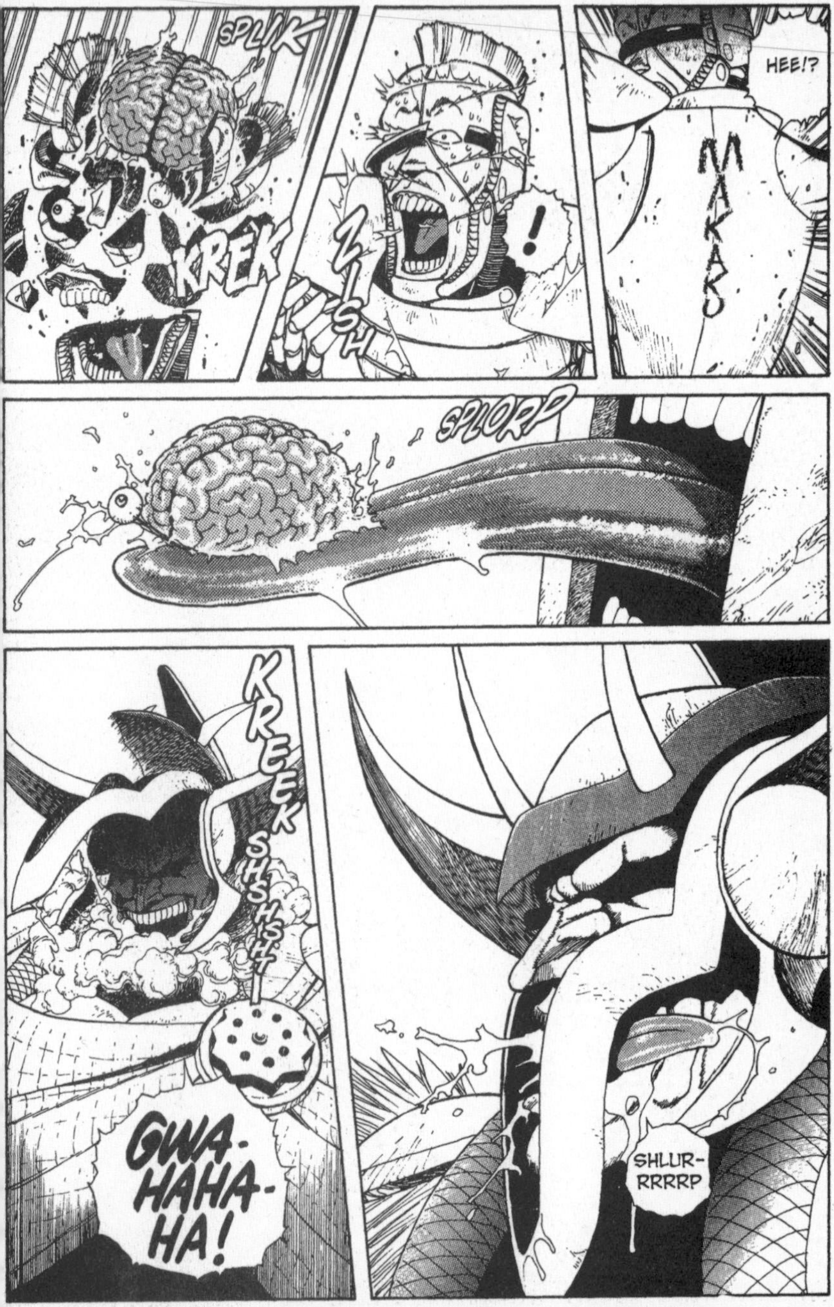
HEE!?
MAKAKU
!
ZISH
SPLIK
KREK
SPLORP
SHLUR-RRRRP
KREEK
SHSHSHT
GWA-HAHAHA-HA!

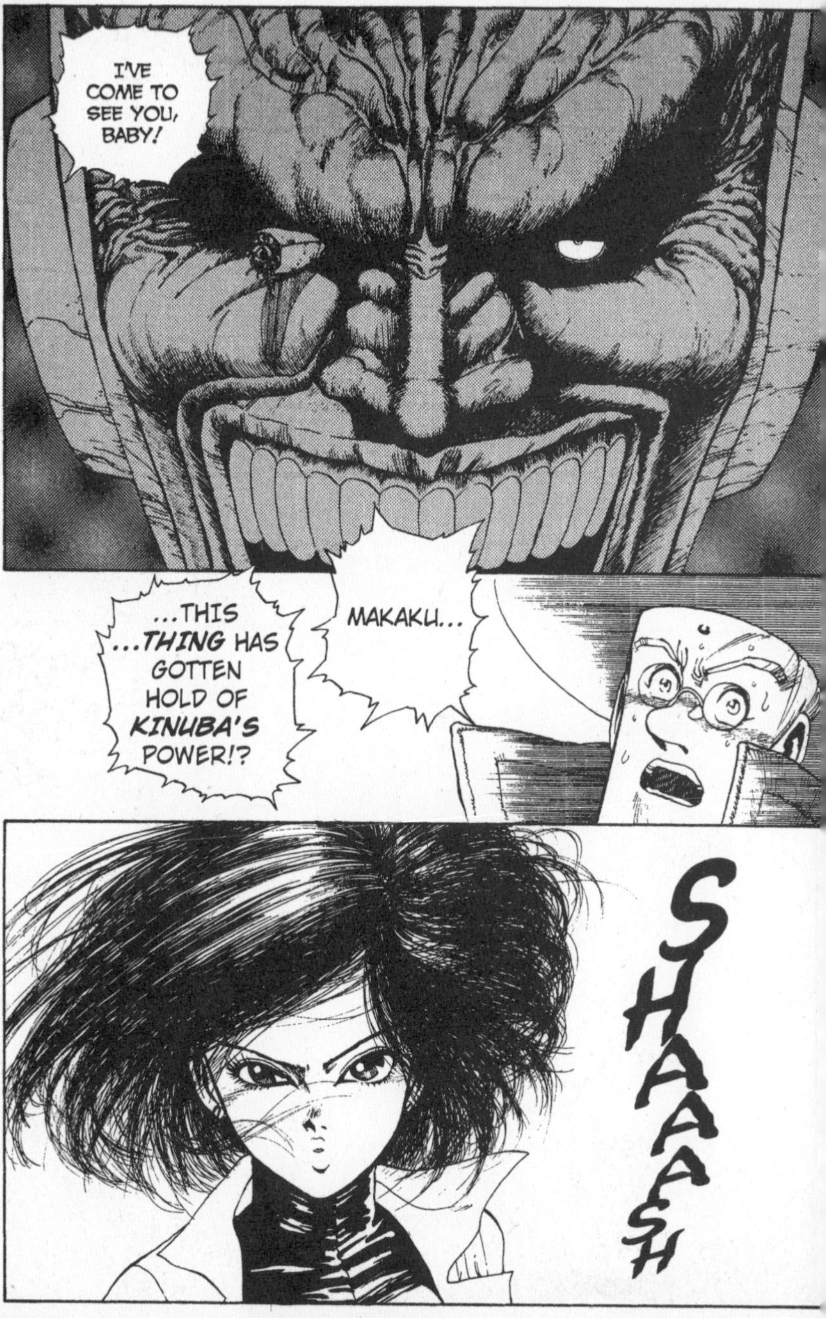
I'VE COME TO SEE YOU, BABY!
MAKAKU...
...THIS ...*THING* HAS GOTTEN HOLD OF *KINUBA'S* POWER!?
SHAAAASH

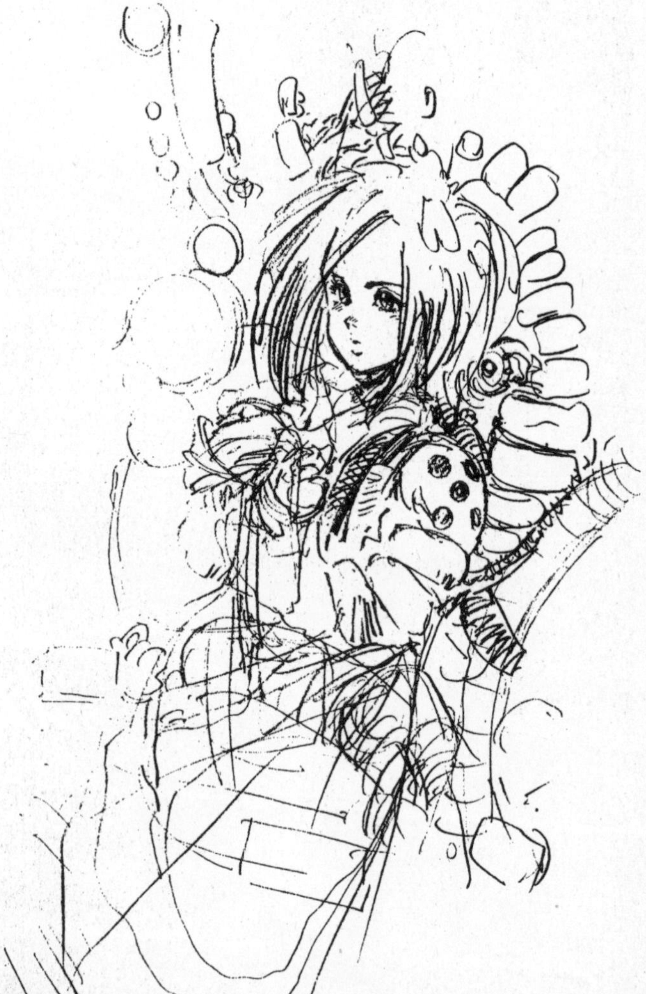

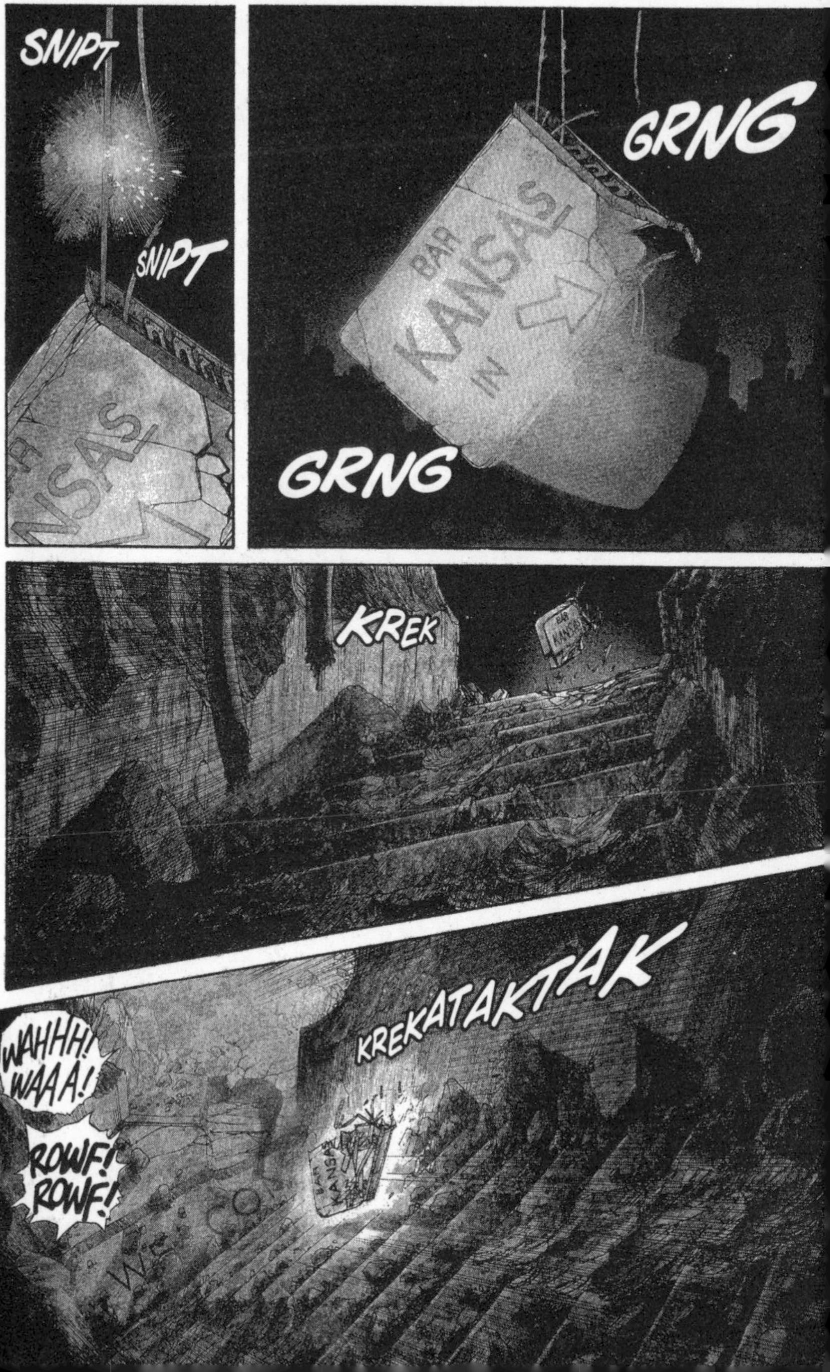
GRNG
BAR KANSAS IN
GRNG
SNIPT
SNIPT
KREK
BAR KANSAS
KREKATAKTAK
WAHHH! WAAA!
ROWF! ROWF!

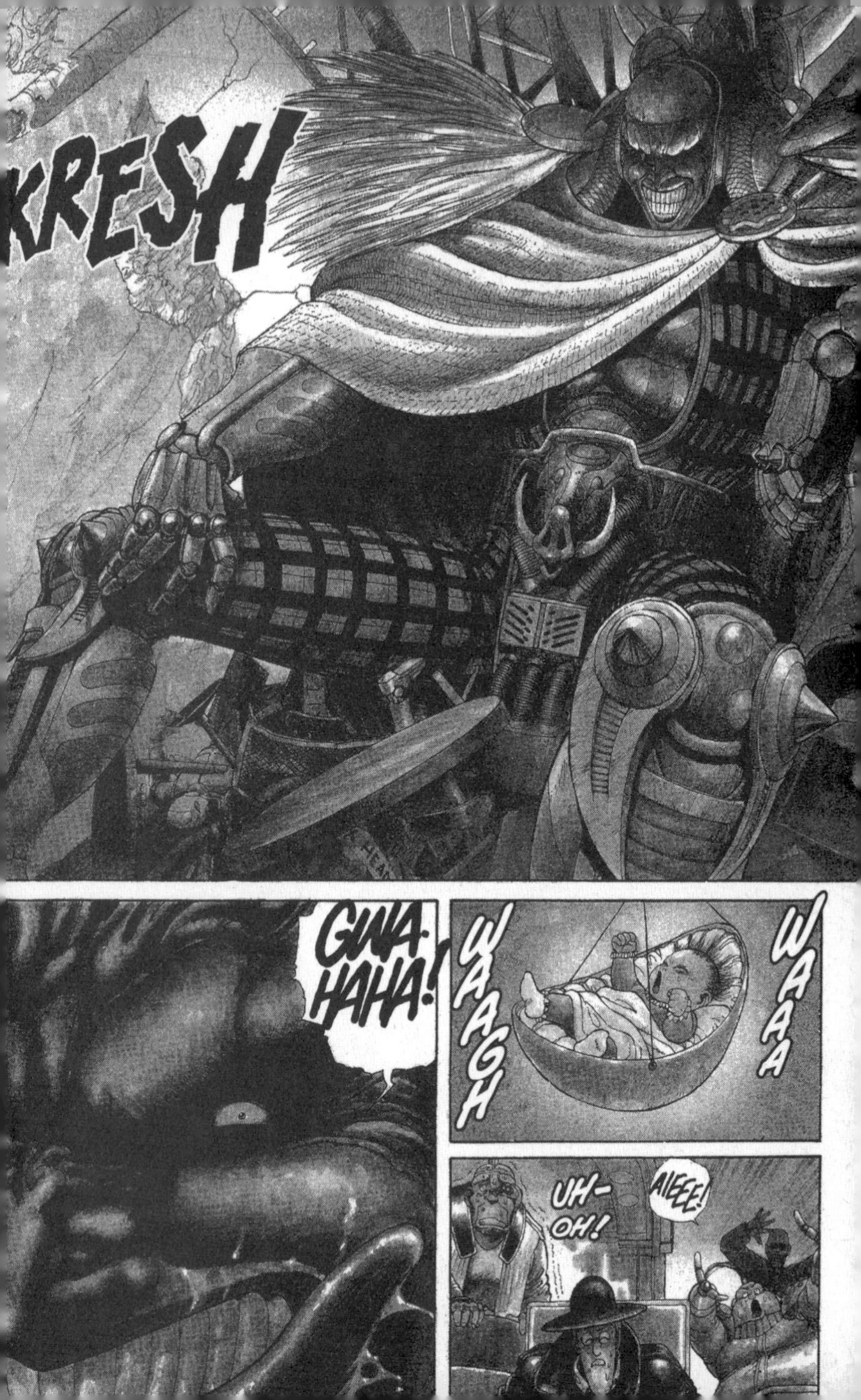
KRESH
WAAAA
WAAAGH
AIEEE!
UH-OH!
GWA-HAHA!

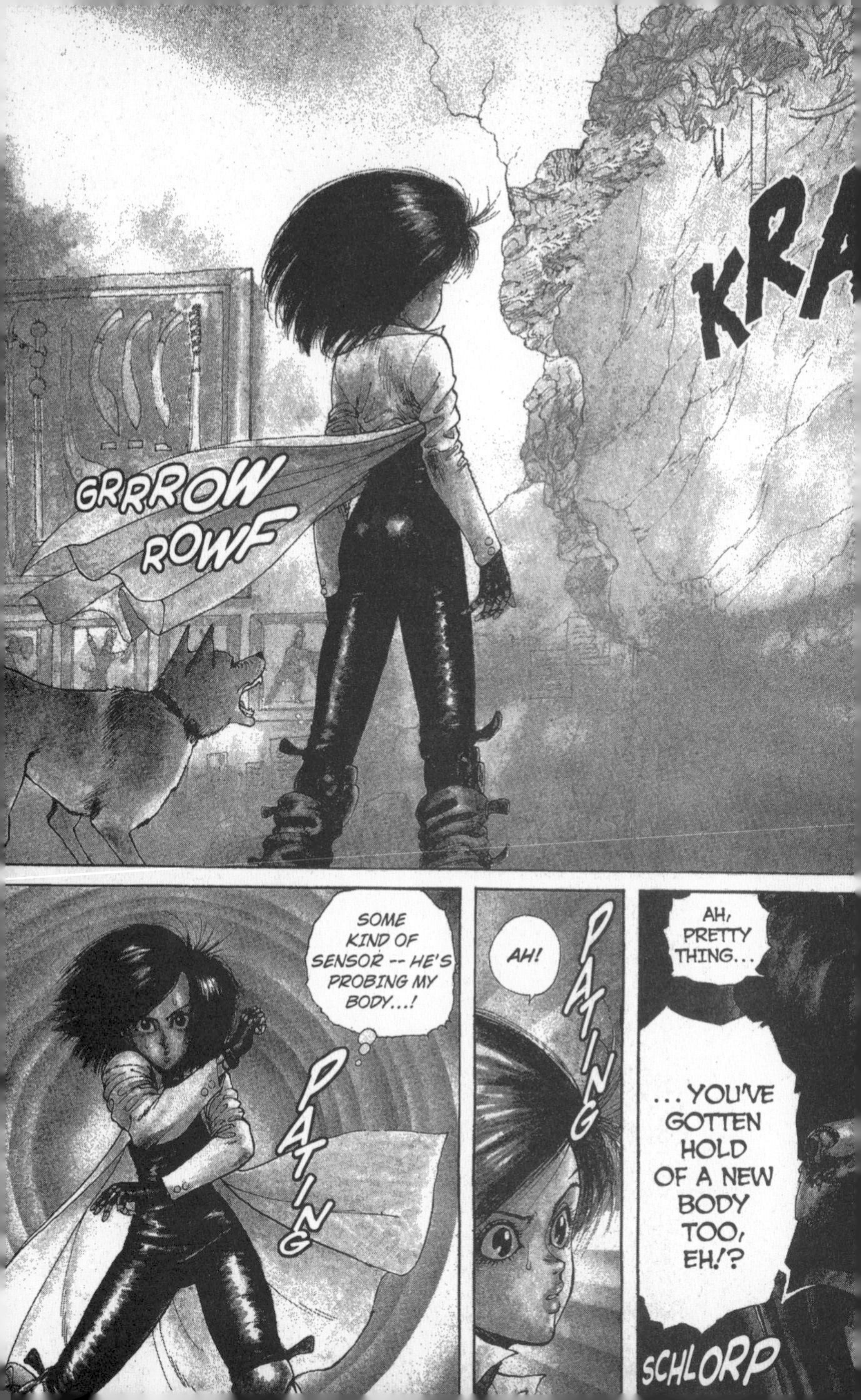
KRA
GRRROW ROWF
AH, PRETTY THING...
...YOU'VE GOTTEN HOLD OF A NEW BODY TOO, EH!?
SCHLORP
AH!
PATING
SOME KIND OF SENSOR -- HE'S PROBING MY BODY...!
PATING

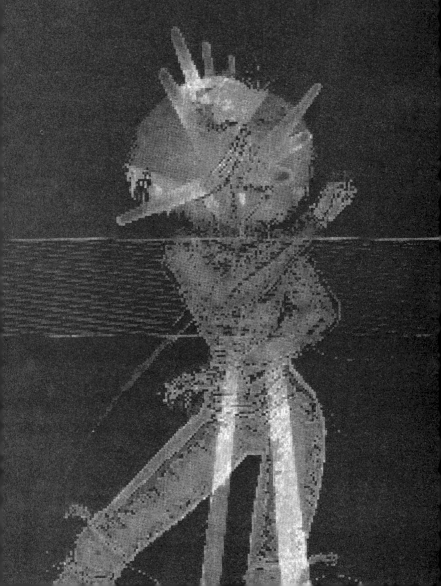

HELL TRAP

Battle 5: Responsibility

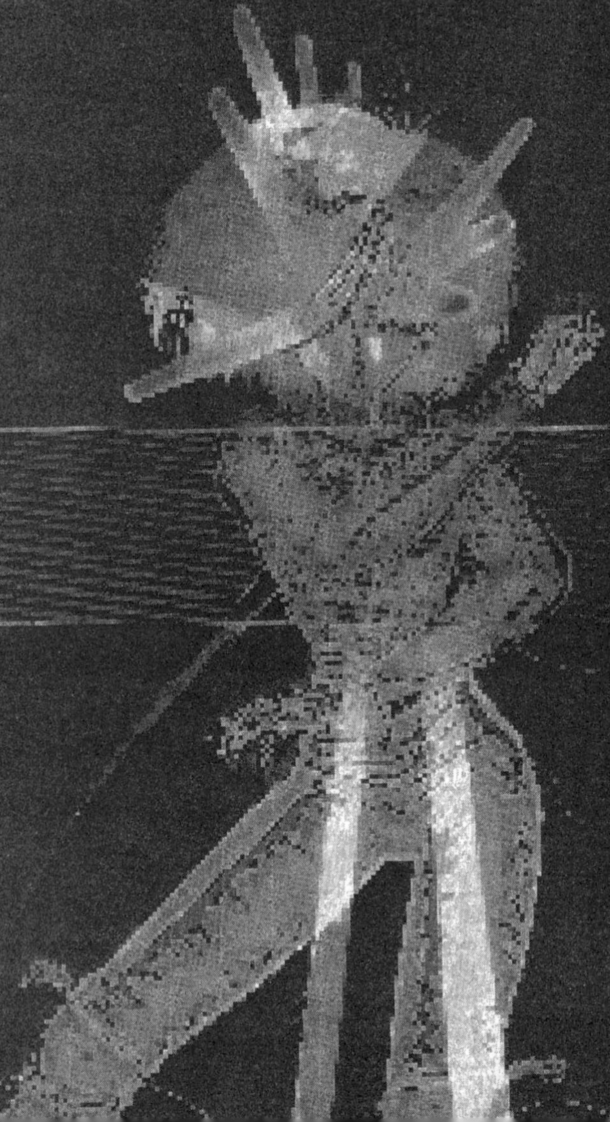

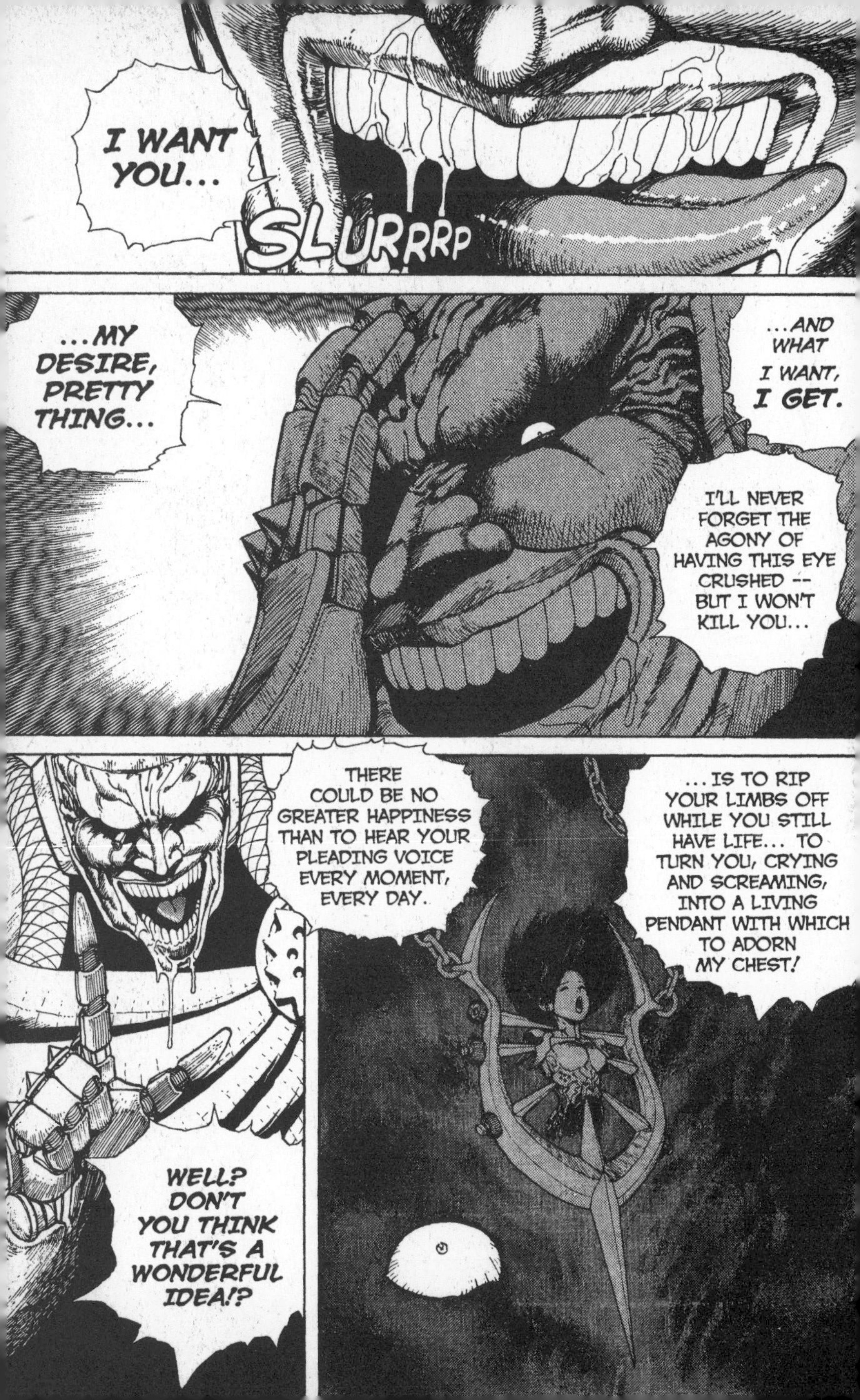
I WANT YOU...
SLURRRP
...MY DESIRE, PRETTY THING...
...AND WHAT I WANT, I GET.
I'LL NEVER FORGET THE AGONY OF HAVING THIS EYE CRUSHED -- BUT I WON'T KILL YOU...
...IS TO RIP YOUR LIMBS OFF WHILE YOU STILL HAVE LIFE... TO TURN YOU, CRYING AND SCREAMING, INTO A LIVING PENDANT WITH WHICH TO ADORN MY CHEST!
THERE COULD BE NO GREATER HAPPINESS THAN TO HEAR YOUR PLEADING VOICE EVERY MOMENT, EVERY DAY.
WELL? DON'T YOU THINK THAT'S A WONDERFUL IDEA!?

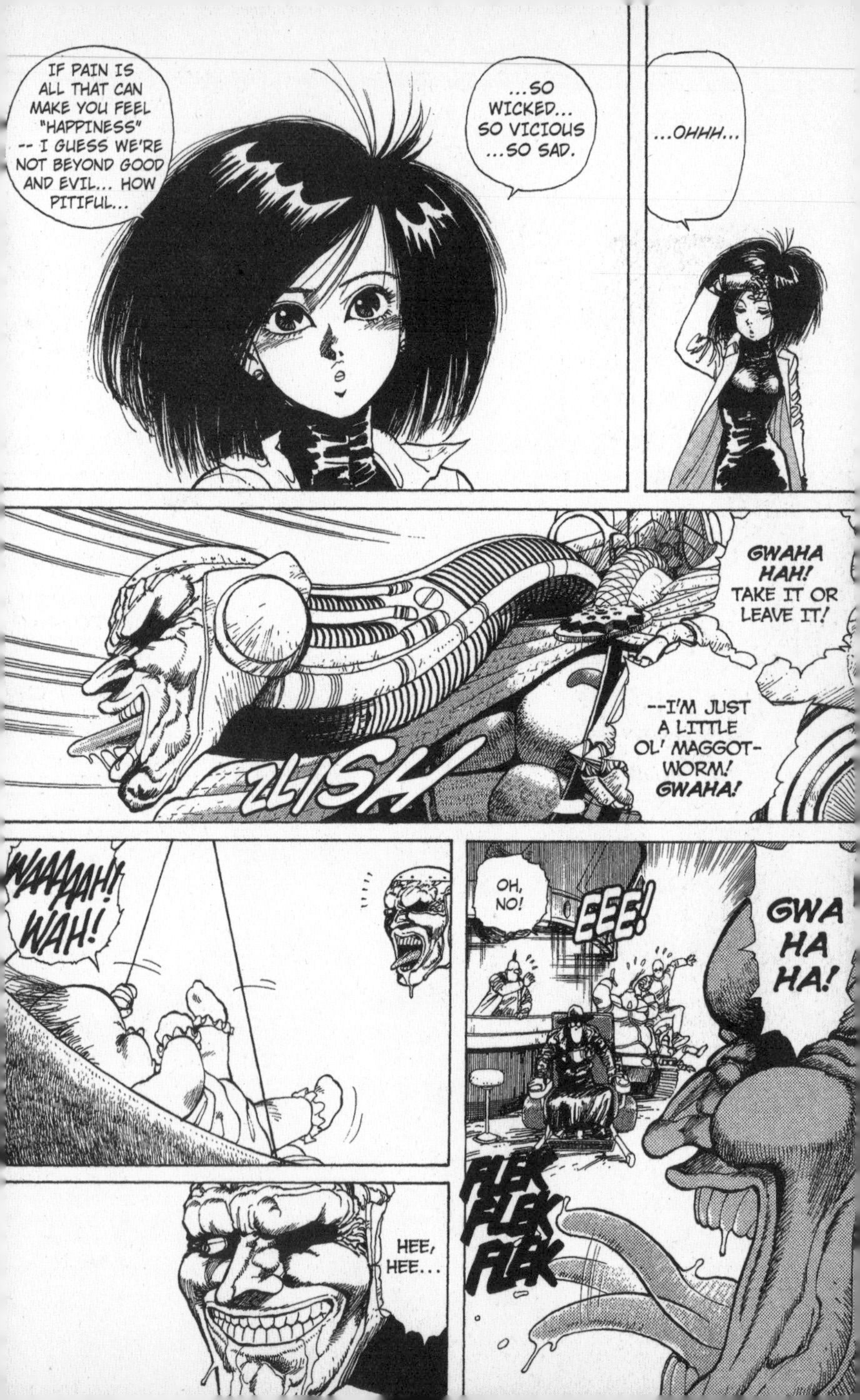
...OHHH...
...SO WICKED... SO VICIOUS ...SO SAD.
IF PAIN IS ALL THAT CAN MAKE YOU FEEL "HAPPINESS" -- I GUESS WE'RE NOT BEYOND GOOD AND EVIL... HOW PITIFUL...
GWAHA HAH! TAKE IT OR LEAVE IT!
--I'M JUST A LITTLE OL' MAGGOT-WORM! GWAHA!
ZLISH
GWA HA HA!
EEE!
OH, NO!
FLEK FLEK FLEK
WAAAAAH! WAH!
HEE, HEE...

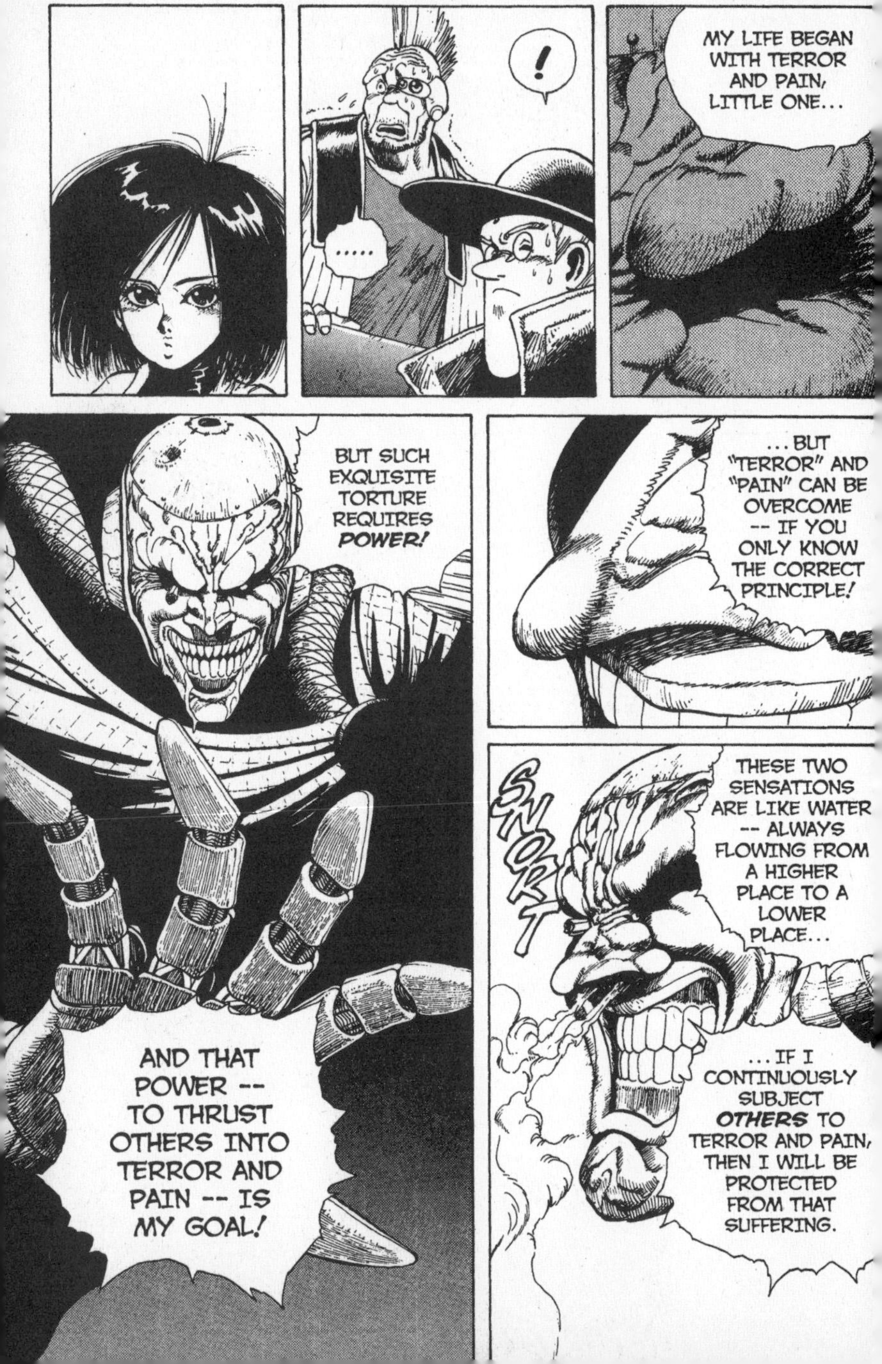
MY LIFE BEGAN WITH TERROR AND PAIN, LITTLE ONE...
!
......
...BUT "TERROR" AND "PAIN" CAN BE OVERCOME -- IF YOU ONLY KNOW THE CORRECT PRINCIPLE!
SNORT
THESE TWO SENSATIONS ARE LIKE WATER -- ALWAYS FLOWING FROM A HIGHER PLACE TO A LOWER PLACE...
...IF I CONTINUOUSLY SUBJECT *OTHERS* TO TERROR AND PAIN, THEN I WILL BE PROTECTED FROM THAT SUFFERING.
BUT SUCH EXQUISITE TORTURE REQUIRES *POWER!*
AND THAT POWER -- TO THRUST OTHERS INTO TERROR AND PAIN -- IS MY GOAL!

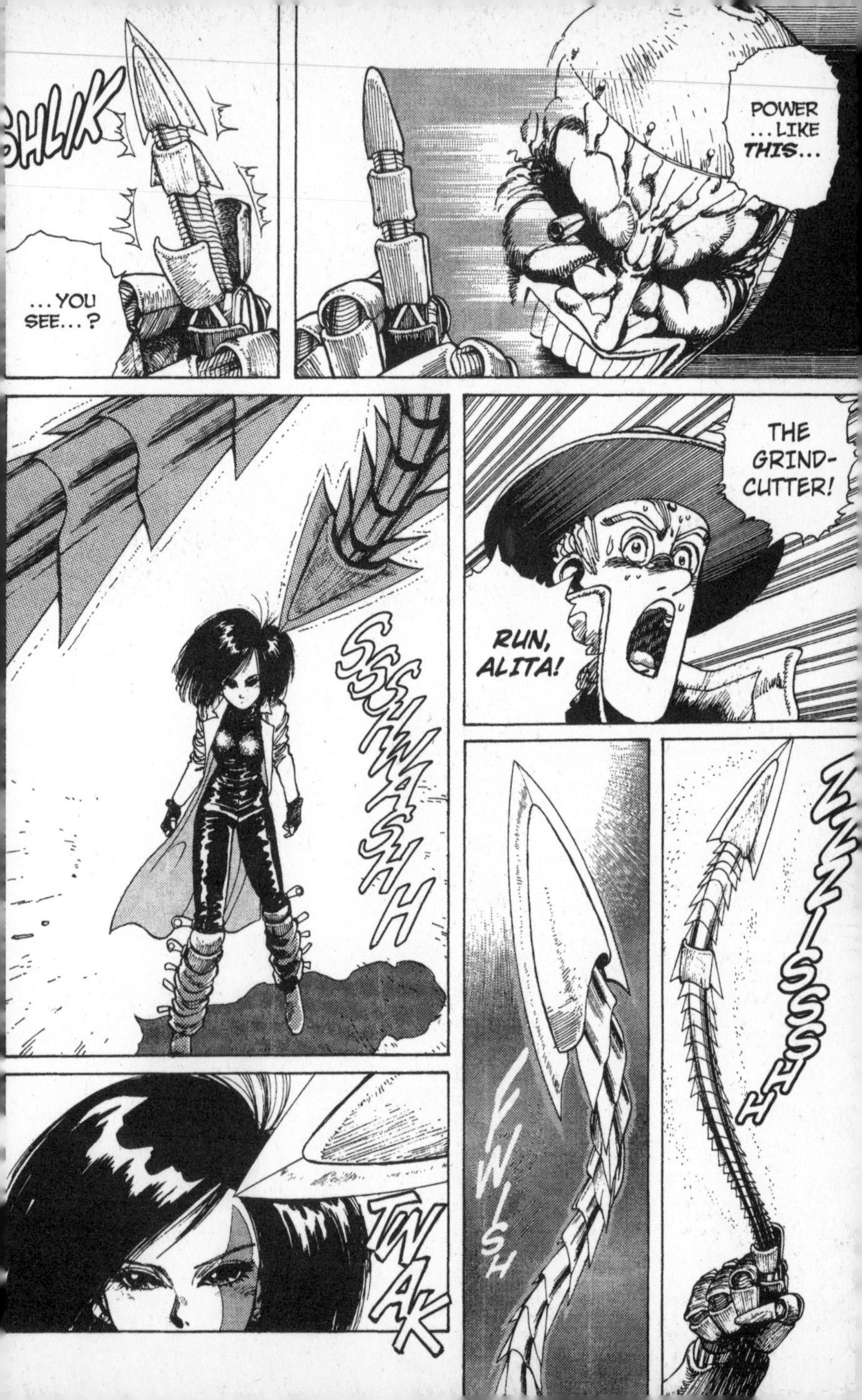
POWER ...LIKE THIS...
SHLIK
...YOU SEE...?
THE GRIND-CUTTER!
RUN, ALITA!
WWWI-SSSSHH
WWISH
SSSHWASSHH
TWAK

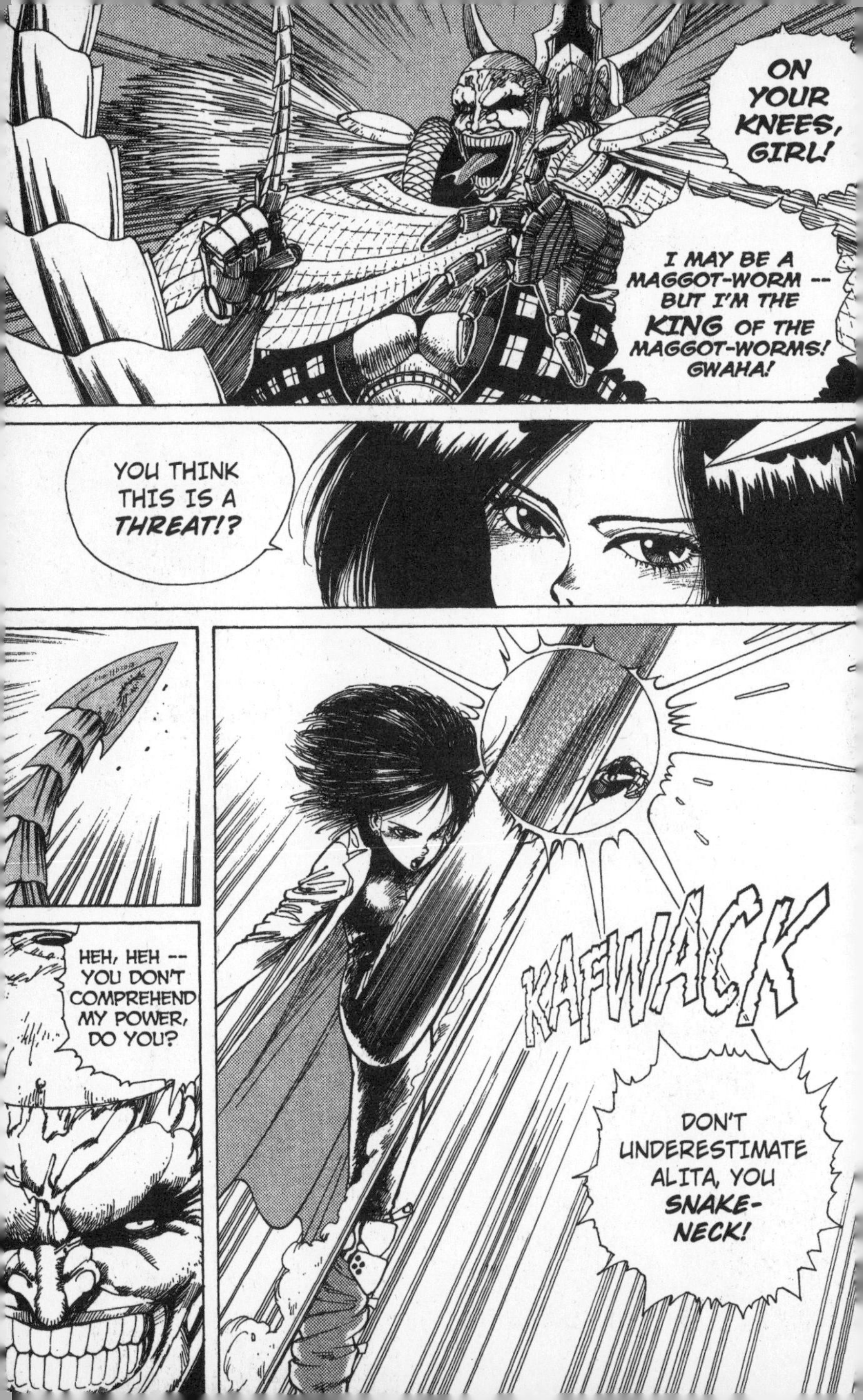
ON YOUR KNEES, GIRL!
I MAY BE A MAGGOT-WORM -- BUT I'M THE KING OF THE MAGGOT-WORMS! GWAHA!
YOU THINK THIS IS A THREAT!?
KAFWACK
DON'T UNDERESTIMATE ALITA, YOU SNAKE-NECK!
HEH, HEH -- YOU DON'T COMPREHEND MY POWER, DO YOU?

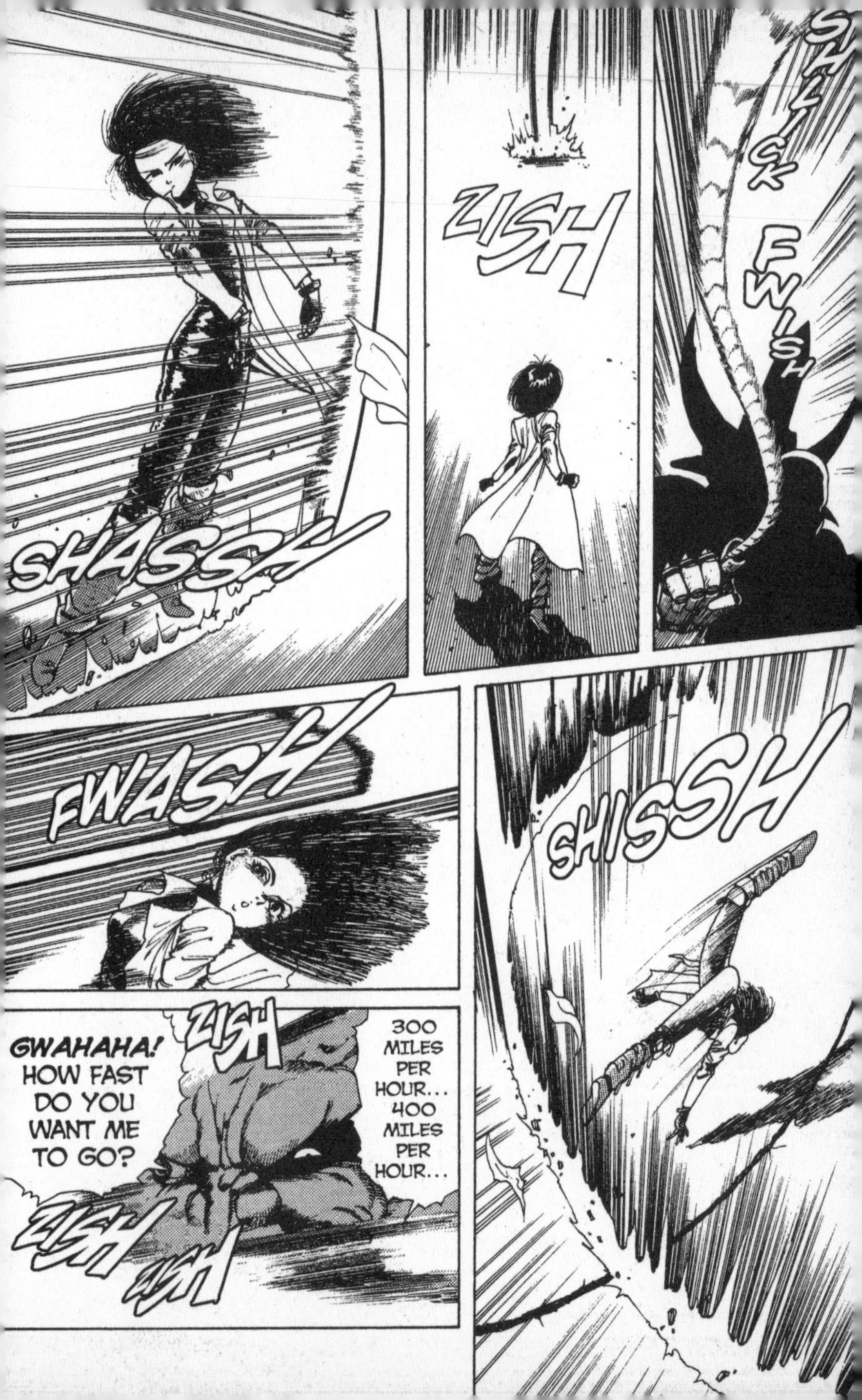
SHLICK
FWISH
ZISH
SHASSH
SHISSH
FWASH
300 MILES PER HOUR... 400 MILES PER HOUR...
ZISH
GWAHAHA! HOW FAST DO YOU WANT ME TO GO?
ZISH
ZISH

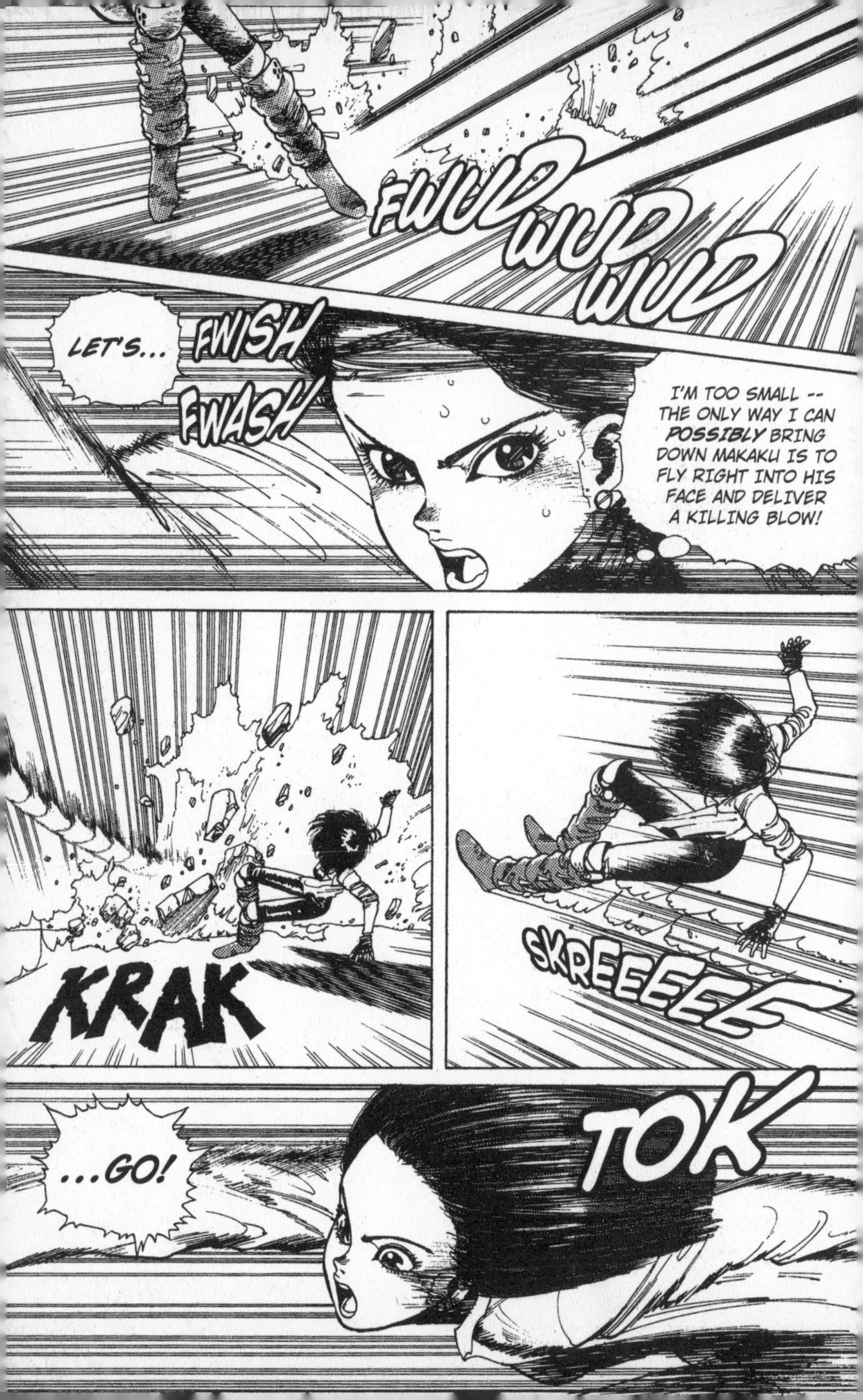
FWUUD WUUD WUUD
I'M TOO SMALL -- THE ONLY WAY I CAN POSSIBLY BRING DOWN MAKAKU IS TO FLY RIGHT INTO HIS FACE AND DELIVER A KILLING BLOW!
LET'S...
FWISH
FWASH
SKREEEEEE
KRAK
TOK
...GO!

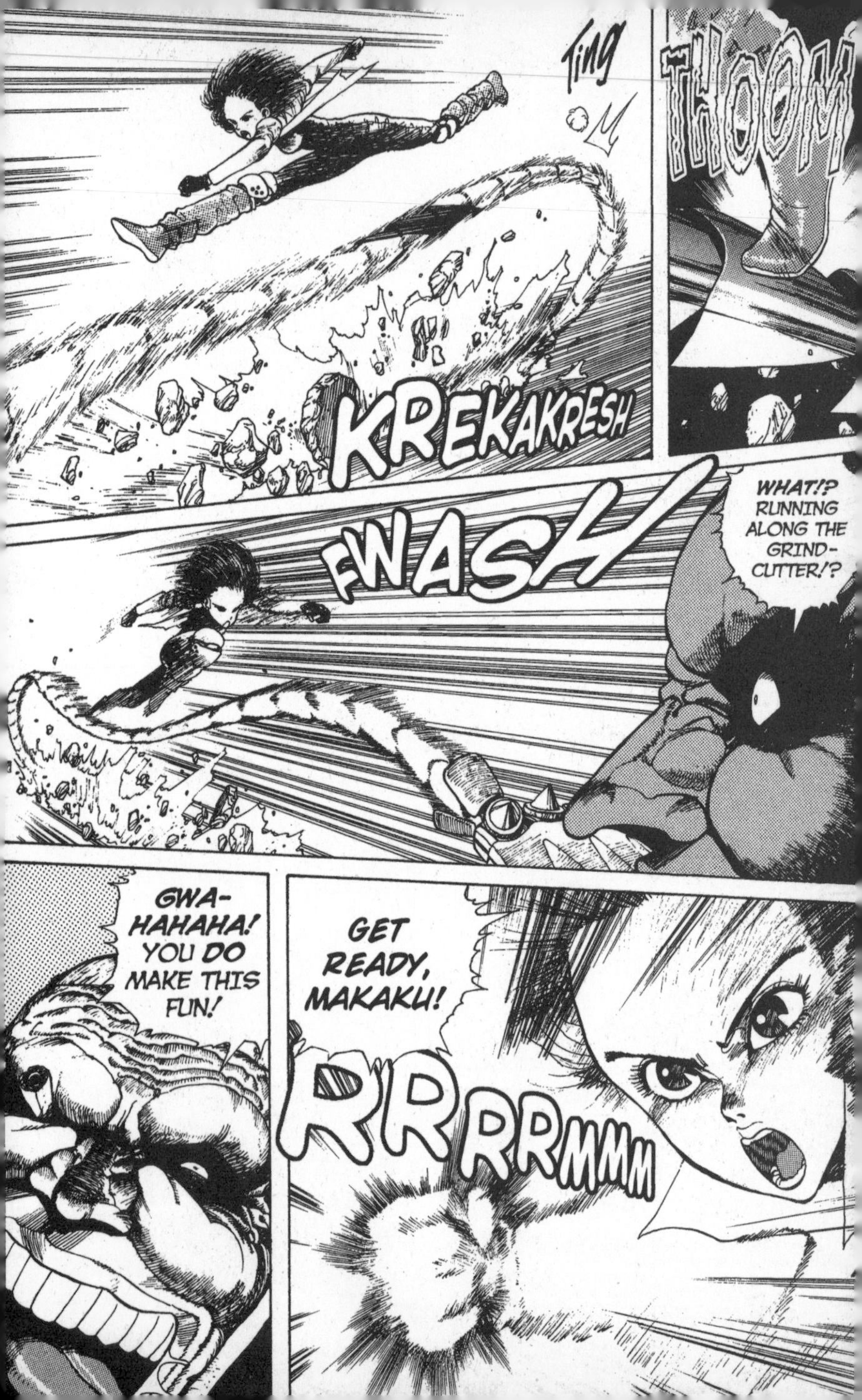
THOOM
Ting
KREKAKRESH
WHAT!? RUNNING ALONG THE GRIND-CUTTER!?
FWASH
GET READY, MAKAKU!
RRRRMMM
GWA-HAHAHA! YOU DO MAKE THIS FUN!

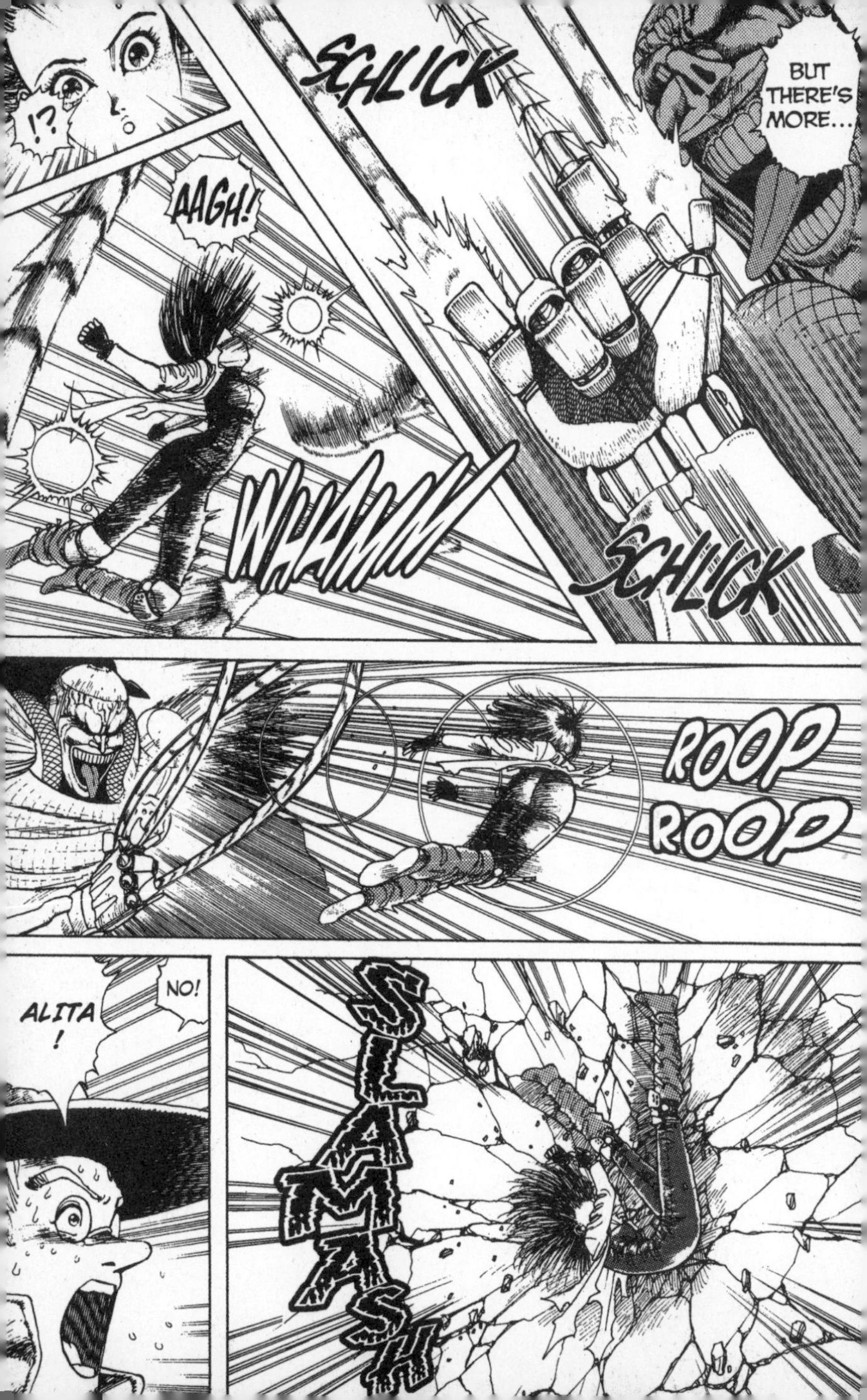

SCHLICK
BUT THERE'S MORE...
SCHLICK
!?
AAGH!
WHAMM
ROOP ROOP
SLAMASH
NO!
ALITA!

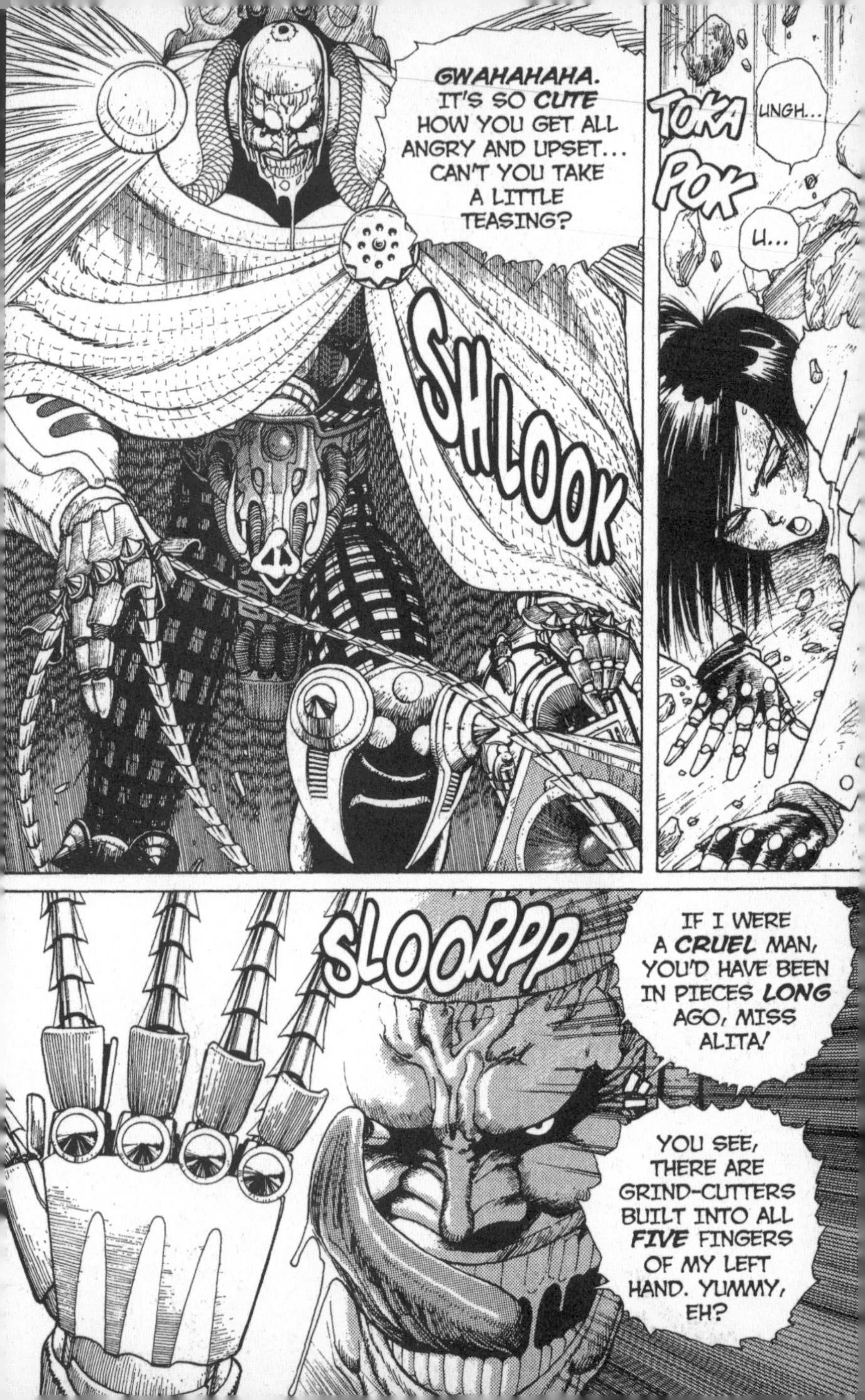
TOKA
UNGH...
POK
U...
GWAHAHAHA. IT'S SO CUTE HOW YOU GET ALL ANGRY AND UPSET... CAN'T YOU TAKE A LITTLE TEASING?
SHLOOK
SLOORPP
IF I WERE A CRUEL MAN, YOU'D HAVE BEEN IN PIECES LONG AGO, MISS ALITA!
YOU SEE, THERE ARE GRIND-CUTTERS BUILT INTO ALL FIVE FINGERS OF MY LEFT HAND. YUMMY, EH?

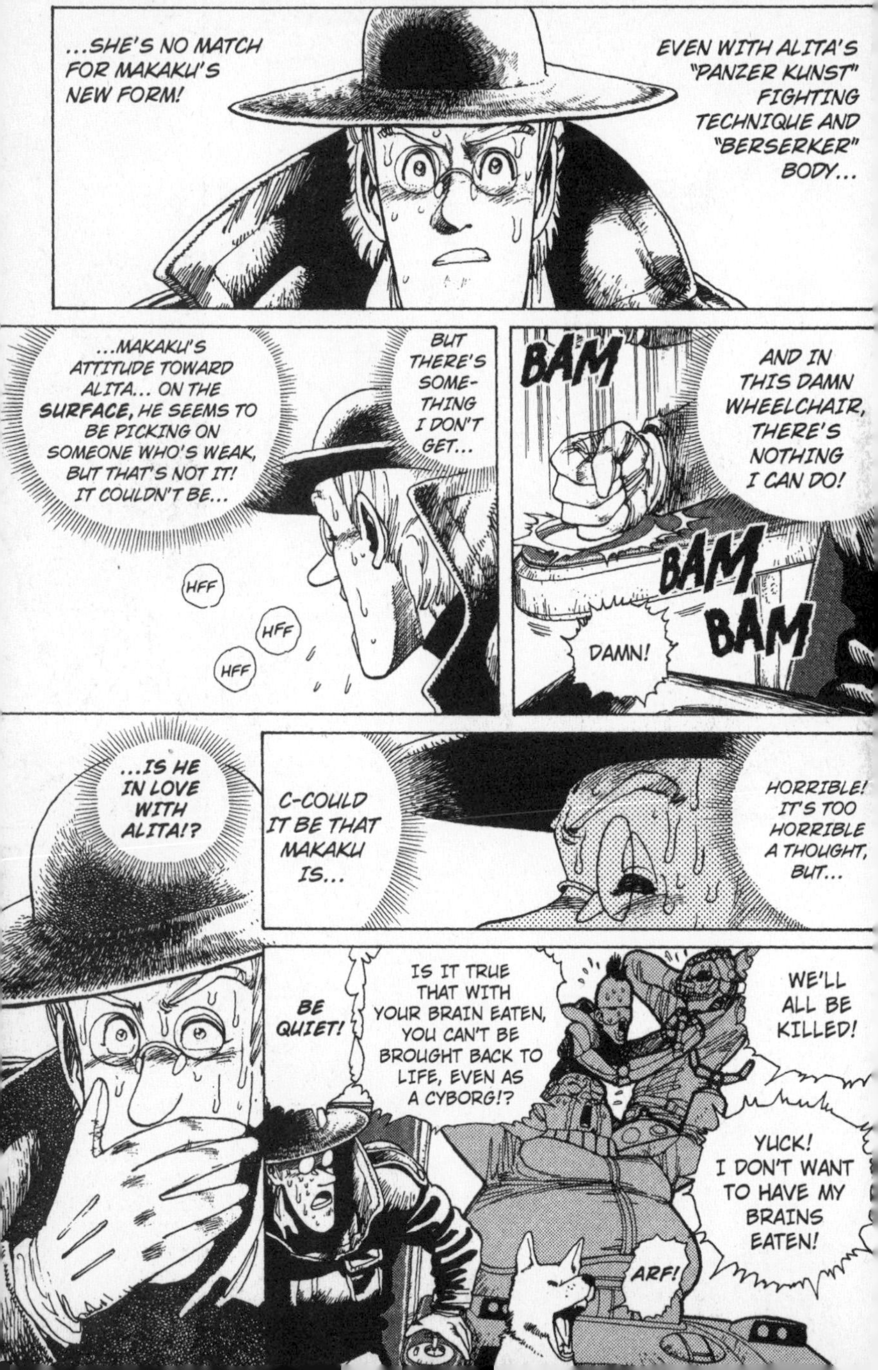
EVEN WITH ALITA'S "PANZER KUNST" FIGHTING TECHNIQUE AND "BERSERKER" BODY...
...SHE'S NO MATCH FOR MAKAKU'S NEW FORM!
BAM
AND IN THIS DAMN WHEELCHAIR, THERE'S NOTHING I CAN DO!
BAM
BAM
DAMN!
BUT THERE'S SOME-THING I DON'T GET...
...MAKAKU'S ATTITUDE TOWARD ALITA... ON THE SURFACE, HE SEEMS TO BE PICKING ON SOMEONE WHO'S WEAK, BUT THAT'S NOT IT! IT COULDN'T BE...
HFF
HFF
HFF
HORRIBLE! IT'S TOO HORRIBLE A THOUGHT, BUT...
C-COULD IT BE THAT MAKAKU IS...
WE'LL ALL BE KILLED!
IS IT TRUE THAT WITH YOUR BRAIN EATEN, YOU CAN'T BE BROUGHT BACK TO LIFE, EVEN AS A CYBORG!?
BE QUIET!
YUCK! I DON'T WANT TO HAVE MY BRAINS EATEN!
ARF!
...IS HE IN LOVE WITH ALITA!?

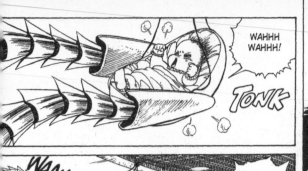

WAHHH WAHHH!

TONK

WAAHH!

K- KOYOMI!

SHLICK

!

GWA- HAHAHA!

P-PLEASE! THE BABY! GIVE KOYOMI BACK!

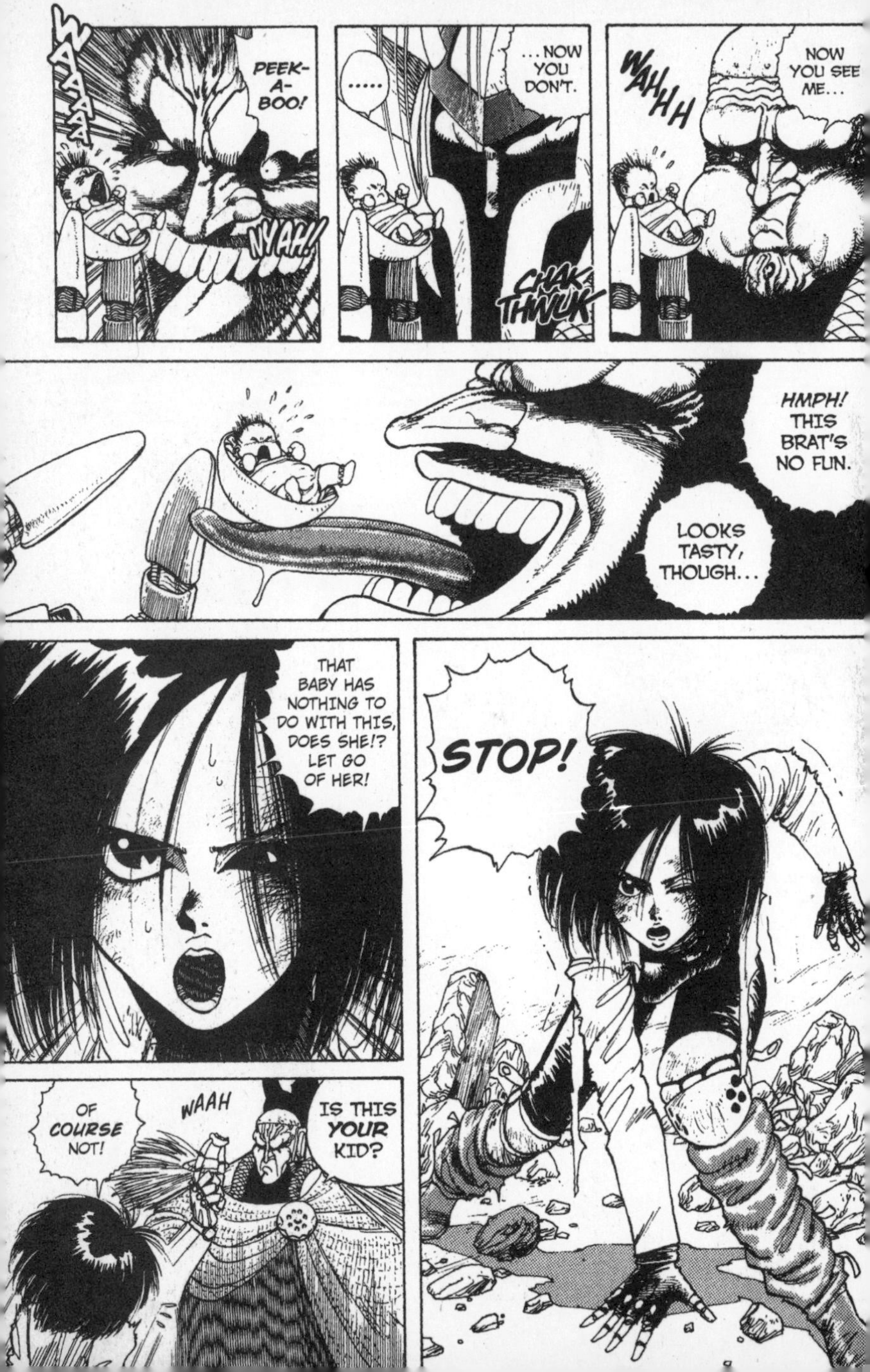

WAHHH
NOW YOU SEE ME...
......
...NOW YOU DON'T.
CHAK THWUK
WAAAAA
PEEK-A-BOO!
NYAH!
HMPH! THIS BRAT'S NO FUN.
LOOKS TASTY, THOUGH...
STOP!
THAT BABY HAS NOTHING TO DO WITH THIS, DOES SHE!? LET GO OF HER!
IS THIS YOUR KID?
WAAH
OF COURSE NOT!

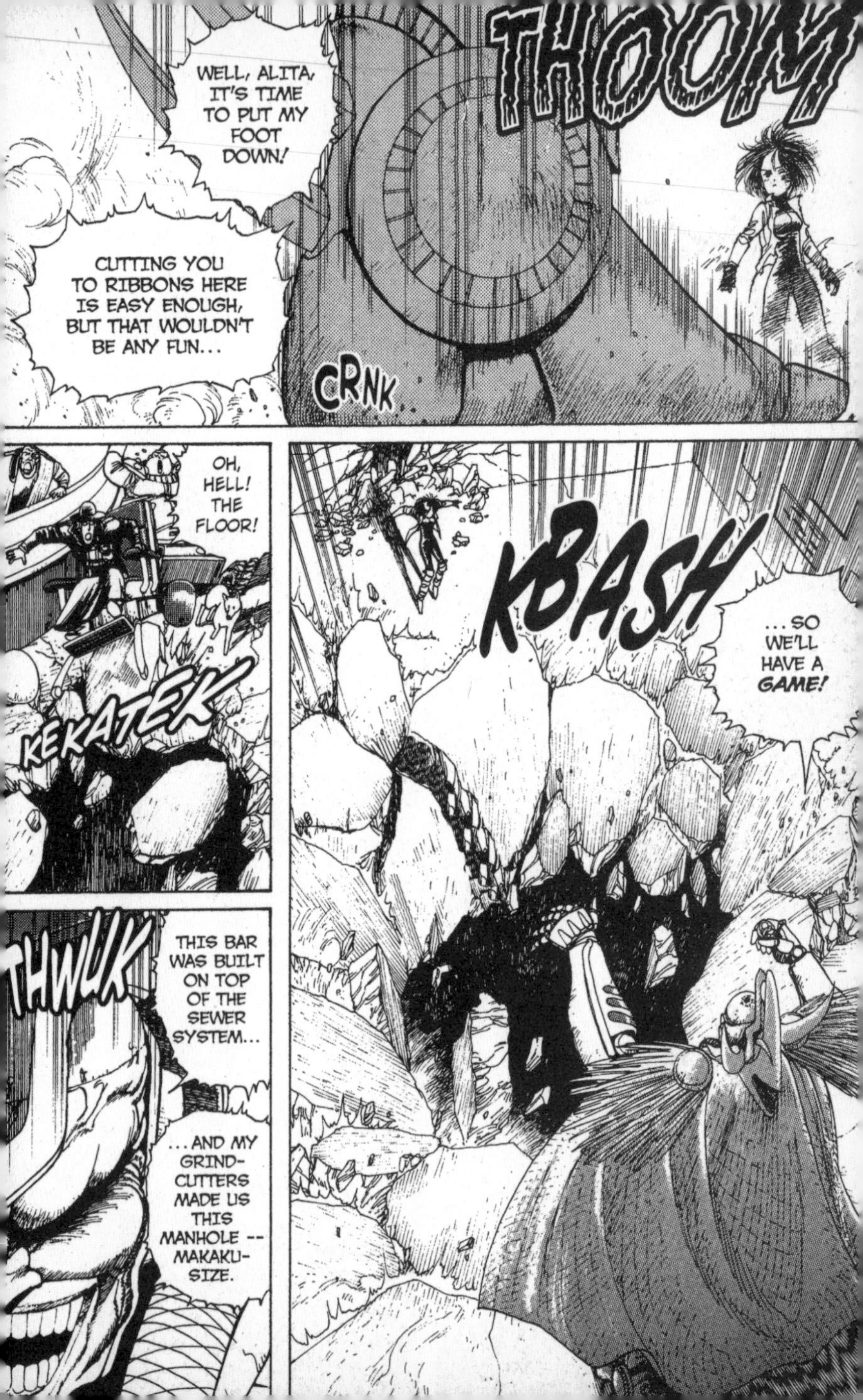
THOOM
WELL, ALITA, IT'S TIME TO PUT MY FOOT DOWN!
CUTTING YOU TO RIBBONS HERE IS EASY ENOUGH, BUT THAT WOULDN'T BE ANY FUN...
CRNK
KBASH
...SO WE'LL HAVE A GAME!
OH, HELL! THE FLOOR!
KEKATEK
THWUK
THIS BAR WAS BUILT ON TOP OF THE SEWER SYSTEM...
...AND MY GRIND-CUTTERS MADE US THIS MANHOLE -- MAKAKU-SIZE.

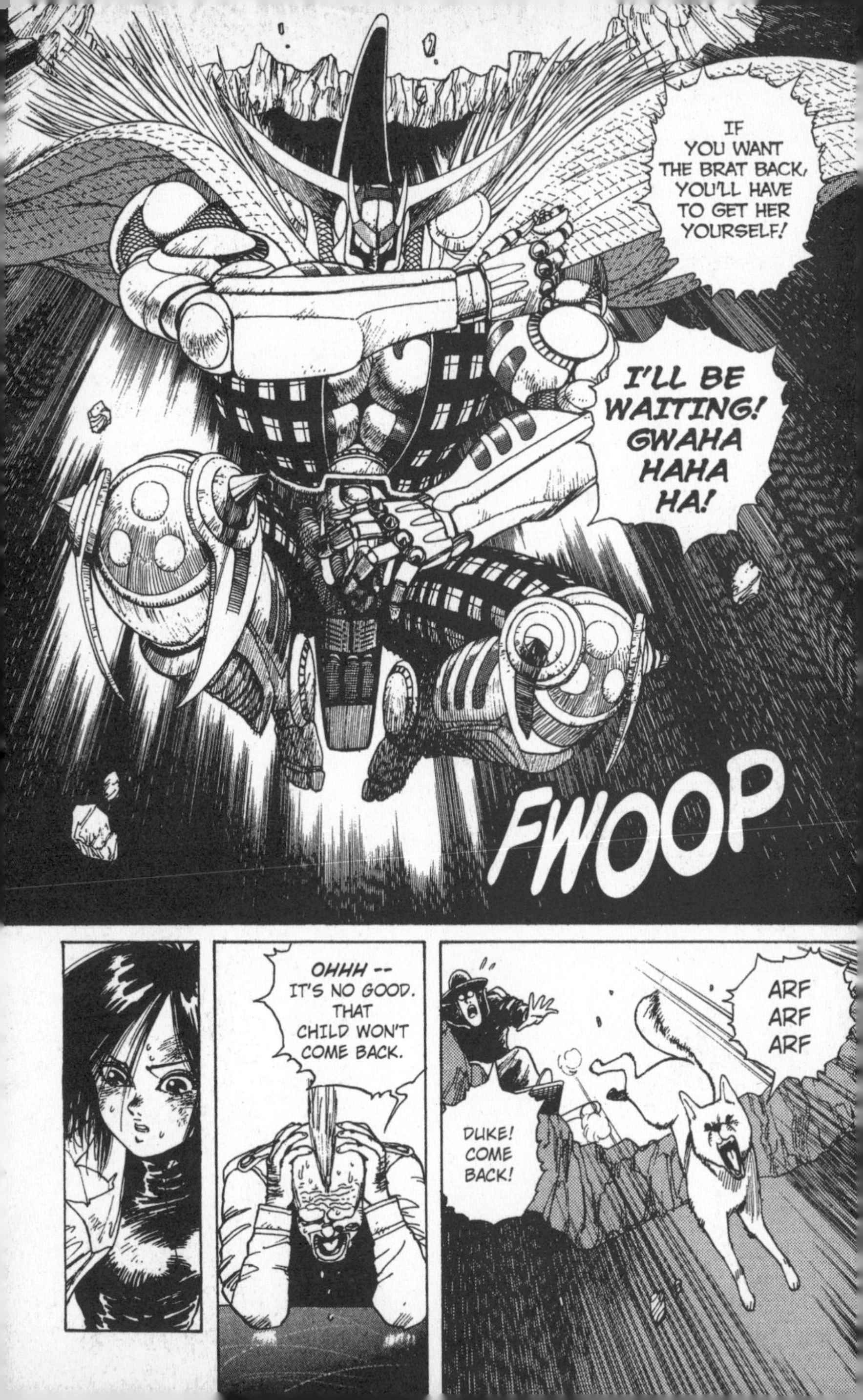
IF YOU WANT THE BRAT BACK, YOU'LL HAVE TO GET HER YOURSELF!
I'LL BE WAITING! GWAHA HAHA HA!
FWOOP
ARF ARF ARF
DUKE! COME BACK!
OHHH -- IT'S NO GOOD. THAT CHILD WON'T COME BACK.

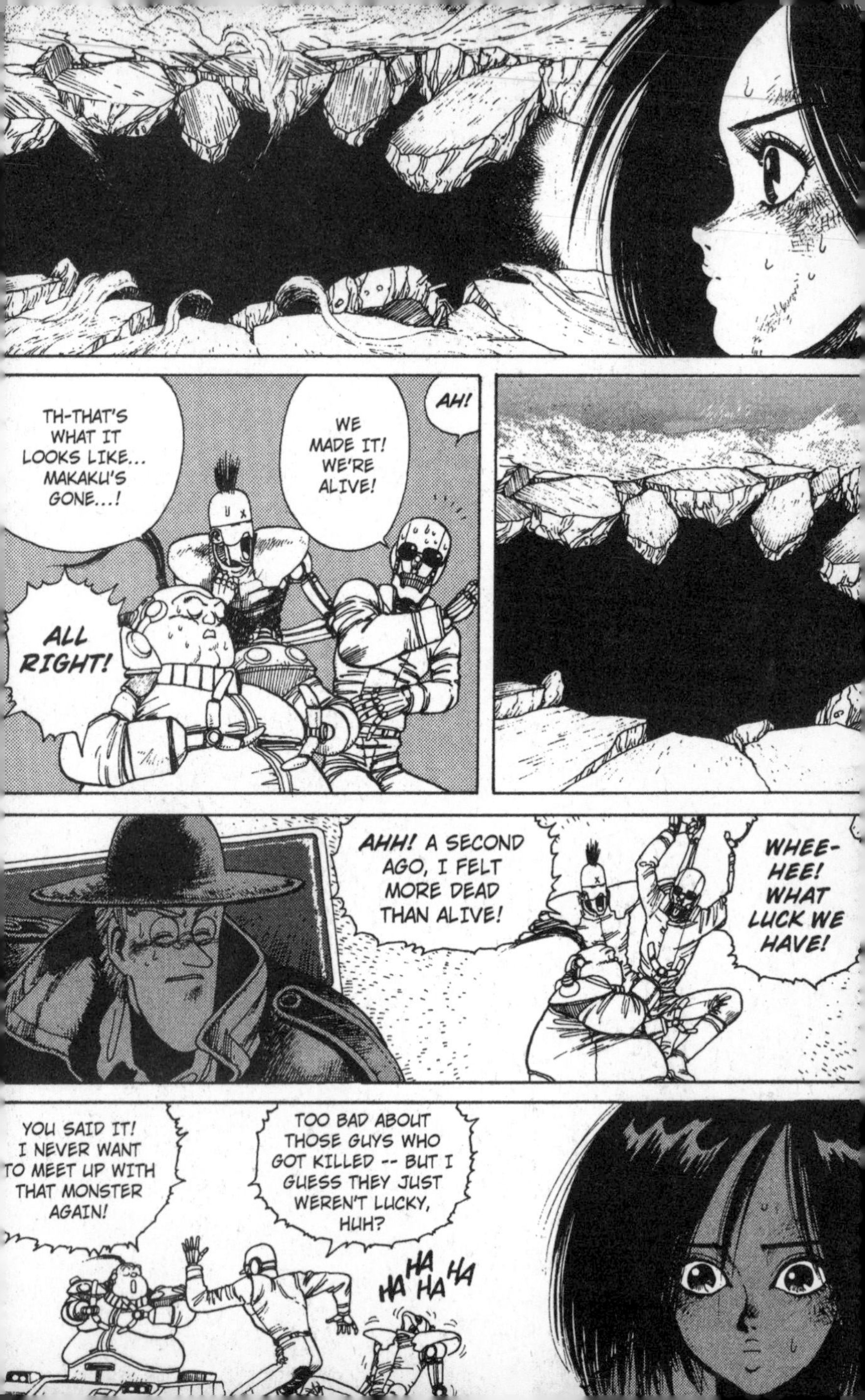
AH!
WE MADE IT! WE'RE ALIVE!
TH-THAT'S WHAT IT LOOKS LIKE... MAKAKU'S GONE...!
ALL RIGHT!
WHEE-HEE! WHAT LUCK WE HAVE!
AHH! A SECOND AGO, I FELT MORE DEAD THAN ALIVE!
TOO BAD ABOUT THOSE GUYS WHO GOT KILLED -- BUT I GUESS THEY JUST WEREN'T LUCKY, HUH?
YOU SAID IT! I NEVER WANT TO MEET UP WITH THAT MONSTER AGAIN!
HA HA HA HA

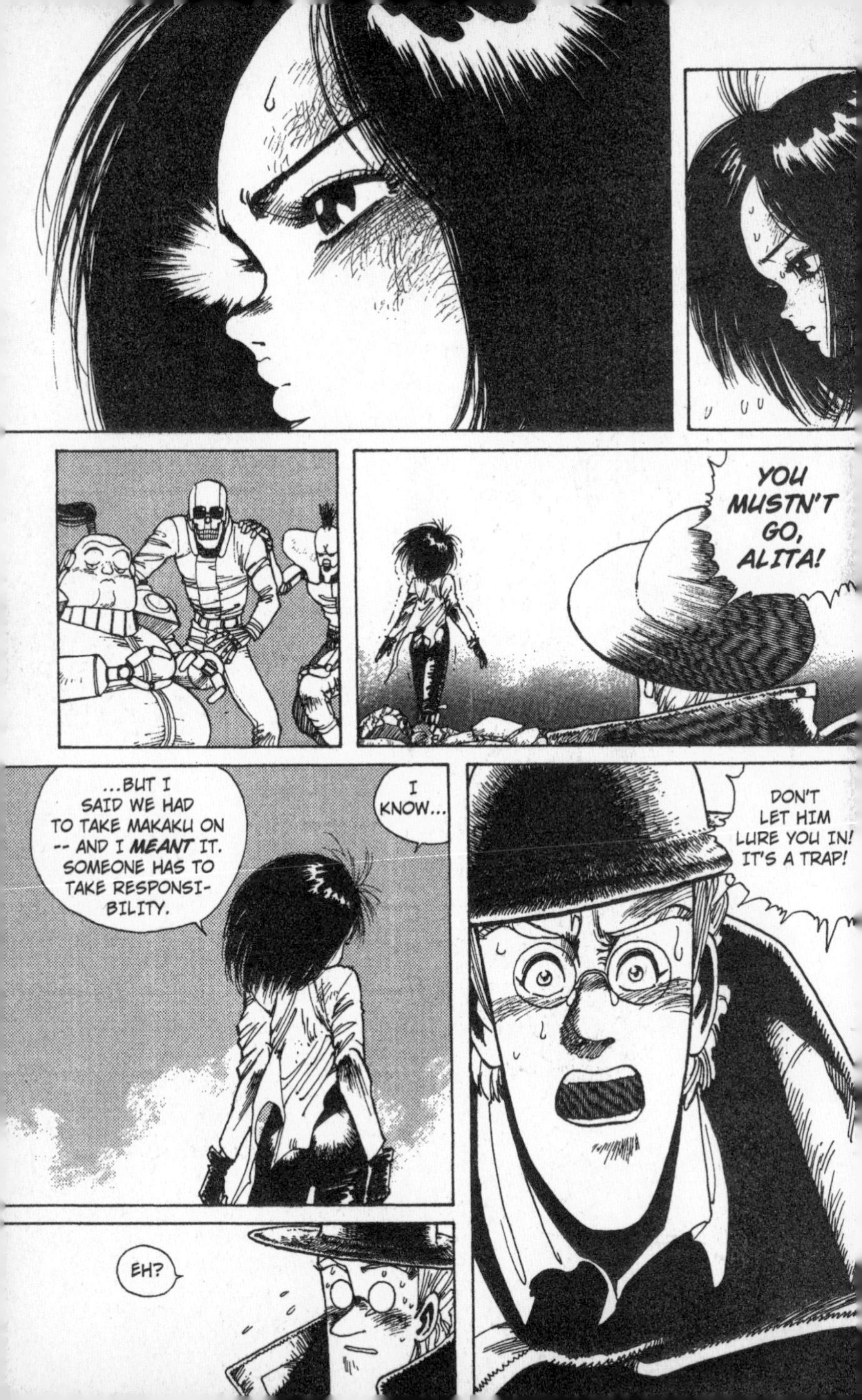
YOU MUSTN'T GO, ALITA!
DON'T LET HIM LURE YOU IN! IT'S A TRAP!
I KNOW...
...BUT I SAID WE HAD TO TAKE MAKAKU ON -- AND I MEANT IT. SOMEONE HAS TO TAKE RESPONSI-BILITY.
EH?

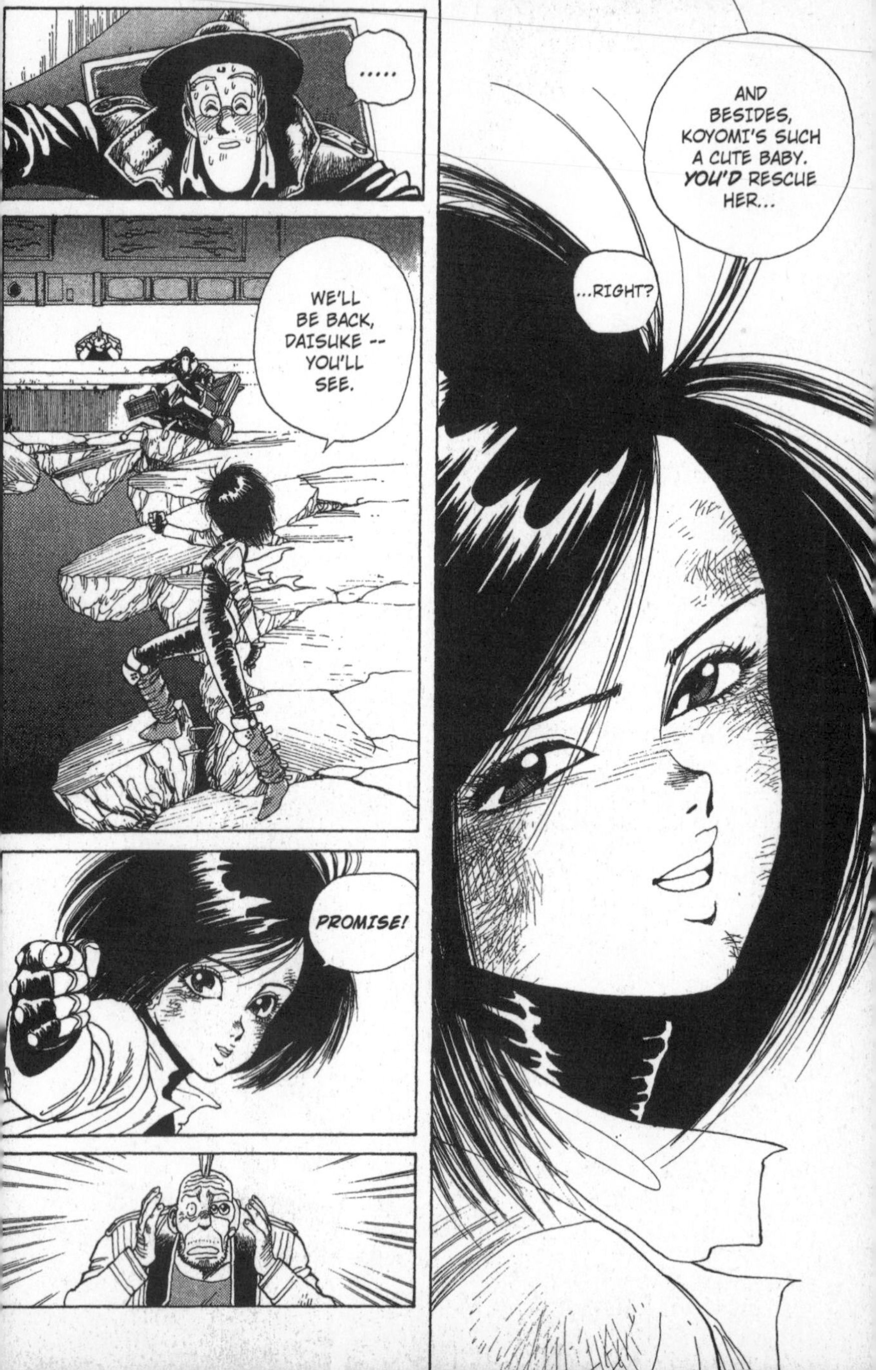

AND BESIDES, KOYOMI'S SUCH A CUTE BABY. ***YOU'D*** RESCUE HER...
...RIGHT?
.....
WE'LL BE BACK, DAISUKE -- YOU'LL SEE.
PROMISE!

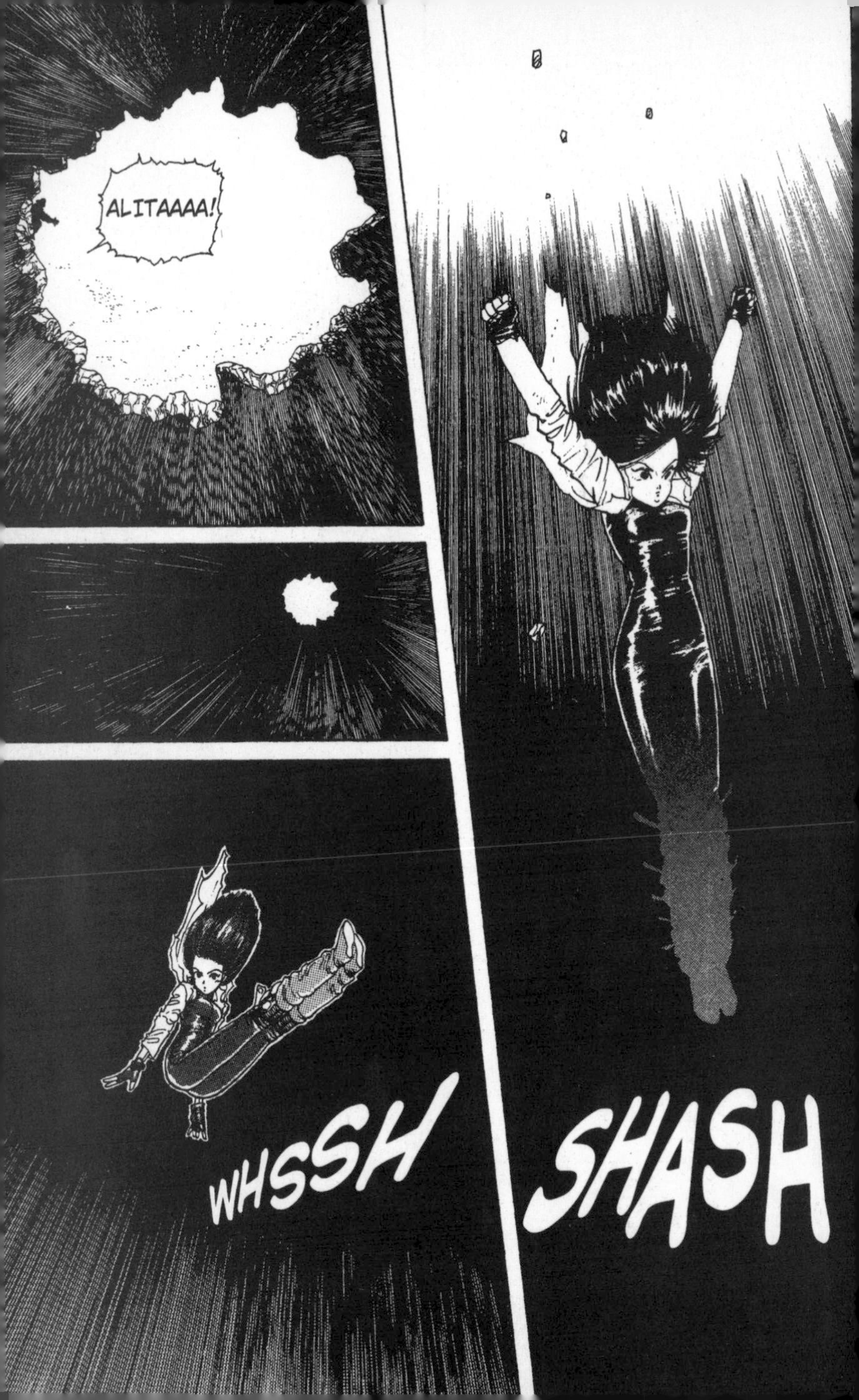
SHASH
ALITAAAA!
WHSSH

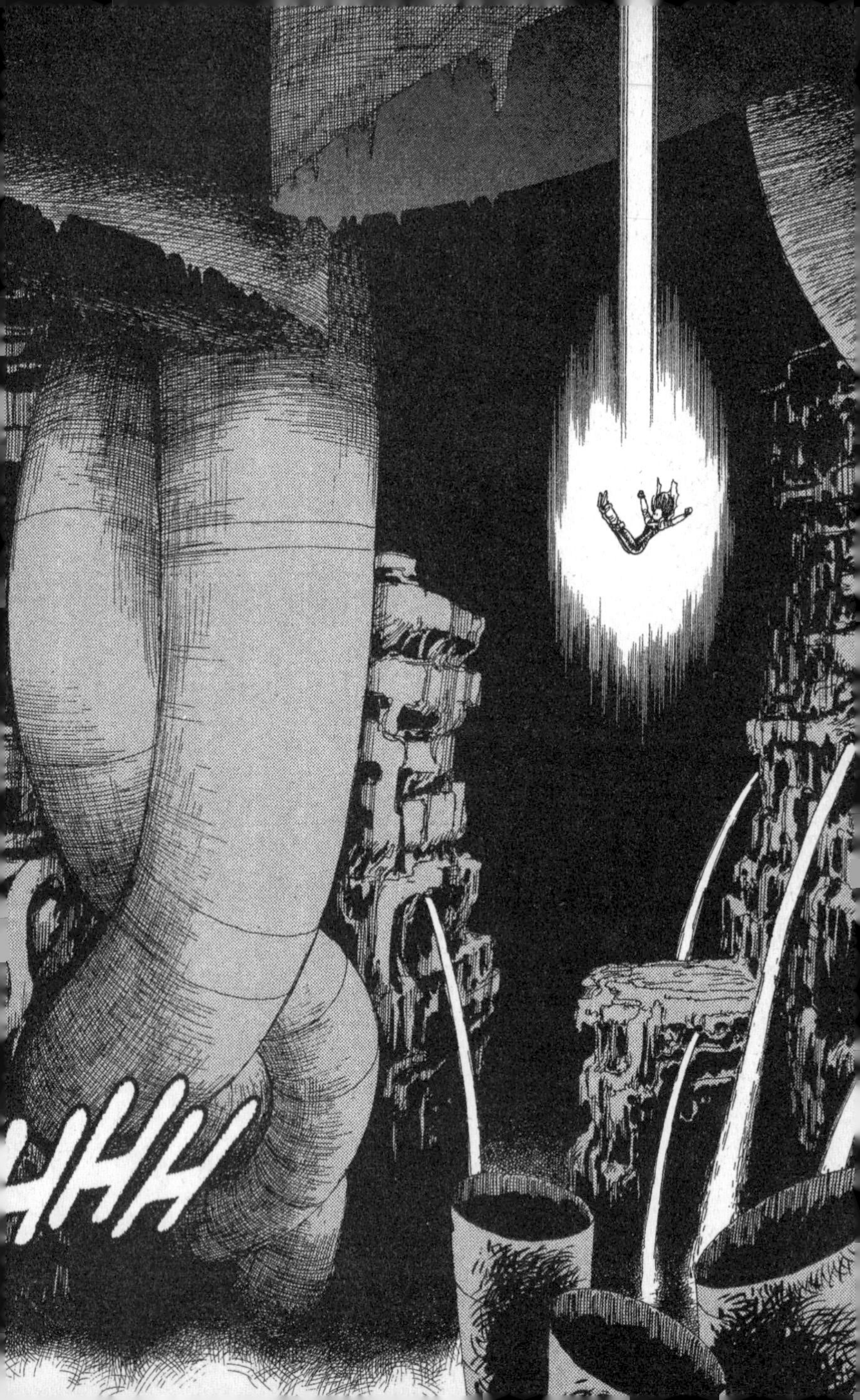
HHH

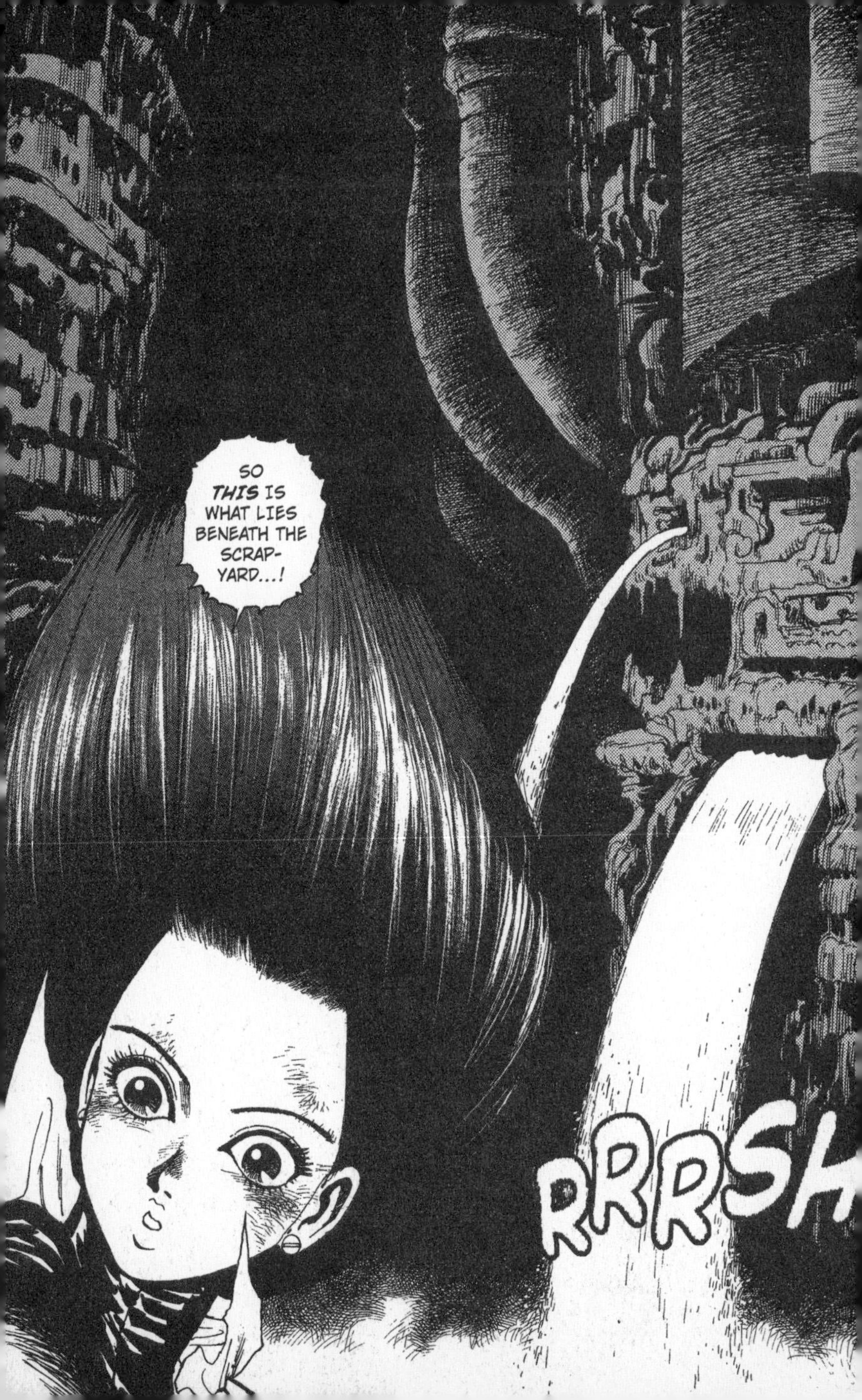
SO *THIS* IS WHAT LIES BENEATH THE SCRAP-YARD...!
RRRSH

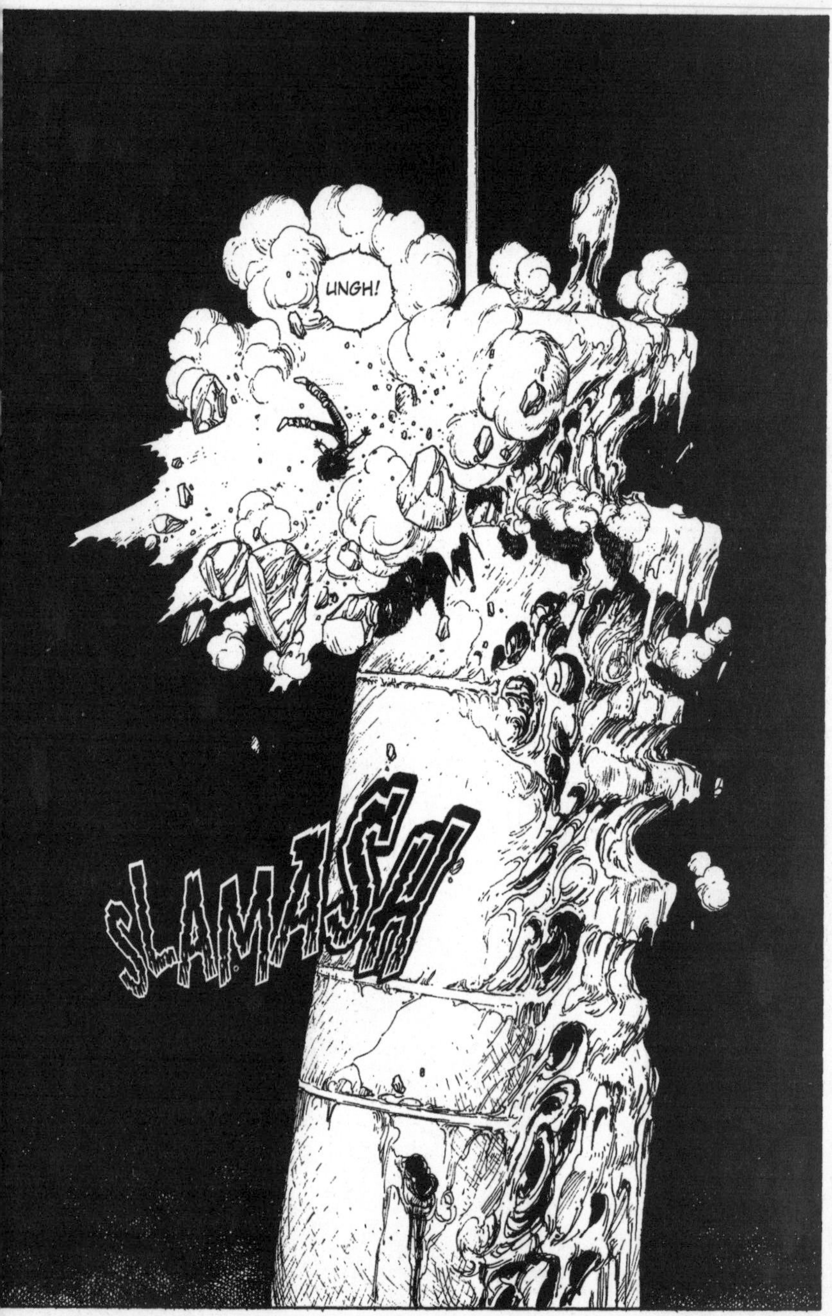
UNGH!
SLAMASH

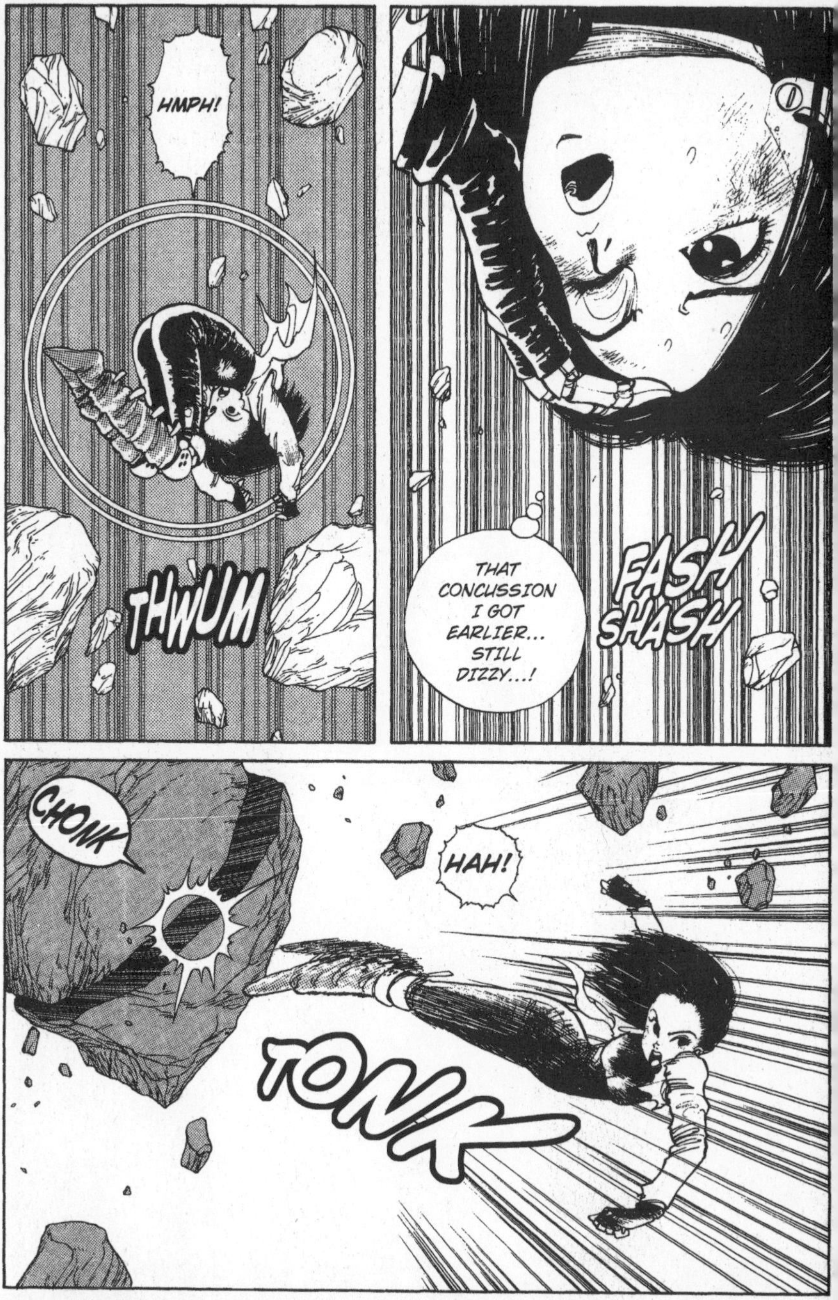
THAT CONCUSSION I GOT EARLIER... STILL DIZZY...!
FASH SHASH
HMPH!
THWUM
HAH!
CHONK
TONK

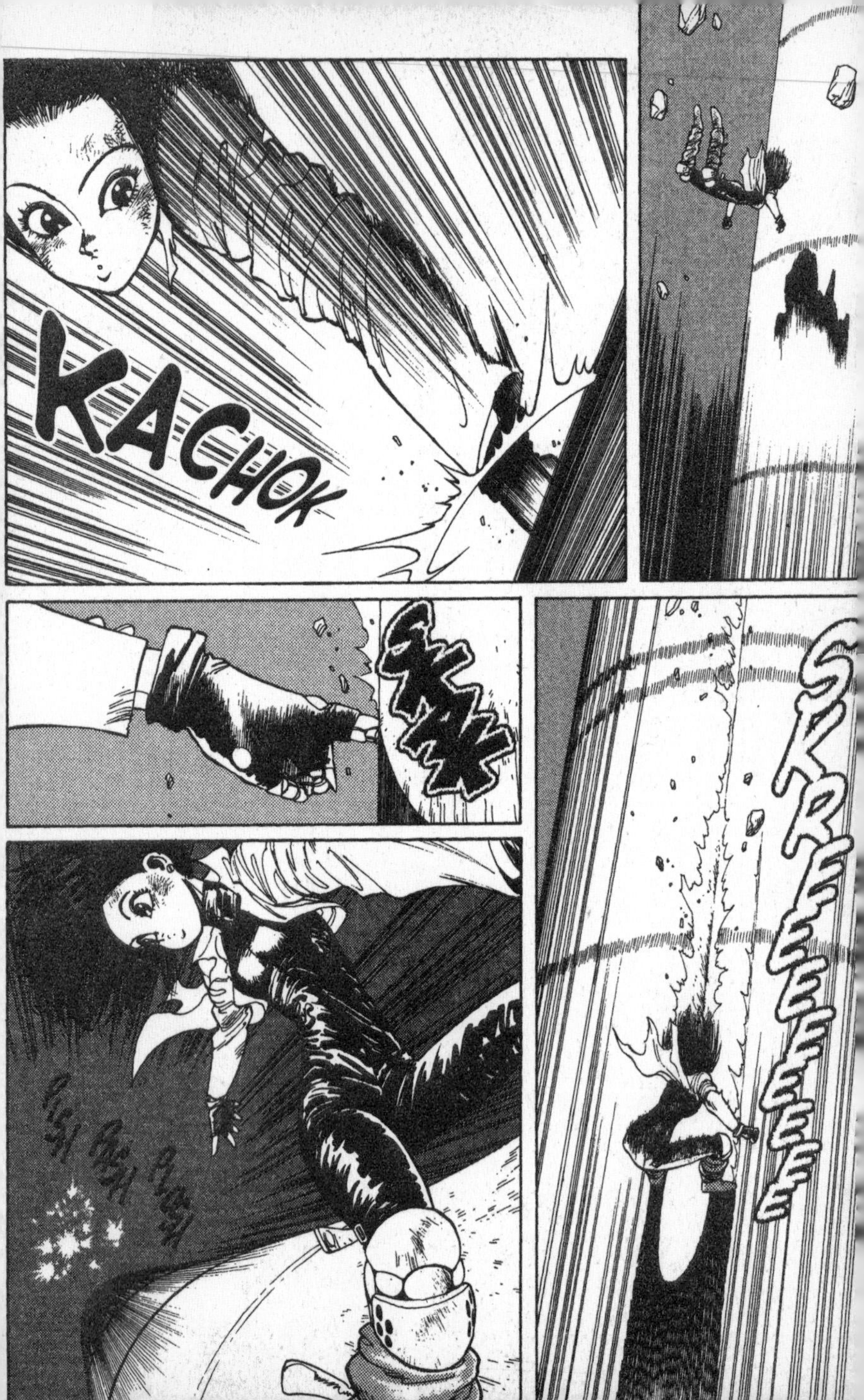
KACHOK
SKREEEEEEEE

KREEEK

MAKAKU...

...WHERE ARE YOU?

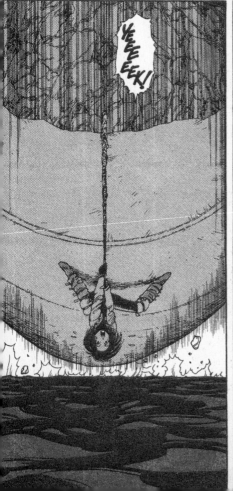

YEEEEEK!

!?

KREKRESH

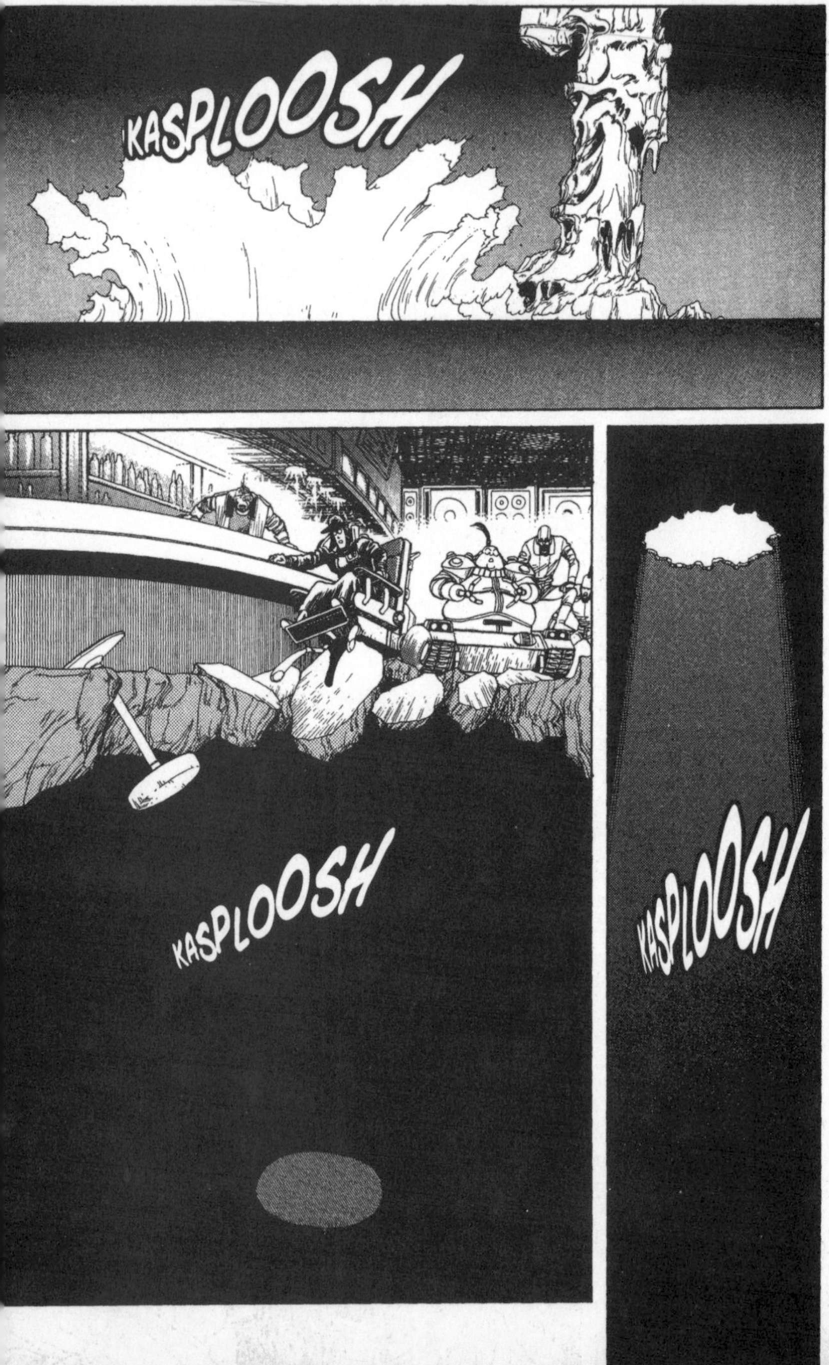
KASPLOOSH
KASPLOOSH
KASPLOOSH

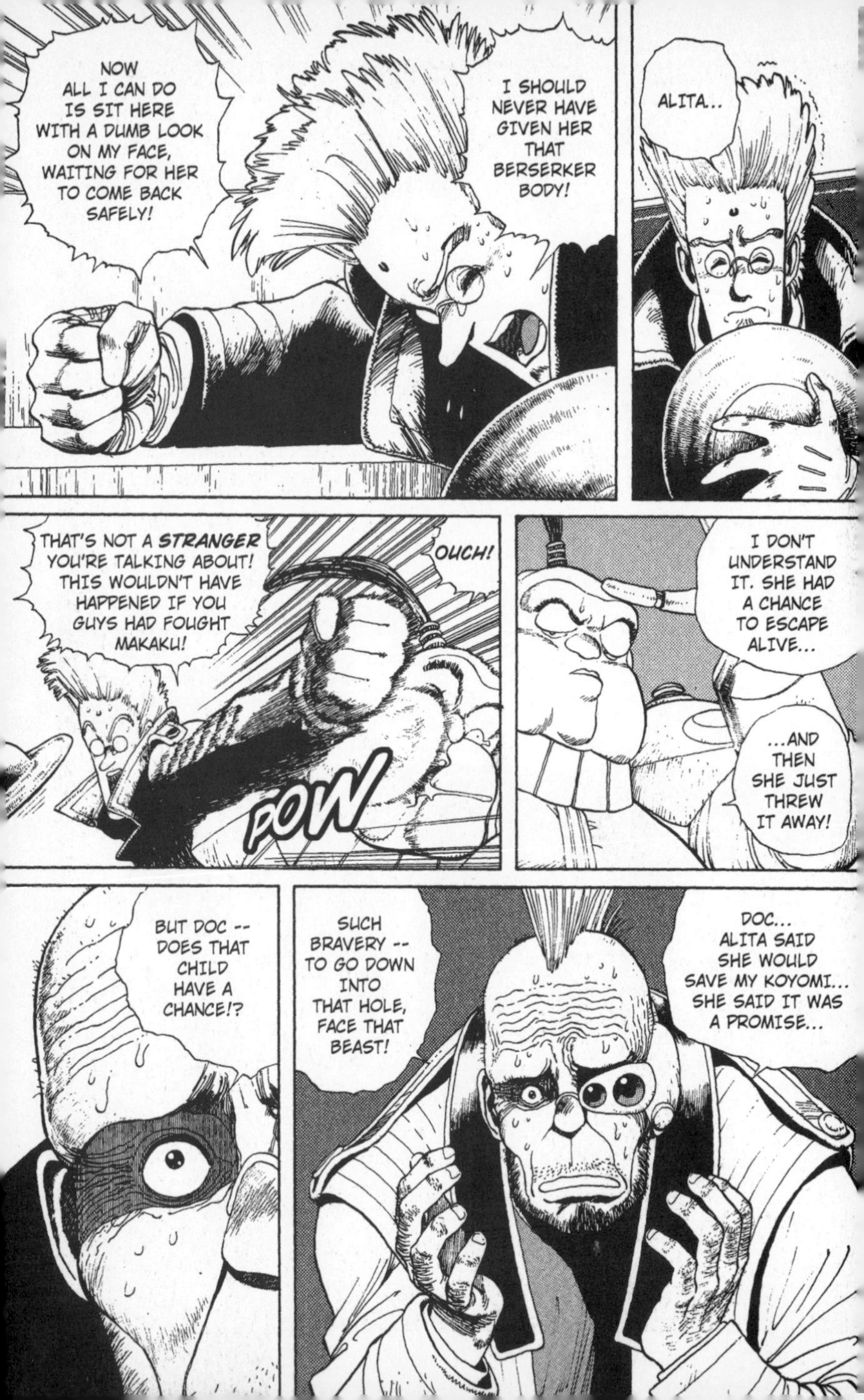
ALITA...
I SHOULD NEVER HAVE GIVEN HER THAT BERSERKER BODY!
NOW ALL I CAN DO IS SIT HERE WITH A DUMB LOOK ON MY FACE, WAITING FOR HER TO COME BACK SAFELY!
I DON'T UNDERSTAND IT. SHE HAD A CHANCE TO ESCAPE ALIVE...
...AND THEN SHE JUST THREW IT AWAY!
OUCH!
THAT'S NOT A STRANGER YOU'RE TALKING ABOUT! THIS WOULDN'T HAVE HAPPENED IF YOU GUYS HAD FOUGHT MAKAKU!
POW
DOC... ALITA SAID SHE WOULD SAVE MY KOYOMI... SHE SAID IT WAS A PROMISE...
SUCH BRAVERY -- TO GO DOWN INTO THAT HOLE, FACE THAT BEAST!
BUT DOC -- DOES THAT CHILD HAVE A CHANCE!?

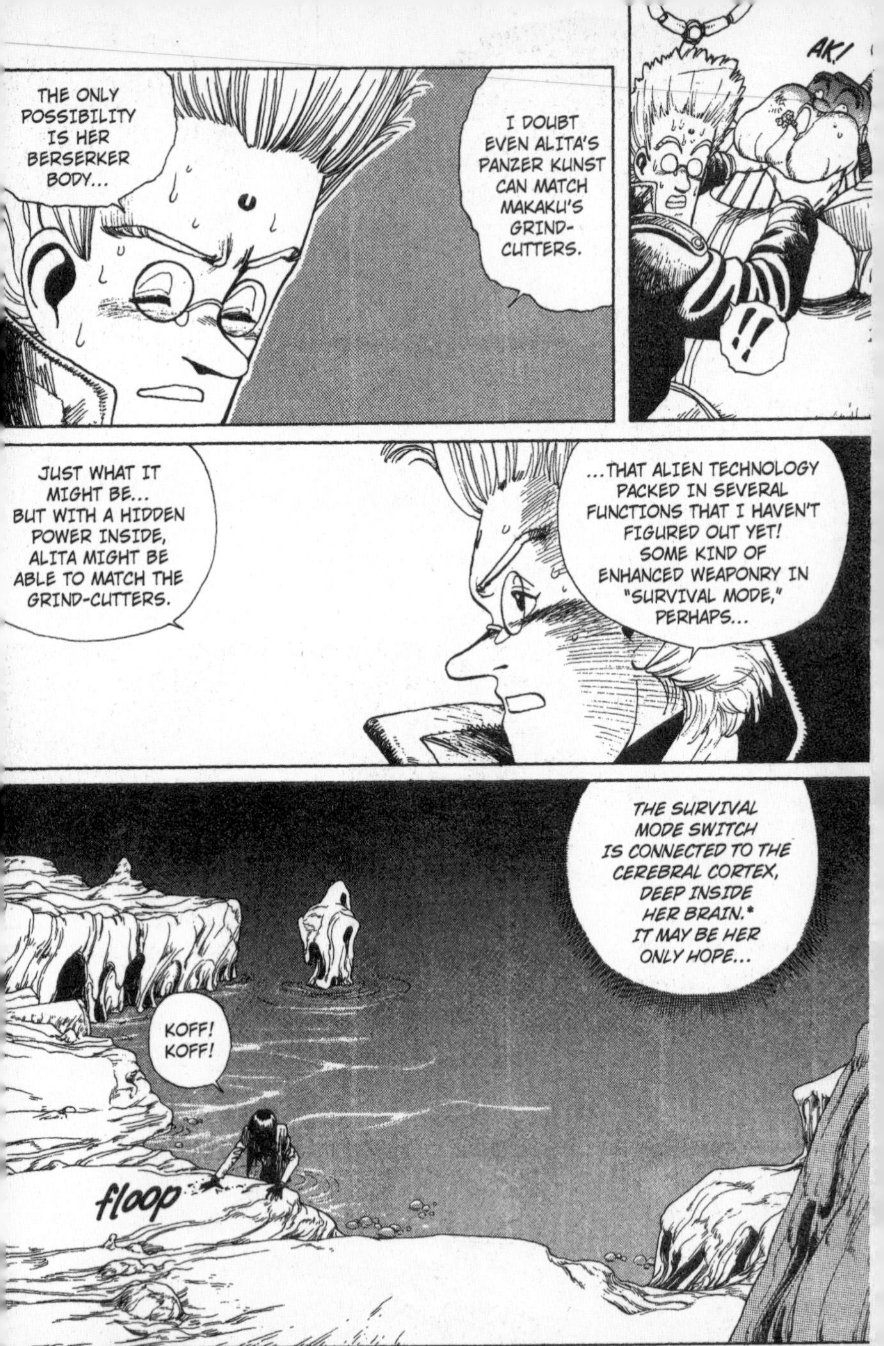
AK!
!!
I DOUBT EVEN ALITA'S PANZER KUNST CAN MATCH MAKAKU'S GRIND-CUTTERS.
THE ONLY POSSIBILITY IS HER BERSERKER BODY...
...THAT ALIEN TECHNOLOGY PACKED IN SEVERAL FUNCTIONS THAT I HAVEN'T FIGURED OUT YET! SOME KIND OF ENHANCED WEAPONRY IN "SURVIVAL MODE," PERHAPS...
JUST WHAT IT MIGHT BE... BUT WITH A HIDDEN POWER INSIDE, ALITA MIGHT BE ABLE TO MATCH THE GRIND-CUTTERS.
THE SURVIVAL MODE SWITCH IS CONNECTED TO THE CEREBRAL CORTEX, DEEP INSIDE HER BRAIN.* IT MAY BE HER ONLY HOPE...
KOFF! KOFF!
floop

CEREBRAL CORTEX: THE REGION OF THE BRAIN THAT CONTROLS LARGE-SCALE MOVEMENTS OF THE MUSCLES, THIS "CROCODILE BRAIN" MANAGES THE PRIMITIVE REPTILIAN INSTINCTIVE ACTIONS.

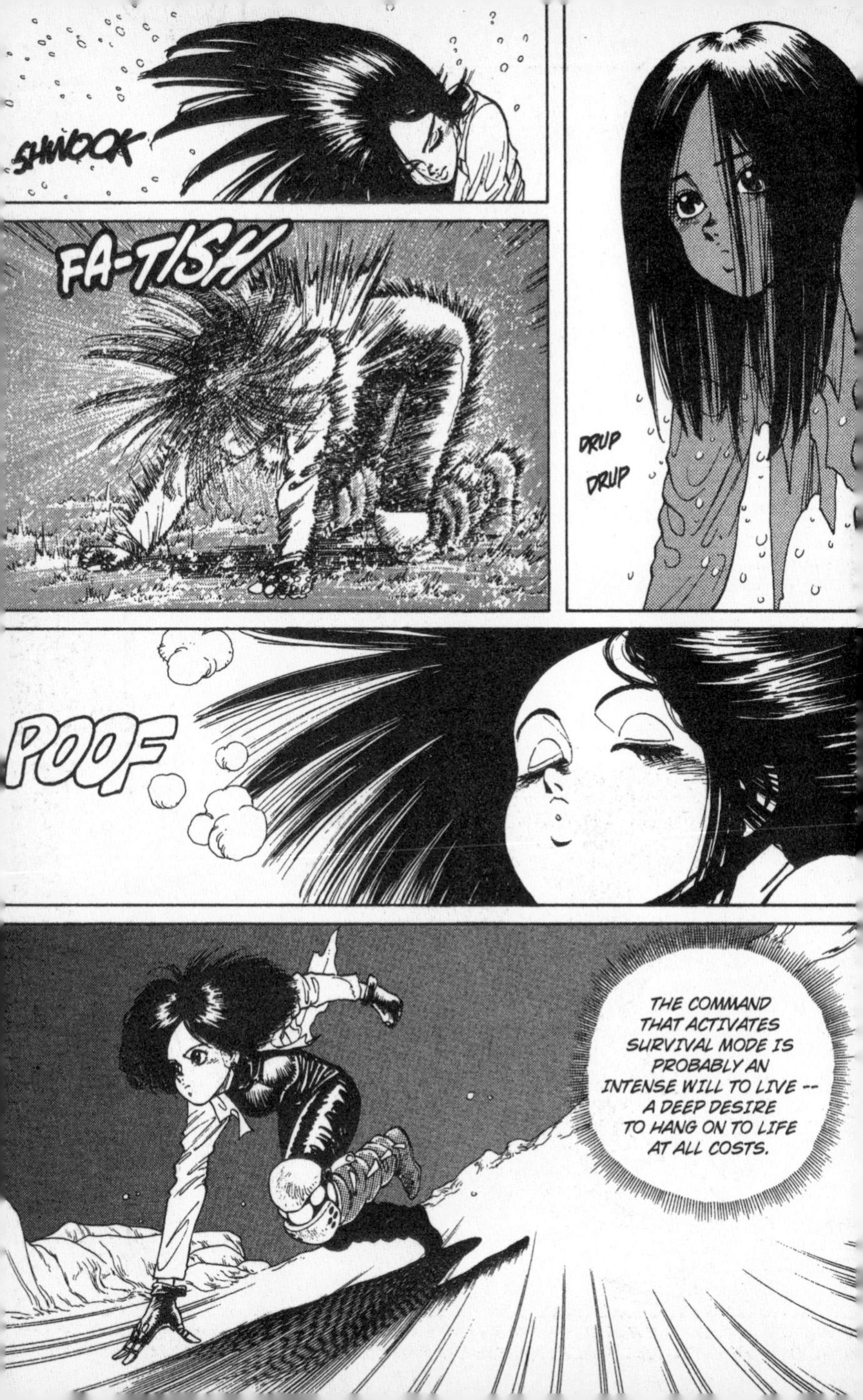
DRUP
DRUP
SHWOOCK
FA-TISH
POOF
THE COMMAND THAT ACTIVATES SURVIVAL MODE IS PROBABLY AN INTENSE WILL TO LIVE -- A DEEP DESIRE TO HANG ON TO LIFE AT ALL COSTS.

SHAAA

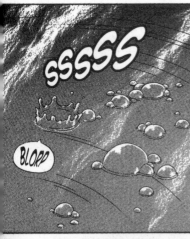

SSSSS

BLORP

I GAVE MY WORD I'D DELIVER THE BABY TO SAFETY...

BLUB

BLUB

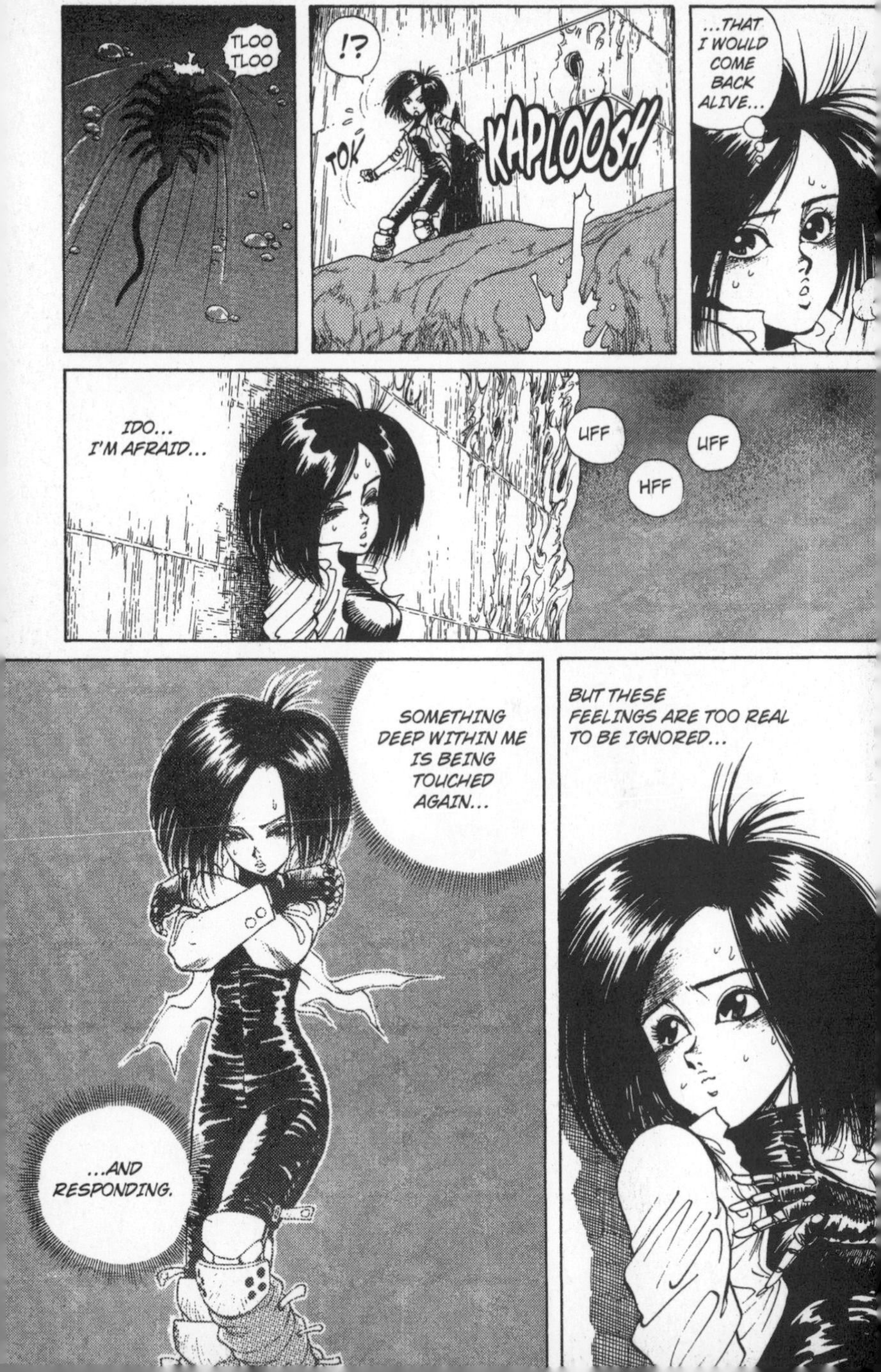
...THAT I WOULD COME BACK ALIVE...
!?
TOK
KAPLOOSH
TLOO TLOO
IDO... I'M AFRAID...
UFF
UFF
HFF
BUT THESE FEELINGS ARE TOO REAL TO BE IGNORED...
SOMETHING DEEP WITHIN ME IS BEING TOUCHED AGAIN...
...AND RESPONDING.

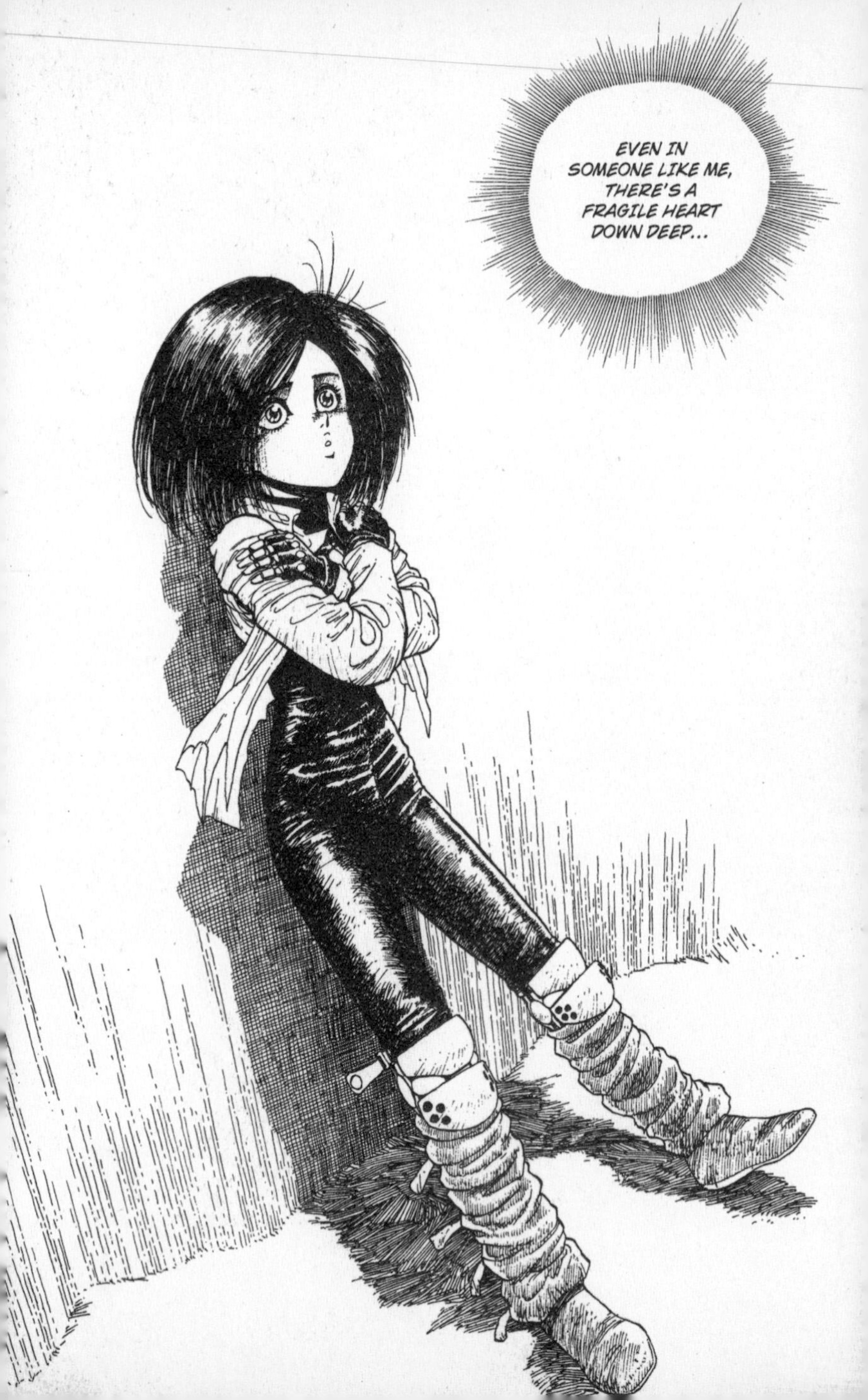
EVEN IN SOMEONE LIKE ME, THERE'S A FRAGILE HEART DOWN DEEP...

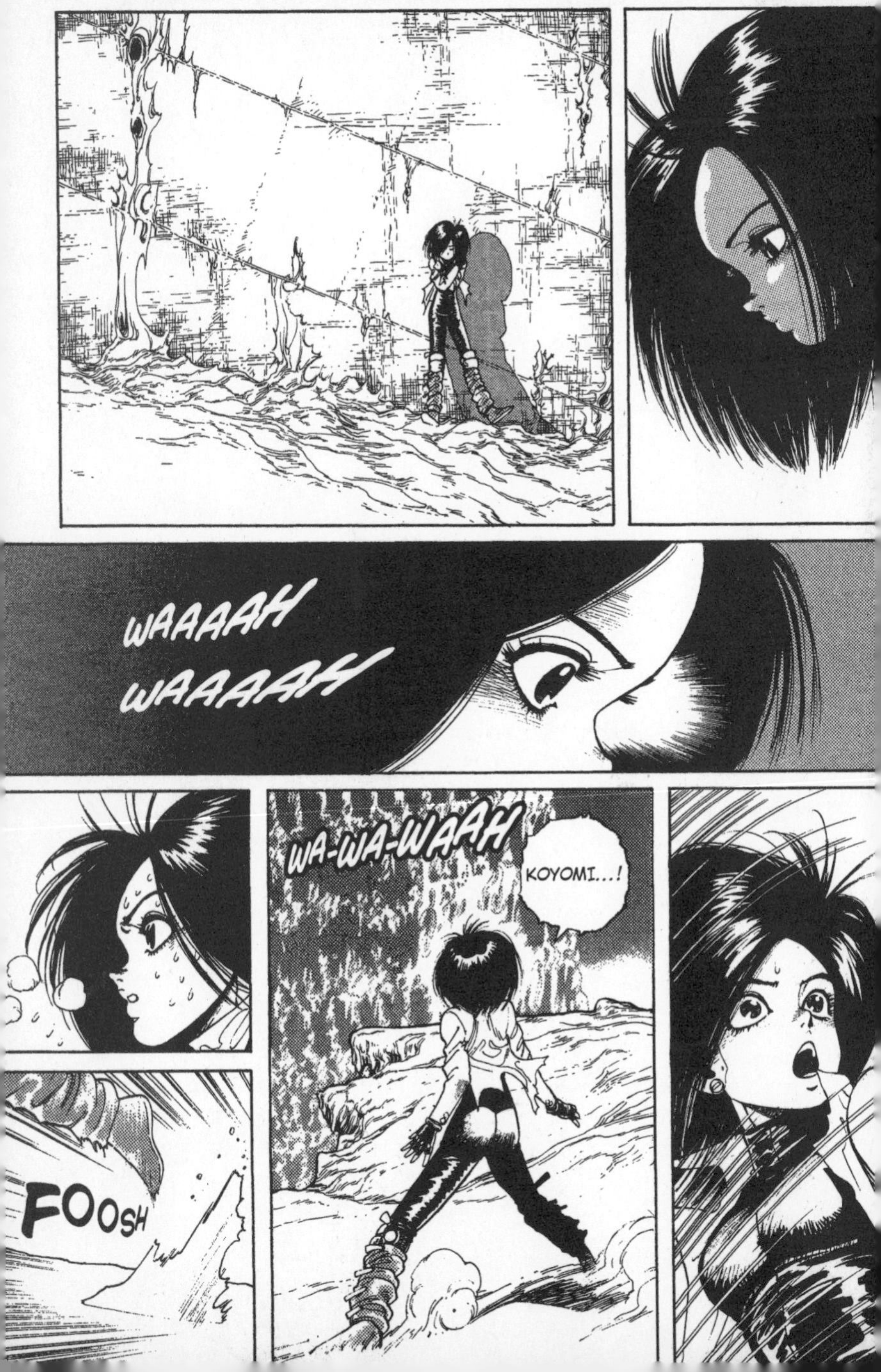
WAAAAAH
WAAAAAH
WA-WA-WAAH
KOYOMI...!
FOOSH

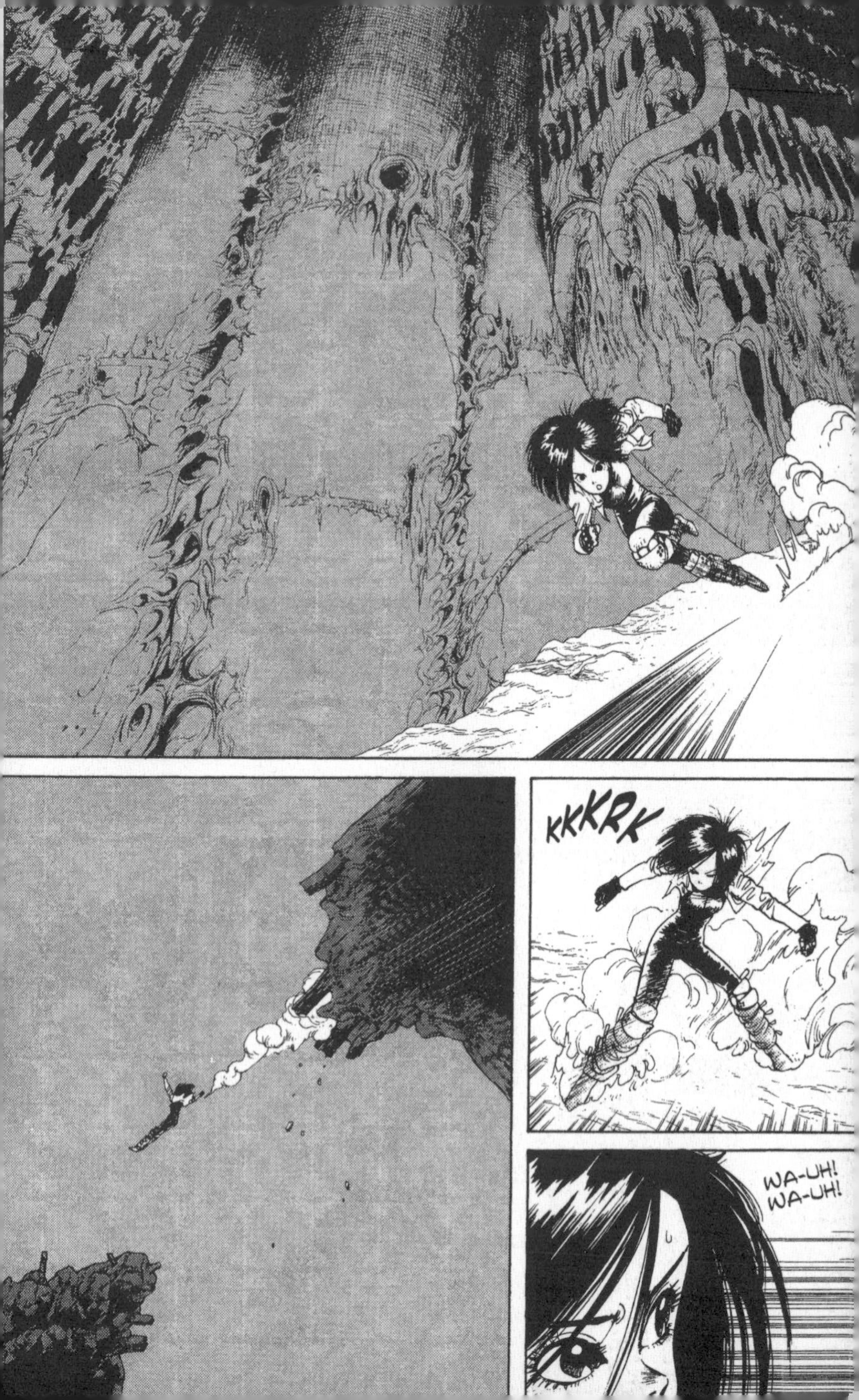
KKKRK
WA-UH!
WA-UH!

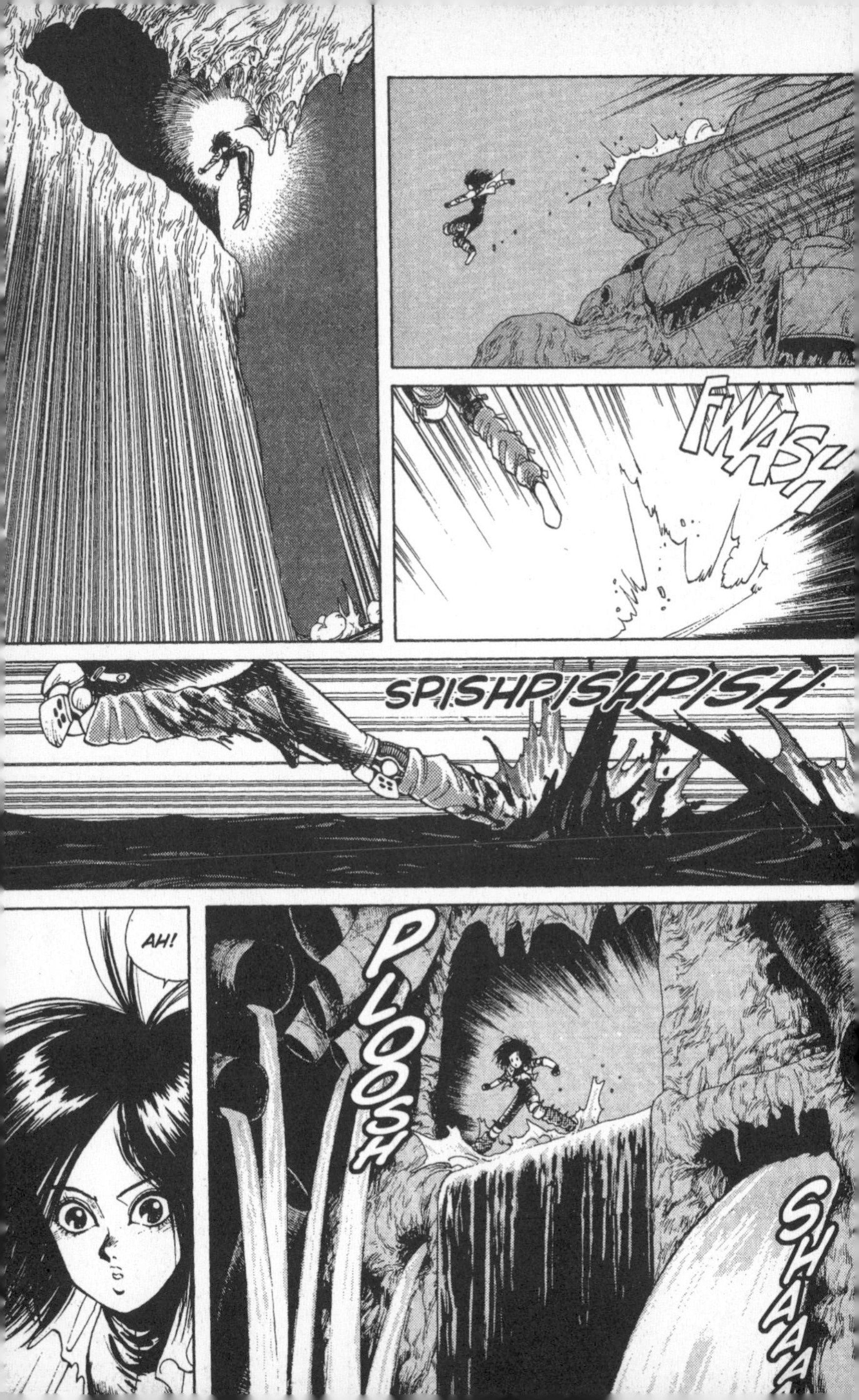
FWASH
SPISHPISHPISH
PLOOSH
SHAAAA
AH!

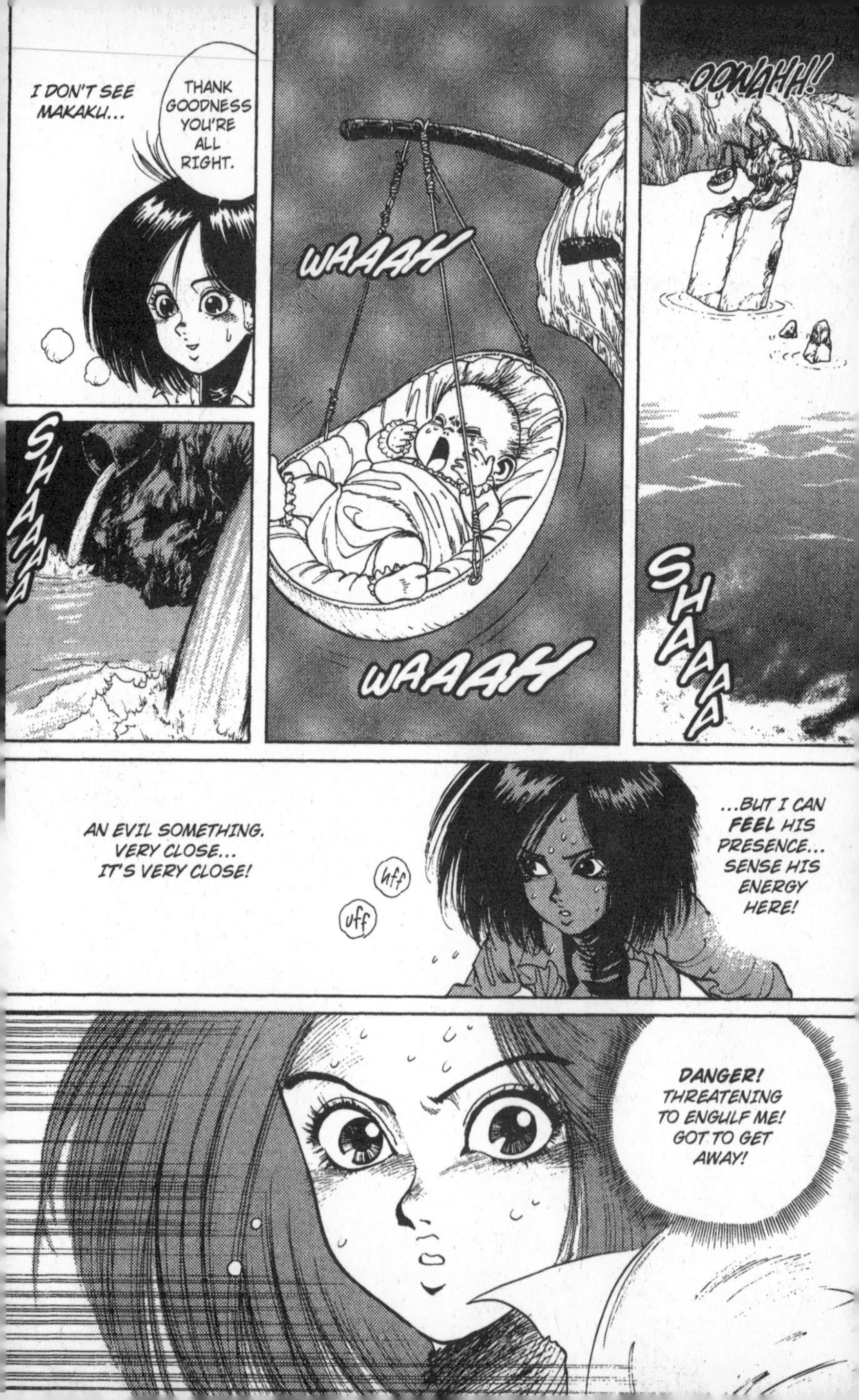
OOWAHH!
SHAAAAA
WAAAH
WAAAH
THANK GOODNESS YOU'RE ALL RIGHT.
I DON'T SEE MAKAKU...
SHAAAAA
...BUT I CAN FEEL HIS PRESENCE... SENSE HIS ENERGY HERE!
uff
uff
AN EVIL SOMETHING. VERY CLOSE... IT'S VERY CLOSE!
DANGER! THREATENING TO ENGULF ME! GOT TO GET AWAY!

ZISH

FWI
SHIT

TONG

Tang

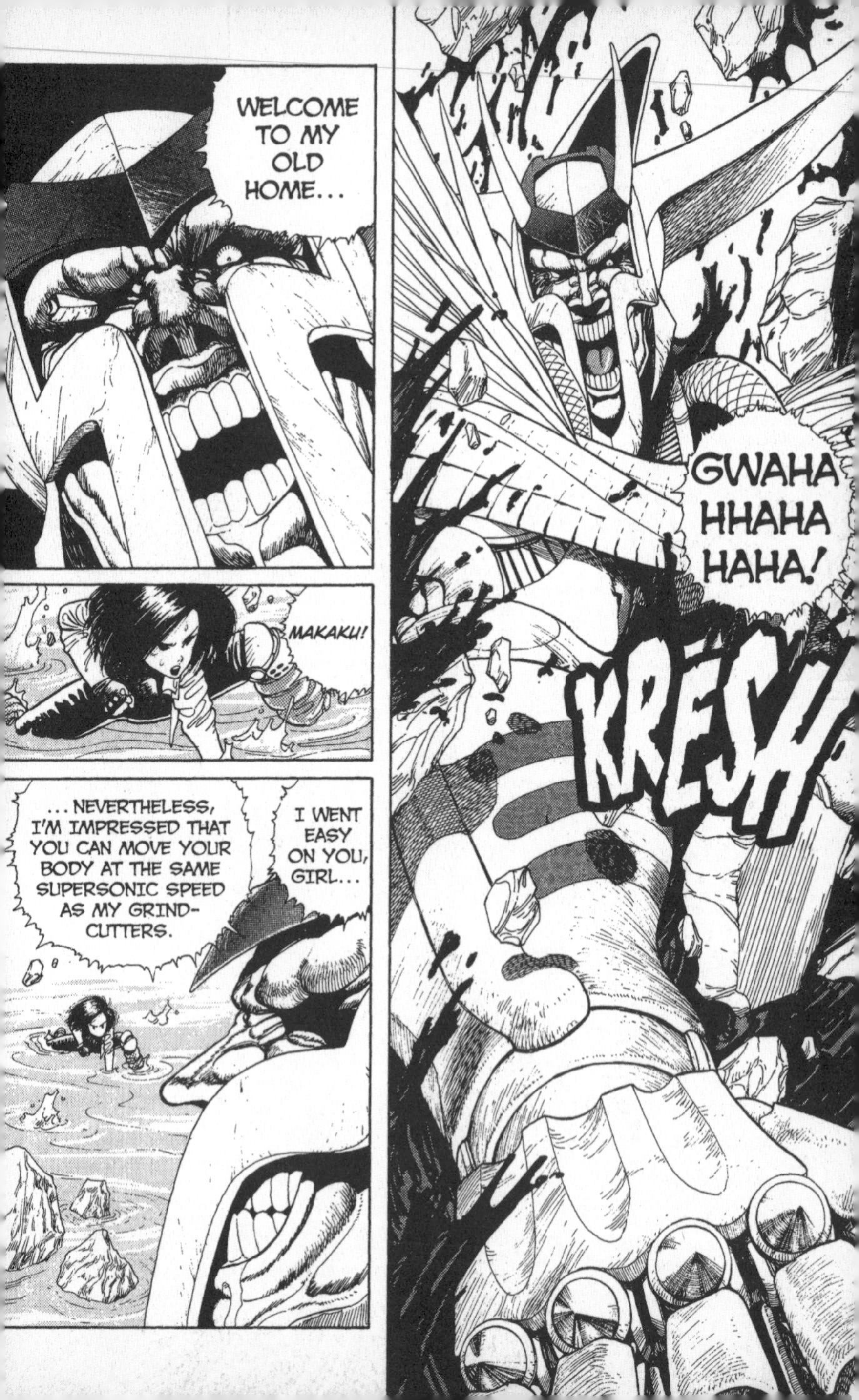
GWAHA HHAHA HAHA!
KRESH
WELCOME TO MY OLD HOME...
MAKAKU!
I WENT EASY ON YOU, GIRL...
... NEVERTHELESS, I'M IMPRESSED THAT YOU CAN MOVE YOUR BODY AT THE SAME SUPERSONIC SPEED AS MY GRIND-CUTTERS.

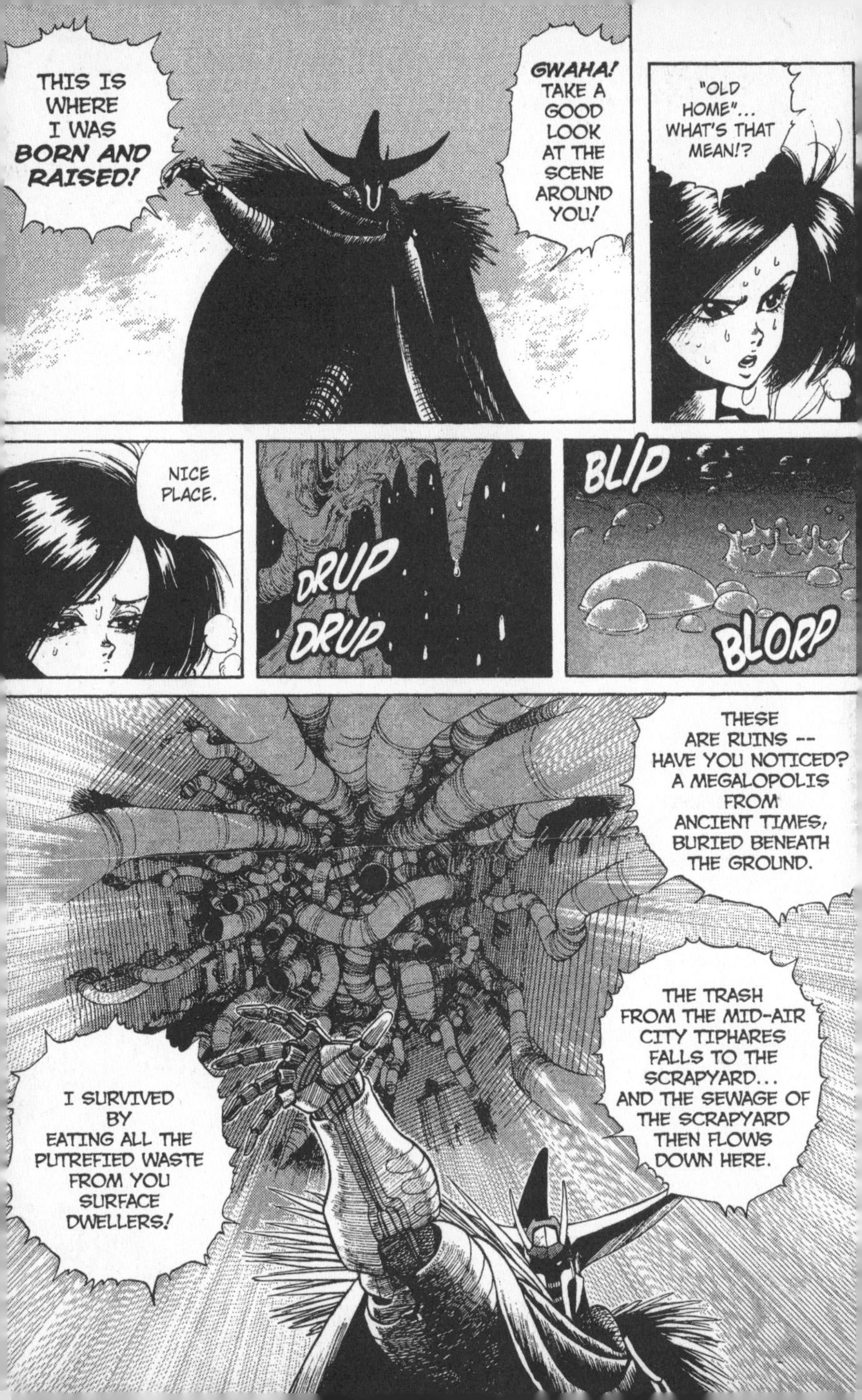
"OLD HOME"... WHAT'S THAT MEAN!?
GWAHA! TAKE A GOOD LOOK AT THE SCENE AROUND YOU!
THIS IS WHERE I WAS BORN AND RAISED!
BLIP
BLORP
DRUP
DRUP
NICE PLACE.
THESE ARE RUINS -- HAVE YOU NOTICED? A MEGALOPOLIS FROM ANCIENT TIMES, BURIED BENEATH THE GROUND.
THE TRASH FROM THE MID-AIR CITY TIPHARES FALLS TO THE SCRAPYARD... AND THE SEWAGE OF THE SCRAPYARD THEN FLOWS DOWN HERE.
I SURVIVED BY EATING ALL THE PUTREFIED WASTE FROM YOU SURFACE DWELLERS!

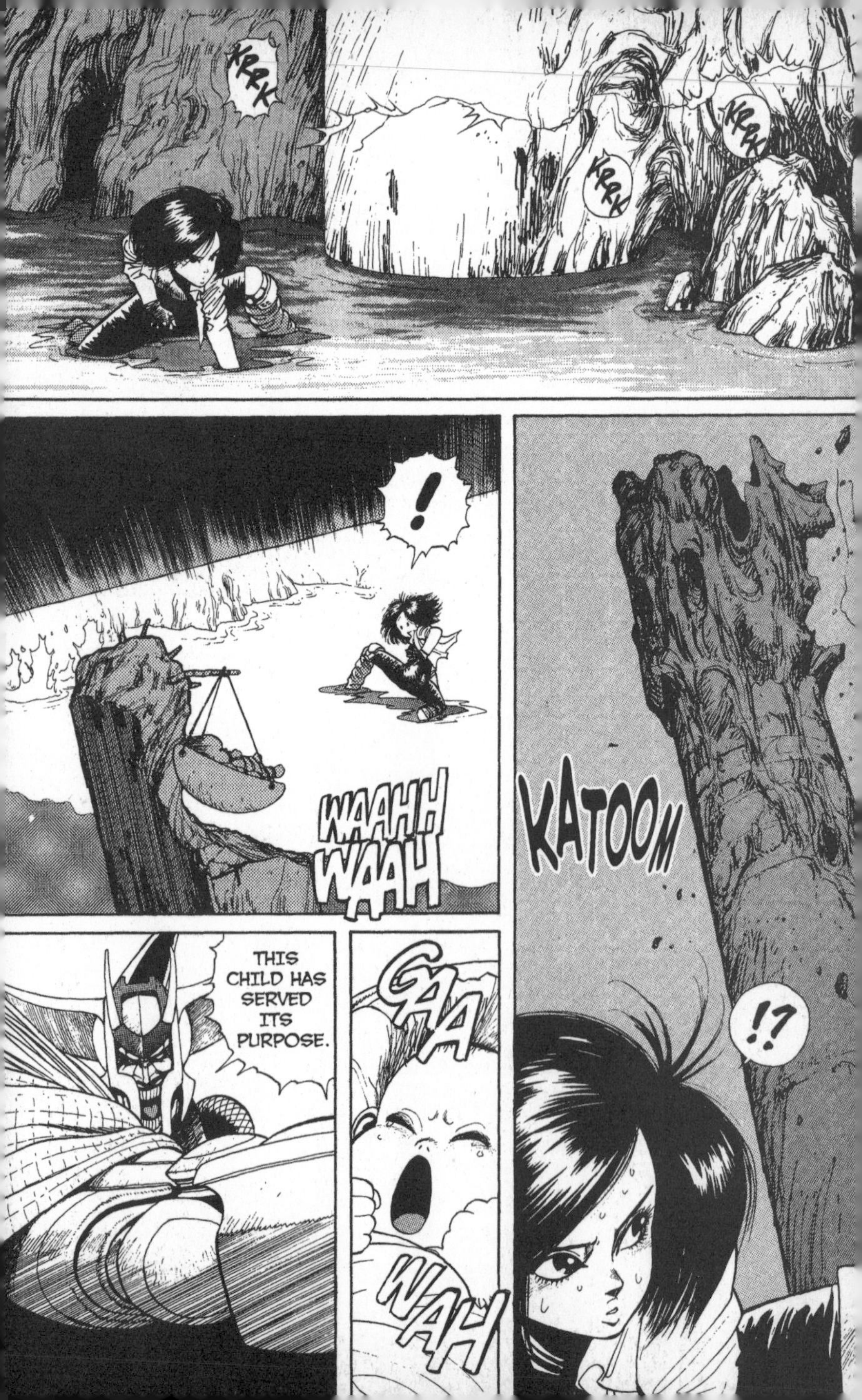
KRRK
KRRK
KRRK
KATOOM
!?
!
WAAHH WAAH
GAA
WAH
THIS CHILD HAS SERVED ITS PURPOSE.

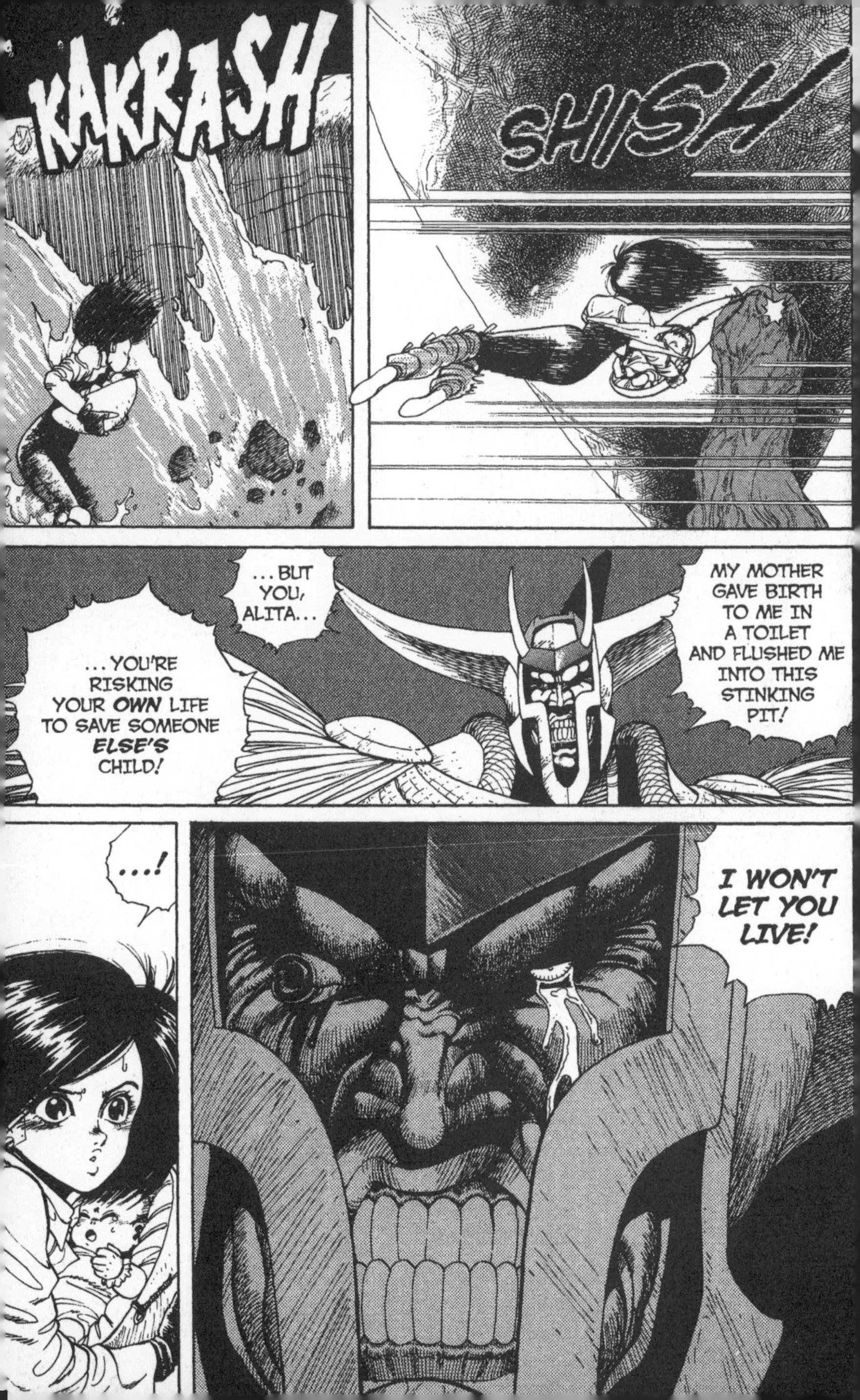
SHISH
KAKRASH
MY MOTHER GAVE BIRTH TO ME IN A TOILET AND FLUSHED ME INTO THIS STINKING PIT!
...BUT YOU, ALITA...
...YOU'RE RISKING YOUR **OWN** LIFE TO SAVE SOMEONE ***ELSE'S*** CHILD!
I WON'T LET YOU LIVE!
...!

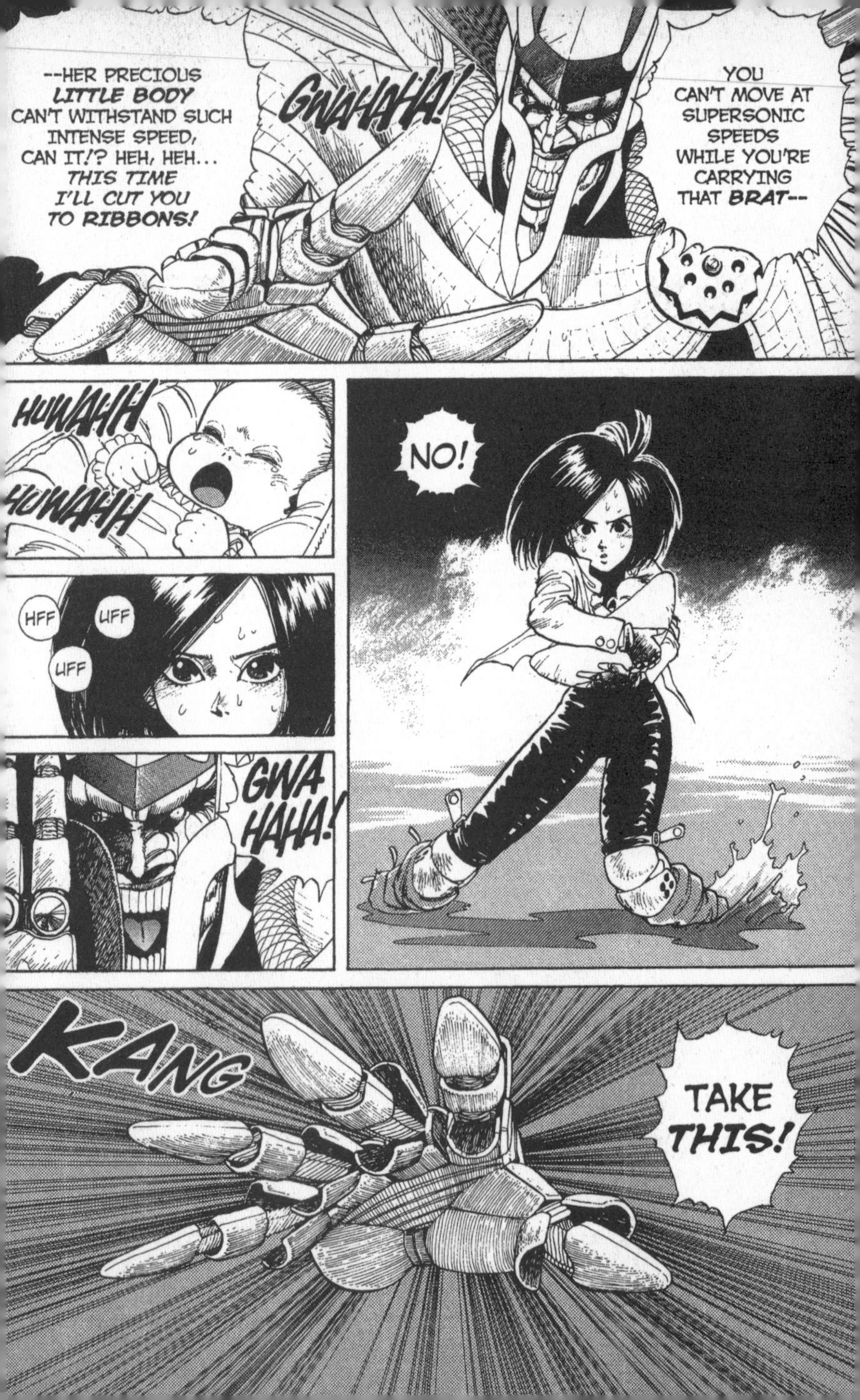
YOU CAN'T MOVE AT SUPERSONIC SPEEDS WHILE YOU'RE CARRYING THAT BRAT--
GWAHAHA!
--HER PRECIOUS LITTLE BODY CAN'T WITHSTAND SUCH INTENSE SPEED, CAN IT!? HEH, HEH... THIS TIME I'LL CUT YOU TO RIBBONS!
NO!
HUWAHH
HUWAHH
HFF
UFF
UFF
GWA HAHA!
TAKE THIS!
KANG

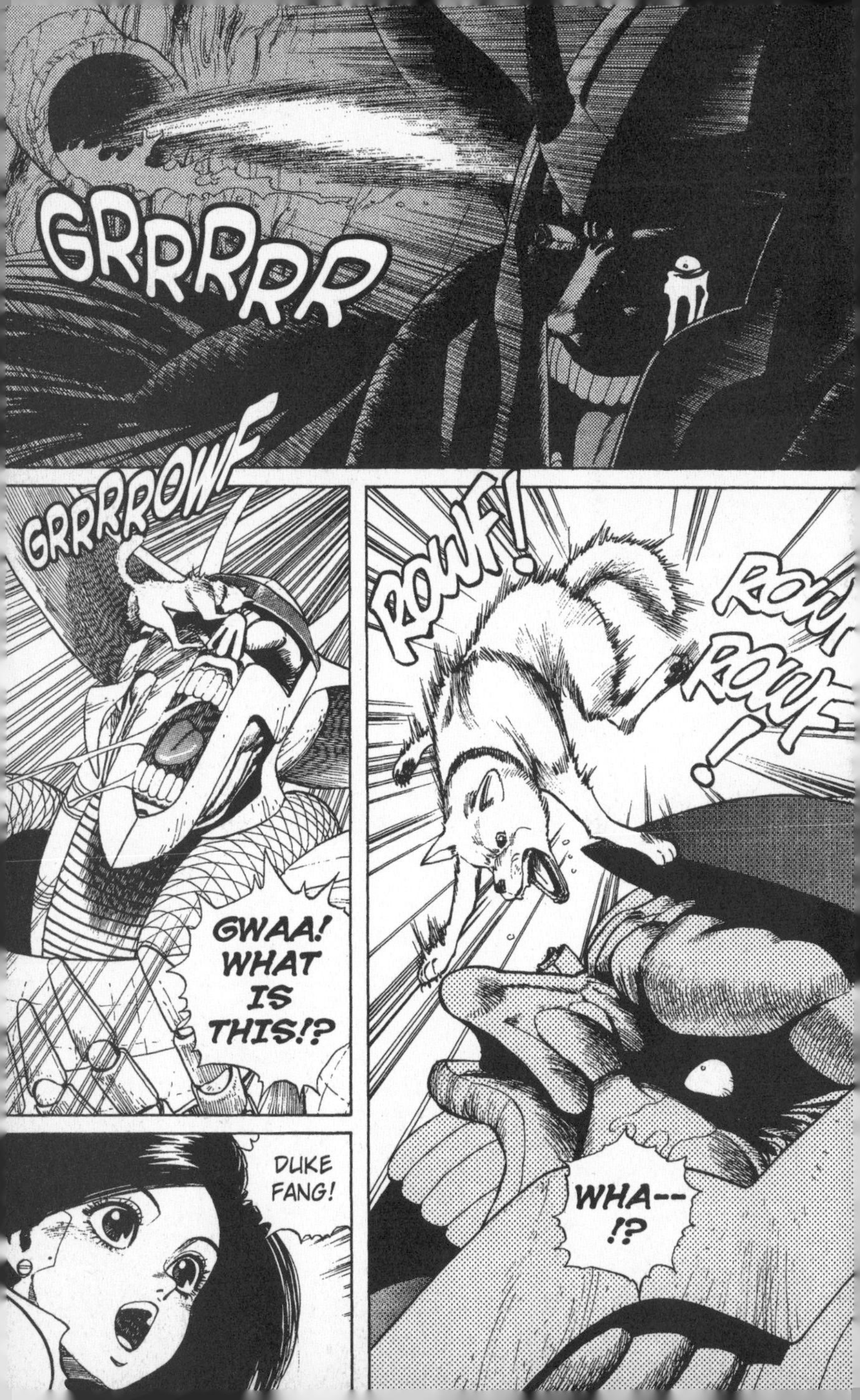
GRRRRRR
ROW ROWF!
ROWF!
WHA--!?
GRRRROWF
GWAA! WHAT IS THIS!?
DUKE FANG!

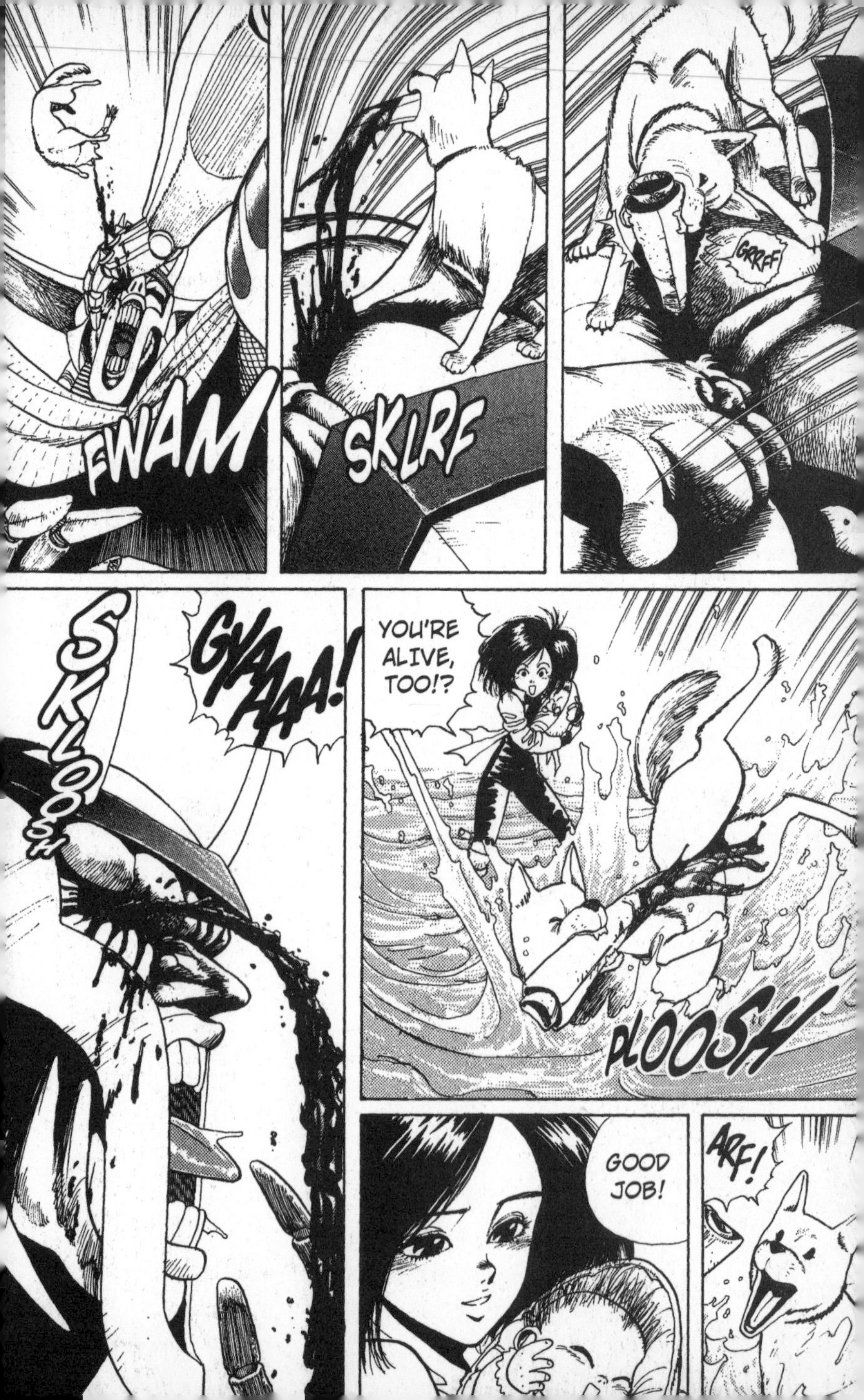
GRRFF
SKLRF
FWAM
YOU'RE ALIVE, TOO!?
PLOOSH
ARF!
GOOD JOB!
GYAAAAA!
SKLOOSH

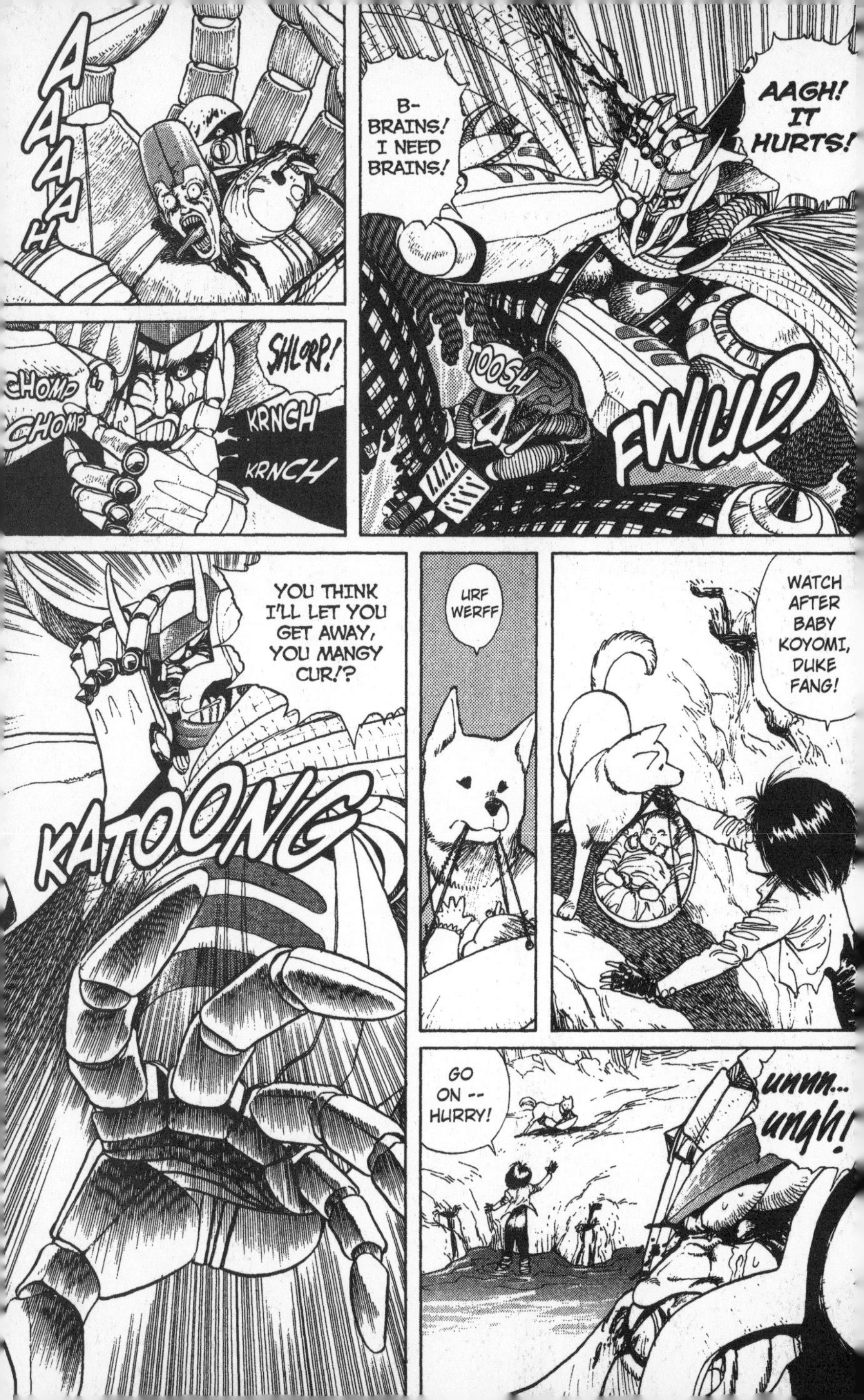
AAGH! IT HURTS!
B-BRAINS! I NEED BRAINS!
TOOSH
FWUD
AAAAAH
SHLORP!
CHOMP CHOMP
KRNCH KRNCH
WATCH AFTER BABY KOYOMI, DUKE FANG!
URF WERFF
GO ON -- HURRY!
unnn... ungh!
YOU THINK I'LL LET YOU GET AWAY, YOU MANGY CUR!?
KATOONG

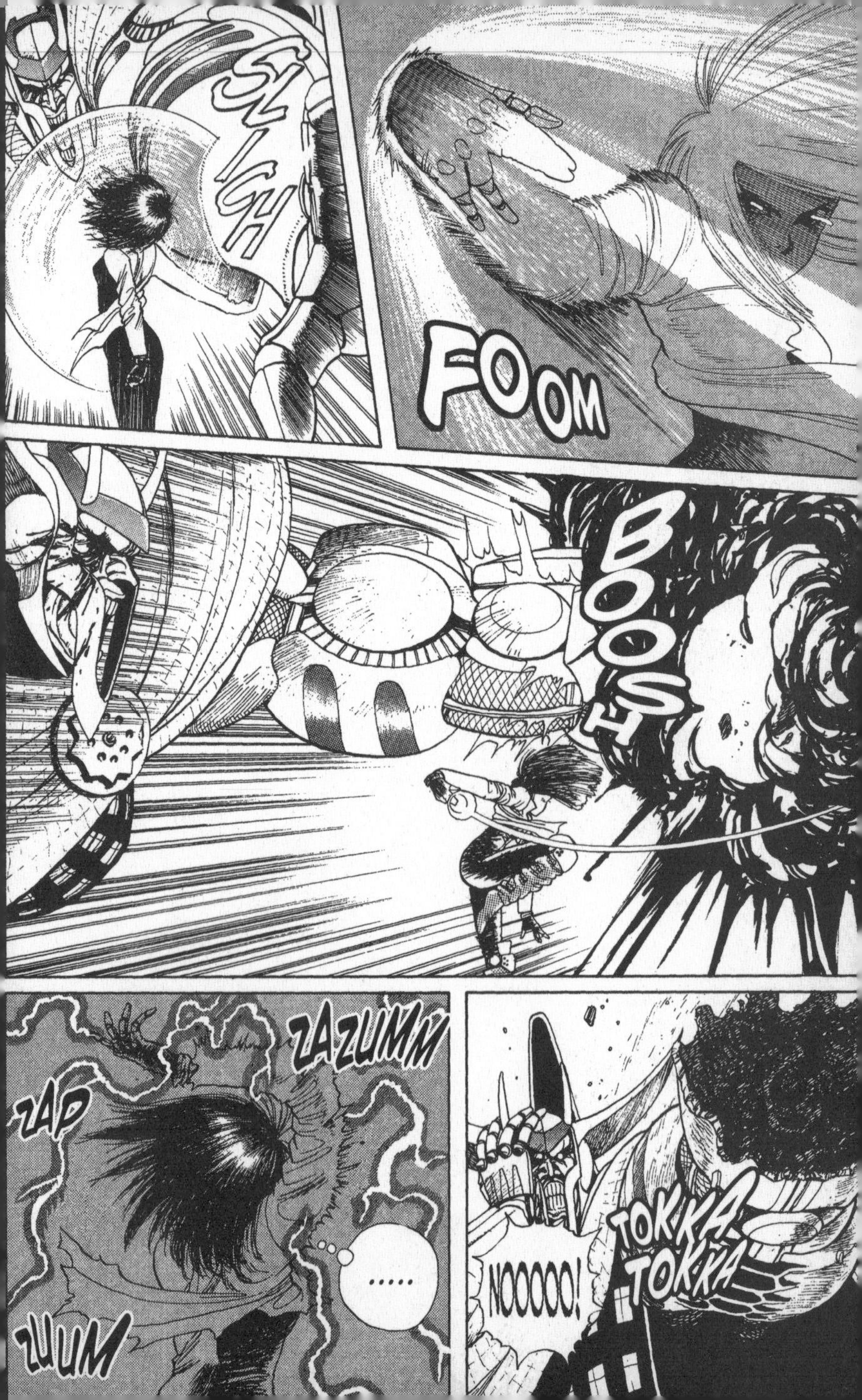
FOOM
SHIGH
BOOOSH
NOOOOO!
TOKKA TOKKA
ZA ZUMM
ZAP
.....
ZUUM

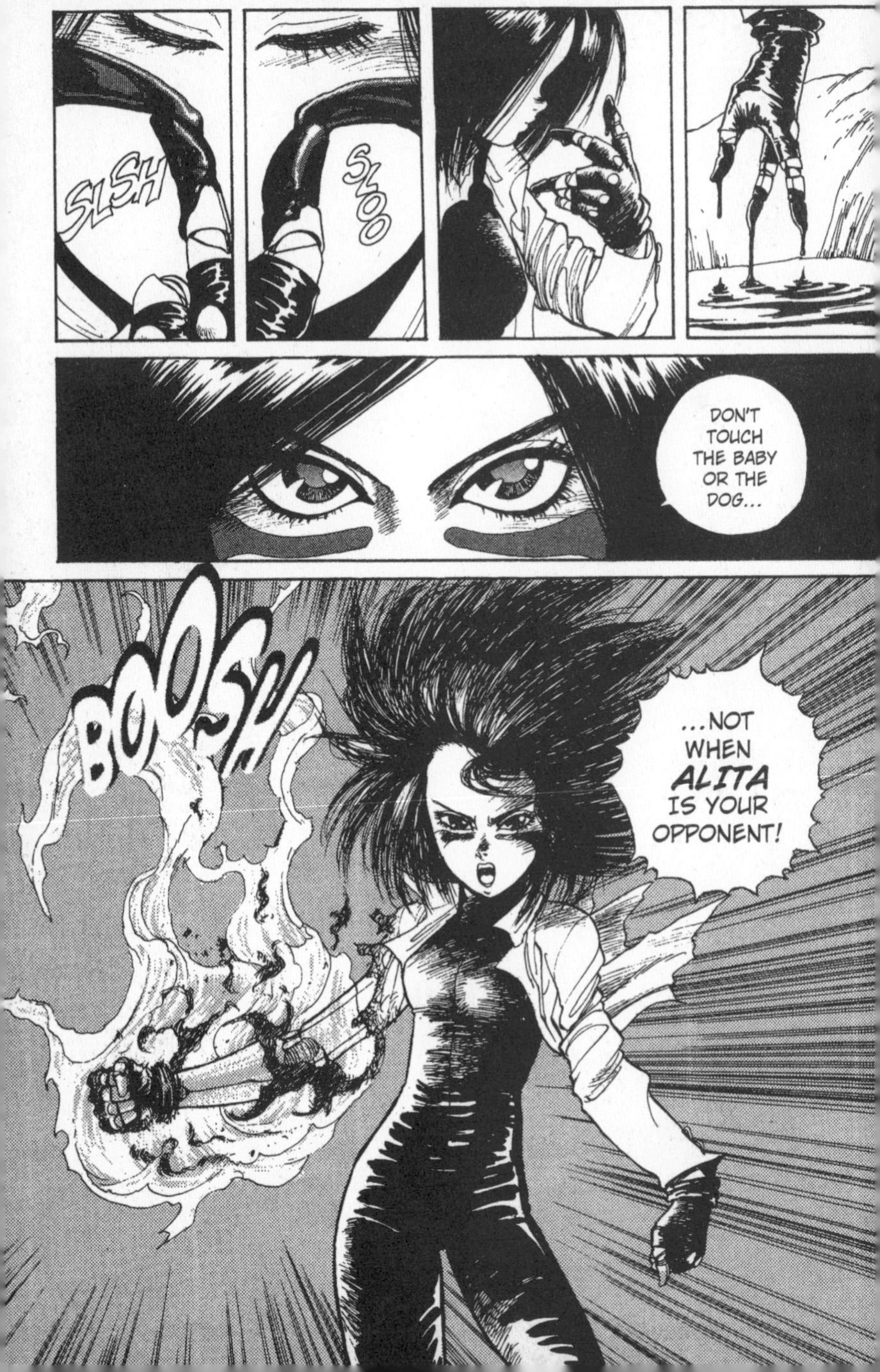
SLOO
SLSH
DON'T TOUCH THE BABY OR THE DOG...
...NOT WHEN ALITA IS YOUR OPPONENT!
BOOSH

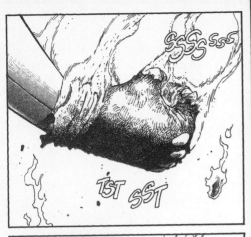

SSSss

TST SST

FWASH

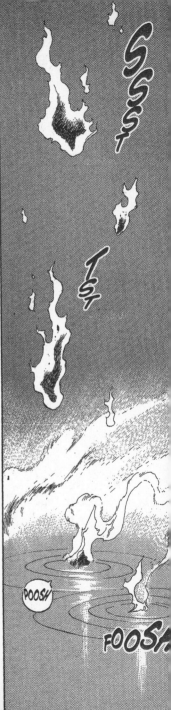

SSSst

TST

POOSH

FOOSH

CONQUERING ANGEL
Battle 6: Struggle

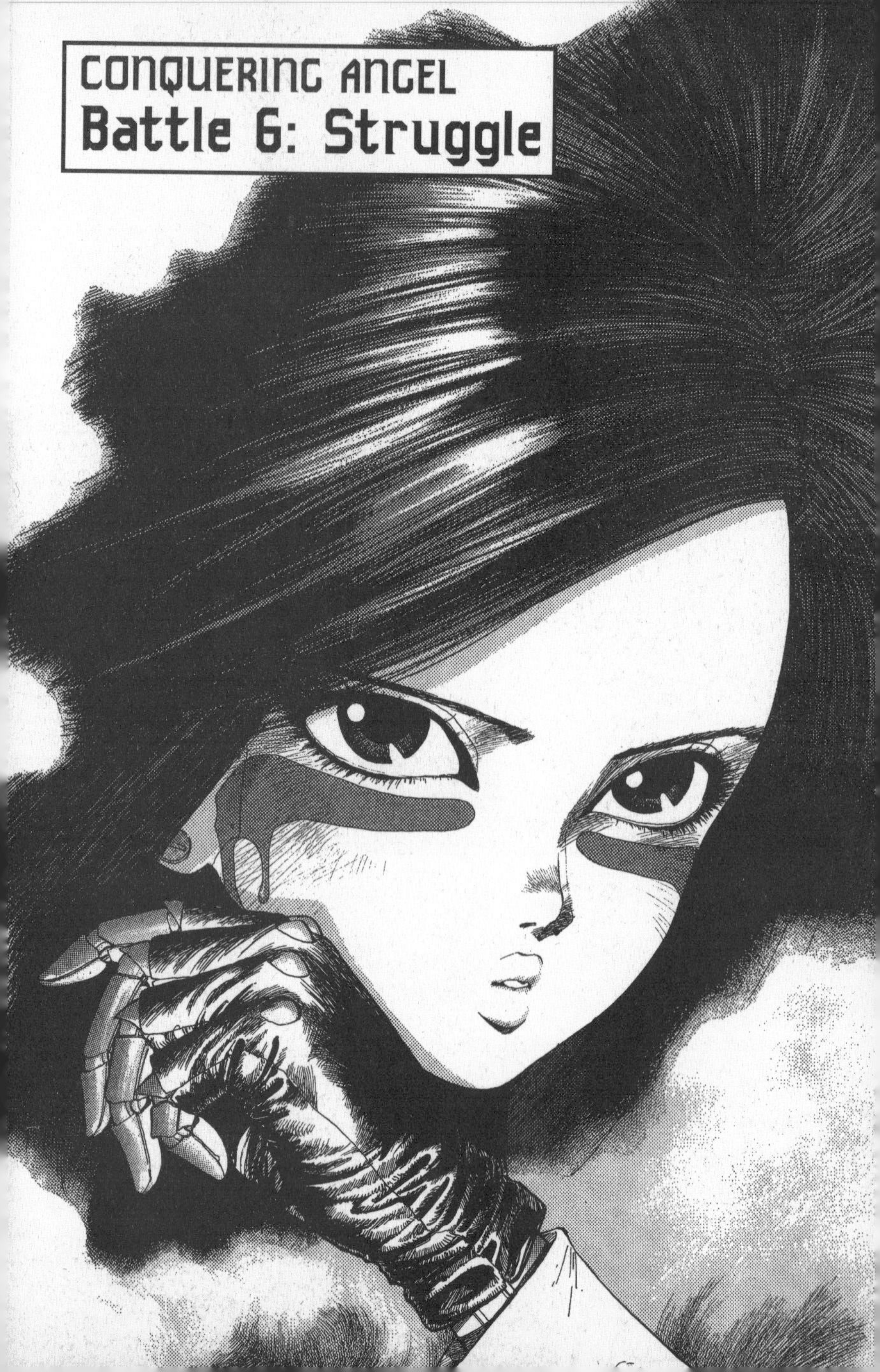

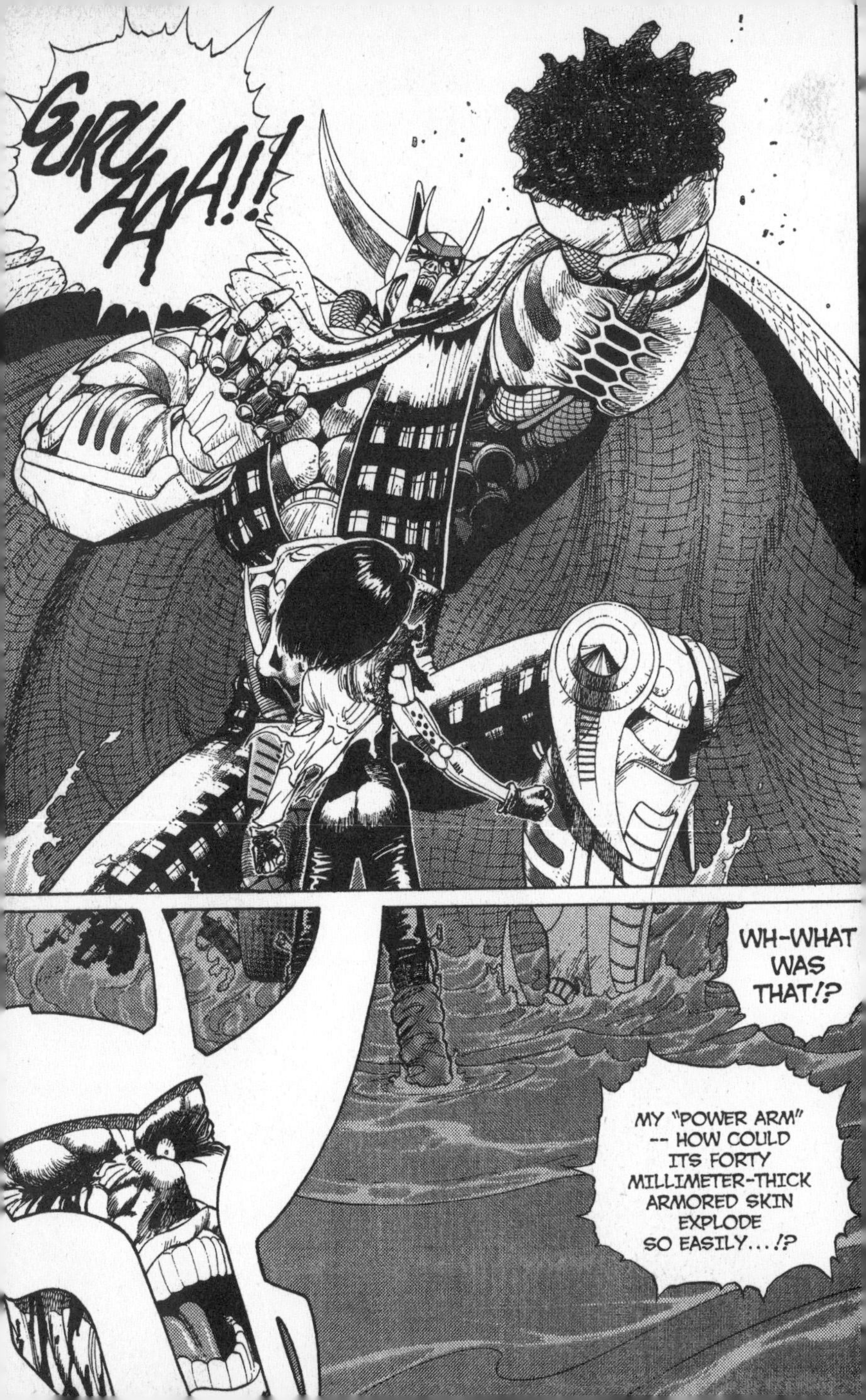
GURU AAA!!
WH-WHAT WAS THAT!?
MY "POWER ARM" -- HOW COULD ITS FORTY MILLIMETER-THICK ARMORED SKIN EXPLODE SO EASILY...!?

THOSE MOVES -- I JUST NATURALLY RESPONDED THAT WAY...

AT THAT MOMENT, I DIDN'T UNDERSTAND MYSELF.

--IT WASN'T SOMETHING I DID CONSCIOUSLY... IT -- IT WAS JUST WHAT I HAD TO DO!

...LIKE STREAKING THE TAN UNDER MY EYES--

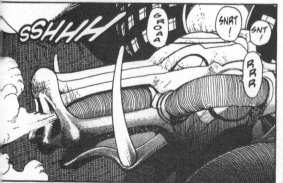

SSHHH

GROA

SNRT!

SNT!

RRR

HER NEW FUNCTIONS -- CODIFY THEM, BOARHEAD!

196

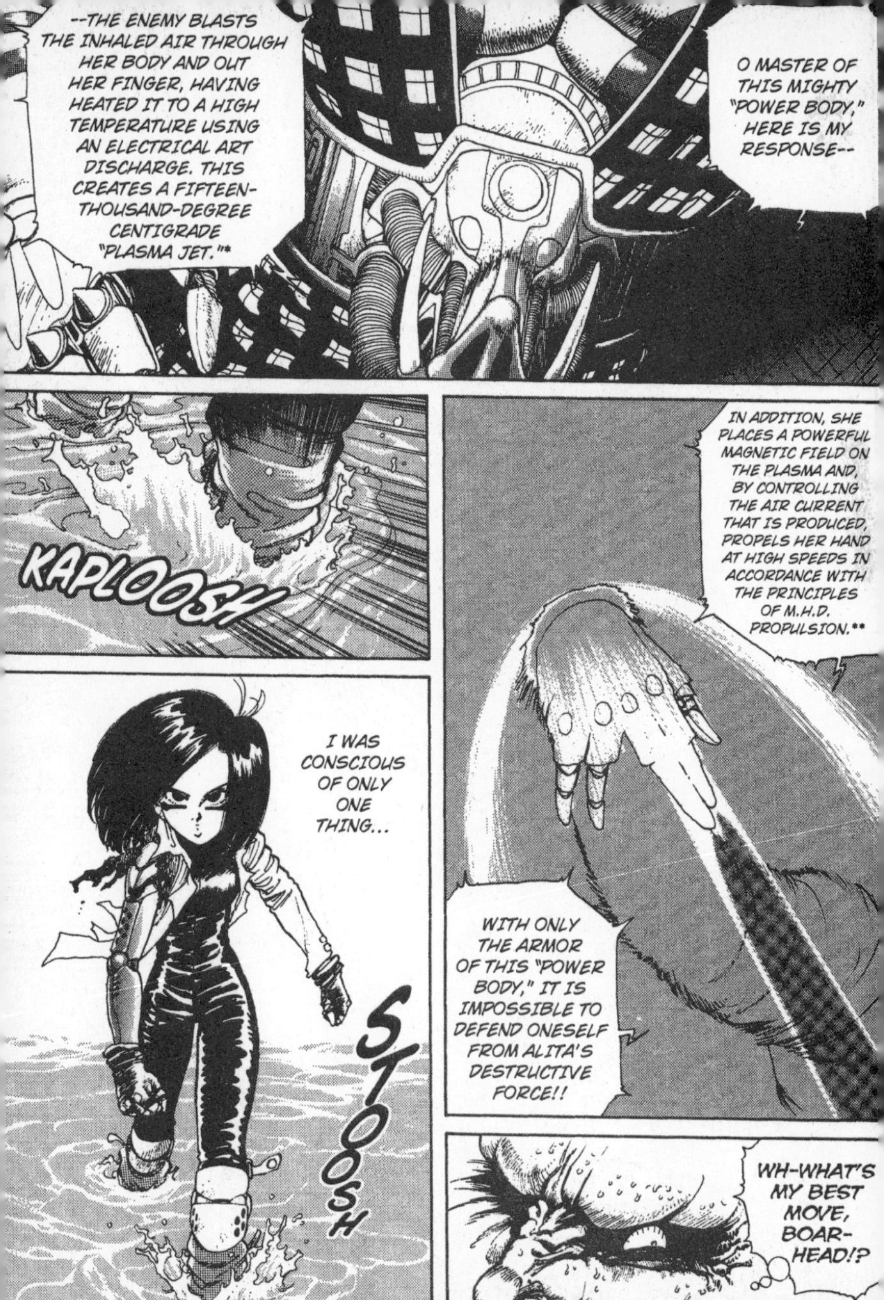
O MASTER OF THIS MIGHTY "POWER BODY," HERE IS MY RESPONSE--
--THE ENEMY BLASTS THE INHALED AIR THROUGH HER BODY AND OUT HER FINGER, HAVING HEATED IT TO A HIGH TEMPERATURE USING AN ELECTRICAL ART DISCHARGE. THIS CREATES A FIFTEEN-THOUSAND-DEGREE CENTIGRADE "PLASMA JET."*
IN ADDITION, SHE PLACES A POWERFUL MAGNETIC FIELD ON THE PLASMA AND, BY CONTROLLING THE AIR CURRENT THAT IS PRODUCED, PROPELS HER HAND AT HIGH SPEEDS IN ACCORDANCE WITH THE PRINCIPLES OF M.H.D. PROPULSION.**
WITH ONLY THE ARMOR OF THIS "POWER BODY," IT IS IMPOSSIBLE TO DEFEND ONESELF FROM ALITA'S DESTRUCTIVE FORCE!!
WH-WHAT'S MY BEST MOVE, BOAR-HEAD!?
KAPLOOSH
I WAS CONSCIOUS OF ONLY ONE THING...
STOOOSH

*PLASMA JET: A HIGH-SPEED JET OF HIGH-TEMPERATURE IONIZED GAS. A TECHNOLOGY USED IN HEAT-CUTTING AND CASTING.

**M.H.D. PROPULSION: A TYPE OF PROPULSION WHICH APPLIES MAGNETOHYDRODYNAMICS TO ELECTRICITY-CONDUCTING PLASMA.

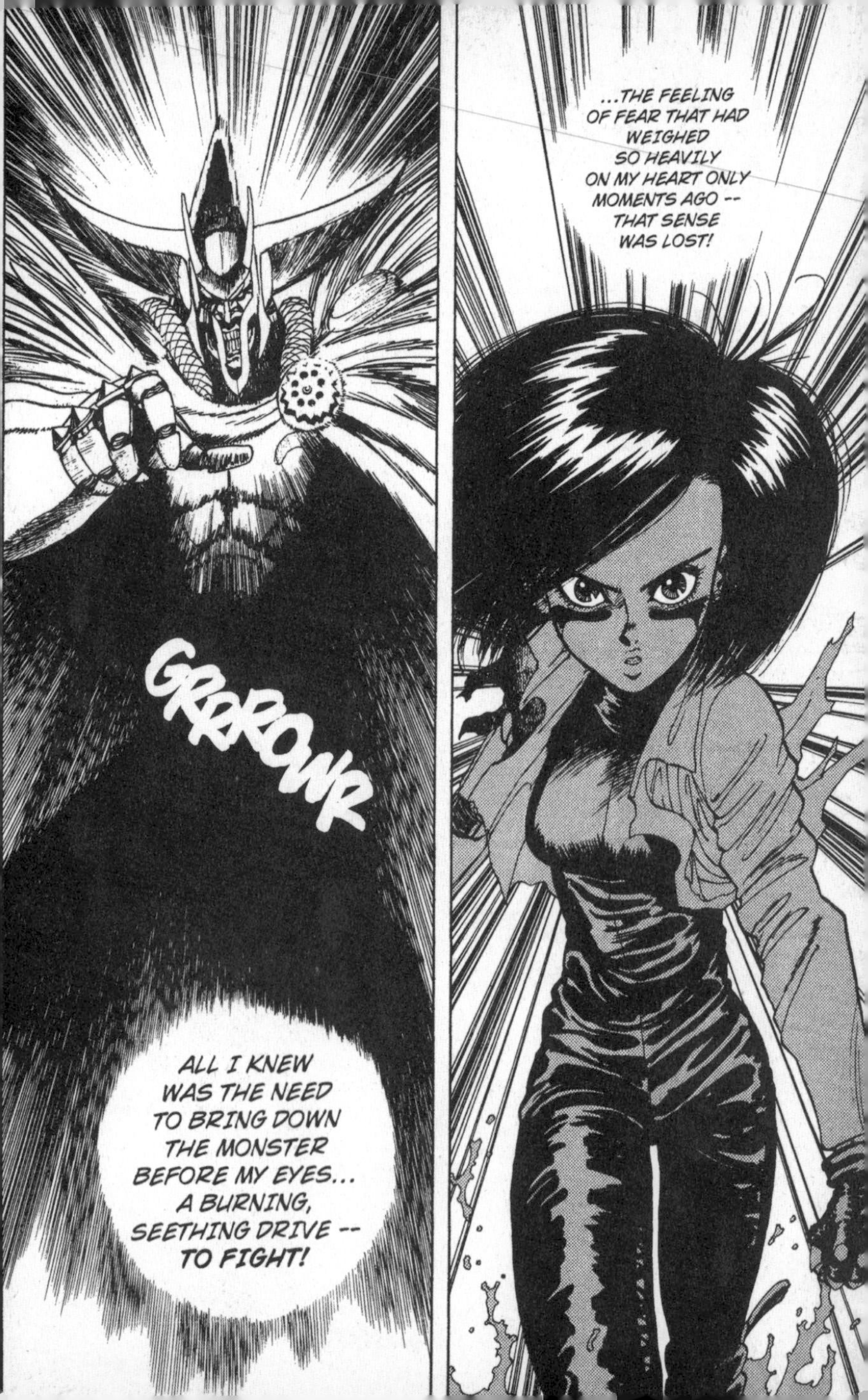
...THE FEELING OF FEAR THAT HAD WEIGHED SO HEAVILY ON MY HEART ONLY MOMENTS AGO -- THAT SENSE WAS LOST!
GRRROWR
ALL I KNEW WAS THE NEED TO BRING DOWN THE MONSTER BEFORE MY EYES... A BURNING, SEETHING DRIVE -- TO FIGHT!

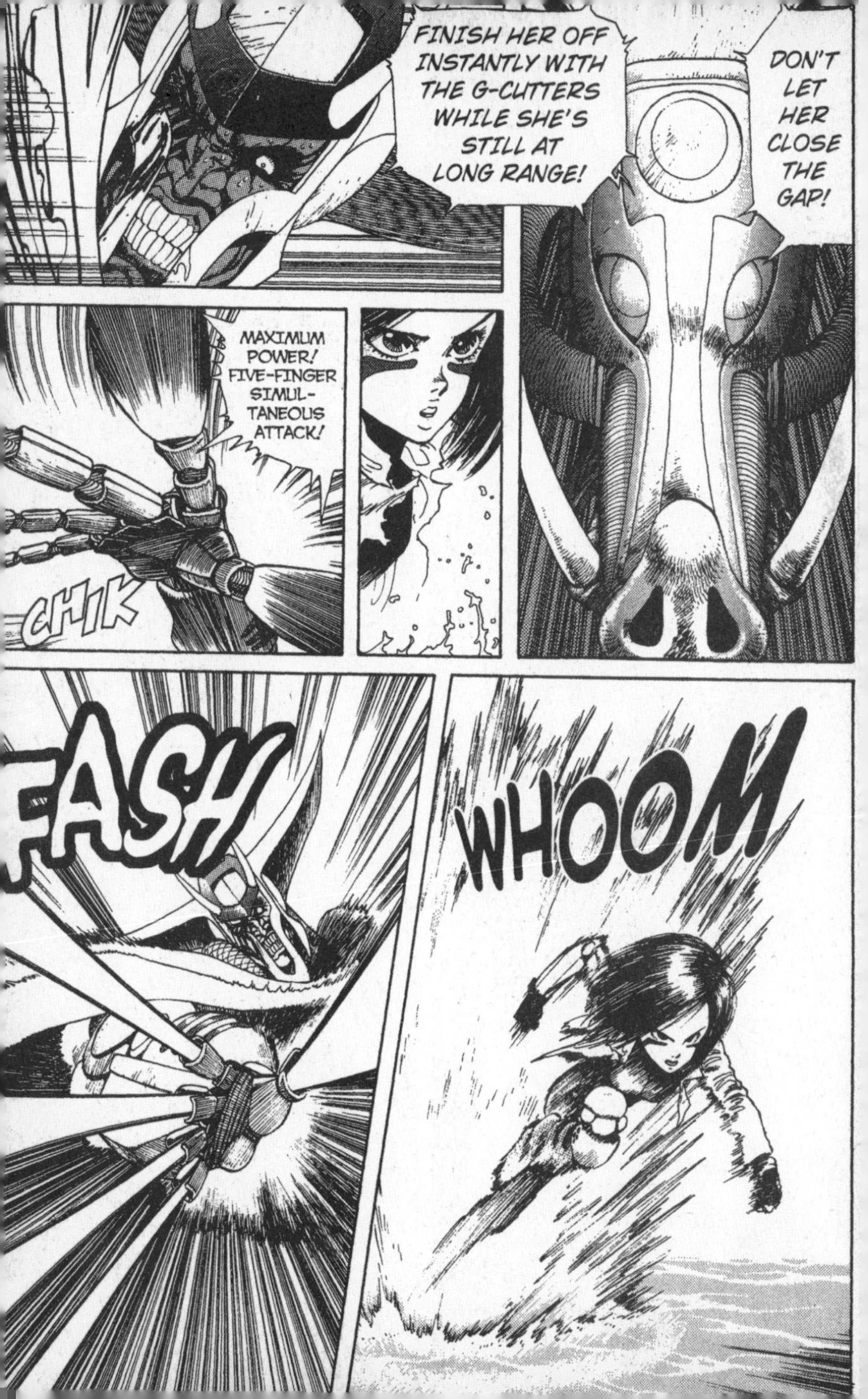
DON'T LET HER CLOSE THE GAP!
FINISH HER OFF INSTANTLY WITH THE G-CUTTERS WHILE SHE'S STILL AT LONG RANGE!
MAXIMUM POWER! FIVE-FINGER SIMUL-TANEOUS ATTACK!
CHIK
WHOOM
FASH

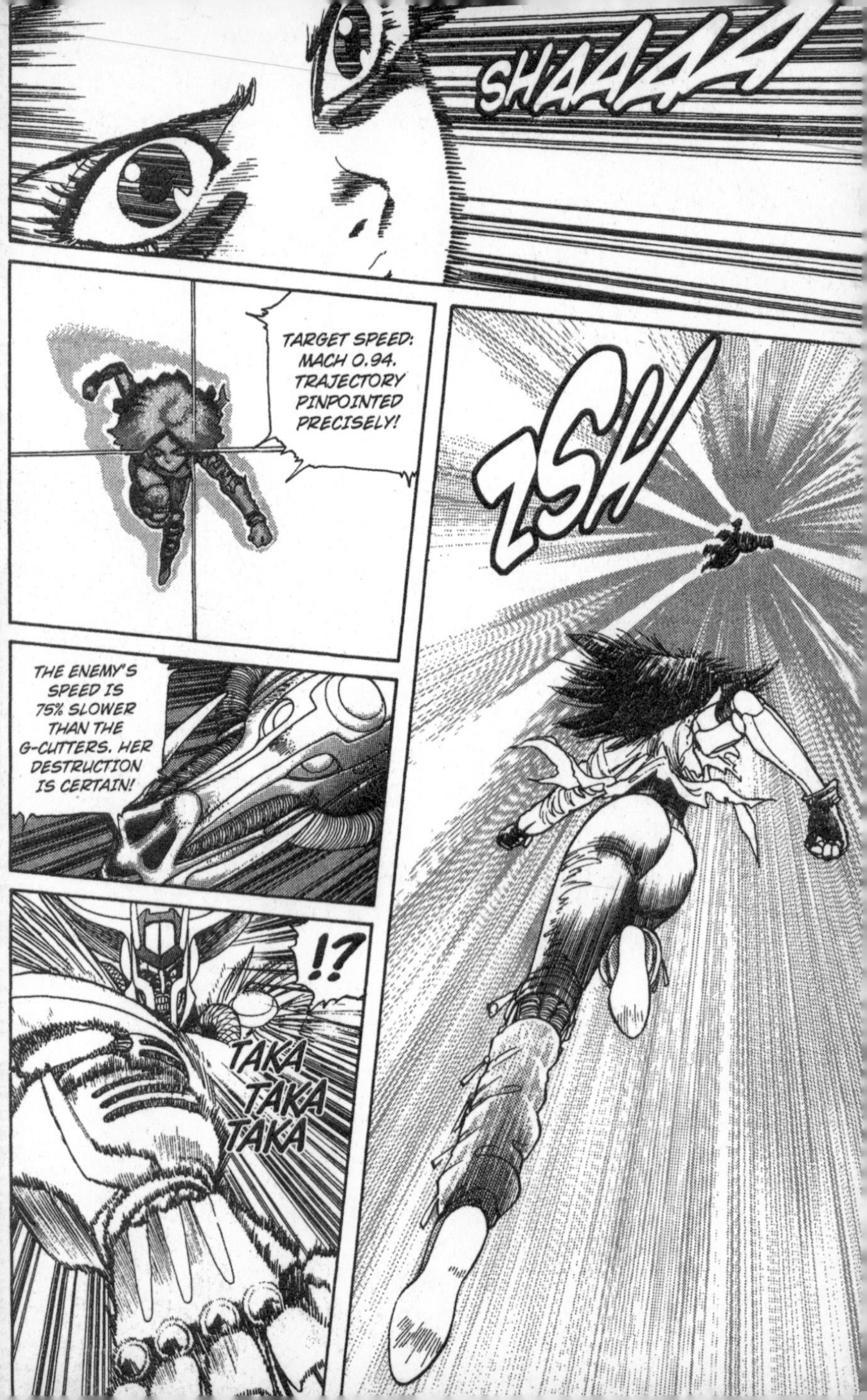
SHAAAAH
ZSH
TARGET SPEED: MACH 0.94. TRAJECTORY PINPOINTED PRECISELY!
THE ENEMY'S SPEED IS 75% SLOWER THAN THE G-CUTTERS. HER DESTRUCTION IS CERTAIN!
!?
TAKA TAKA TAKA

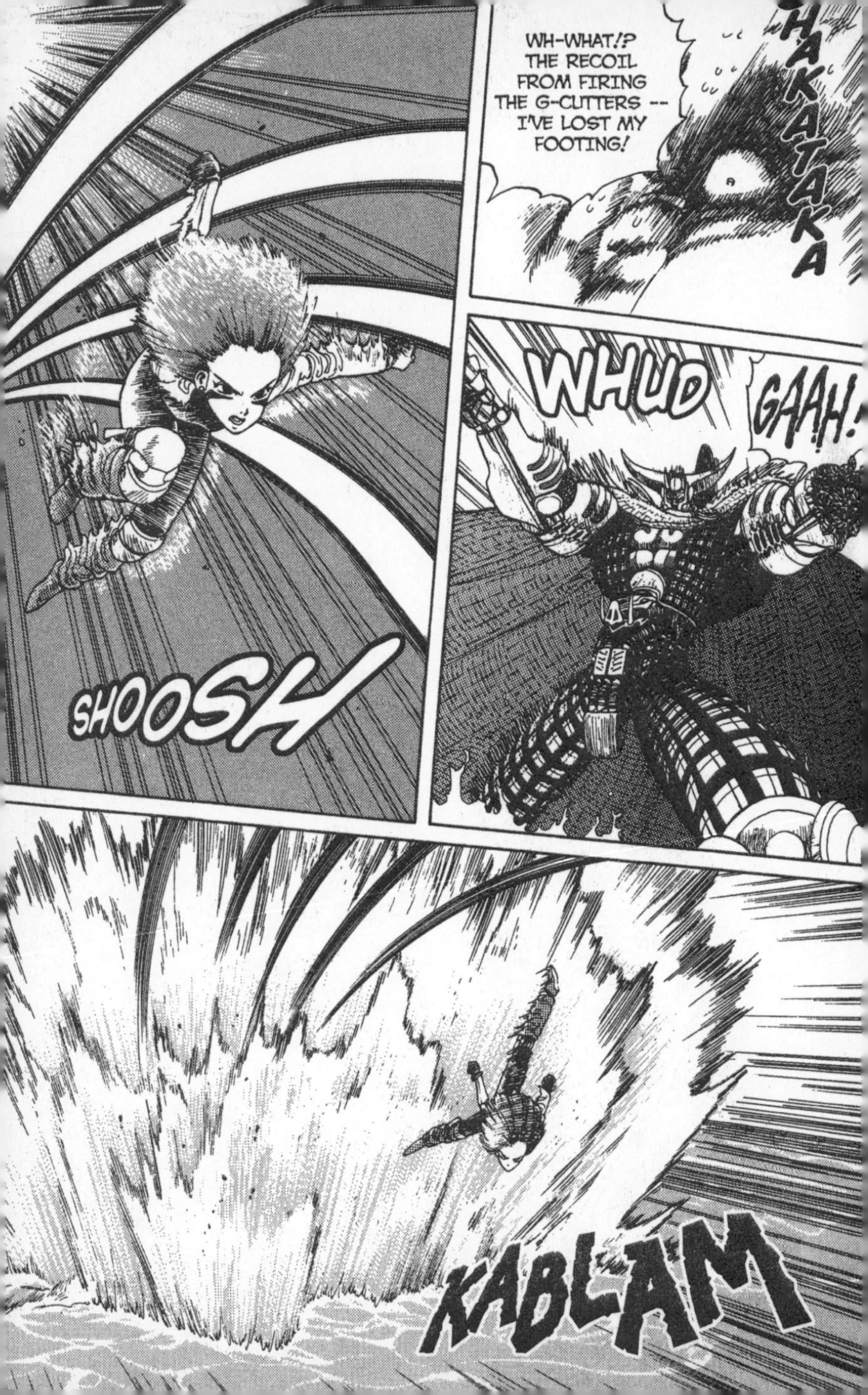
WH-WHAT!? THE RECOIL FROM FIRING THE G-CUTTERS -- I'VE LOST MY FOOTING!
HAKATAKA
GAAH!
WHUD
SHOOSH
KABLAM

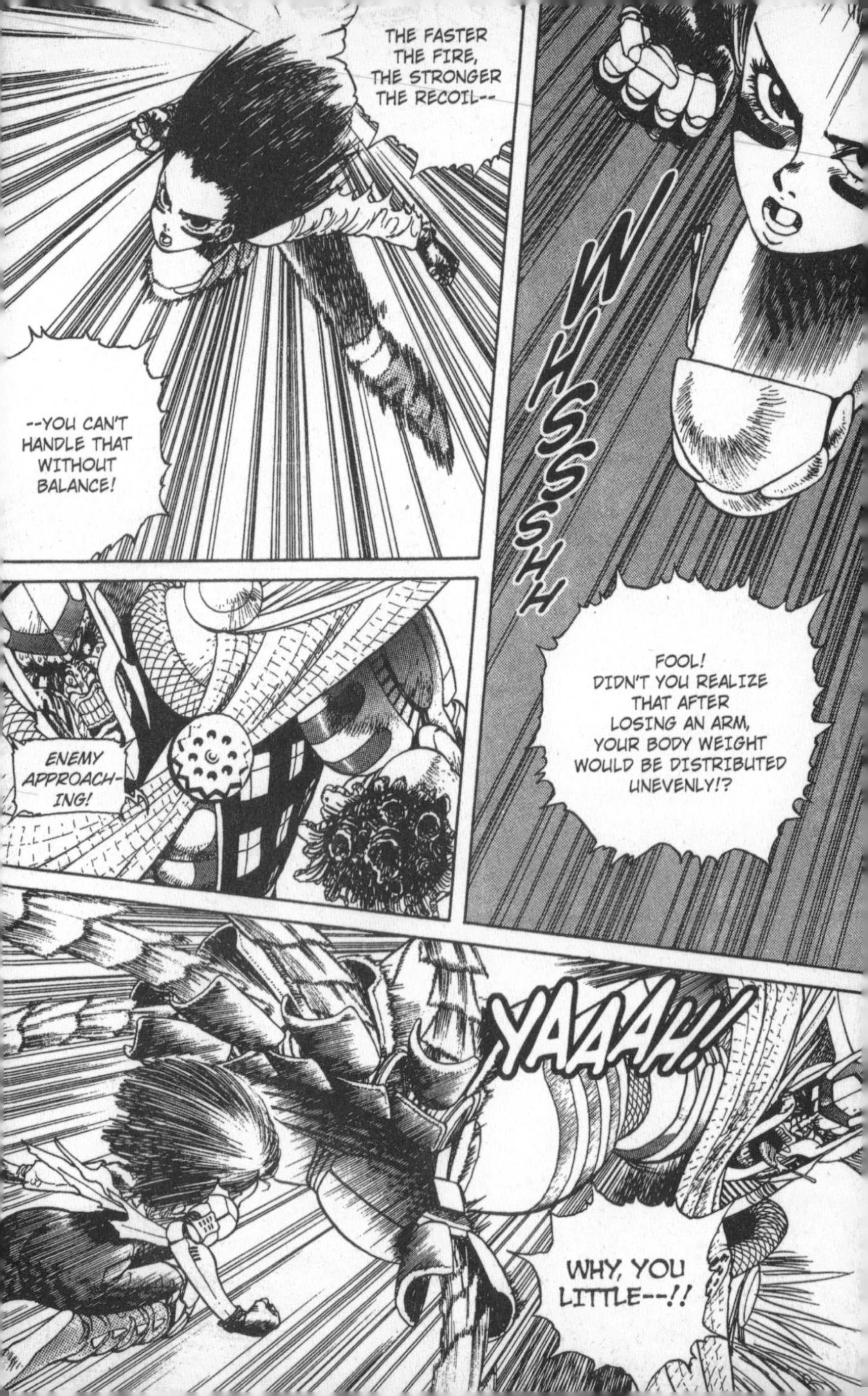
WHHSSSHH
FOOL! DIDN'T YOU REALIZE THAT AFTER LOSING AN ARM, YOUR BODY WEIGHT WOULD BE DISTRIBUTED UNEVENLY!?
THE FASTER THE FIRE, THE STRONGER THE RECOIL--
--YOU CAN'T HANDLE THAT WITHOUT BALANCE!
ENEMY APPROACH-ING!
YAAAH!
WHY, YOU LITTLE--!!

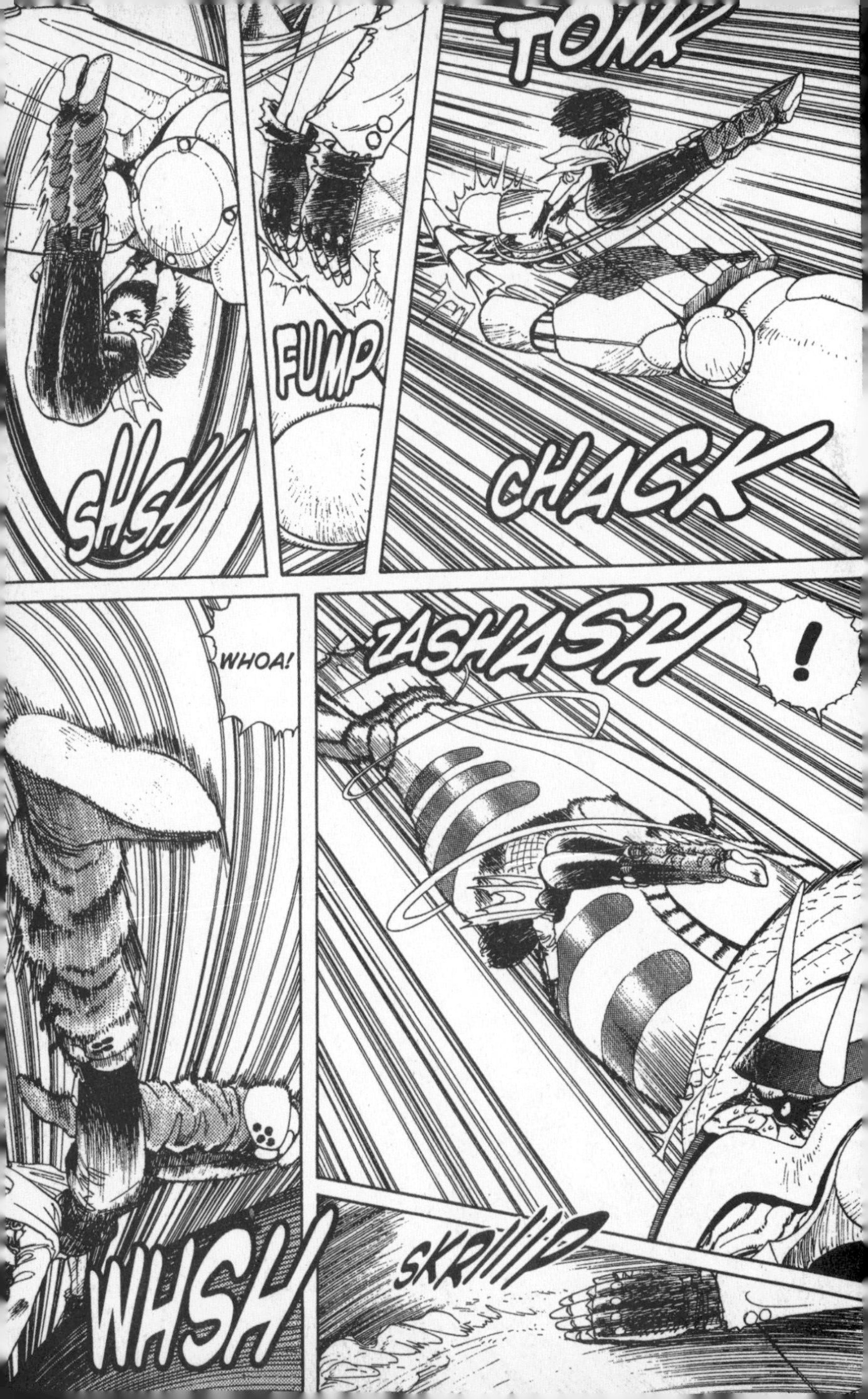
TONK
CHACK
FUMP
SHSH
!
ZASHASH
SKRIIID
WHOA!
WHSH

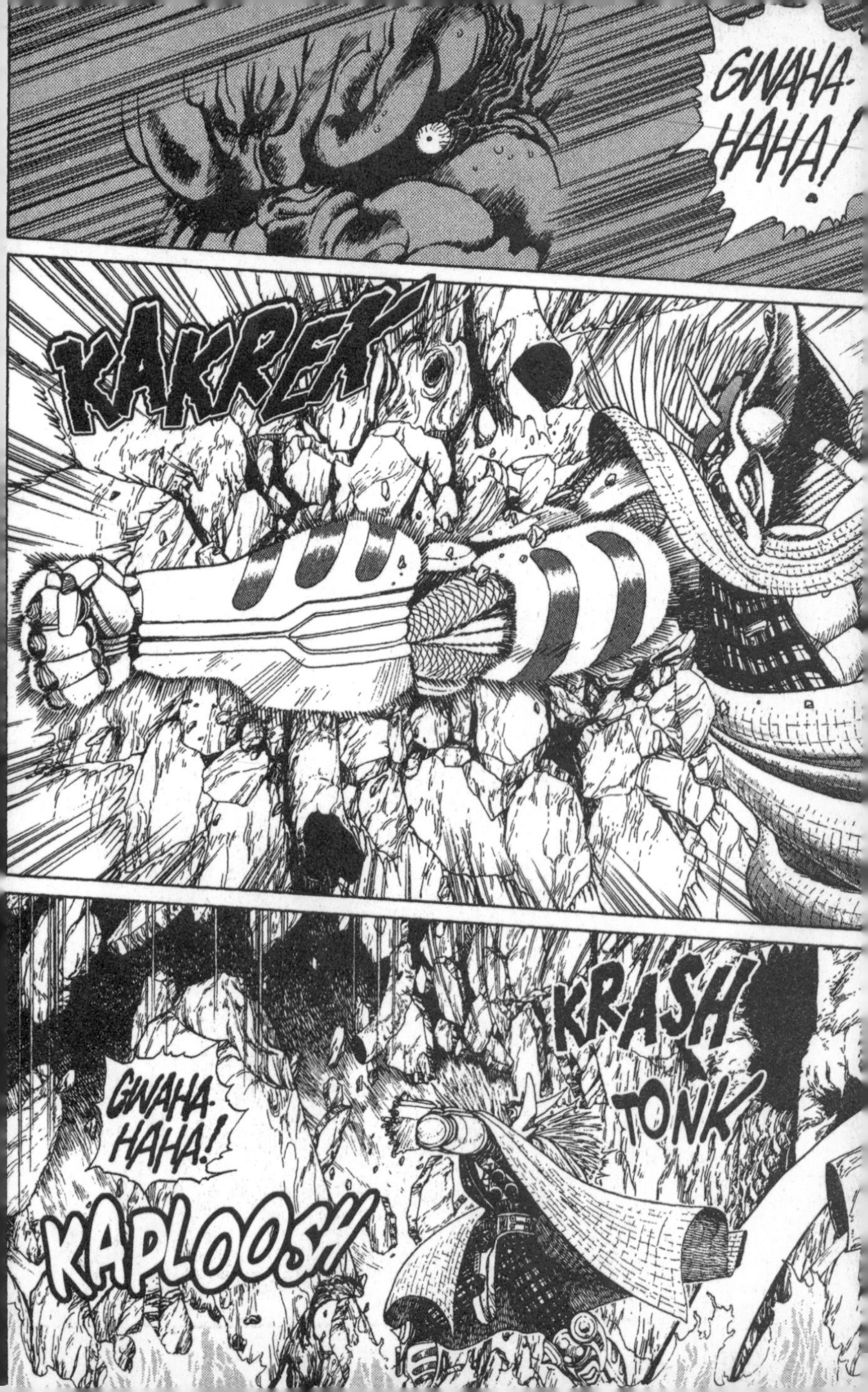
GWAHA-HAHA!
KAKREK
KRASH
TONK
GWAHA-HAHA!
KAPLOOSH

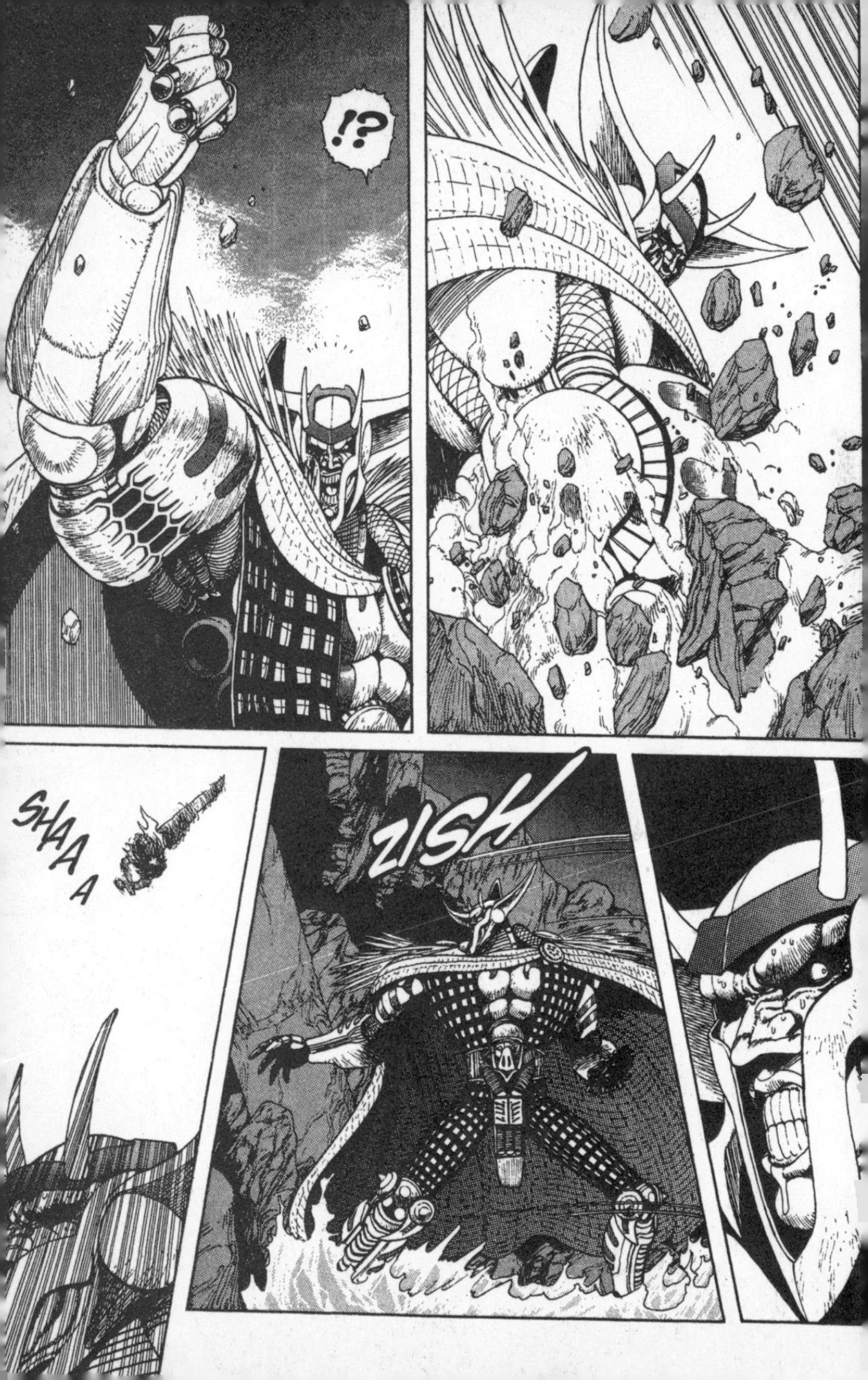
!?
ZISH
SHAAAA

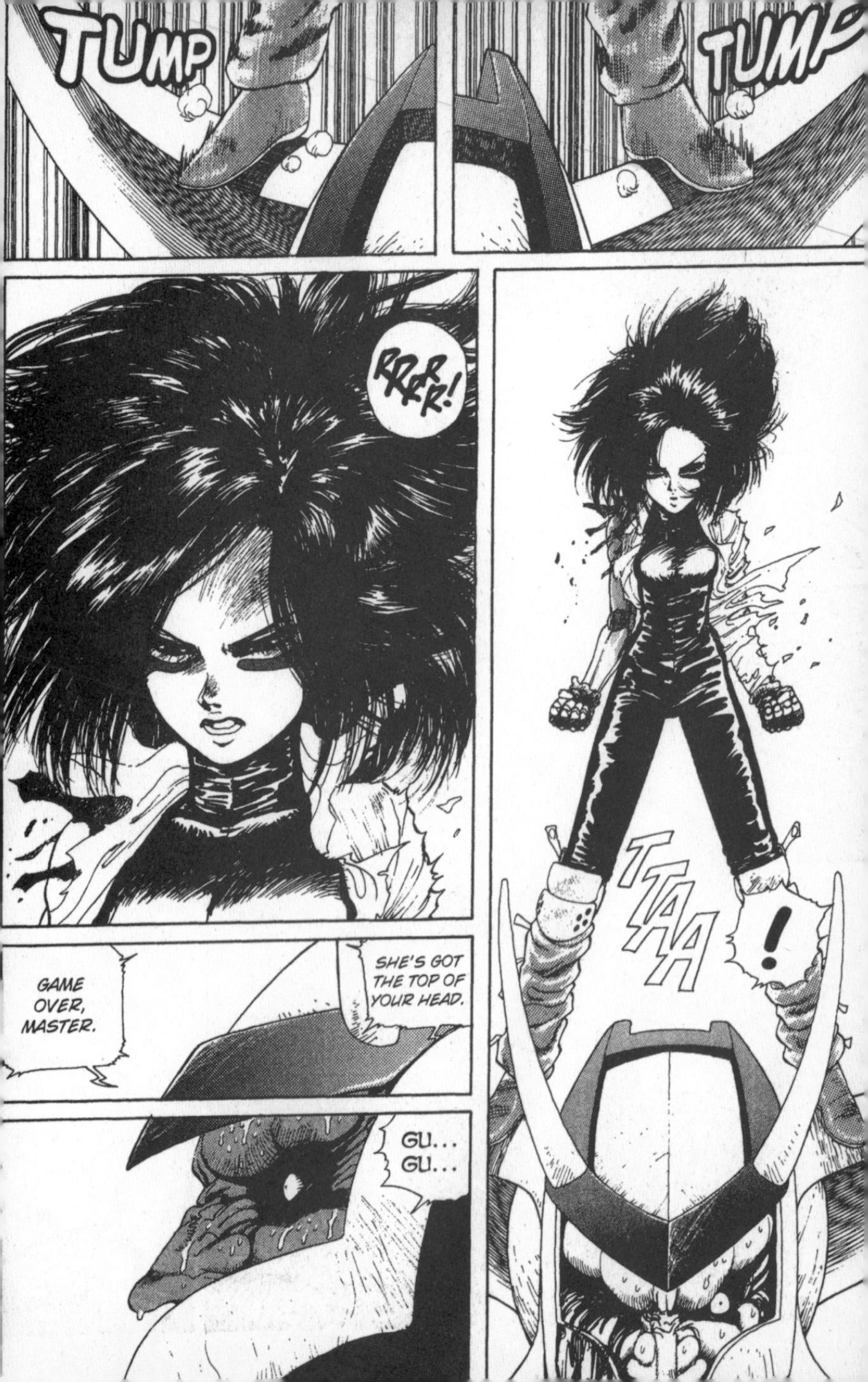
TUMP
TUMP
TTAAA!
RRRRR!
SHE'S GOT THE TOP OF YOUR HEAD.
GAME OVER, MASTER.
GU... GU...

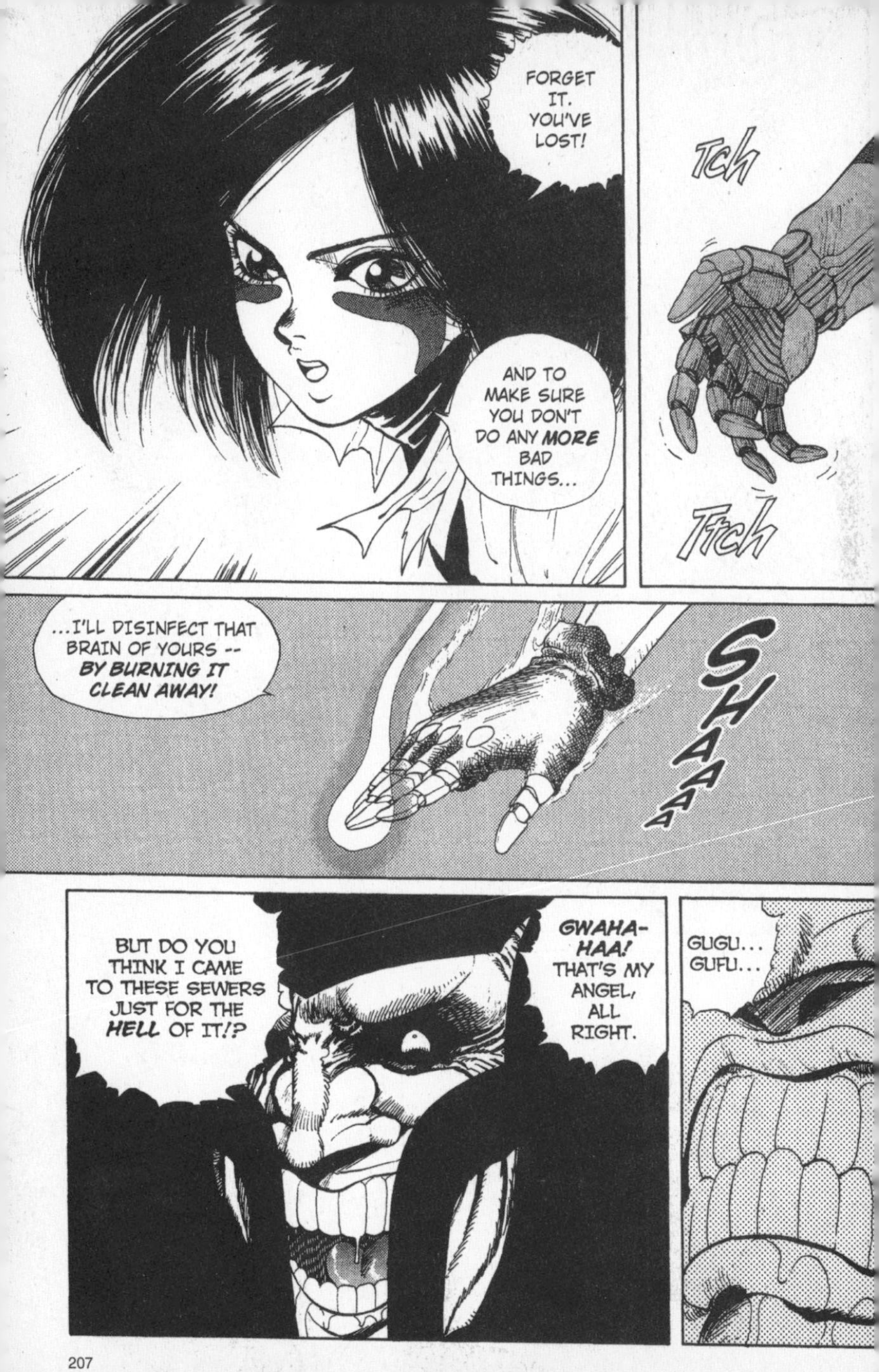
Tch
Tfch
FORGET IT. YOU'VE LOST!
AND TO MAKE SURE YOU DON'T DO ANY ***MORE*** BAD THINGS...
SHAAAA
...I'LL DISINFECT THAT BRAIN OF YOURS -- ***BY BURNING IT CLEAN AWAY!***
GUGU... GUFU...
GWAHA-HAA! THAT'S MY ANGEL, ALL RIGHT.
BUT DO YOU THINK I CAME TO THESE SEWERS JUST FOR THE ***HELL*** OF IT!?

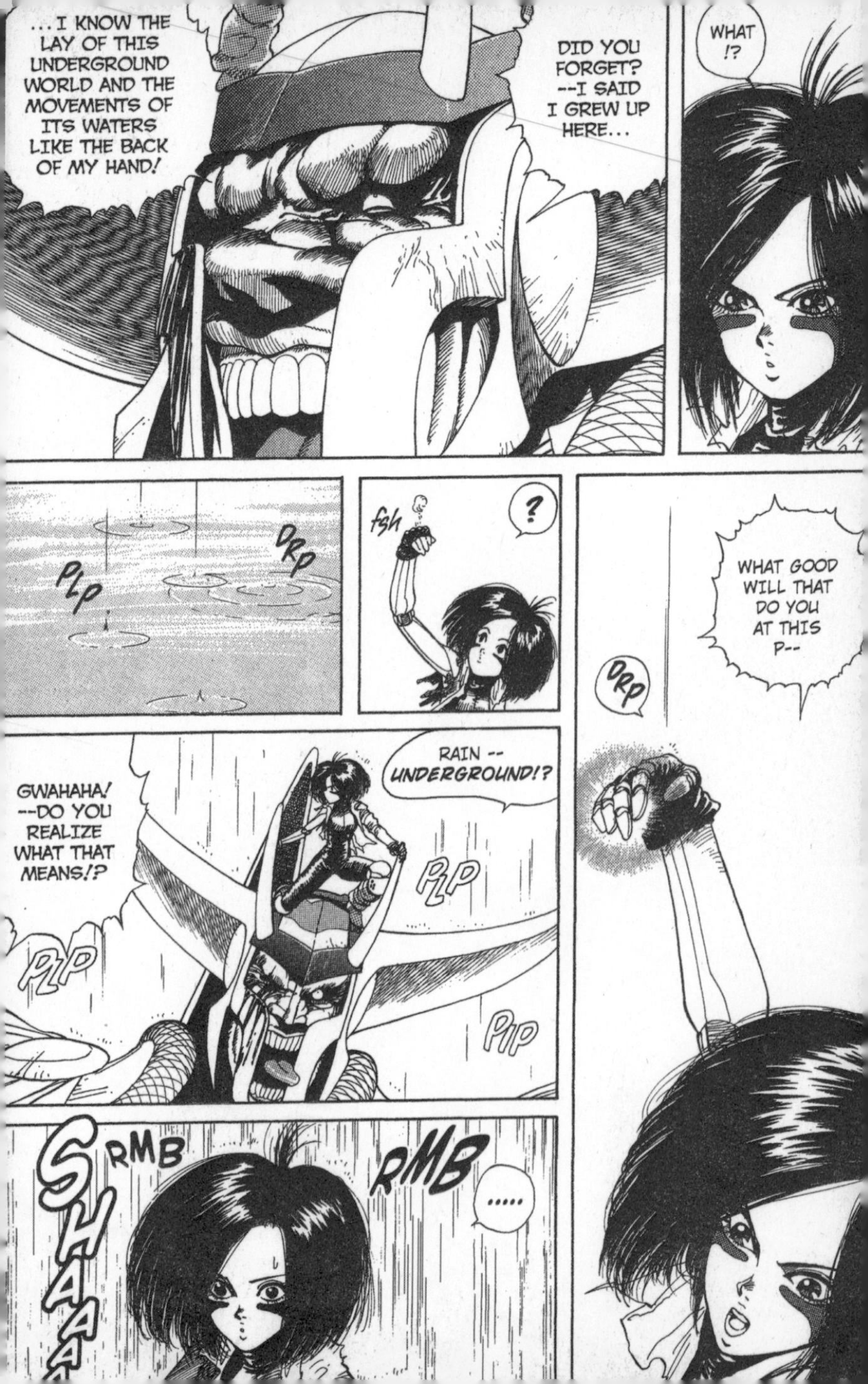

WHAT !?
DID YOU FORGET? --I SAID I GREW UP HERE...
...I KNOW THE LAY OF THIS UNDERGROUND WORLD AND THE MOVEMENTS OF ITS WATERS LIKE THE BACK OF MY HAND!
WHAT GOOD WILL THAT DO YOU AT THIS P--
DRP
?
fsh
DRP
PLP
RAIN -- UNDERGROUND!?
GWAHAHA! --DO YOU REALIZE WHAT THAT MEANS!?
PLP
PLP
PIP
RMB
......
RMB
SHAAAA

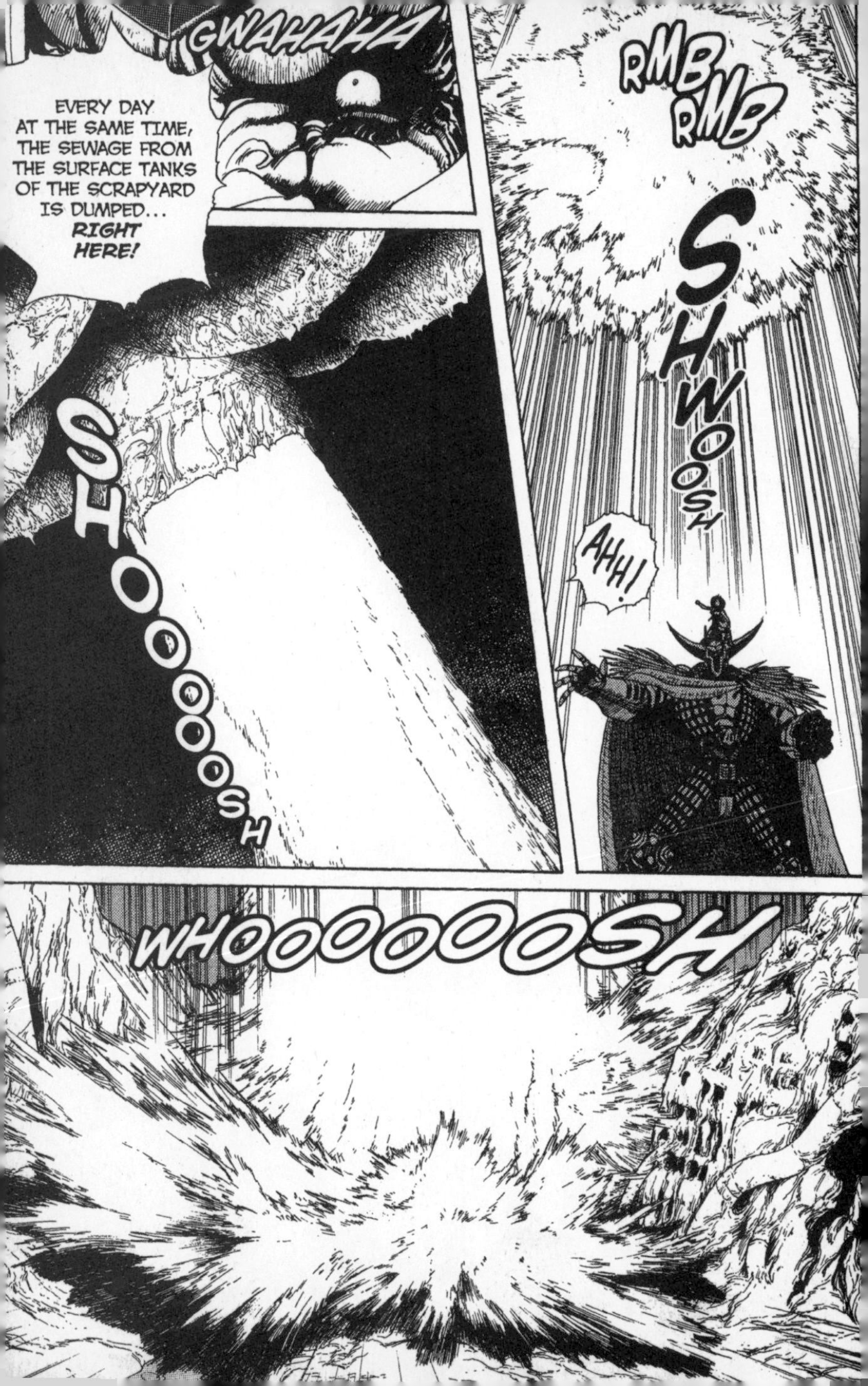
RMB RMB
SHWOOSH
AHH!
GWAHAHA
EVERY DAY AT THE SAME TIME, THE SEWAGE FROM THE SURFACE TANKS OF THE SCRAPYARD IS DUMPED... RIGHT HERE!
SHOOOOOOSH
WHOOOOOOOSH

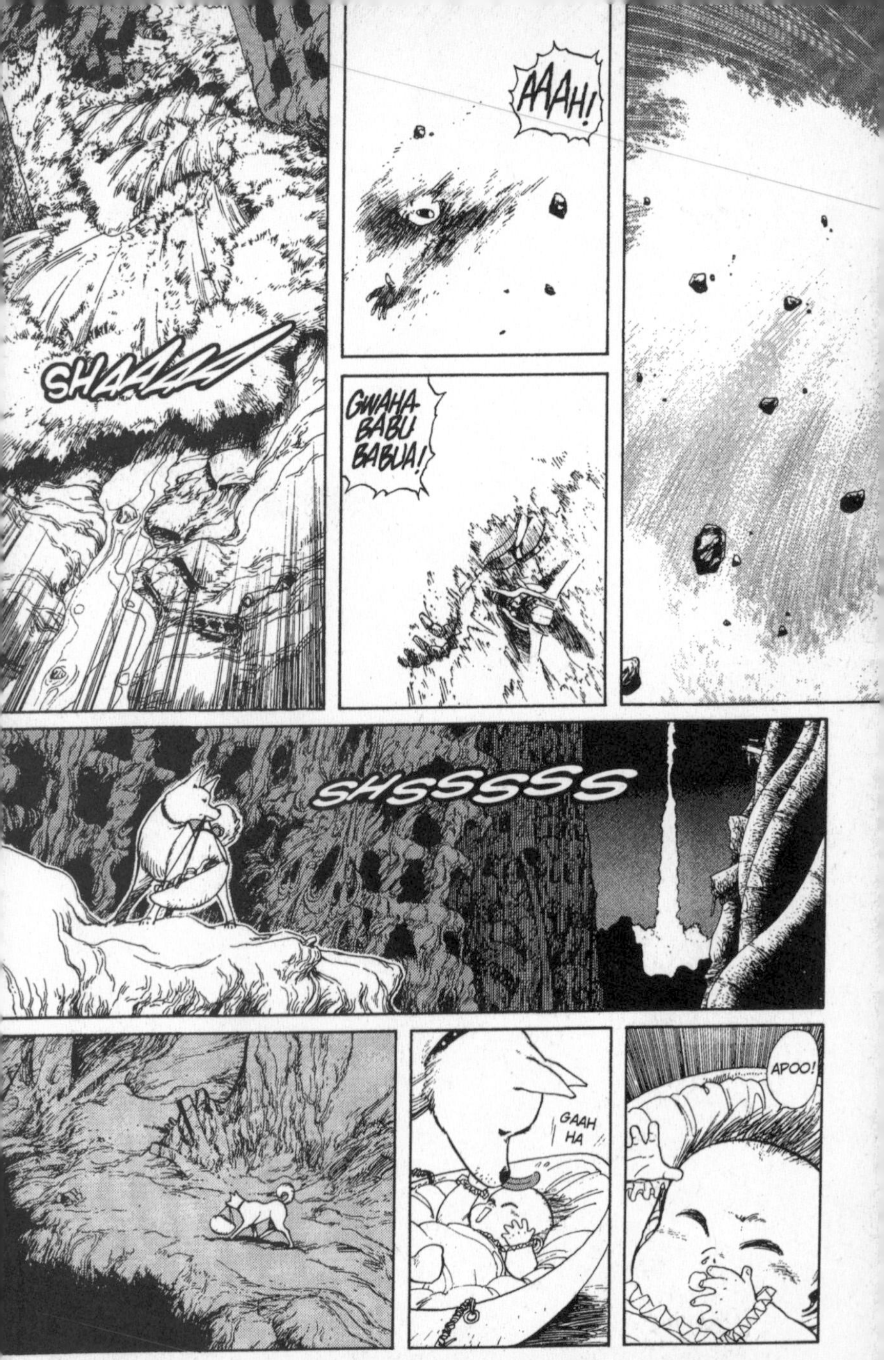
AAAH!
GWAHA BABU BABUA!
SHAAAA
SHSSSSS
APOO!
GAAH HA

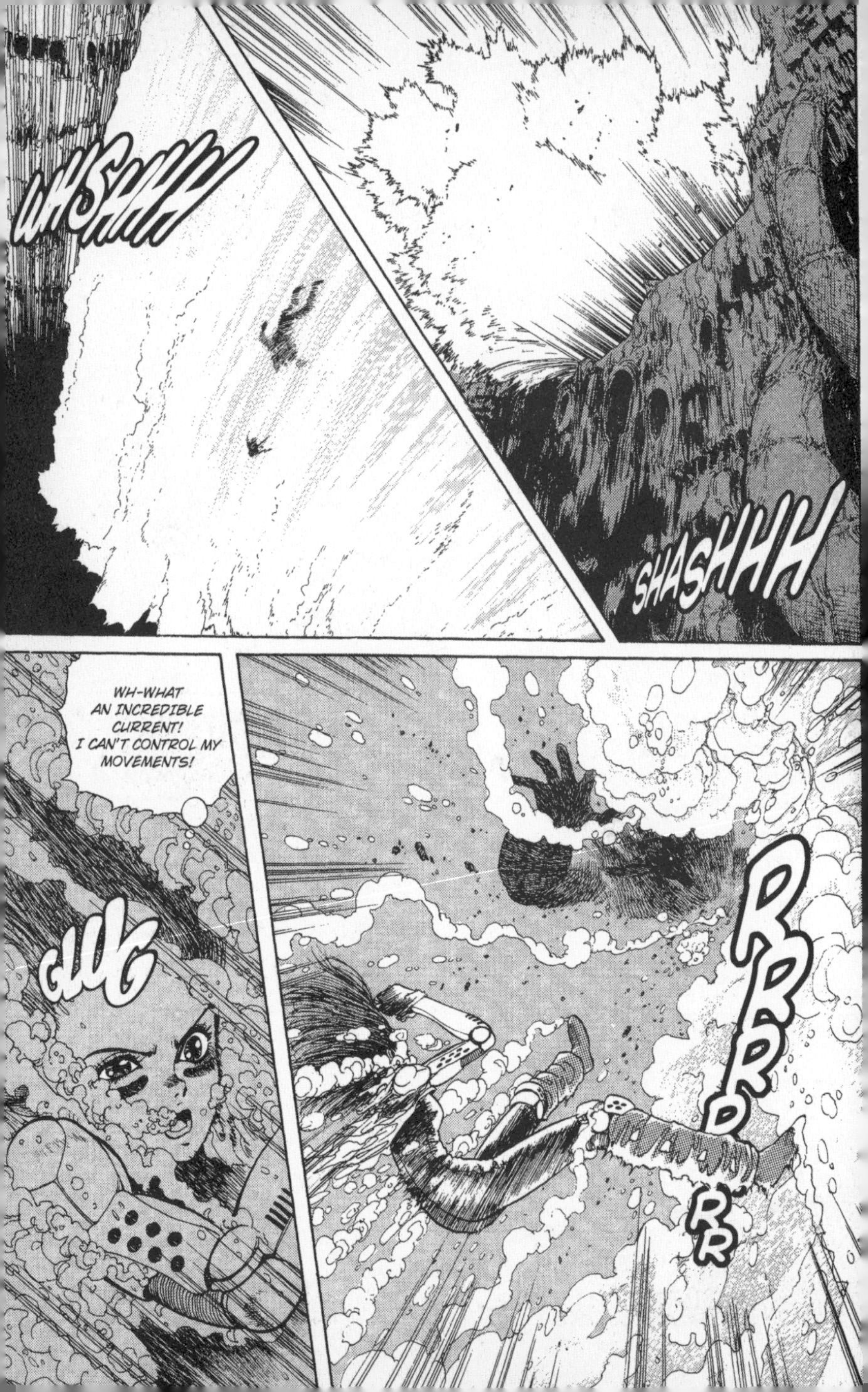
SHASHHH
WHSHHH
WH-WHAT AN INCREDIBLE CURRENT! I CAN'T CONTROL MY MOVEMENTS!
GULP

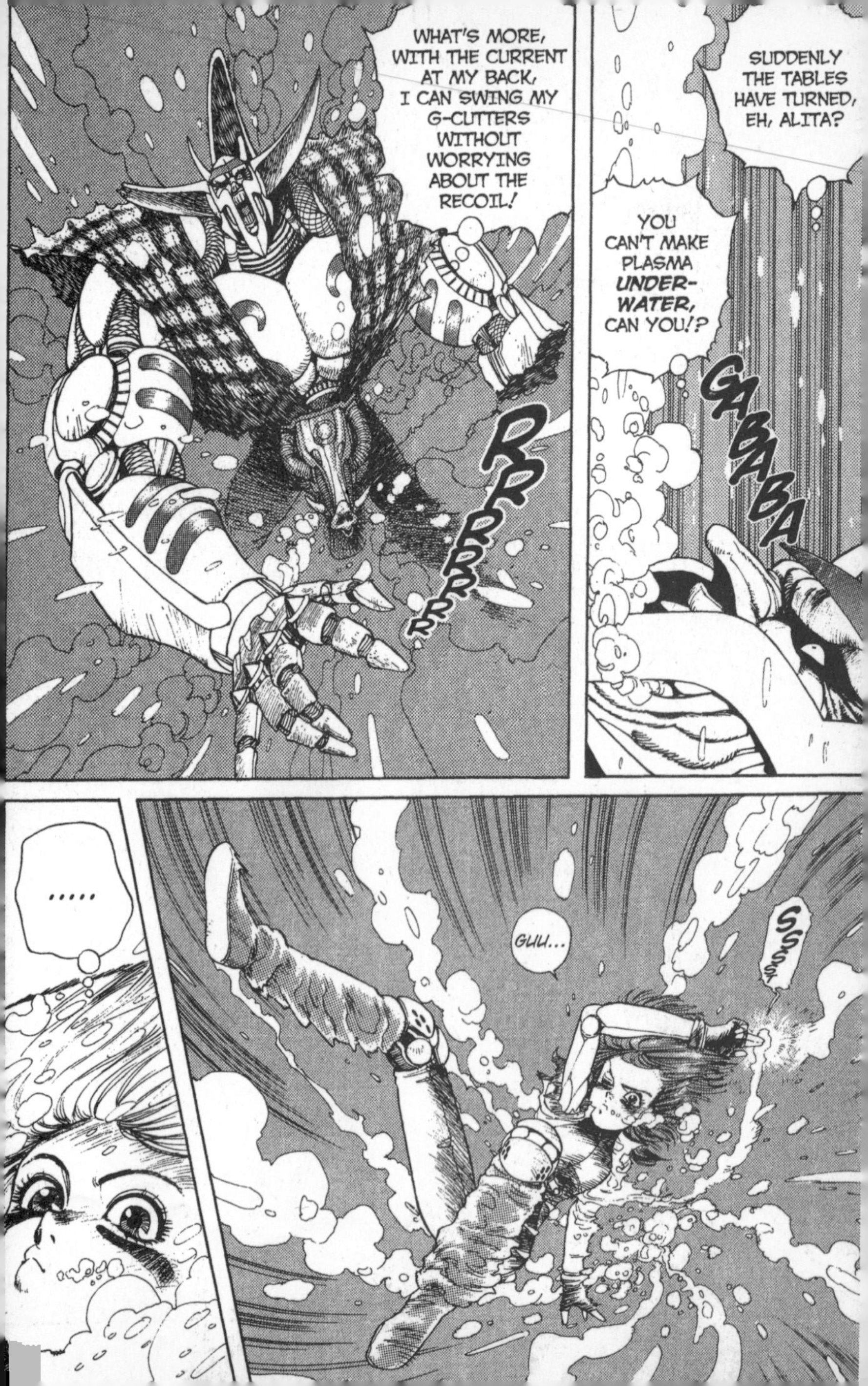
SUDDENLY THE TABLES HAVE TURNED, EH, ALITA?
YOU CAN'T MAKE PLASMA UNDER-WATER, CAN YOU!?
GABABA
WHAT'S MORE, WITH THE CURRENT AT MY BACK, I CAN SWING MY G-CUTTERS WITHOUT WORRYING ABOUT THE RECOIL!
RRRRRRRR
SSSSSK
GUU...
.....

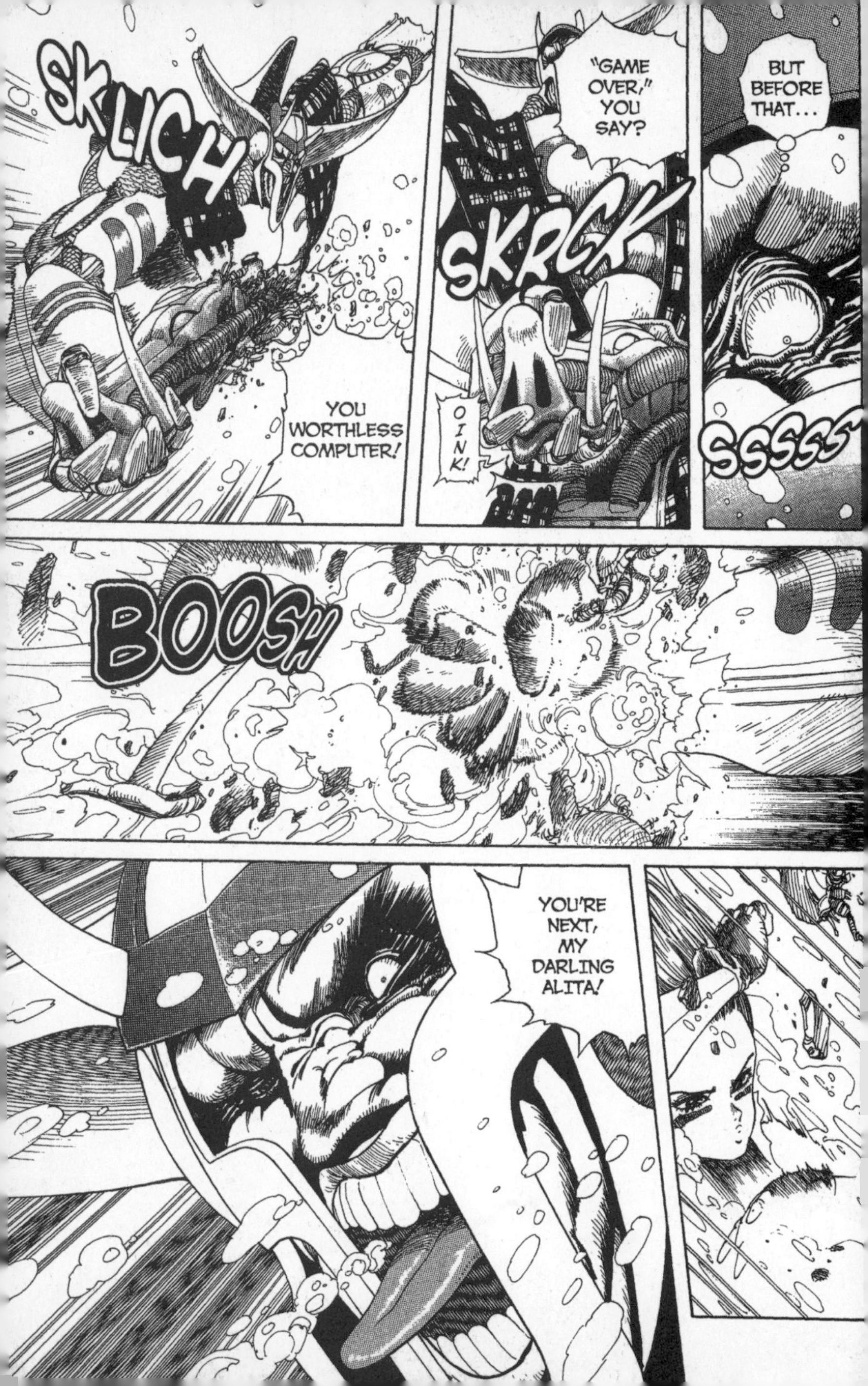
BUT BEFORE THAT...
SSSSS
"GAME OVER," YOU SAY?
SKRCK
OINK!
SKLICH
YOU WORTHLESS COMPUTER!
BOOSH
YOU'RE NEXT, MY DARLING ALITA!

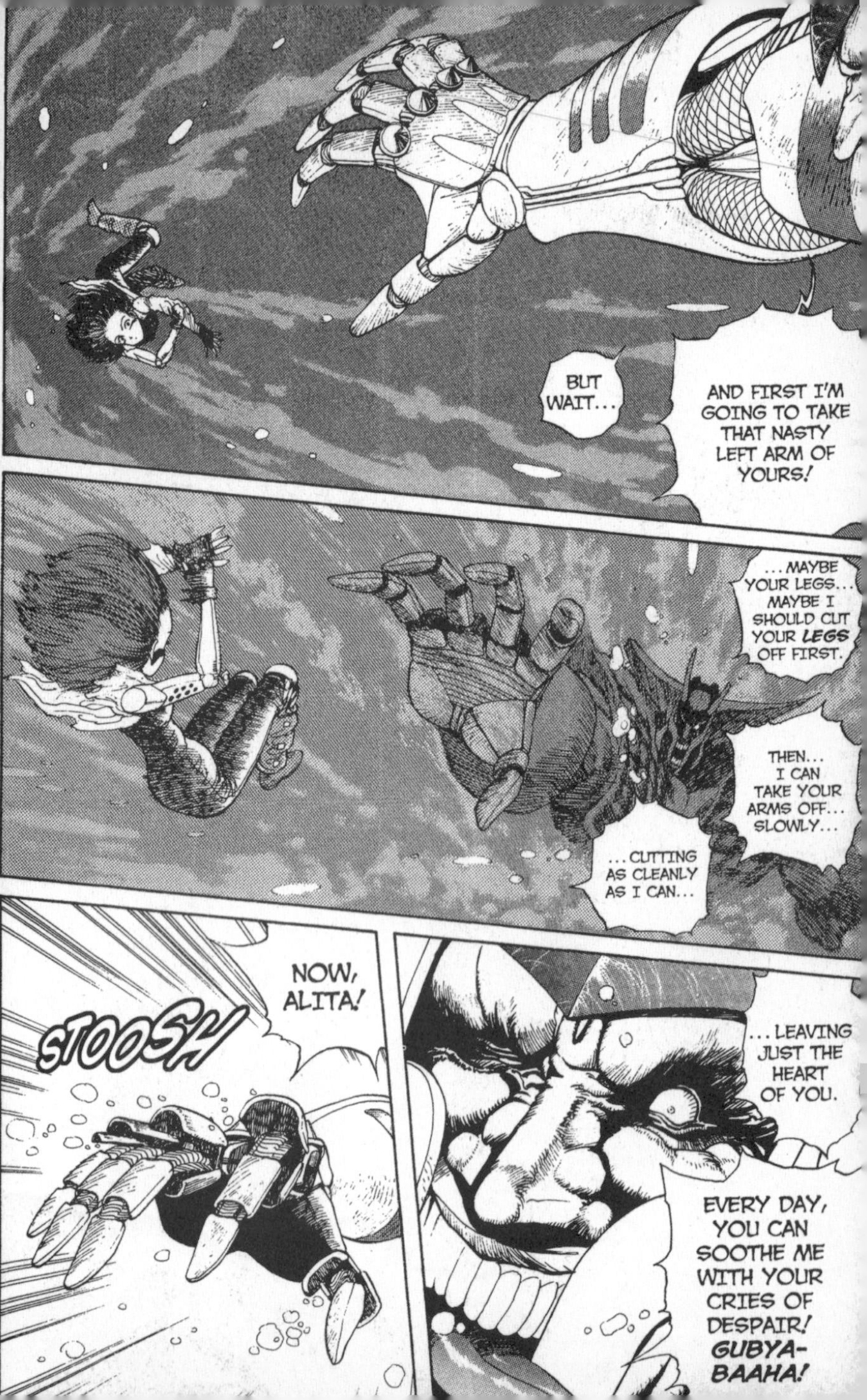
AND FIRST I'M GOING TO TAKE THAT NASTY LEFT ARM OF YOURS!
BUT WAIT...
...MAYBE YOUR LEGS... MAYBE I SHOULD CUT YOUR *LEGS* OFF FIRST.
THEN... I CAN TAKE YOUR ARMS OFF... SLOWLY...
...CUTTING AS CLEANLY AS I CAN...
...LEAVING JUST THE HEART OF YOU.
EVERY DAY, YOU CAN SOOTHE ME WITH YOUR CRIES OF DESPAIR! *GUBYA-BAAHA!*
NOW, ALITA!
STOOSH

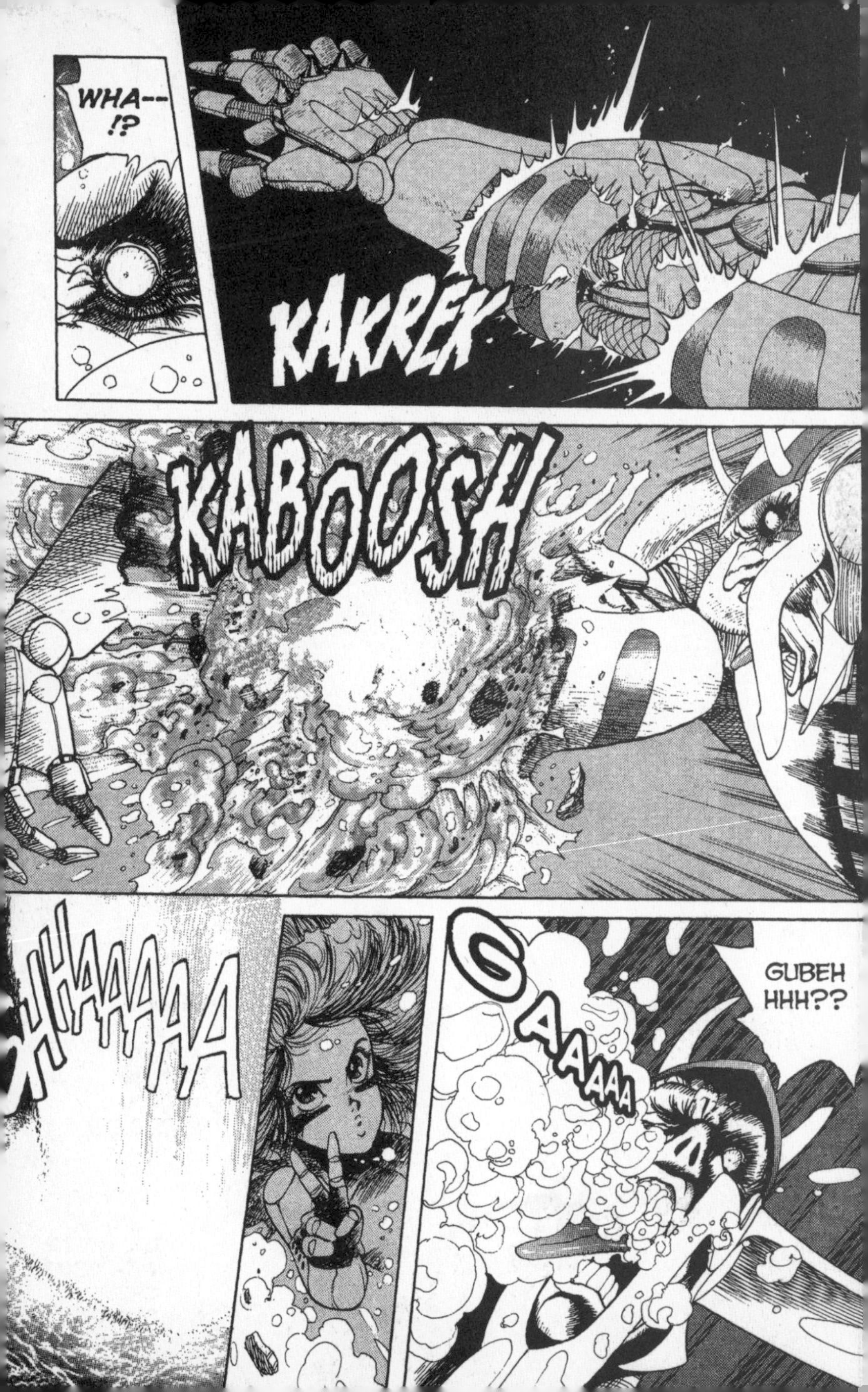
KAKREK
WHA--
!?
KABOOSH
GUBEH
HHH??
GAAAAA
HAAAAAA

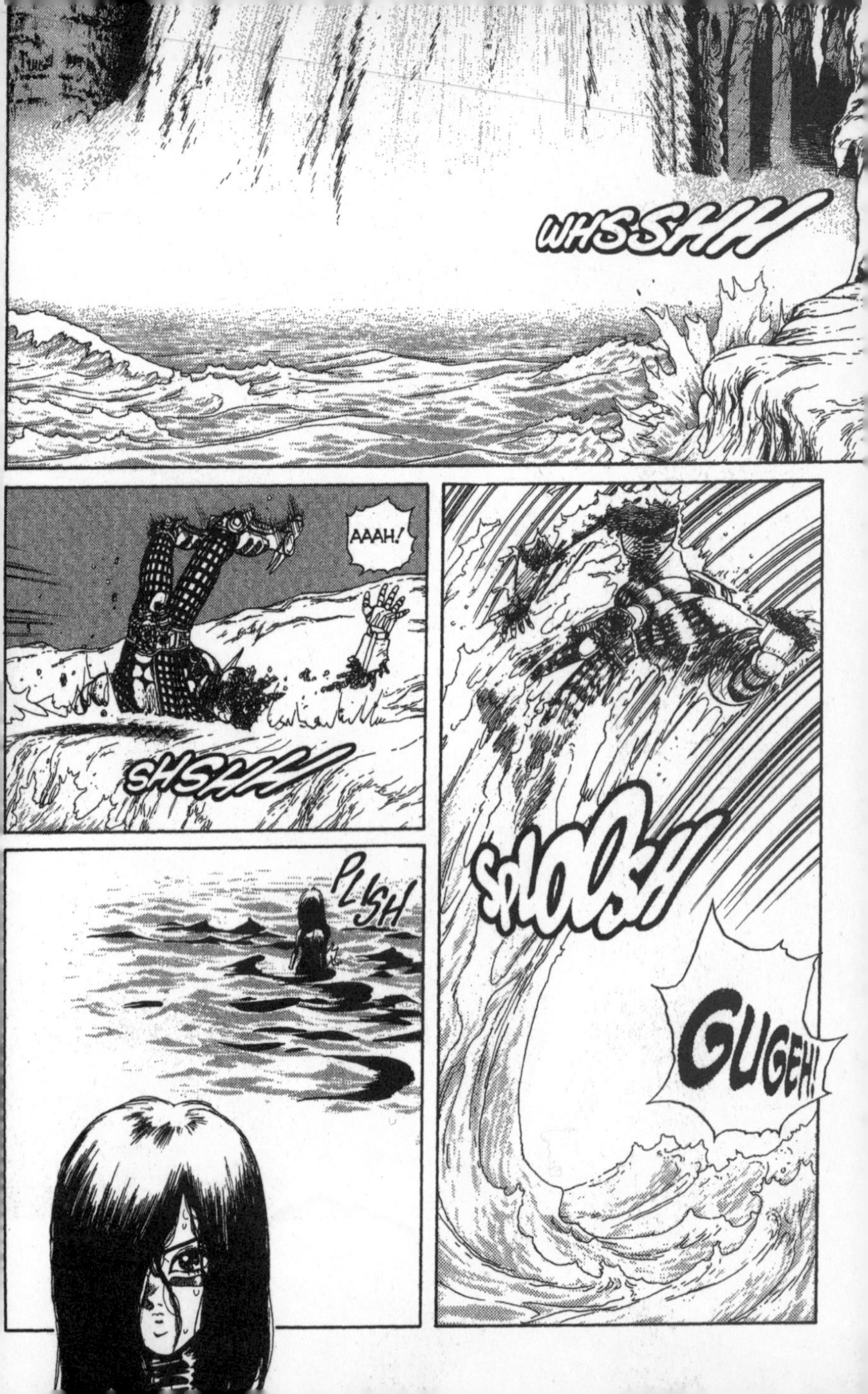
WHSSHH
SPLASH
GUGEH!
AAAH!
SHSHH
PLISH

YOU IDIOT! *I* DID IT.

TMP

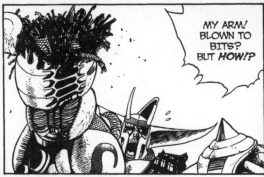

MY ARM! BLOWN TO BITS? BUT *HOW!?*

I CARVED AN INCISION INTO THE ACTUATORS OF YOUR ARM...

...SO THAT THE NEXT TIME YOU SENT POWER THROUGH IT, IN ORDER TO FIRE YOUR G-CUTTERS, YOUR ARM WOULD EXPLODE.

WITH THESE FINGERS -- SEE!?

Factories and Deckmen

Exposé!

Factories are literally "facilities for manufacturing," but, in the Scrapyard, the word Factory is also synonymous with "government."

The Factories serve as the administrative centers for the Scrapyard's industrial complex, and exist solely for the benefit of Tiphares. Most of the food and industrial goods processed in the Scrapyard is sent to Tiphares via the Factories.

There are 11 administrative centers, numbered from 11 to 1111, in the Scrapyard. There are no people in the administrative centers, and special cyborg units called Deckmen are used for customer service.

Operational Cylinder Deckman

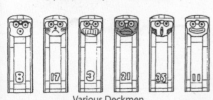

Various Deckmen

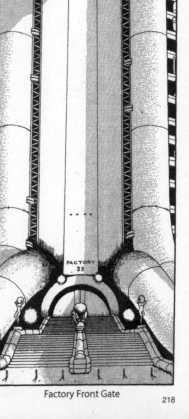

Factory Front Gate

The Birth of Deckman No. 10

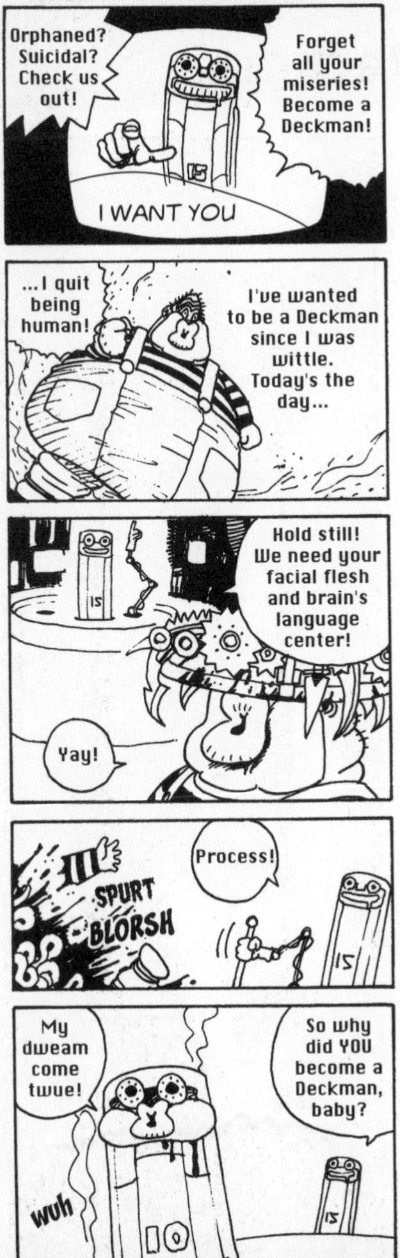
Forget all your miseries! Become a Deckman!
Orphaned? Suicidal? Check us out!
I WANT YOU
I've wanted to be a Deckman since I was wittle. Today's the day...
...I quit being human!
Hold still! We need your facial flesh and brain's language center!
Yay!
Process!
SPURT
BLORSH
So why did YOU become a Deckman, baby?
My dweam come twue!
wuh

The End

Deckmen use a live brain instead of a bio-chip, but they are simple robots, slaves to Tiphares with neither human will nor desire.

The core Deckman bodies are transported via linear tubes and link to the system instruments, which function as their limbs.

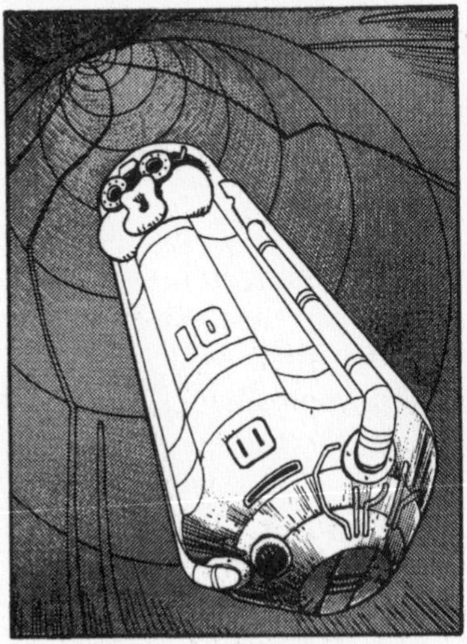

A Deckman zooming the tubes

Much about the Factories and Tiphares remains shrouded in mystery, but their secrets will be revealed as the story progresses.

Battle Royale

The best-selling novel that shocked Japan is now available in the U.S. exclusively from VIZ. A field trip becomes sick and twisted when junior high students are taken to a deserted island and forced to play a deadly game of survival. It's kill or be killed in this winner-take-all contest.

The Big O

In Paradigm City, it's as if time never existed prior to 40 years ago. Or, at least no one can remember it because they've all lost their memories before that date in this film noir-like manga. Negotiator Roger Smith tries to find clues to the past, but often runs into conflict that must be resolved by the Big O, a giant robot he pilots.

© 1999 Hajime Yatate, Hitoshi Ariga
© 1999 Sunrise

© 2000 YUKITO KISHIRO/SHUEISHA Inc.

Battle Angel Alita: Last Order

Creator Yukito Kishiro brings back cyborg Battle Angel Alita, along with some of her friends and foes, and introduces new bizarre, tormented characters. Desty Nova resurrects Alita in a biomechanical body, which makes her even more powerful. However, while she was "gone," Nova revealed the horrific secret of Tiphares. Killer robots are hunting down anyone who knows the truth about the floating city, including children. Will Alita be able to save them?

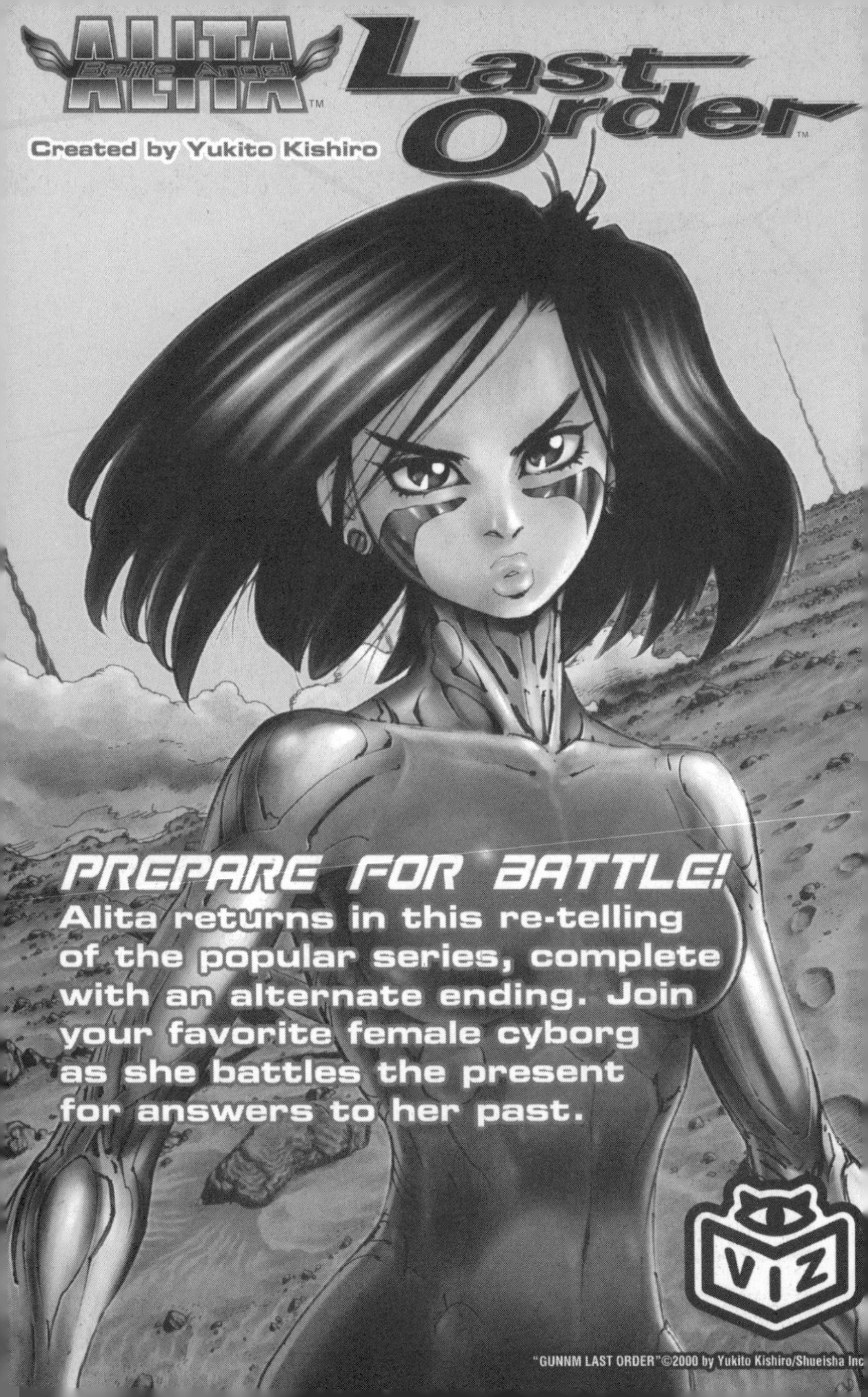
ALITA Battle Angel ALITA™
Last Order™
Created by Yukito Kishiro
PREPARE FOR BATTLE!
Alita returns in this re-telling of the popular series, complete with an alternate ending. Join your favorite female cyborg as she battles the present for answers to her past.
VIZ
"GUNNM LAST ORDER"©2000 by Yukito Kishiro/Shueisha Inc

COMPLETE OUR SURVEY AND LET
US KNOW WHAT YOU THINK!

☐ Please check here if you DO NOT wish to receive information or future offers from VIZ

Name: _____

Address: _____

City: _____ State: _____ Zip: _____

E-mail: _____

☐ Male ☐ Female   Date of Birth (mm/dd/yyyy): ___/___/___   (Under 13? Parental consent required)

What race/ethnicity do you consider yourself? (please check one)

☐ Asian/Pacific Islander   ☐ Black/African American   ☐ Hispanic/Latino

☐ Native American/Alaskan Native ☐ White/Caucasian   ☐ Other: _____

What VIZ product did you purchase? (check all that apply and indicate title purchased)

☐ DVD/VHS _____

☐ Graphic Novel _____

☐ Magazines _____

☐ Merchandise _____

Reason for purchase: (check all that apply)

☐ Special offer   ☐ Favorite title   ☐ Gift

☐ Recommendation   ☐ Other _____

Where did you make your purchase? (please check one)

☐ Comic store   ☐ Bookstore   ☐ Mass/Grocery Store

☐ Newsstand   ☐ Video/Video Game Store ☐ Other: _____

☐ Online (site: _____)

What other VIZ properties have you purchased/own? _____

_____

How many anime and/or manga titles have you purchased in the last year? How many were VIZ titles? **(please check one from each column)**

ANIME	MANGA	VIZ
☐ None	☐ None	☐ None
☐ 1-4	☐ 1-4	☐ 1-4
☐ 5-10	☐ 5-10	☐ 5-10
☐ 11+	☐ 11+	☐ 11+

I find the pricing of VIZ products to be: **(please check one)**

☐ Cheap ☐ Reasonable ☐ Expensive

What genre of manga and anime would you like to see from VIZ? **(please check two)**

☐ Adventure ☐ Comic Strip ☐ Science Fiction ☐ Fighting

☐ Horror ☐ Romance ☐ Fantasy ☐ Sports

What do you think of VIZ's new look?

☐ Love It ☐ It's OK ☐ Hate It ☐ Didn't Notice ☐ No Opinion

Which do you prefer? **(please check one)**

☐ Reading right-to-left

☐ Reading left-to-right

Which do you prefer? **(please check one)**

☐ Sound effects in English

☐ Sound effects in Japanese with English captions

☐ Sound effects in Japanese only with a glossary at the back

THANK YOU! Please send the completed form to:

NJW Research
42 Catharine St.
Poughkeepsie, NY 12601

All information provided will be used for internal purposes only. We promise not to sell or otherwise divulge your information.